KOLKATA IN
SPACE, TIME, AND IMAGINATION
VOLUME 1

Kolkata in
Space, Time, and Imagination

Volume 1

edited by

ANURADHA ROY

MELITTA WALIGORA

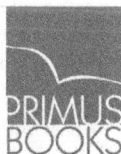

PRIMUS
BOOKS

PRIMUS BOOKS

An imprint of Ratna Sagar P. Ltd.

Virat Bhavan

Mukherjee Nagar Commercial Complex

Delhi 110 009

Offices at

CHENNAI LUCKNOW

AGRA AHMEDABAD BENGALURU COIMBATORE DEHRADUN GUWAHATI
HYDERABAD JAIPUR JALANDHAR KANPUR KOCHI KOLKATA MADURAI
MUMBAI PATNA RANCHI VARANASI

First published 2019

ISBN: 978-93-5290-786-1 (hardback)
ISBN: 978-93-5290-787-8 (POD)

Published by Primus Books

Laser typeset by Mithu Karmakar
mithu.karma@gmail.com

CONTENTS

The City in Time
The Eventful Twentieth Century and Beyond

PREFACE

This book titled *Kolkata in Space, Time, and Imagination* has emerged from a research-cum-publication project based on a formal tie-up between Humboldt University and Jadavpur University. The project was entrusted to two editors, one from each university. One of the editors, having spent all her life in Kolkata, is tied to the city through a sort of primordial bond and this serves as one of the essential foundations of her identity. The other one, a German and a Berliner, has come to know Kolkata and developed a fondness for it primarily through a conscious academic interest. The Calcutta-born editor loves the city for the intense life and love she has found here as much as she hates it for all its wickedness, discriminations, corruptions, pretensions, and its frantic efforts towards superficial and hypocritical glosses (which is becoming increasingly prominent day by day). The German editor, having been compelled to adjust her identity through the division and reunification of her country and her city, perhaps feels the fleetingness of identity more strongly and is more open about its spatial determination. This has gradually helped her to make Calcutta a part of her identity, maybe a comparatively small part, but genuine and sincere nevertheless. And because thoughtful identities generate both love and criticism (in contrast to blind and bigoted identities), she too loves and critiques the city simultaneously. She loves it because it is a source of intellectual and emotional gratifications for her, and critiques it for its often mindless and self-destructive ways that reminds her of her own country and city (though, the context and nature of these ways may be very different). We begin this foreword on a personal note, because we think this will help explain our planning of the book that is caring, critical, and above all, motivated by an urge to know the city in depth which is actually an urge to know ourselves. Alongside, we do hope that this endeavour will contribute not only to a better understanding of Calcutta, but also to a mutual understanding of different people across countries and thus, to the making of a better world.

Even within the limits of academics with its claim of objectivity (though not detachment), we feel that scholars and intellectuals must try and understand each other at the international level. Even if it is a regionally or locally limited subject, just one city in this case, it should interest scholars far and wide and they should engage with some general questions and methodology to understand it. They should also try and develop some common ideas and theories in the process (preferably through a healthy give and take). After all, it is not that an idea or theory based upon a certain experience would describe only that one experience; it should be able to explain other experiences, at least up to a point. While experiences are not identical world over, they have some definite similarities. Urban experiences certainly do have similarities; so do colonialism, modernity, class disparities, gender, the rage for 'development' in today's neoliberal globalized world order, and some other phenomena that have to be understood for understanding Calcutta. At the end of the day, humanity is universal and amenable to a remarkable convergence in several crucial aspects. Such convergence requires academics to develop a common epistemology, and thus, strengthen and consolidate their intellectual pursuits to ensure excellence. This book project, involving scholars from India, Germany, and beyond is a small attempt in this direction.

There already exist several books on the city of Kolkata, both individually authored and edited volumes, and both in English and Bengali. Even if we consider English books only, the two-volume *Calcutta: The Living City* (edited by Sukanta Chaudhuri) is regarded as a standard reference work on the city, covering more than eighty vital aspects of city life. So what is the need for yet another book on the subject? Our project explores areas, not covered earlier: in terms of both topics and time. It includes novel and interesting topics related to both the outer spaces and inner recesses of the city's existence. Also, Chaudhuri's book was published in the early 1990s, on the occasion of the city's so-called tercentenary and much water has flown down the Ganges since then. The city has been undergoing drastic changes since the turn of the century. Our book is largely a response to the crucial conjuncture that the city seems to have reached as a result of these changes and tries to address them at least partly. By the way, of all the recent changes, the renaming of Calcutta as Kolkata in 2001 seems to be the most nominal indeed; all the more so, because it is not much of a change for the localites—Bengalis in particular—who had always called this city Kolkata. The contributors to our book have used both Calcutta and Kolkata, as they have thought fit. No strict editorial policy has been adopted in this regard and the reader will often find the two names used interchangeably in the book, even in this 'Preface'.

We have conceived the two-volume book quite broadly. Urbanity is a dynamic process rooted in history and constantly reconfigured and restructured by politics, economy, and changing sociocultural norms. We explore the entire process by focusing on certain selected aspects only. Thus, rather than a comprehensive volume, what we aimed at was a collection of some interesting, insightful, and offbeat essays that would be related to some significant aspects of the city and based on thorough research. We had a wide range of themes in mind within the overarching theme of Kolkata, but all of them were chosen carefully to make the book meaningful; and scholars with expertise in the relevant areas were invited to write on them. However, we could not and indeed did not want to ensure a uniform research methodology. And alongside established historical sources like archival materials, literature, images, interviews, etc., we urged our contributors to use their own memories as far as possible, particularly while writing on the recent past. After all, memories are a legitimate source of history-writing. Also, we do hope that the resultant collection will promote overall a fuller understanding of the city, its past, present, and perhaps also the future. Here are some of the general thoughts that were behind the planning of the book along with an outline of its contents.

For many years Calcutta was famous as the first capital of British India and the second city of the British Empire and is widely perceived as a colonial city even today. This, of course, is a colonial perception, but is true of much of our received body of knowledge about the city's past. We feel that this calls for serious interrogation, though at the same time we do not intend to deny that the colonial rulers did play a vital role in the making of the city.

In the very first essay of the first volume, Michael Mann studies the early official architecture and urban design as an expression of the political will of colonial rulers. In the second essay, Kaustubh Mani Sengupta unpacks the colonial spatial imagination as shaped by the metropolitan bourgeois values and the imperial vision in the late-nineteenth century and also reveals the inherent tension between different official visions, even though they all aimed at a beautiful, cleaner, and healthier city. But the process of Calcutta's urbanization did not exclude the agency of many others: of foreign merchants of other nationalities (Dutch, French, Portuguese, Armenians, etc.) in its earliest phase, and of course of the natives throughout its history. A major part of the book tries to understand how colonialism indigenized in the city gave birth to a new society and culture which cannot really be understood within the convenient framework of an impact-response model. We thus treat the city as a centre of 'colonial modernity' (not a colonizers' modernity) with a very active, local participation in the process of urban transformation, constantly generating new values and thoughts; some of these are quite radical. Thus, the book stresses the creative role of the colonized in different fields even during the colonial period. The natives claimed the city as their own and accommodated it within their own aesthetic sense, ethical norms, their idea of the nation, and so on. The postcolonial history of the city, of course, brings forth the agency of the natives all the more prominently.

Any history straddles both time and space. But the first volume of our book has two different sections on these: 'Negotiating Space: From the Formative Years towards Mega Urbanity' and 'The City in Time: The Eventful Twentieth Century and Beyond', respectively. These are not just about spectacular sites and big events, but more about small spaces and small times of everyday life-worlds and their social practices entailing considerable contestations and transgressions. The first section foregrounds space, its gradual expansion and transformation through time, a process that has recently become unprecedentedly profound and rapid. Here we have one essay written by Swati Chattopadhyay on the rooftop terraces, a ubiquitous, unprogrammed space in residential buildings in the dense urban fabric of the 'native' town, revealing an interesting history of sociality that had a predominantly gendered character and also provided an interface between the private and public. The rest of this section is about the spatial planning and expansion of the city in a more recent period. Anuradha Roy seeks to understand how space and culture implicate each other by tracing the history of Salt Lake, a 40–50 year old middle-class township, with which began Calcutta's eastward growth that has now become the overwhelming spatial reality of the city and is also indicative of big transformations in middle-class lifestyle. Stressing both continuities and changes in the Bengali middle-class culture, her essay presents Salt Lake as a bridge between the old Calcutta and the new in spatial, temporal, cultural, and metaphorical senses. While it is a take on the middle-class culture in the main, the poor people who got evicted to make room for the middle-class Salt Lake and still serve as the township's labour market lurk around in the essay. Sukanya Mitra writes about the even more recent phenomenon of shopping malls and helps in our understanding of the linkages between the evolution of physical sites and the culture of consumption. She also talks about the petty shopkeepers and hawkers who have managed to survive the growing shopping-mall culture in the city. This section ends with a vignette from the pen of a keenly observant Alka Saraogi (who, by the way, is a noted fiction writer) on how the social and topographical character of the old cosmopolitan locality of Bhowanipore where she lives has been changing radically in the recent times goaded by the 'ferocious beast of development' and yet, how the beast has been unable to devour the past and the poor of the city completely.

The second section of the volume tries to understand how the city has negotiated the changing times and in the process changed itself. During the twentieth century in particular, the city experienced the stirrings of the national movement which in course of time broadened into socialism for many people. The twentieth century also saw Calcutta negotiating several catalytic events, including the two World Wars, a devastating famine, Independence, Partition, the Naxalite uprising, and so on. Our book provides glimpses into this negotiating process, sometimes through very unusual lenses, again to stress the ordinary and everyday underside of the city. The time of the First World War is captured here by Suchetana Chattopadhyay through a study of the impressions that the ships anchoring (or expected to anchor) at the Calcutta docks left on both the crisis-ridden colonial authority and the popular mind-triggering multilayered anxieties, expectations, and excitements; and generating a lot of rumours. The popular here includes the bottom of the social hierarchy. The city in the late 1920s, caught between the colonial governance and the nationalist assertion as well as between the ideologies of nationalism and communism, has come alive through Tanika Sarkar's account of two scavengers' strikes that took place in 1928. She brings out the caste-class ramifications of being scavengers and the way they tried to translate this as a source of strength through their own agency (with *methranis* or women scavengers finding a special mention). The scavengers who used to provide an essential service to the city and yet, whom the city wanted to excise from its sight could make themselves visible only by stopping this service. The turbulent 1940s has featured in the book so far as it impacted the field of health and hygiene in the essay jointly penned by Srilata Chatterjee, Ritwika Biswas, and Avirup Sinha. They show how big events like the Second World War, Bengal Famine, communal violence, and refugee influx affected not only the public health condition of the city, but also changed the attitude of the varied social and occupational groups living in the city towards the matters related to health and medicine. This section also includes an essay on the city during the days when a revolutionary dream was nurtured by a substantial section of its youth, i.e. the days of the Naxalites which has been written by a participant-observer Amit Bhattacharyya. This is followed by Parimal Ghosh's essay about the end of this dream and the shift towards pragmatism during the rule of the Left Front whose capitulation to the existing order became more obvious in the post-liberalization days. Towards the end, the essay touches upon the city in the post-Left Front regime too and shows how the retreat of socialism has left its mark on society and culture (how the character of the old *paras* or localities has changed, for example) aided by other factors such as the expansion and changing composition of the middle class.

The second volume continues with the theme of the ordinary and everyday, with special attention paid to the underclasses of the city. The first section has articles on certain categories of labouring people serving the city, including women labourers. Such people have always been marginalized in the city's history and are getting more and more invisible in the flush of the recent developments towards mega urbanity, even though the city continues to live off their labour. We are proud to say that our book gives them their due. We hope to have made it clear by now that when we dispute Kolkata's epithet as a colonial city, we do not essentialize the natives, nor try to elide the experiences of the Bengali middle-class males into the urban experience as a whole. The Calcutta presented in our book is not a city of 'phallic solitude', to use a phrase coined by Henri Lefebvre, the famous philosopher and sociologist who also propounded the concept of the 'right to the city' meaning the right of the underprivileged to access the city's resources and to shape the process of urban development, a right we felt should be reflected and recognized in our book too.[1]

However, the book seeks to understand the city not only in space and time, but also in imagination. But of course, imagination can be called an ideational space of images, representations, and broadly speaking, cultural productions floating in time. The second section of the second volume deals with the efflorescence of creative imagination in the city's culturescape which, even while nurturing 'rural romance', has always been rooted in urbanity. In a sense, the city itself is an imagined existence, albeit a pluralistic one. So this section also seeks to understand the city as it has been imagined in some private letters, stories, poems, and songs. The fourth and final section of the second volume shows how the perceptions of the city's past are also largely determined by imagination, sometimes even myth-making. These two sections provide glimpses into the wide-ranging and heterotopic cultural world of the city, and also show how aesthetics and politics implicate each other.

The above outline is just to tell the reader very broadly what was in the editors' minds when they planned the volume and about the outcome of this planning. It hardly does justice to the rich contents and the nuanced arguments of each article. We would, moreover, like to state that even the planning has not been fully fructified. For example, we would have liked to include more articles on the micros and the margins, say, related to the Calcutta Muslims; the workers of the locked-out factories; the street urchins; also on the ponds, trees, and other features of nature that still survive in the city; the night life of Calcutta; the impact of Calcutta on other areas of Bengal and even beyond Bengal; and so on. Our book does not seal but only hope to further open up the future scholarship on Kolkata.

And now we must acknowledge our debt to the past scholarship on the city. This book builds on a rich tradition of studies reflecting on Kolkata and should be treated as complementary to the existing works on the city's history. We have already pointed out how it should complement *Calcutta: The Living City*, dealing as it does with some offbeat topics that are missing there and also extending the history well into the most recent times.

Our book should also complement some of the more recent anthologies on the city that highlight certain specific aspects or phases of the city life; for example, *Calcutta Mosaic: Essays and Interviews on the Minority Communities of Calcutta* (edited by Nilanjana Gupta, 2009). Our volume, however, is not focused on any one aspect of the city. We have not directly addressed the issue of minorities, but Alka Saraogi's piece does talk about a highly cosmopolitan part of the city where trading communities like Gujaratis and Marwaris reside in large numbers alongside old Bengali families. It reveals how a domiciled Marwari views the changes happening in her part of the city today.

Another interesting collection *Strangely Beloved: Writings on Calcutta* (edited by Nilanjana Gupta, 2014), avowedly stresses some aspects of the city which make Calcuttans love it, despite many a horrifying thing about it. Not that we disavow love for the city, but we approach our subject more objectively. Indeed, one of our aims is to make people critically rethink and question some dimensions of the city's history, particularly the 'developmental' process it has been undergoing since the 1990s under the impact of the neo-liberal economy and culture.

Calcutta: The Stormy Decades (edited by Tanika Sarkar and Sekhar Bandyopadhyay, 2015) and dealing with the 1940s and 1950s is an important contribution to the critical understanding of the city's history at a crucial historical juncture. The temporal scope of our book is much broader and though it touches upon those stormy decades, it does so by addressing some aspects of the history which are not there in the book edited by Sarkar and Bandyopadhyay.

A number of individually authored works on Kolkata (or some aspects of city life) have come out in recent times. We situate our volume in that historiography and hope to further enrich it. Let us mention just a few of them here. Sumanta Banerjee's *The Wicked City: Crime and Punishment in Colonial Calcutta* (2009) is about the city's underworld of criminals. Anindita Ghosh's *Claiming the City: Protest, Crime and Scandals in Colonial Calcutta, c.1860–1920* (2016) offers a view of urbanization from below by reflecting on the popular culture of the city. Such books seek to expose the seams of Kolkata's history and a number of essays in our book try to do the same.

Partho Dutta's book *Planning the City: Urbanization and Reform in Calcutta, c.1800–c.1940* (2012) has disputed the 'chance-erected, chance-directed' image of the city and established that 'colonial Calcutta was not only planned, it had been severely planned. The ignorance has arisen because the history of Calcutta planning was not written about before'. The first two articles of our volume are in tune with this assertion and throw more light on the city's planning in its early phases.

Swati Chatterjee in her *Representing Calcutta: Modernity, Nationalism and the Colonial Uncanny* (2005) has problematized the idea of representing the city—both the colonialist and nationalist—and explored the structures of power and knowledge that underlie different representations of the city. She refuses to see Calcutta as a failure of modernity which is supposed to be found in its authentic and original form only in the West, and shows how colonial encounters led to both accommodations and conflicts with several Western ideals of modernity, how in the process the city was rendered uncanny in both the colonialist and nationalist imagination by repressing and resurrecting traces of an unreasoning modernity. Unreason here does not refer to a lack of reason, but to a realm of memory, myth, etc. Our book treads the same path in understanding the perceptions of the city, not only in literature and arts but also in the popular mind. Swati Chatterjee's own article on the spatial imagination of the indigenous population centred on the terraces, included in the section 'Negotiating Space' in the first volume, is a major contribution in this regard.

Of course, many more serious academic works deserve to be mentioned along with the aforementioned ones. A number of them randomly come to mind, starting from somewhat old books like Pradip Sinha's *Calcutta in Urban History* (1978) and *The Urban Experience, Calcutta: Essays in Honour of Professor Nisith R. Ray* (edited, 1987); *Kolkata 1981: The City, Its Crisis and the Debate on Urban Planning and Development* (edited by Jean Racine, 1990) to Siddhartha Sen's *Colonizing, Decolonizing and Globalizing Kolkata: From a Colonial to a Post-Marxist City* (2017). The essays in our book have engaged with such scholarly works on Kolkata, as and when needed.

This book on Kolkata also engages with, and hopes to take its place in the scholarly works on urban history and urbanism in general. It is said that the twenty-first century will witness an urban revolution in the developing world and India will be at the forefront of this revolution.[2] From the way, Calcutta has been developing in the recent times, it seems that it will not lag behind in the process. Whether it will accelerate economic growth, reduce poverty, and ensure a dignified living for everybody, as is often expected, is, however, doubtful. On the other hand, Marxist scholars sometimes argue that cities promoting an awareness of common lived experience and a kind of sharing has a disalienating effect. According to them, urbanism today is a truly cosmopolitan culture, to which everybody is coming and which everybody is somehow shaping, even if always unevenly, and this makes today's global citizen a universal citizen rooted in place. They argue that this is why Marx lobbied for the coming of the urban culture. However, this description seems to be not quite applicable to Calcutta. Here urban-consciousness has led to fractures—social, cultural, temporal—rather than 'urban consolidates' based on universality (a kind of sociality as described by Henri Lefebvre). Urban consciousness has perhaps sharpened class-consciousness in the city, but it hinders bonding, rather drives a wedge among people. The survival instinct of people is, however, universal. So Kolkata survives, Kolkata goes on.

Whose city is Kolkata really? And whither is it bound? It is the intention of the book to raise these questions as sharply as possible, though it does not claim to have found definitive answers to these questions.

ANURADHA ROY
MELITTA WALIGORA

Notes

1. Henri Lefebvre, 'The Right to the City', in *Writings on Cities*, ed. Eleonore Kofman and Elizabeth Lebas, Cambridge, Massachusetts: Wiley-Blackwell, 1996. Actually, he had put forward this idea way back in 1968 in a book written in French. Swati Chattopadhyay has engaged with Lefebvre's phrase 'phallic solitude'; see Swati Chattopadhyay, 'Introduction', in *Representing Calcutta: Modernity, Nationalism and the Colonial Uncanny*, London and New York: Routledge, 2005, pp. 1–20.
2. For example, see Prasanna Kumar Mohanty, *Cities and Public Policy: An Urban Agenda for India*, New Delhi: Sage Publications, 2014.
3. Benjamin Fraser, ed., *Marxism and Urban Culture*, UK: Lexington, 2014.

The editors would like to acknowledge the support and encouragement they have received from their colleagues of the Department of History, Jadavpur University, the Department for South Asian Studies, Humboldt University and also some of their colleagues at Centre for Studies in Social Sciences, Kolkata.

Negotiating Space

From the Formative Years towards
Mega Urbanity

1

BUILT SOVEREIGNTY

Designing Calcutta between 1772 and 1824

Michael Mann

The Setting

After the capital city of British India was shifted from Calcutta to New Delhi in 1912, the entirely planned and newly built city eventually completed in 1934, the former capital fell into oblivion. Today, Calcutta is rarely remembered as the capital of the East India Company and the British Raj, between 1772 and 1912. This also holds true to a large extent for the scientific engagement with the city's history. There are of course numerous volumes and articles on the history of Calcutta, but they mainly deal with the history of the early East India Company settlement or the city's political history in the eighteenth century as part of the established narrative that emphasizes the British conquest of Bengal.[1] Only a few books engage with the city's economic and social history during the eighteenth century and there is only one study which for the first time explicitly deals with town planning in the nineteenth and early-twentieth centuries,[2] belonging, however, to a—likewise established—colonial urban sanitary discourse.[3]

Some light has been shed on depicting Calcutta between scientific accuracy and picturesque representation, and the meaning of public urban space at the turn of the eighteenth century.[4] A well-edited coffee-table book on Calcutta as the *City of Palaces* (1998), provides a rich treasure of maps, pictures, and drawings as well as texts from various travelogues, diaries, and memoires. The book is, however, a rather descriptive account of Calcutta's development between 1698 and 1858, reflecting the still existing British imaginations of Calcutta within the context of the city's alleged foundation 300 years ago.[5] Despite the wonderful illustrations, both books lack the wider political context of town planning, urban design, and urban art as well as the highly symbolic meaning of Calcutta's architecture of public buildings. Calcutta's urban morphology has not been viewed as the history of an intentionally designed and gradually evolving capital of the British Empire in India. As historically proven, this process already commenced in the 1760s and, as will be seen, culminated in the three decades after the turn of the eighteenth century.

So far, academic research has not touched upon the entanglement(s) of politics, town planning, and architecture but rather treated Calcutta's early urban design as a singular, isolated phenomenon. Numerous books deal with colonial architecture in India but the idea of official architecture as a means and expression of political will is almost completely absent. Besides the often available wonderful pictures and drawings, books remain fairly focused on graphic/visual descriptions as authors do not analyse the political and cultural implications of architecture and urban design.[6] Exceptions to the rule emphasize the function and consciousness with regard to the architecture of representative public buildings in a colonial context but eventually fail to explain the importance of the topographical distribution of buildings which are projected as being accidentally dispersed in Calcutta's urban landscape.[7] To various degrees, all the earlier mentioned books treat the architecture of public buildings as being, more or less, seemingly isolated and self-sufficient structures within an urban space devoid of any historical, political, and cultural context.

This article argues, first, that Calcutta's representative public buildings were carefully designed according to the then prevailing British understanding of representational architecture, and second, that they were located at carefully selected places within the urban landscape. They, thus, indicate how the state's representative architecture is symptomatic of a morphology of power: how does the aesthetics of power become manifest, and how are the coordinates of power shaped and structured in the form of these buildings? It is particularly argued that after 1772 when authorities in Calcutta were ordered to take over the direct management of revenue collection and civil jurisdiction according to the *diwani*, granted to the Company by the Gurkaniya-Padshah[8] Shah Alam II (r.1759–1806), there seems to have been no concrete plan for the future urban development of the city as a capital. It was only between 1798, i.e. with the beginning of Richard Wellesley's term as Governor General in Calcutta (until 1805), and the establishment of the Lottery Committee in 1803 for raising money and to eventually implement a comprehensive building programme in the first-half of the 1820s, some sort of a general outlay of Calcutta as a capital city was developed.

Next to Calcutta's street pattern, realized between 1800 and 1825, architecture was the central means for the British to organize the colonial urban space. Theoretically viewed, urban spaces are socially produced, sequentially made, and historically constituted. As any other city, Calcutta's urban space(s) were historically produced and invented, and the city was the symbol of its society's culture and civilization.[9] In other words, cities have never been the work of a moment but the product of continuous social interactions, of persistent encounters, assemblies, and the simultaneity of order and disorder by means of self-presentation and self-representation. '[I]t is a society's practical capabilities and sovereign powers to have at their disposal special places: religious and political sites.'[10] Buildings, especially their façades, as well as monuments are of special importance in this context because they express rhythm and symmetry as parts of politically coordinated symbols.[11] It is against this background that Calcutta's public buildings that were erected between 1800 and 1825 have to be viewed as an expression of 'built sovereignty'.[12]

The term 'built sovereignty' originally referred to forts and fortresses of the early modern European State, making a monarch's newly-gained military power of standing armies that enabled him to wage war at any time visible. More generally, the term should be understood as a political regime's building programme to architecturally represent supreme power and might. In the context of this article, the term is, therefore, applied to Calcutta's major public buildings as an immediate expression of the British political and economic ruling class' or oligarchic elite's will to dominate the city and rule its inhabitants. At the same time built sovereignty was meant to create a distance between the few who ruled and the many that were ruled. The elite comprised the upper echelons of the emerging colonial State's civil administration and military officers, as well as prominent merchants, businessmen, bankers, and lawyers. According to the Police Census of 1837, out of 229,714 persons living within the boundaries of Calcutta, there were 3,138 British, 4,746 Eurasians, 181 Portuguese, 160 French, and 636 Armenians. The census also distinguished between 'Upcountry Muhammedans' and 'Bengali Muhammedans', next to Parsees, Mughals, Arabs, Maghs, Madrassis, and 19,000 inhabitants of 'Unspecified Lower orders'.[13] In all, British residents made up a mere 1.50 per cent of the urban population and the members of the said elite comprised less than 0.50 per cent of it.[14]

Without doubt, Calcutta was a Bengali city, not simply on the ground of the composition of its inhabitants but also depending on how space was ordered and put to use by its inhabitants. However, Calcutta was often depicted as a British city in India. The distinction between what was called a 'white town' and a 'black town', based on how Calcutta was represented in sanitation plans during the second-half of the nineteenth century, also belongs to this colonial legacy. This distinction produced the persistent picture of a densely populated, congested, and filthy northern 'Black' and a rather spacious, clean, and prosperous 'White' southern Calcutta.[15] It, however, does not make any sense to distinguish Calcutta's residential quarters along ethnic lines, as the anatomy of the town constantly changed and people persistently transgressed city quarters to pursue their businesses and settle.[16] Besides, not a single city ward seems to have been exclusively inhabited by a certain ethnic group.[17] What can be distinguished to some extent is the economic, residential, and political functions of the urban landscapes. Beyond these functions was the layer of public buildings as a means of the built sovereignty that penetrated more or less, all city quarters.

This essay concentrates on the public and governmental buildings of Calcutta's new political centre between Tank Square and the Esplanade. The function and meaning of art and architecture applied in the city centre will also be analysed. Yet it has to be made clear here that the edificial display of power, prestige, and sovereignty did only to a limited extent address the Bengali inhabitants of Calcutta as the built sovereignty rather spoke to the British residents, as rulers of the country, who were more or less familiar with the latest developments of European urban design and architecture. Whether Bengalis would perceive this built sovereignty in the same way, or in any other way, was not on top of the British urban planners' and urban designers' agenda. With its monumental architecture, the entire building programme was self-referential without any 'missionary' impetus, i.e. any intended improvements for the local population. To what extent the Bengalis appreciated or rejected the Palladian and Classical architectures remains obscure yet and although, an important question to pose, it is beyond the scope of this article.

Classical and Palladian Architectures as a Means of the Built Sovereignty

When arriving in Calcutta in 1823, Bishop Reginald Heber enthusiastically described the neoclassical architecture of the city's public buildings, especially mentioning their façades that were painted white, and their Palladian porticoes.[18] Heber especially mentioned the grandiose appearance of Esplanade Row towards the River Hugli.[19] When, in the middle of the 1830s, Leopold von Orlich described Calcutta, he also referred to the magnificent buildings on Esplanade Row stating '[v]iewed from the Hooghly, Calcutta has the appearance of a city of palaces. A row of large superb buildings extend from the princely residence of the Governor-General, along the Esplanade, and produce a remarkably striking effect, by their handsome verandas, supported by columns'.[20] What impressed all the contemporary visitors of Calcutta and the British inhabitants alike was the Palladian and Classical styles of architecture. The almost coherent ensemble of representative public edifices along the Esplanade was at that time unique in the British Empire, even London had nothing comparable to exhibit.

During the eighteenth century, Palladianism and neoclassical architecture became an essential part of the emerging British

modern state's material means of self-representation, in contrast
to many European mainland states, which to a large extent—at
least until the nineteenth century—preferred baroque style. In
England, Palladianism became the architectural taste, expressing
the emerging self-understanding of the Whig aristocracy, after
the Glorious Revolution of 1688–9. Whigs then developed strong
beliefs in their own capacities and strong disbeliefs in the Stuart
Dynasty, the Roman Church, and most foreign things. They were
looking for an architecture that could adequately represent this self-
esteem and, to some extent, also become a means of distinction
and national representation. At the beginning of the eighteenth
century, two trendsetting books appeared in the market which
deeply influenced British architecture and urban design. The
first was Colen Campbell's *Vitruvius Britannicus* and the second,
a translation of Andrea Palladio's *Il Quattro Libri dell Architettura*,
originally published in 1570.[21] The two books provided the essential
means for introducing the new Italianate architecture embodying
ancient Roman principles, though representing an 'Anglicized' style
in many respects.[22]

At the beginning of the eighteenth century, Roman architecture
represented a grandiose empire in Britain which was then lost
but whose cultural achievements were still visible in the form of
monumental ruins. Later in the eighteenth century, ancient Hellenic
architecture was also discovered and included in the canon of
Europe's cultural heritage and the members of the British oligarchy
regarded themselves as its most qualified curators. Beside its
aesthetic value, ancient architecture also stood for an idealized and
stable political order which was regarded as an appropriate means for
giving expression to the modern British state, given that it emerged
during the turbulent times between the Glorious Revolution and
the end of the Continental (European) and Subcontinental (Indian)
Wars of 1815–18. Within a then recently established cultural
discourse, neoclassical architecture was seen not only as a means for
architecturally representing Britain's domestic political order but
also as an adequate means for representing colonial order in India
and elsewhere within the empire.[23]

In the middle of the eighteenth century, Edward Gibbon's
monumental history of the decline and fall of the Roman Empire,[24]

which was received enthusiastically, added to the question of whether the commercial British Empire was in some way or the other a modern successor of the Roman Empire 'albeit nobler and with a more defined sense of moral purpose'.[25] It is against this background that in England as well as in the overseas colonies, large public and private buildings of the Georgian Era were designed according to the Palladian or Classical principles.[26] After the Greek revival emerged in England at the turn of the eighteenth century, Doric classicism partially replaced the hitherto favoured Roman-Corinthian order of columns.[27] In Calcutta, this architectural transformation became visible in all public buildings erected between 1780 and 1824 which again graphically confirms the idea that Calcutta, in the eyes of the British elites, was in no way lagged behind the contemporary European and English artistic and architectural developments at all.

Built Sovereignty in the Colonial Capital City

The relocation of Fort William, a mile to the south of the old fort, as ordered by the Council in 1758, deployed a far-reaching reorientation and reconstruction of the original settlement.[28] The town of Calcutta (Kalikata, a separate municipal entity, next to Dihi Calcutta, Sutanati, and Govindpur), with Tank Square as its centre, was then transformed into a city with numerous administrative and representative buildings. However, as the space around the Tank Square was limited, the city was expanded some 400 yd. towards the creek that was filled-up, and the new representative edifices of Government House, Council House, the Accountant General's House, and the new Court House among others were erected on the northern end of the Esplanade between 1764 and 1784, facing the new Fort William.[29] The commercial centre remained in the vicinity of Tank Square where the remnants of the old fort were gradually turned into warehouses and living quarters for writers, and where the new Custom House was eventually housed. With their plain classical façades, the Government House and Council House represented contemporary Georgian architecture whereas the new Court House, with its long row of columns on the piano nobile's veranda, clearly showed the new plain classical, rather Palladian style that was soon to dominate Calcutta's representational morphology.

Two historical developments caused the fundamental
reorientation of Calcutta's edificial and architectural appearance, as
well as that of its accompanying street pattern, i.e. the reorganization
of the urban space in the city. First, the Court of Director's
decision in 1771 to take over direct administration of Bengal and
the Parliament's Regulation Act of 1773 which reorganized the
Company's administrative structure refer in particular to the creation
of the post of a governor general residing in Calcutta: an act,
definitely demanding more political representation of the Company
within the concert of Bengali-Indian powers, not only in terms of
personnel, including a growing number of British residents in town,
but also in terms of the architecture of representative buildings.
Second, after the defeat and death of Tipu Sultan of Mysore in
1799; the victorious Gurkha War in northern India during 1814–
16; and finally, the ultimate defeat of the Maratha Confederation
in 1818, the British claimed a paramount presence in India. They
now regarded their military and political power in South Asia as
insurmountable. By 1820, the days when Calcutta and Bengal were
administered by a factory's administrative staff were long gone.

Superiority found its expression in the pompous architecture
of four government buildings housing the judiciary (Court House,
1784), the public representation of the colonial elite of the city
(Town Hall, 1813), the auditing authority (Accountant General's
House, 1780s), and legislative-cum-executive of the country (New
Government House, 1803) on Esplanade Row. The sequence and
morphology of governmental edifices can be viewed as an Axis
of Power. Furthermore, Esplanade Row connected the New
Government House with Chandpal Ghat, then the colonial state's
official place of disembarkation. State representatives and prominent
visitors landing at Chandpal Ghat were escorted from the ghat to
the main entrance of the Government House—on the northern
side of the building—thus, ceremonially walking alongside the
impressive sequence of porticoes of the aforementiond buildings.

In addition to the Axis of Power, Governor General Richard
Wellesley and the architect of the New Government House, Captain
Charles Wyatt (1759–1818), an engineer officer who belonged to the
well-known Wyatt family of architects, most likely conceptualized
what may be called an Axis of Might when planning the monumental

FIGURE 1.1: *Esplanade Row Calcutta towards Chandpal Ghat, through the west gate of Government House.* Anonymous drawing, *c.*1830. On the right side from front to background: Accountant General's House, Town Hall, and Court House. *Source*: © British Library Board (followed by Photo 867), see http://ogimages.bl.uk/images/019/019PZZ000000867U00000000[SVC1].jpg, accessed 15 September 2016

FIGURE 1.2: 'Southern Gates and Porticoes of Government House', *c.*1865. *Source*: © British Library Board (followed by Photo 394) https://i2.wp.com/ogimages.bl.uk/images/019/019PHO000000394U00063000%5BSVC2%5D.jpg, accessed 15 September 2016

edifice in 1798. This urban design eventually consisted of three projects: first, an enlarged and improved Tank Square framed by a stone balustrade and gates completed in 1805, and the southern façade of the Writers' Building towards Tank Square which was dramatically upgraded architecturally and eventually accomplished in 1821;[30] second, turning the New Government House by 180 degrees and designing its monumental flight of steps that led to a huge propylaeum-like portico on the edifice's northern façade. Third, the demolition of numerous houses and expropriation of land between the Government House and Tank Square for creating a wide road and a magnificent vista between the central portico of the Writers' Building and the entrance portico of the Government House, built between 1803 and 1805.[31]

In fact, Lord Valentia, visiting Calcutta in 1803, must have known about such plans as he envisaged the potential of this axis, stating 'the space now to be cleared will have a noble effect; and the Writers' Building being newly repaired, form a good object from the end of the street that leads from the northern front [of Government House]'.[32] This effect was created keeping the spectators' view in mind. The landing of the flight of steps and the balcony of the Government House, the new seat of power, were visually and virtually linked to the old town centre, represented by the Writers' Building. The impression was soon to be enhanced with the erection of the Marquis of Hastings Monument in 1824 on the southern side of Tank Square, and the already existing St Andrew's Kirk completed in 1818, situated east of the Writers' Building. It is the grandiose ensemble of a government building, an ecclesiastical edifice, and a public monument that underlines the symbolic importance of the Axis of Might. The most interesting effect, however, was the Government House becoming the hinge joint of the two axes. The building, thus became a unique symbol representing the morphology of power.[33]

The similarities between Calcutta's Tank Square and London's Trafalgar Square are quite obvious. It seems that the architect of London's National Gallery, William Wilkins (1778–1839), had, two decades earlier, in some way or the other, deeply influenced the reconstruction of the Writers' Building in Calcutta. Wilkins was also the architect who had designed the Haileybury and Imperial Service College, built in 1806, that was the Company's educational institution for its future employees. From the English neo-Palladian elements, Wilkins took the tripartite division of the main front, as it had been established by London's meanwhile famous façades of the Adelphi and of Somerset House. Besides this, at Haileybury, he also emphasized monumental Greek elements like Doric porticoes modelled on the propylaeum of the Acropolis of Athens.[34] Comparing the façade of Haileybury with that of the Writers' Building, it is quite striking how the latter's refurbishing resembles the former's architecture. Immediate evidence is, however, missing. Drawing a conclusion in some cases is henceforth, rather ex silentio than based on documented facts.

In London, the first steps to improve the impoverished urban area which was to become Trafalgar Square, took place in 1812 when architect John Nash (1752–1835) projected the overall development of the site near Pall Mall, the Royal Mews built by William Kent in 1732, James Gibbs' St Martin-in-the-Fields completed in 1726, and Charing Cross. However, except the new road opening up St Martin-in-the-Fields in 1825, thus making the church's portico

FIGURE 1.3: *The south front of Haileybury College, Herts*, 1810.
Source: Anthony Farrington, ed., frontispiece. *The Records of the East India College, Haileybury, & Other Institutions*, London: HMSO, 1976

visible from afar and seen from Pall Mall East, a *point de vue*, most
of the urban design had to be shelved due to the lack of financial
means.[35] After much ado about Trafalgar Square's future size,
shape, design, and buildings, including a National Gallery, work on
the latter eventually began in 1832.[36] Wilkins had offered a cost-
saving plan for the building that saved him the contract, but the
lack of financial means was the reason why the building's design
was eventually rather poor.[37] He again proposed a long tripartite
building with protruding porticos in the neoclassical style. The
National Gallery was finally completed in 1837; however, it took
until 1843 to erect 'Nelson's Column' and, last but not the least, the
two fountains, built in 1845, to complete the 'Emblem of Empire'.[38]

In contrast to the badly proportioned façade of the National
Gallery followed by the rather solitary edifice of St Martin-in-
the-Fields squeezed out of the square in the corner of Trafalgar
Square, the monumental and well-proportioned tripartite façade of
the Writers' Building facing Tank Square, followed by the four-
columned portico of St Andrew's Kirk which is visible from the
square's southern side, defines its harmonious size. In addition,
the portico-cum-tower of St Andrew's Kirk, an obvious imitation
of St Andrew Church in Edinburgh, one of the many copies
of St Martin-in-the-Fields, which meanwhile had become the
prototype for multiple copies in the British Empire and English
speaking Protestant communities elsewhere,[39] represents an urban
landmark. This is highlighted by the fact that the façade of the
church symmetrically stands on the axis of the Old Court House
Street and serves as a *point de vue* into the city's streetscape, thereby,
linking two main road axes, namely the Writers' Building and Lal
Bazar (east-west), and the Old Court House Street (north-south).[40]

What has become evident is the importance, the British
administration gave to an urban space defined by architecture, in
particular the façades of buildings. It is the arrangement of façades
along the sides of a place that creates harmony and at the same time
documents the great power of a particular façade or a combination
of façades. They bring certain acts to the realm of what is visible,
whether such acts occur 'on' the façade itself (windows, balconies,
balustrades, porticoes, staircases, etc.) or are to be seen 'from' the
façade (processions, parades, public receptions, demonstrations,

FIGURE 1.4: 'Writers' Building, Calcutta', *c*.1860s.
Source: http://1.bp.blogspot.com/-eMhXfzAhf3I/TtE6yU3MuEI/
AAAAAAAAMtE/E2g8YyqI-LM/s1600/Writer%2527s+Buildings+-+Calc
utta+%2528Kolkata%2529+1878.jpg, accessed 15 September 2016

FIGURE 1.5: Trafalgar Square, London, National Gallery and
St Martins-in-the-Fields; © Michael Mann, 2017

revolutions, etc.). Numerous acts occur 'behind' façades where they are actually condemned to clandestineness, at least partially. Such indoor acts lose their function as a means to render power and public presence visually and instead, become a means of power that produces exclusion and separation.[41] This is particularly true for a State's political elite's representative acts which gain a sense of reassurance through stately ceremonies and rituals.

Two buildings in Calcutta will demonstrate the importance of architecture and design in understanding the social meaning attached to urban space. They will exemplify the morphology of power produced through urban representative buildings on the one hand and the idea of built sovereignty culminating in a single edifice on the other hand. The first is St John's Church that was consecrated in 1786 and became a highly symbolic edifice because of the material used to build it and also because it became the church of the bishop of Calcutta after 1813. The second is the already mentioned New Government House, completed in 1803, the seat and symbol of the country's (and the colony's) supreme administration. Both these edifices reveal the colonial elite's self-understanding as not just being the inhabitants of a remote outpost of the British Empire, and therefore, of a city as well as citizens, of negligible importance; but as one of the British Empire's prime cities that was carefully planned and magnificently as well as meaningfully designed.

St John's Church

The construction of St John's Church started in 1784.[42] Interestingly, the church was not financed by the Church of England or the Company but the land was donated by Raja Nabakrishna Deb (1733–97) of Shobhabazar Rajbari and the money was raised through a committee headed by the then Governor General Warren Hastings.[43] The church was opened on 24 June 1787 and the consecration ceremony was attended by Hastings' successor Lord Cornwallis.[44] Located on the former Powder Magazine Yard which adjoined the old burial ground outside the settlement, 'the foundations [of the church] were laid among the mouldering remains of scores upon scores of those who had died during the ninety years of the English occupation'.[45] Of the old mausoleums, only those of Job Charnock, Head of the East India Company in Bengal and founder of the

English factory in the vicinity of the villages, Kalikata and Sutanati, and Admiral Watson, the Commander of the Royal Navy ships who recaptured Calcutta together with Robert Clive's Company troops in 1757, were left undisturbed and kept in memory of Calcutta's 'founding father' and 'saviour', respectively.

Lieutenant James Agg of the Bengal Engineers, son of a Gloucestershire stonemason, was the church's architect who had arrived in Calcutta in 1777.[46] The church's design was neoclassical with a portico of six Doric columns. Originally, the apsis and altar were behind the main entrance, a misconception that was corrected in 1797 when the entrance, including the newly constructed portico was shifted to the western side, right under the spire.[47] The nave was constructed in brick and plaster and the columns were covered with *chunam*—an Indian type of brightly-shining plaster made from shell lime and sand—whereas, the steeple was completed in the pinkish-brown ashlar stone from Chunar.[48] At first glance, the steeple reminds one of James Gibbs's St Martins-in-the-Fields. However, due to the building material's weight and Calcutta's soft alluvial soil, the construction had to be reduced accordingly in height, giving the spire a fairly compressed appearance. The floor of the nave was laid out with the bluish-grey shining stone from ruined Gaur, the residence of the Bengal rulers from 1457 until 1565. Due to its stone steeple and stone floor, St John's Church was commonly known as the *pathure girja* or stone church.[49]

The colloquial Bengali denomination indicates the building's significance. Using the former capital city of Gaur as a quarry to gain an extraordinary material for building St John's Church is a remarkable episode of claiming succession to an old dynasty or polity and, at the same time, legitimacy as the rulers of Bengal. The fact that the stone slides were used as the floor covering, thus literally and highly symbolically subduing the former famous polity by walking on its appropriated remnants is highly interesting. It also indicates the new rulers' claim to the right, as conquerors of the country, to requisition from the subdued people whatever they deemed fit for establishing their power, including, most importantly, the former symbols and signs of might. Of special significance is the widely visible lithic spire because, like every tower or tall building, it is a clear and at the same time a phallic sign of power and might. What is nonetheless more important from a geographical and geological context is the fact that procuring and using stone as a construction material in a landscape generally devoid of stone, impressed the Bengali inhabitants of Calcutta and came to signify the power of the new rulers, as was most certainly intended by the British.

There are plenty of analoguous examples of such demonstration of the succession of power and the claim to legitimacy by usurping and transforming former signs and symbols of power and might. The relocation of the Egyptian obelisk in Rome in 1586 from its original position next to St Peter's, right into the middle of Bernini's colonnaded square, the technical task then deemed almost unsolvable, is a telling example. Pope Sixtus V viewed himself in an

FIGURE 1.6: St John's Church, Calcutta; © Michael Mann, March 2017

imagined line of continuity from the most ancient civilization known in Europe at that time, indicating at the same time Christianity's superiority over Egyptian and Roman antiquities. The obelisk had been transported to Rome in CE 37 and erected on the spina of the Circus Caligula, later known as Circus Nero, the site covering the present-day St Peter's Cathedral and Bernini's Square, with a cross placed on its peak.[50]

Another example is a form of the Russian Orthodox Church's cross introduced after the battle on the Kulikovo Field in 1380. In the cultural memory of the Russian nobility and the Orthodox Church, the battle indicated the end of the Tartar tyranny in Russia that had lasted since CE 1240.[51] Since members of the 'Golden Horde', as the Tartars called themselves and were to a large extent followers of Islam, victory over the Tartars was also seen as a victory over Islam which was symbolized by the Russian Orthodox cross triumphantly standing on, one may also view it as pronging, the Islamic crescent. In the nineteenth century, Russian

FIGURE 1.7: 'Obelisk on St Peter's Square',
Source: See http://2.bp.blogspot.com/-3wzSLeMYZik/T4R0pW_yc0I/
AAAAAAAAAYQ/7eCngKxAlP8/s1600/obelisk+petersplatz.JPG,
accessed 15 September 2016

national historiography instrumentalized this cultural memory, now
claiming that the Kulikovo Battle bears evidence of Russia being
a civilized 'Western' power which defended and protected Europe
from an expanding, uncivilized and Islamic 'Eastern' power. The
only comparable example to this is the Battle of Poitiers and Tours
in CE 732 that stopped Moorish expansion in Western Europe. The
commemoration monument on the Kulikovo Field expresses this
interpretation with the somehow forgotten cross on the crescent
making a reappearance.[52]

It is this translocal cultural context of representing power and
might through simple and unambiguous means that was immediately
comprehended by the inhabitants of the sixteenth-century Rome
and of the fourteenth-century Russian ecclesiastical and princely
elites, as well as the British population and the visitors of Calcutta
at the end of the eighteenth century. Managing technology whilst
erecting the Egyptian obelisk in Rome or building a stone spire
on Calcutta's soft alluvial soil as well as symbolically subduing
a conquered civilization as in the case of the new cross of the
Russian Orthodox Church, the cross on top of the obelisk in Rome

FIGURE 1.8: 'Terem Palace, built in 1635–7, the main residence of the
Russian Tsars in Moscow's Kremlin during the seventeenth century'.
See the traditional cross of the Russian Orthodox Church on the
cupola on the right side.
Source: see https://tse3.mm.bing.net/th?id=OIP.Mdd1021f4e783ef9ae110df
fd32664ab2H0&pid=15.1, accessed 15 September 2016

and the British feet on the Bengali stone floor of St John's Church were acts of power and gestures of might, well understood by the victors and may have been perceived as impressive signs of mastery by the local population.[53]

Government House

Construction work started in February 1799 and the edifice was inaugurated in August 1802.[54] Wellesley commissioned Captain Wyatt to design the New Government House. The model for the floor plan was the original plan of Lord Scarsdale's Kedleston Hall, namely a central main building with four pavilions connected by flat-curved corridors and built in the Palladian style, mainly to the designs of James Paine (1717–89) and with amendments by Robert Adam (1728–98) in the 1760s.[55] This floor plan was, however, far from being unique given that similar floor plans existed since Andrea Palladio's time (1508–80) and had been taken up by various British architects, e.g., by William Kent (1685–1748) for conceptualizing Holkham House.[56] Similarities between Kedleston Hall and Government House in Calcutta are but a few.[57] The outer design of Government House differs fundamentally from Kedleston Hall. As the former's curved corridors were of the same height as the central building and the pavilions, in contrast to the latter's one-storied corridors and small pavilions, the Government House's northern closed front, given that the pavilions were as such not distinguishable, formed an open court reminiscent of European baroque palaces.[58]

Shortly after Wellesley had arrived in Calcutta in May 1798 to take up his post as governor general, he decided to build a representative house for the head of the colonial state. The palatial appearance of the edifice was raised by the impressive lithic flight of steps in front of the central portico-cum-pediment protruding from the façades of the pavilions. In terms of its dimensions, the flight of steps has only a few precedents in European representative architecture which may have influenced Wyatt's design. Most prominent among these is Andrea Palladio's prototype of a temple-like façade with its huge protruding straight stairway of the Villa Badoer, built during 1556–63. The villa's plan and description were available in his *Four Books on Architecture*.[59] Here, for the first time, a basic element of

sacral architecture was applied to a secular building. Wyatt may have
also heard or seen a plan of Stowe House's palatial southern front
with its flight of thirty-three steps, built during 1771–9.[60] Whether
the huge flight of steps in front of the propylaeum on Athens'
Acropolis influenced Wyatt's stairway in front of the temple-like
entrance of the Government House, remains obscure.

However, Wyatt and/or Wellesley may have been familiar with
the huge flight of steps in front of the main entrance gate of Akbar's
capital city/residence-fortress at Fatehpur Sikri or the great stairways
in front of the gates of Jama Masjid in Delhi. The dramatic effect
of the latter was drawn by Thomas Daniell and William Daniell,
and published as the first picture in their series *Oriental Scenery:*
Twenty-Four Views in Hindoostan in March 1795, just a year after their
return from India, and the set of prints became available in India
in 1796.[61] The purpose of the flight of steps of the Government
House was clear, given that the ritual function of a palace's indoor
stairway was defined in the context of European courtly culture
since the seventeenth century as the place to ceremonially receive
diplomats, princes, and monarchs. In this way, the staircase became

FIGURE 1.9: 'Government House, Calcutta'.
Source: Francis Frith, *Photographs of India*, see
https://commons.wikimedia.org/wiki/Category:Photographs_of_India_by_
Francis_Frith, accessed 15 September 2016

the space of a hierarchical and politically charged space, regulating access to prince and power.[62] As staircases in South Asia were only known outside a few palaces and mosques, the significance of Calcutta's staircase was enhanced in two ways. First, it became the outdoor place of stately receptions, now virtually performed in public; second, north Indian princely visitors would be reminded of a culturally familiar scenery, namely to climb up a huge stairway to get access to the sovereign or to divine service. Seen against this background, the Government House's flight of steps seems to have been an adaptation and a consequent absorption of South Asian architectural morphology that underlined British claims to power within the still existing Gurkaniya Empire.

In its outer appearance, freely visible from all sides, the Government House had more splendour than any other representative building of the British Empire, including the royal palaces in London and the country houses of the English

FIGURE 1.10: Thomas Daniell and William Daniell, 'Eastern gate of the Jummah Musjid at Delhi', *Oriental Scenery: Twenty-Four Views in Hindoostan*, part 1, plate 1, 1795.
Source: see http://3.bp.blogspot.com/-6etJyhjxemo/VekiROQ9API/ AAAAAAAAArE/q-eVAH3G7E8/s1600/Picture1.png, accessed 15 September 2016

aristocracy. Bishop Heber stated at the beginning of the 1820s that the 'Government House is, to say the least of it, a more shewy palace than London has to produce'.[63] Keeping this in mind, Lord Valentia's well-known statement on the Company to rule India from a palace, with the underlying imagination of a princedom, acquires a more nuanced meaning.[64] It reflects the idea of baroque palaces giving expression to and, at the same time, helping to define the very political structures they house.[65] Government House was more than just a European princely palace built in Bengal. It was also a skilful combination of Bengali/South Asian and British/ European ideas of the morphology of power: the aesthetic of the Government House's open court with its monumental protruding stairway expressing the idea of built sovereignty in a way that was intended so by the architect and the administrators, and also well comprehended by users and observers.

The case of the outer design, the inner design, and particularly the distribution of rooms of the Government House is also fundamentally different from Kedleston Hall and other contemporary four-winged British country houses. Comparing the floor plans of the two buildings, differences are obvious, e.g., the arrangement of rooms being far less dense.[66] The building's corridors and the distribution of rooms provided for a constant current of air which is one of the outstanding features of the edifice as already observed by contemporary visitors of the building. The other one is the lighting of the main hall which, at Kedleston Hall, is direct and done by a glass cupola in the centre of Marble Hall's ceiling whereas in Government House the lighting of Marble Hall on the piano nobile and upstairs Ball Room is indirect and done by five lateral French windows lit on each side by the corresponding number of windows in the outer walls of parallel elongated rooms.[67]

Of particular importance are the two aforementioned staterooms. The Marble Hall was the principal stateroom of Government House. It consisted of a central nave and two sideway corridors, each separated by a row of 10 Doric columns and 2 half columns at its ends. Marble busts of the 'Twelve Caesars', 'replicas of a series not infrequently met with in the adornment of palaces and princely mansions during the classical revival of the 18th century', were ranged along the east and west walls of the aisles.[68] These busts of the 'Twelve Caesars' were actually derived from Gaius Suetonius

Tranquillus' *De Vita Caesarum*, written in CE 121 and consisting of the biographies of Julius Caesar and the following eleven imperators.[69] In an English aristocrat's house, however, the 'Twelve Caesars' may have rather been of decorative importance, at best indicating an owner's knowledge of antique languages. In the colonial context though, they were certainly of particular political significance as they symbolically placed the British Empire, especially the governor generals in Calcutta in line with the imperators, i.e. victorious commanders of ancient Rome, with Hastings, Lord Cornwallis, and of course Richard Wellesley being the most recent successors.[70]

The Ball Room was exactly the same size and had more or less the same arrangements as the Marble Hall. Since its first employment in 1803, the room was used as throne room, in which receptions took place until the middle of the nineteenth century. The adjacent southern anteroom, decorated with large mirrors, served as a drawing room on the occasion of dinner parties and the northern anteroom was used for the buffet at balls.[71] It is the layout of both these

FIGURE 1.11: 'The Marble Hall, Government House'.
Source: The Marquis Curzon of Kedleston, *British Government in India: The Story of the Viceroys and Government Houses*, 2 Volumes, London: Cassel and Co., 1925, pp. 98–9

staterooms in Government House that reminds one of Kedleston
Hall's Marble Hall. The latter's Marble Hall was designed by Robert
Adam around 1772,[72] the original design, however, being York's
Assembly Rooms, drafted by the Earl of Burlington (1694–1753) in
1730.[73] The Marble Hall and Ball Room in Calcutta's Government
House are, again rooms, purposefully designed as an architectural
epitome of British pride and power in Calcutta, skilfully varying
from the original design of York's Assembly Rooms and even
improving it with regard to space and lighting, in response to the
climatic conditions of the colony.[74]

Conclusion

The two representational buildings—one mundane, one
ecclesiastic—clearly indicate the role of architecture as an artful
and wilful combination of style/design, construction material, and

FIGURE 1.12: 'York: Assembly Rooms, designed by Lord Burlington'.
Source: see https://heritagecalling.files.wordpress.com/2015/10/pl-ii-8-
yc_01372.jpg [YC1327 - Interior view of Assembly Rooms, York,
October 1969: Crown copyright: Historic England Archive], accessed
15 September 2016

morphology on the one hand; and location and positioning of the said buildings on the other hand. Besides the importance of the exterior façades, it is the art and decoration of the edifices' interior architecture that underline the political will as well as the historical awareness of the British as the newly established rulers in Bengal and beyond. St John's Church and the Government House are, in a political sense, the most sacred buildings of Calcutta where, in front of and behind the façade, the most important rituals of the state were celebrated: the Sunday Mass, just like state entries, may be viewed as political rituals of the colonial elite.

In addition, the two buildings were purposely and meaningfully distributed within the urban landscape of the colonial capital city. Calcutta's political space was, as has been demonstrated, demarcated by the Government House and the Writers' Building on the one side, and by the earlier mentioned government buildings along the Esplanade on the other. Whilst the latter constitutes the Axis of Power, the former forms an Axis of Might, with St John's Church, most symbolically, embraced and protected by the two axes. It is this concert of artful architecture, conscious selection of location, and reciprocal referencing that constructed and, at the same time, ordered the political space of Calcutta as British India's capital city after the turn of the eighteenth century. In conclusion, it is apt to state that it was the morphology of power (embedded in the materialization of architecture) and the topography of might (as graphic in the assignment of locations) that constituted Calcutta's, as any other capital's built sovereignty. The latter, as pointed out at the beginning of this article, is understood as a political regime's building programme to express and to represent its supreme power and might.

Further evidence will have to document the function of additional representative buildings within that setting, for example Calcutta's Town Hall on Esplanade Row or St Andrew's Kirk at the upper end of the Old Court House Street. In addition, the street pattern of Calcutta, as planned and partially executed by the Lottery Committee, deserves a close scrutiny to understand how far and according to which principles, Calcutta's urban space was actually ordered.[75] To what extent was the Lottery Committee as well as the colonial government involved, not only in planning streets and

places but also in their edificial design, would be one of the most
important questions to pose. This would clearly promote the idea
that built sovereignty was part of a comprehensive town-planning
scheme that was designed and executed in Calcutta between 1772
and 1825.

Notes

1. Soumitra Sreemani, *Anatomy of a Colonial Town: Calcutta, 1756–1794*,
   Calcutta: Firma KLM, 1974; and Samaren Roy, *Calcutta: Society and
   Change, 1690–1990*, Calcutta: Rupa & Co., 1991.
2. Raja Binaya Krishna Deb, *The Early History and Growth of Calcutta*, Calcutta:
   Romesh Chandra Ghose, 1905; Suresh Chandra Ghosh, *The British in
   Bengal: A Study of the British Society and Life in the Late Eighteenth Century*,
   Leiden: E.J. Brill, 1970, repr. New Delhi: Munshiram Manoharlal, 1998;
   and Pradip Sinha, *Calcutta in Urban History*, Calcutta: Firma KLM, 1978.
3. Partho Datta, *Planning the City: Urbanization and Reform in Calcutta, c.1800–
   1940*, New Delhi: Tulika, 2012.
4. Swati Chattopadhyay, *Representing Calcutta: Modernity, Nationalism, and the
   Colonial Uncanny*, London and New York: Routledge, 2005.
5. Jeremiah P. Losty, *Calcutta, City of Palaces: A Survey of the City in the Days
   of the East India Company, 1690–1858*, London: British Library Arnold
   Publishers, 1990.
6. Sten Nilsson, *European Architecture in India, 1750–1850*, New York:
   Taplinger, 1969; Philip Davies, *Splendours of the Raj: British Architecture
   in India, 1660 to 1947*, London: John Murray, 1985; and Jan Morris,
   Stones of Empire: The Buildings of British India, Oxford: Oxford University
   Press, 1983.
7. Thomas R. Metcalf, *An Imperial Vision: Indian Architecture and Britain's Raj*,
   Berkeley and California: University of California Press, 1989, pp. 1–23.
8. Gurkaniya, literally son-in-law, is the self-denomination of the Indian
   Padshah, whereas Mughal or Mogul is a European appellation, see
   Beatrice Forbes Manz, *The Rise and Rule of Tamerlane*, Cambridge:
   Cambridge University Press, 1989, pp. 14–16. Son-in-law refers to the
   constructed legitimization of Timur Tamerlan's imperial rule as son-in-
   law of Genghis Khan. Padshah is the official title of the monarch, like
   the shah-i-shah in Persia, or the emperor of the Holy Roman Empire.
9. Henri Lefebvre, 'The Production of Space', tr. Donald Nicholson-Smith,
   Malden (USA), Oxford (UK), Victoria (Aus.): Blackwell, 1991, pp. 71–
   4, 101–2, 110.
10. Ibid., p. 34.

11. Ibid., p. 224.

12. The phrase is taken from Henning Eichberg, 'Ordnen, Messen, Disziplinieren: Moderner Herrschaftsstaat und Fortifikation', in *Staatsverfassung und Heeresverfassung in der europäischen Geschichte der frühen Neuzeit*, ed. Johannes Kunisch, Berlin: Duncker & Humblodt, 1986, pp. 347–75, esp. p. 350.

13. 'Samachar Darpan', 25 February 1837; as reproduced in B.N. Bandopadhyay, 'Sangbadpatre Sekaler Kata', vol. 2, 1949, p. 625; repr. Sinha, *Calcutta in Urban History*, p. 43.

14. Public balls at Government House were often attended by up to 800 persons, see George Viscount Valentia, *Voyages and Travels in India, Ceylon, the Red Sea, Abyssinia, and Egypt, in the Years 1802, 1803, 1804, 1805, and 1806*, 4 vols. (1789, 1790, 1791, and 1792), vols. 1 and 2, London: F.C. and J. Rivington, 1811, pp. 37–8 and 6 December 1792, p. 236.

15. Datta, *Planning the City*, pp. 171–288; and Partha Chatterjee, *The Black Hole of Empire: History of a Global Practice of Power*, Ranikhet: Permanent Black, 2012, pp. 225–8.

16. Chattopadhyay, *Representing Calcutta*, pp. 28–33, 76–80.

17. Carl H. Nightingale, 'Before Race Mattered: Geographies of the Color Line in Early Colonial Madras and New York', *American Historical Review*, vol. 13, no. 1, 2008, pp. 48–71.

18. Reginald Heber, *Narrative of a Journey through the Upper Provinces of India; from Calcutta to Bombay, 1824–25 (With Notes upon Ceylon): An Account of a Journey to Madras and the Southern Provinces, 1826, and Letters Written in India*, 3 vols., London: John Murray, 1828; Reginald Heber, 'Correspondence'; and Reginald Heber, 'To Miss Dod', Calcutta, 15 December 1823, pp. 237–42, esp. p. 240.

19. Heber, *Narrative of a Journey through the Upper Provinces of India*, vol. 1, pp. 28–9.

20. Leopold von Orlich, *Travels in India, Including Sinde and the Punjab*, vol. 2, tr. H. Evans Lloyd, London: Longman, Brown, Green and Longmans, 1845, p. 175.

21. Colen Campbell, *Vitruvius Britannicus, or the British Architect*, vol. 1 (London, 1715); vol. 2 (London, 1717); and vol. 3 (London, 1725) had the most far-reaching impact on British architecture during the Georgian period; Isaac Ware, ed., *Andrea Palladio: The Four Books of Architecture*, London, 1737; with a new introduction by Adolf K. Placzek, New York: Dover, 2014.

22. John Summerson, *Architecture in Britain, 1530–1830*, New Haven and London: Yale University Press, 1993, pp. 296–309. In fact, between 1715 and 1725, Campbell set up the models upon which the whole of Palladianism in England was to depend.

23. On the debate, whether modern Britain was comparable with ancient Rome and whether a Greater Britain was similar to an imagined Greater Rome, which started in the middle of the eighteenth century and lasted until the beginning of the twenty-first century; see Phiroze Vasunia, *The Classics and Colonial India*, Oxford: Oxford University Press, 2013, pp. 119–55.

24. Edward Gibbon, *The Decline and Fall of the Roman Empire*, 6 vols., London: W. Straham and T. Cadell, 1776–87.

25. Chattopadhyay, *Representing Calcutta*, p. 29.

26. For example, William Chamber's theoretical reflections in *A Treatise on the Decorative Part of Civil Architecture*, 3rd edn, London: Joseph Smeeton, 1741 had a deep impact on the classical design of edifices. See Mildred Archer, 'Aspects of Classicism in India: Georgian Buildings of Calcutta', *Country Life*, 3 November 1966, pp. 1142–6. For the second generation of Neoclassical architects and the Greek revival, see Summerson, *Architecture in Britain, 1530–1830*, pp. 410–26.

27. Metcalf, *An Imperial Vision*, p. 9.

28. There is no proof of either a decision-making process or that of a single decision by the Calcutta Council on Fort William. That decision will remain one of the missing documented links.

29. Losty, *Calcutta*, pp. 58–61; R.R. Choudhury, *The Lord Sahib's House, Sites of Power: Government Houses of Calcutta 1690–1911*, Kolkata: Wild Strawberry Books, 2010, pp. 61–74, 102. Proceedings, 15 October 1764, comp. J. Long, *Selections from Unpublished Records of Government for the Years 1748 to 1767 Inclusive Relating Mainly to the Social Condition of Bengal, with a Map of Calcutta in 1748*, vol. 1, London: N. Trübner & Co., 1869, pp. 384–5.

30. Government of Bengal, Judicial Criminal, no. 23, 25 July 1805; quoted in Datta, *Planning the City*, pp. 26–7. W.S. Seton-Karr and H.D. Sandeman, eds., *Selections from Calcutta Gazettes*, Thursday, 9 August 1821, vol. 9, Calcutta: O.T. Cutter, Military Orphan Press, 1816–23 (in two parts), p. 418.

31. *Calcutta Gazette*, 22 October 1796.

32. Valentia, *Voyages and Travels in India*, vol. 1, p. 195.

33. Nilsson, *European Architecture in India*, p. 66. Nilsson realizes the comprehensive restructuring but fails to explain the changes in a wider context of contemporary ideas of European town planning and urban design, thereby, missing the importance of the transformation.

34. R.W. Liscombe, *William Wilkins, 1778–1839*, Cambridge: Cambridge University Press, 1980, pp. 46–50.

35. J.P. Malcolm, writing in 1807, said that the west front of St Martin-in-the-Fields '. . . would have a grand effect if the execrable watch-house and sheds before it were removed . . .' and described the sides of the church as '. . . lost in courts, where houses approach them almost to

contact . . .'. James Peller Malcolm, *Londinium Redivivium, or, an Ancient History and Modern Description of London*, vol. 4, London: Nichols; Son et al., 1803–7, p. 202. See also 'The New Opening to St. Martin's Church (1825)', in *The National Gallery: An Illustrated History*, ed. Alan Crookham, London: National Gallery Company, 2009, p. 15.

36. On the origins of the National Gallery, see Charles Saumarez Smith, *The National Gallery: A Short History*, London: Frances Lincoln Limited, 2009, pp. 12–30.

37. Liscombe, *William Wilkins*, pp. 180-4.

38. Rodney Mace, *Trafalgar Square: Emblem of Empire*, 2nd edn, London: Lawrence and Wichert, 2005.

39. Bryan Little, *The Life and Work of James Gibbs, 1682–1754*, London: B.T. Batsford, 1955, pp. 181–8.

40. Nilsson, *European Architecture in India*, p. 128; Davies, *Splendours of the Raj*, p. 70.

41. Lefebvre, 'The Production of Space', p. 99.

42. Seton-Karr and Sandeman, eds., *Selection from Calcutta Gazettes*; Office of the Superintendent of Government Printing and Calcutta Central Press Company Limited 1864–69, reprinted with an Introduction by N.R. Ray, Calcutta: Bibhash Gupta, 1987, vol. 1, 1784, p. 13.

43. For a detailed account of the lottery's various receipts from Calcutta's British and Bengal residents, see Long, *Calcutta and Its Neighbourhood*, p. 189.

44. Seton-Karr and Sandeman, eds., *Selections from Calcutta Gazettes*, vol. 1, Thursday, 28 June 1787, p. 203.

45. Kathleen Blechynden, *Calcutta: Past and Present*, London: W. Thacker & Co., 1905, p. 138.

46. Davies, *Splendours of the Raj*, p. 58.

47. Halder, *Colonial Architecture of Kolkata*, pp. 109–12. Later changes, such as the addition of the verandas on the northern and southern exterior walls in 1811 and the removal of galleries in the interior in 1901, altered the church's inner and outer appearances fundamentally; see Evan Cotton, *Calcutta, Old and New: A Historical & Descriptive Handbook to the City*, Calcutta: W. Newman & Co., 1907, p. 473.

48. Nilsson, *European Architecture in India*, p. 167.

49. Folio 153, dated 1 June 1784; Folio 161, dated 9 June 1784, 15 June 1784, 26 June 1784, 8 July 1784, 10 July 1784, 'Minutes of the Kirk Sessions of St John's Church', as quoted in Soumitra Das, 'Gour to St. John's', *The Telegraph*, Calcutta, 22 June 2008, see http://www.telegraphindia.com/1080622/jsp/calcutta/story_9421910.jsp, accessed 24 July 2015.

50. Ernst Batta, *Obelisken: Ägyptische Obelisken und ihre Geschichte in Rom*, Frankfurt a. M.: Insel Verlag, 1986, pp. 15–16, 23–50.

51. Janet Martin, *Medieval Russia, 980–1584*, Cambridge: Cambridge University Press, 1995, pp. 213–16.

52. The memorial, designed by Alexander Brullov and erected on the Kulikovo battlefield in commemoration of the battle in 1848, is a black column capped by a golden Russian Orthodox cross on a crescent.

53. Historical evidence is however missing as no contemporary source mentions how the stone floor of St John's Church was perceived by the Bengal inhabitants of Calcutta.

54. The Marquis Curzon of Kedleston, *British Government in India: The Story of the Viceroys and Government Houses*, vol. 1, London: Cassel and Co., 1925, p. 44; Blechynden, *Calcutta*, p. 109.

55. For the history of planning and designing Kedleston Hall, see Joseph and Anne Rykwert, *The Brothers Adam: The Men and the Style*, London: Collins, 1985, pp. 64–8.

56. Ware, ed., *Andrea Palladio*, pp. 54–5; Rudolf Wittkower, *Palladio and English Palladianism*, London: Thames and Hudson, 1983, p. 122, plate 148.

57. This is in contrast to almost all descriptions of Government House which seem to be based on Curzon's description. Exception to the rule is Chattopadhyay, *Representing Calcutta*, pp. 111–18.

58. Little, *Life and Work of James Gibbs*, p. 35.

59. Ware, ed., *Andrea Palladio*, vol. 2, p. 49 and plate 31.

60. Michael Bevington, *Stowe House*, Stowe: Capability Books, 1990, revised repr., London: Paul Holberton, 2002, pp. 11–13, 29–30.

61. Thomas Daniell, *Oriental Scenery: Twenty-Four Views in Hindoostan*, vol. 1, London: Longman, Hurst, Rees, Orme and Brown, 1795. See also Archer, *Early Views of India: The Picturesque Journeys of Thomas and William Daniell, 1786–1794: The Complete Aquatints*, London: Thames and Hudson, 1980, Plate 36; *Calcutta Gazette*, 22 October 1796, advertised 'twenty-four views of Hindoostan from the drawings of Thomas Daniell and engraved by himself' for a set price of 200 *sicca* rupees; see also Thomas Sutton, *The Daniels: Artists and Travellers*, London: The Bodley Head, 1954, pp. 89–90.

62. John Adamson, 'Introduction: The Making of the Ancien Régime Court 1500–1700', in *The Princely Courts of Europe: Rituals, Politics and Culture under the Ancien Régime, 1500–1750*, London: Weidenfeld & Nicolson, 1999, pp. 7–41, esp. pp. 12–14.

63. Heber, *Narrative of a Journey through the Upper Provinces of India*; Heber, 'Correspondence'; and Heber, 'To Miss Dod', pp. 237-42, esp. p. 238.

64. Valentia, *Voyages and Travels in India*, vol. 1, p. 192.

65. Hugh Murray Baillie, 'Etiquette and the Planning of State Apartments in Baroque Palace', *Archaeologia*, vol. 101, 1967, pp. 169–99, esp. p. 172.

66. Chattopadhyay, *Representing Calcutta*, pp. 112–15.

67. See the two floor plans, ibid., pp. 112–13; and Cotton, *Calcutta, Old and New*, pp. 667–8.

68. Curzon, *British Government in India*, vol. 1, p. 94, fn. 1; pp. 97–100; quoted from p. 100.
69. The eleven following Caesars are: Augustus, Tiberius, Caligula, Claudius, Nero, Galba, Otho, Vitellius, Vespasian, Titus, and Domitian. *De Vitae Caesarum* is considered a primary source on Roman history. The book discusses the significant and critical period of the Principate from the end of the Republic to the reign of Domitian; see Andrew Wallace-Hadrill, *Suetonius: The Scholar and his Caesar,* London: Duckworth, 1983.
70. After the victorious war against Tipu Sultan of Maisur, Wellesley, like a Roman imperator claiming triumphal procession from the Roman Senate, made unmistakably clear that 'I must claim the *sole* and *exclusive* merit of whatever is honourable, proud and commanding, in our present situation in India'. 'The Earl of Mornington to the Rt. Hon. Henry Dundas, 16 May 1799, Fort St. George', in *Two Views of British India: The Private Correspondence of Mr Dundas and Lord Wellesley, 1798–1801*, ed. Edward Ingram, Bath: Adam Dart, 1970, p. 154.
71. Curzon, *British Government in India*, vol. 1, pp. 108–10.
72. Rykwert, *The Brothers Adam*, pp. 64–77.
73. Isaac Ware, ed., 'Chapter 10', in *Andrea Palladio: The Four Books of Architecture*, London: 1737; with a new Introduction by Adolf K. Placzek, vol. 2, New York: Dover, 2014, pp. 44–5.
74. The Assembly Rooms in York lacked space behind the rows of columns and the space between the columns was too narrow for the ladies wearing hoop petticoats; see Wittkower, *Palladio and English Palladianism*, pp. 135–44.
75. Datta, *Planning the City*, pp. 38–9.

2

MAKING THE CITY BEAUTIFUL

Open Space, Imperial Culture, and the Modern Market

Kaustubh Mani Sengupta

Throughout the nineteenth century, like any other city in the world, Calcutta underwent a series of changes that were supposed to alter the face of the city and make it beautiful, cleaner, and healthier. Concerns over health and hygiene of the population were the driving forces behind the various planning initiatives of the colonial government of the city. Linked to the projects of constructing hospitals, markets, and sewers is the question of opening up congested areas as well as preserving the open spaces of the city. This essay looks at the issues regarding the vast open space or maidan of Calcutta, and how the spatial imagination of this tract was intimately connected to the imperial might and colonial governance. A curious tussle ensued in the 1860s when the Dalhousie Institute was proposed to be constructed on one part of the maidan. Through a discussion around the debate of establishing a building encroaching on some parts of the 'lung of the city', this essay elaborates the inherent tension among the various initiatives and vision of the colonial officials regarding the nature of the beautiful city. Further, with a study of the building of the New Market, the essay will focus on the imperial vision in another context that was directly linked to the wider currents of metropolitan thought which promoted the bourgeois values of health, hygiene, and aesthetics in a colonial city. Through a study of these two sites—the Dalhousie Institute and the New Market—the essay tries to unpack the colonial spatial imagination that shaped the cities of the colonies in the nineteenth century. An exploration of these sites will also help in analysing the materiality of the colonial spatial imagination.

In recent years, historians of colonial urbanism have argued for a reappraisal of the stark binary division of the White Town/Black Town. They urge us to look for instances of 'blurring' of these racial boundaries and to see the production of the urban space as a 'joint enterprise' of both the colonizer and the colonized. In case of Calcutta, Swati Chattopadhyay has forcefully argued that the representation of the city as a 'pathological space' was linked to the continuing justification and legitimization of the colonial rule. The persistence of an image of unhealthy, congested, and unplanned Black Town was a strategic lever of colonial power.[1] However, these 'images' also informed the planning initiatives of the state. Partho Datta has convincingly shown how lopsided notions of 'improvement' guided the planners in Calcutta, which further reproduced the inequalities between various spaces of the city.[2]

In Calcutta, the various planning initiatives conceived during the nineteenth century speak of a distinct vision of what a good city ought to look like and how it should be governed. The two basic axes of the enterprise were to shape the city according to plan and to know the various spaces more intimately, and be able to represent them in an objective manner. Environmental issues became crucial to the development of a 'healthy' city. Piecemeal efforts at shaping the settlement were part of the eighteenth-century East India Company governance. But systematic planning programme for the town began at the turn of the nineteenth century. Generally, Lord Richard Wellesley's regime is seen as ushering in a new period of town planning. His minutes (1803) on the improvement of the town chalked out the basic tenet of the programme which continued to serve as a model for many years to come.[3] The issues of urban health and town-improvement were intricately linked with specific material, political, and cultural contexts in the metropolitan centres of Britain. The rapidly industrializing cities housed enormous populations at close quarters, giving rise to problems of health and sanitation. Democratic ideals and electoral exigencies made sure that demands were put to the government to ameliorate the condition on the ground. And the belief that foul odour exacerbates epidemic diseases like cholera ensured incessant search for the perfect urban system, devoid of congestion and free of filth.[4] These concerns were equally, if not more (from the perspective of the colonial government), valid in the case of cities in the tropical colonies. Before going into the discussion of the Maidan, the Dalhousie Institute, and the New Market, let us first briefly look at the condition of Calcutta in the first-half of the nineteenth century. The reports of the colonial administration and the medical personnel point towards the pathetic state of urban affairs. We will try to figure out some of the key features of these reports and how that guided the vision of the planners, the administration, and in some cases, the general public.

Diseased Body of the City

James Ranald Martin's *Notes on the Medical Topography of Calcutta* (1837) was an important contribution to this field of literature. Medical topographies, as Mark Harrison points out, gained prominence after the huge loss of British soldiers in the Anglo-Burmese War of 1824.[5] Uncharted territories of the subcontinent were to be described and analysed to move on with the project of extensive colonization. Harrison argues that the optimism of the earlier period regarding the ability to adapt to a tropical climate gave way to a more pessimistic outlook in these initial decades of the nineteenth century. Tropical climates were now regarded as unsuitable for north European constitutions. The climatic theory also gave rise to new racial distinctions, as people bred in the tropics were seen as lazy and slothful, and generally averse to any labour. The internal logic of colonization made it an imperative to move into these new territories and 'civilize' the people. Thus, the sense of optimism did not entirely disappear: the 'ideology of improvement' that marked the 'liberal' mission of the colonial rulers was premised on the idea of the possibility of transformation. However, the sanitary question of a city was something different.

The innate climatic deficiencies of Bengal (or Calcutta) were not the only hindrance in building up a healthier environment in the city. Martin's text reveals a tension between the climatic aspects and the social/cultural issues. Natural and social issues were combined to depict the prevalence of disease in the city. He put the causes of all predominant diseases under the following heads: '1. Vitiated exhalations and secretions of human body, 2. Noxious exhalations of the earth, 3. Depraved habits of life.'[6] The solutions were simple: 'The injury from human exhalations is removed simply by prevention of crowding, by exposure to sun and wind, cleanliness; and that from terrestrial exhalations, by draining, clearing, leveling.'[7] However, if one persists with the theory of climatic determinism, then it is difficult to agree with the fact that any improvement is possible. Thus, climate was soon linked to other aspects of life.

Employments, customs and amusements are likewise powerfully influenced by climate and form of government: the effects of both these are everywhere conspicuous in Asia. The languid and slothful habits of the Hindoos together with the absence of motive for labour are all rightly ascribed by Mill to their 'wretched government, under which the fruits of labour were never secure'.[8]

Not surprisingly, climate and the form of government were acting on social issues of 'native' inhabitants which made them a lazy bunch of people.[9] Martin believed in the axiom that it is 'Man who makes his climate'. He mentioned that 'even epidemicks [*sic*], though we cannot prevent their visitations, are generally modified by states of locality; and they are found in all countries to fasten *with peculiar tenacity, and remain longest* in such localities as are neglected'.[10] Ishita Pande suggests that the 'sanitary city' for Calcutta was conceived during the 1830s and 1850s 'to replace the dual city of the days of Company's *nabobs*'.[11] With the spread of cholera, the model of the dual city received a blow. Pande shows that from being a disease of climate only, cholera, in the nineteenth century transformed into a disease of culture.[12] The filth of the native town was no longer to be neglected. The measure to be adopted, thus was, to render the city, salubrious through sanitary reforms. Sanitary regulations would serve to separate sickness that was a consequence of poverty or biological fate from that which was simply a question of bad urban governance. The Fever Hospital Committee, constituted to establish a hospital in Calcutta after severe bouts of cholera in the 1820s and 1830s, prepared a set of questions and gave it to select inhabitants of the city. The committee inquired about the state of the sewerage system, markets, burial grounds, privies, native huts, roads, and interestingly, 'any native habits which you consider injurious to health'.[13] The idea was not to reform the native habits but to create certain self-regulating measures in the process of 'naturalization' or 'normalization'. This process can be considered in terms of the realization of the city as a place of free circulation, and the social imaginary that was involved in this was that of what is called 'sanitary city'.[14]

Linked to this idea of good governance and public health was the issue of circulation. Circulation was also the keyword for free trade liberalism. In a corporeal sense as well, circulation became important. Richard Sennett argues that William Harvey's discovery of circulation of blood in a human body in the seventeenth century, with the simultaneous rise of capitalism and focus on the idea of free trade, had profound influence on urban planning in the western European countries in the eighteenth and nineteenth centuries. Burdened by the working-class population in the rapidly industrializing cities, urban planners started emphasizing the idea of easy circulation of air and the necessity of open spaces for the general health of the city. This moment in the history of the Western civilization, according to Sennett, irrevocably altered the perception of both the individual and the city whereby the medieval pattern of the intimate urban spaces with unexpected encounters with strangers ceased to exist.[15] This analogy of the body and the city is crucial for understanding the concerns of the nineteenth-century urban planners. According to Patrick Joyce, 'In viewing the city as a body, the natural systems that were invoked at that time [nineteenth century] were marked most emphatically by the medical gaze. The "sanitary economy" of the town was like that of the body. Both were characterized by a dynamic equilibrium between living organisms and their environment'.[16] For the urban planners, the most important aspect of a healthy urban environment was the constant flow of air, water, people, and commodities within the city. However, the circulation of liquid did not mean washing so much as *draining*. As Alain Corbin mentions in the context of the western

European cities, 'the primary goal was to ensure the discharge, the evacuation of rubbish'. Corbin too sees the connection between Harvey's discovery and the planning of a city as 'his [Harvey's] model of circulation of the blood created the requirement that air, water and products also be kept in a state of movement. Movement was salubrious'.[17]

The concerns in Calcutta moved along similar lines. Climate, culture, and circulation became the keywords for the urban planners. Along with these, the idea of aesthetics gained prominence from the middle of the nineteenth century. Improvement of the city did not only mean development of the public health; the 'second city of the Empire' should also boast of a refined culture and beautiful edifices. We will see how all these concerns came together during the construction of the Dalhousie Institute and New Market.

Maidan

> The existence of the great Maidan, having an area of about 2 sq. mi., is a factor of immeasurable importance to the city. Apart altogether from the facilities for recreation it affords, it is of the greatest possible value as a 'lung' in purifying the air of the town. The importance of such an open space can hardly be overestimated, and Calcutta owes a great debt to the past, which in this instance has left unspoiled her greatest asset.
>
> —JAMES MADEN and ALBERT DE BOIS SHROSBREE, *Calcutta Improvement Trust—City and Suburban Main Road Projects*, 1986.

Generations of urban planners have emphasized the importance of the 'great Maidan' to the general health of Calcutta. Even today, it often becomes a battleground between the environmentalists and various shades of general public: the wayfarers, sports enthusiasts, political parties holding huge rallies, or hopeless romantics yearning for fairs. From its inception, the vast open space between the new Fort William and the city became an issue of contention among various actors. At different stages, disputes arose regarding the control of this space between the military and civil authorities, the Government of India and that of Bengal. For some, it was the ideal locale for entertainment and amusement while others jealously guarded against any encroachment or appropriation to

create and maintain a salubrious and healthy town. The Maidan
was created when in the second-half of the eighteenth century,
the new Fort William was built in the village of Gobindapore
in the southern outskirts of the town. Dense jungle and native
dwellings were cleared away to produce the esplanade of the fort.
The open space was necessary for reasons of security: a clear
range of visibility was essential to locate any advance from the
enemies. The English East India Company was more than eager to
safeguard its fort and people in the wake of the recent massacre of
the population by the country power. The lack of a proper defence
mechanism was exposed when Siraj-ud-Daula sacked the town in
1756. After defeating him in Plassey in 1757 and becoming the
de facto ruler of the province, the Company officials, especially
Robert Clive, pursued the building of the new fort with great zeal.
Military considerations played a crucial role in the creation of the
maidan. Health and environmental concerns came later.[18] The new
fort irrevocably altered the morphology of Calcutta. In a sense, it
etched the new pattern of settlement by forcing people to move
out of Gobindapore and resettle in the northern part of the town,
thereby, creating the template for the 'Black Town' of the later
days. The esplanade also gave the Calcutta cityscape an enduring
feature for years to come. Though the fort itself did not feature in
the urban everyday (apart from the cannon shots proclaiming the
hours), the Maidan or esplanade became the place where the city
would breathe and relax. As C.R. Wilson remarks in early twentieth
century,

Fort William is the largest fortification in India and in its day an excellent
piece of military engineering. Its area is two square miles; its full garrison,
ten thousand men. Its ditches and ramparts, its piles of shot, and six hundred
guns are a perpetual wonder to the stranger from the country. But the ordinary
citizen who trudges round it afoot, or skims round it on his bicycle, cares for
none of these things. To him the fort suggests thoughts of golf, football,
cricket, hockey, races, anything rather than military defence: for the common
which forms the glacis of the fort is the play-ground of Calcutta.[19]

The Maidan acted as a pasture and grazing ground, open park
for Europeans, hosted some of the sporting clubs of the town,
and became a site for recreation and temporary amusements like
circus shows. During all these times, it was also subject to intense

debates among various arms of the governments and often the general European public whenever any new structure was proposed to be added to the landscape of Calcutta. When a proposal was put forward to build the General Post Office on a part of the Maidan, the Court of Directors wrote from London to the Council at Calcutta that

The Governor-General of India strongly objected to all encroachments on the Esplanade before the fort both for military reason and because he considered that this open space contributed essentially to the healthiness of the Calcutta town. He had, therefore, rejected all applications for permissions to build upon it . . . we entirely concur with His Lordship in the necessity of keeping Esplanade untouched and we desire that no further encroachment upon this space may be permitted in future.[20]

Against this backdrop, let us look at the history of the building of the Dalhousie Institute and New Market. For both the projects, initially the Maidan was proposed as a favourable site. The conservationist sentiment overrode the idea on both the occasions, but the fact that it was thought of, in the first instance also, perhaps indicates the paucity of large open spaces in the city. Calcutta, by the middle of the nineteenth century, was already a densely packed settlement. It needed new areas to incorporate within the city which would happen later in the century with the amalgamation of the southern suburbs of Bhowanipore.

Dalhousie Institute

The website of the Dalhousie Institute states that it was established,

to promote the literary and scientific improvement of members by means of lectures, library, reading room, and other sources as may from time to time be devised; to foster a spirit of goodwill and sociability among the members; to provide amusements; to take part in and promote sports and games, and to embark upon any activities calculated to benefit the Institute or to advance the welfare of the members.[21]

A brief sketch of the history of the institute written in 1872 mentions that in 1859, members of the Committee of the Trades' Association decided to establish an institute in Calcutta that would 'promote the moral, social, and intellectual improvement of the youths of this city', and that which would be beneficial 'not only to its resident young men, but also to newcomers who would have to make acquaintance with the people of India'.[22] Leading trading firms agreed to send in subscriptions of Rs.100. Members of the Committee of Calcutta Tract and Book Society supported the scheme and offered to supply a number of books from the Society's depot at a reduced rate for the Institute's library.[23] The Calcutta Institute, as it was called initially, was established in a house on Old Court House Street on 1 November 1859. The building was taken on a lease for three years. Meanwhile, the Institute committee came to know that a large surplus of the 'Dalhousie Testimonial Fund', which was established to build a statue of Lord Dalhousie, was available for public enterprises. The Committee successfully bid for this fund. They proposed to construct a new building for the Institute that would also house statues and monuments. The fund was granted to the committee on two conditions—the statue of Lord Dalhousie should be placed at a suitable location in the building and the name of the institute should be changed from 'Calcutta Institute' to 'Dalhousie Institute'.[24]

For this purpose, in December 1859, the Calcutta Institute applied to the government for a piece of land to set up an institute to 'commemorate the administration of the Marquis of Dalhousie, to receive memorials of other distinguished men, to serve as an Institute for the advancement of Science and Literature and certain other purposes of public utility.'[25] They put forward a proposal to the government, mentioning the favourable spot to set up the building. Initially the Governor-General of India assented to their scheme and granted them a portion on the Maidan to erect the institute. This raised a hue and cry from several quarters of the government which brought forth the issue in the general circulation of various departments of the administration. It was soon found out that hardly any wing of the local government was consulted before sending the matter to the governor-general. No engineers, medical officers, police commissioners or even the municipal commissioners of the town were aware of the situation. It was evident that the property owners, adjoining the proposed site, had no clue about this building. Only the military department knew of the proposal. The Council, headed by two 'members of another Presidency', James Outram and Bartle Frere, sent the matter to the governor-general for his opinion. This line of action led people in the Bengal administration to question the validity of the judgement of the Council. The question of 'local knowledge' came up. Outram and Frere could not assess the importance of the open space of the Maidan and the sentiment of the people of Calcutta in guarding the pristine patch from this sort of encroachments. They consulted the matter solely from the viewpoint of the military, totally neglecting any opinion of the civil authorities.

Leaving aside the sanitary or civic issues, financial considerations were also raised; and curiously, this got entwined with the question of beauty and aesthetics. The funds at the disposal of the Calcutta Institute were hardly enough to erect a building worthy of the location, it was argued. Indeed, as an argument in favour of the encroachment of the green space, it was stated that the building for the new institute would be of one storey only. But, while cleared by the military authorities, crucial questions were raised from a completely different angle. This strand of objection gives us an insight to the way the urban centre was being perceived by a section of the authorities, where not only medical or sanitary issues warranted the opinion of the planners. The city must also look beautiful. As was questioned:

. . . what sort of a one-storied building can be erected there [on *maidan*] which, while unobjectionable for its height on military grounds, shall bear a contrast with such edifices as Government House and the Town Hall? And for what purpose is the fine façade of the Esplanade now to be obscured and its remarkable capacity for architectural improvement to be destroyed forever? . . . any building which the Committee can raise on this site with the means at their disposal, besides its incongruency with the surrounding objects, standing out as it were lopsided, in advance, on the right wing of one of the grandest frontages in the world, will be a mean and unworthy object in itself, and an eyesore to the place.[26]

An alternative spot was proposed at the intersection of the Sudder Street and Chowringhee Road, opposite the Maidan. The site consisted of a portion of the compound of the Small Cause Court. The municipal commissioners were already contemplating of buying the adjacent land to widen Sudder Street. The portion of Sudder Street that fell between Madge Lane and Chowringhee Road was bought off by the government to widen it and provide a good entrance to the Small Cause Court. This opened up an empty space between the court and Chowringhee Road, which was offered to Calcutta Institute to erect their new building. The Institute was asked to submit a definite plan by 1 May 1861 and to prove that they had enough provision of funds for the building.[27] However, this did not work out and the Institute had to wait till 1865 to lay the foundation stone at a different spot. But, meanwhile, keeping this site in mind, the work for the building started.

First, the advertisement for a specific design for a suitable structure was put out in *The Times* and *The Builder* in England and in several other Indian publications. A cash prize was announced for the first two selected designs.[28] An amount of Rs.3,000 would be awarded for the best design and an amount of Rs.1,000 would be awarded for the second best design. The last date for entry in the competition was 31 March 1861. Detailed instructions were given in the advertisement regarding the specific requirements of the Institute. At first, it clearly mentioned the location:

The building must be designed with a view to its being erected in a wholly detached position, on the plot of ground to the eastward of the Government House-gardens, and bounded on the westward by the main road in prolongation of Government-place, on the eastward by the Dhurrumtollah Tank, on the north by part of Esplanade Row, and on the south by the cross road from Government Place road to the head of Juan Bazaar street, Chowringhee.[29]

The designer was free to choose the style of architecture but it was mandatory that the building should be of only one-storey with a basement. The basic features required for the building included a central hall, 'for the reception of statues and busts, and suited for public meetings, concerts, and the like'.[30] The hall should accommodate at least a thousand people at a time with provision made for a large organ and orchestra. Apart from the hall, other necessities included a lecture room for an audience of 200 people, a reading and library room, two rooms for committee meetings and other organizational activities, two retiring rooms, and accommodation for the servants in the basement.[31]

In all, seventeen applications were submitted, five from England and the rest from various parts of India. Initially, in the first meeting of the committee, five of these were shortlisted. In the second meeting the winners were declared. The first prize of Rs.3,000 went to the Executive Engineer of Ramghur Division in Hazareebagh Christopher G. Wray. The second best design was submitted by Walter L. Granville from Harrington Street, Calcutta. He received an honorarium of Rs.1,000. It was decided that a sub-committee would carefully discuss these two plans and then submit its report to the government.[32] When the committee took a long time to report, on either the plan or the estimated budget and the source of fund, the government told them that it was ready to grant some more time provided they ensured that the building would commence in that calendar year according to a plan agreed upon by the governor-general. The Committee should also clearly mention their position on acquiring the necessary funds for the project. On the insistence of the government, the civil architect was taken on-board for the project, as he would be able to provide expertise regarding the plan and estimate. The Civil Architect Captain Price, studied the designs and found them inadequate. He agreed to make a new design keeping in mind all the criteria regarding style and finance, but in that case, he would have to take this job as official duty. The government granted him permission and the institute agreed to pay his remuneration.[33] In a few days, Price submitted his design, which was then presented to the governor-general for his approval. The new plan was much reduced in scale. He assented to the plan and, as was reported to the Committee of the Institute, did not object to 'the erection of a building of this character on the Esplanade but having regard to the diminished size of the structure, as compared to what was originally intended, he will reserve for future decision the exact position to be assigned for the building as well as the area to be given for it.'[34]

In 1865, the foundation stone for the Dalhousie Institute was laid on the southern side of the Tank Square, later to be named as the Dalhousie Square. The spot was on the opposite side of the Maidan, located in the central administrative part of the town. Even this spot was highly debated. In 1862, when the site first came up in discussion, some objected that a building on one side of the open square would block the circulation of air, and initially the government declined to provide the site for the Institute.[35] But failing to obtain any other suitable site the building finally started in another three years. Laying the stone for the new building on

4 March 1865, the Lieutenant-Governor of Bengal Cecil Beadon remarked that 'the true value of the building . . . consists in its character as a place where all classes of the community may meet together for instruction in literature, science, and art, and for all purposes of intellectual, moral, and social improvement'.[36]

Markets in Calcutta

Good and hygienic markets have always been a preoccupation with urban planners all over the world. Circulation and proper planning were not only about providing new lease of life to the urban body; they were also about controlling the signs that opposed life. They were concerned with regulating the physical manifestations of death. There was a profound anxiety about blood, excrement, rotting, and dead matter in the nineteenth century.[37] Patrick Joyce talks about markets as liminal spaces within a city that manifested this anxiety with the dead. In Calcutta, similar concerns with markets can be traced. Martin's *Notes* explicitly ordained that:

All butcher's markets and slaughter houses should be removed to the outskirts of the Town, on the river bank, and be constructed on more approved principles than any now extant. The Tiretta's bazaar does little credit to European taste, whether as respects situation or cleanliness. The chief meat bazaars of this city should have a free water-course in every direction, and be paved with Chunar stone.[38]

The concern here clearly reflects what Alain Corbin terms as the 'Tactics of Deodorization'. According to him, paving, draining, and ventilating were the three most crucial aspects of these tactics. Paving 'was a means of sealing off the filth of the soil or the noisomness of underground water. In sheds adjoining markets, paving stones were indispensable.'[39] Smell emitting from the dead matters in a market were a reminder of the inevitable passage of time and a negation of the vitalization process of the body that marked the urban sanitary reforms of the nineteenth century. Disinfection/ deodorization was a plan to conceal 'the evidence of organic time, to repress all the irrefutable prophetic markers of death.'[40]

The colonial authorities complained about the state of the markets in the city from the late eighteenth century—be it regarding the nature of occupancy, proprietary rights of the owners, leasing out the bazaar or the actual spot of it.[41] Above everything else, there were constant complaints regarding the atrocious condition of these places. Before going into the details of the New Municipal Market, let us first look into the attempt by one European to build 'modern' markets in the city which anticipated many features of the municipal market almost a century back.

Edward Tiretta's Market

In eighteenth-century Calcutta 'native' landlords alone did not vie for *sunnuds* from the Company to establish a market. Bazaars were a lucrative property-option and European entrepreneurs were equally enthusiastic about exploring the various opportunities to augment their income from private ventures in the city. In 1782, Edward Tiretta, a Venetian merchant, put forward a proposal to establish three bazaars: 'one for the sale of Fish another for the Sale of Meat and a Third one for Selling Vegetables.'[42] He mentioned that by the order of the by-law passed in 1780,[43] whereby all straw huts in the town were asked to be demolished, the market in Bogden's Garden had been shattered. The land, now in possession of Tiretta, was ideal for establishing a bazaar that would serve the public and also be an 'ornament' to the town. Tiretta wanted to have a bazaar 'consisting of a Pucka Building, divided into three different squares, properly drawn out with Shops and Warandar [verandah] all round, with a Covered Hall or Halls in the middle for the accommodation of the vendors so as to form Three Separate Markets or Bazars. . .'.[44] He wanted the Company to grant him a lease of ninety-nine years, against an annual revenue of Rs.500 payable to the Company. The Superintendent of the Police Mr C.S. Playdell, reported favourably to this proposal of Tiretta, writing that proper market places would remove the meat and vegetable sellers from the streets making life comfortable for commuters and residents of those lanes.[45]

The authorities could see the utility of the project. More than anything else, it proposed to build a well-regulated, healthy market, which, according to them, was not the case with most of the bazaars in the town. Vendors could be removed from the streets and relocated in the new market; roads and drains would be cleared off the dirt arising from the bazaars held on streets. Proper building for the bazaar also ensured the permanency of the structure. The proposal anticipated the municipal markets of the nineteenth century, emphasizing the idea of a regulated market. In that sense, Tiretta's proposal was novel. Markets were to have an instructive role. Linked to the well-ordered, sanitized idea of space was the concern with revenue as well. A fixed spot, with well-maintained, durable structures for a market would also ensure a steady flow of income for the government. This was not the case with most of the bazaars in the town, which shifted places according to convenience, or at the whims of the proprietors of the land. The bazaar on the streets, classified as a 'public nuisance' was difficult to regulate. After charting out the financial details of the proposal, the Committee of Revenue allowed Tiretta to build the market, and it served the European population of the town for a long time. But even this fell into disrepute as we have already noted in Martin's *Notes* cited earlier. Calcutta needed a new market, run by the municipality and not by a profit-seeking private owner.

New Municipal Market

In 1871, the Chairman to the Justices Stuart Hogg, mentioned that:

At present there are only two markets where Europeans can obtain supplies from, namely, the Dhurrumtollah and the Tiretta. Meat and provisions of superior quality are sold only at Dhurrumtollah, and this is the market from whence nearly all the higher classes of Europeans have their table supplied. . . . the area devoted to the market is altogether insufficient and inadequate for the requirements of the public; the market, moreover, is most defective in the important point of ventilation, and the stalls and buildings therein are so low and small as to be altogether unsuited for the sale of provisions; owing also to the confined space and defective structures of the buildings, it is quite impossible to carry out any proper and sufficient conservancy arrangements, the consequence is, that the market presents a most uninviting appearance, and the odours emanating from it are most offensive.[46]

The Dhurrumtollah market was owned by Baboo Hira Lal Seal and was situated at the junction of Chowringhee and Dhurrumtollah Street. S.W. Goode, the municipal historian, also mentions that 'the market was surrounded by houses on all sides, its accommodation was quite inadequate to the crowds which frequented it, and its ventilation and conservancy arrangements were most defective'.[47] The European population of the city constantly urged the government to improve the condition of the market. The government could not do much about these requests regarding a privately-owned market and ultimately thought of establishing a municipal market which would be a clean, healthy modern market and cater to the needs of the European residents. On 16 January 1866, the justices agreed to allot a sum of Rs.1 lakh for this purpose. The government permitted the scheme and a site at the corner of Grant Street and Corporation Street was selected. But soon it was found out that 'nothing short of 2 lakhs would finance the project, and this difficulty . . . proved fatal'.[48]

The Government of India agreed to the fact that the market at Dhurrumtollah was 'a disgrace to the capital of India' and that Calcutta 'does mightily need a reform where markets are concerned . . . '. But doubts were expressed regarding the financial viability of the scheme proposed by the justices. The market needed to yield a profit of Rs.3,000 per mensem to repay the interest on 6 per cent debentures on a sum of 60,000 pounds. This was difficult, according to the men at the higher echelon of the government. Instead, they proposed the Justices of Peace to 'get a site for nothing, erect the market on the maidan, near where the Theatre is. Build a light, elegant iron and glass place with thorough ventilation through and through, whiten earthen-ware slabs for meat, marble for vegetables, open on all sides, thoroughly cleaned up and tidied up by noon daily'.[49] They went on to elaborate the nature of the structure:

. . . far from being an eye-sore, like the Theatre, this structure might be a great ornament to the place, and might be constructed for less than half of what it is proposed to spend. We do not want a lofty pretentious edifice; but a series of light, elegant, comparatively low galleries, running at right angles to each other, open everywhere and with uncovered interspaces between the galleries. . . .[50]

There was nothing wrong with this proposal save for one little but crucial point. The response from Government of Bengal to this scheme of establishing a market on a portion of Maidan was quite blunt. The proposal was summarily dismissed: 'The necessity of preserving the maidan against all permanent encroachment is so strong an article of faith both with the government and the public of Calcutta that the suggestion would . . . have no chance of being accepted.'[51]

Next, a proposal was made to buy the Dhurrumtollah market and establish the municipal market on that spot. The proprietor asked for Rs.6 lakh for the property which was deemed too high by the municipality, as in effect, the sum was only for the site (the value of which was only Rs.1,50,000 according to them) as they had to pull down the existing structures to build the new, modern market. Also, the municipal authorities feared that 'as the tenants of the Dhurrumtollah market have long recognized the present proprietor of the property as their landlord, it would be most difficult to guard against a rival market being established with the money paid for the purchase of the existing market'.[52] The alternative scheme proposed and later accepted entailed in purchasing the large tract of land between Jaun Bazar Street and Lindsay Street, exactly opposite the Opera House, and to build a modern municipal market, completely independent of the old Dhurrumtollah bazaar. Stuart Hogg informed the Government of Bengal that:

the site selected is 17 beegahs in extent, and is at present entirely taken up with huts of small value; this proposal, apart from securing to the public a Municipal Market, will effect a very great town improvement, by the removal of a great number of objectionable, closely-built huts, from a quarter of the town which stands much in need of free ventilation, and also by enabling the Corporation to open out a broad thoroughfare from Grant Street to Magde's Lane.[53]

Thus, apart from a new market, the plan would also ensure the removal of 'objectionable' huts from the centre of the town, and open up spaces for free circulation of air, a preferred mode of planning throughout the nineteenth century to make the town more salubrious.

The scheme of the market caused enormous tension between the European and Indian members of the Calcutta Municipal Corporation, and later on with the owner of the Dhurrumtollah market. So much so, the 'war of the market' became quite a popular story in the media and satires were produced, mocking especially the chairman, Hogg. The two principal speakers for the Indians in the Legislative Council, Jotindra Mohan Tagore and Digumber Mitra, forcefully criticized the idea of the new municipal market. They saw it nothing but a waste of important municipal funds. Tagore sarcastically noted:

It is said that the time might come when Hindoos would equally with the Europeans resort to the new market. One might just as well use municipal funds to build an opera house on the pretext that Native ears might hereafter be trained to appreciate the sweets of Italian music! If this principle is admitted the municipality would be justified in undertaking anything and everything to suit the tastes of any particular section of the community.[54]

The argument that the new market was for a limited number of Europeans in the city was not quite off the mark, but this uneven development of the infrastructure of a colonial city was a pattern almost all over the world. Calcutta was no exception. The whole enterprise of making a beautiful, healthy, and aesthetically pleasing city was a colonial project guided by a particular sense of beauty and aesthetics, complemented by Western medical theories and notions of public health arising from industrial towns of the metropole.

The tussle with the Indian members continued but Hogg went ahead with the plan. R.R. Bayne, architect of East India Railway Company, designed the building for the new market. It was designed in Victorian Gothic style. Bayne was rewarded with a sum of Rs.1,000 for his design. In September 1871, the construction for the building of the new market started. And on 1 January 1874 the market was opened for the public. But new problems ensued. Rivalry with the Dhurrumtollah market turned ugly. There were accusations against the municipality of enticing stall holders and merchants from the old bazaar and forcing them to set up stall at the new market. Hiralal Seal went to the court against Hogg arguing that municipal funds were inappropriately used during the opening ceremony for the market. He lost the case. And after a few years, the municipality bought the Dhurrumtollah market to put an end to the controversy.

Conclusion

The idea of a beautiful city animated the urban discourse in the nineteenth and early-twentieth century all over the world. In Calcutta, this particular aspect manifested itself in a number of instances. Here we discussed two such occasions—the building of the Dalhousie Institute and the new municipal market. These two got entangled with the open tract of the *maidan*. Medical, environmental and aesthetic concerns came together to produce the space of the central district of the city. Finance was also a major issue in any development of the colonial city. In these instances obtaining the adequate fund, buying up the preferred spot or negotiating with dissenting voices were crucial steps in building the edifices. Colonial cities were shaped by the vision of the colonizers, often over-ruling the resistance and dissent of the native population. Specific aesthetic sense, cultural referents, and consumption patterns produced the various spaces of the city. But, as this essay has tried to show, there were difference of opinion and contentious shades of judgement even among the bureaucrats and officials of the state. The state often did not speak in the same voice and a careful reading of the everyday negotiations articulated among the various branches of the government illuminates the way through which abstract concepts like beauty, hygiene, and health were discussed and debated.

Notes

1. Swati Chattopadhyay, *Representing Calcutta: Modernity, Nationalism, and the Colonial Uncanny*, London: Routledge, 2005.

2. Partho Datta, *Planning the City: Urbanization and Reform in Calcutta, c.1800–c.1940*, New Delhi: Tulika, 2012.

3. Ibid. See also, Samita Gupta, 'Theory and Practice of Town Planning in Calcutta, 1817 to 1912: An Appraisal', *Indian Economic and Social History Review*, vol. 30, no. 1, 1993, pp. 29–55.

4. David S. Barnes, 'Confronting Sensory Crisis in the Great Stink of London and Paris', in *Filth: Dirt, Disgust, and Modern Life*, ed. William A. Cohen and Ryan Johnson, Minneapolis, London: University of Minnesota Press, 2005, pp. 51–77.

5. Mark Harrison, *Climates and Constitutions: Health, Race, Environment and British Imperialism in India*, New Delhi: Cambridge University Press, 1999, pp. 119–20.

6. J.R. Martin, *Notes on the Medical Topography of Calcutta*, Calcutta: Bengal Military Orphan Press, 1837; also reproduced in parts in *General Committee of the Fever Hospital and Municipal Improvement: Printed Proceedings of the Governors of the Native Hospital dated 20th May 1835, with notes and proceedings of the General Committee from 18th June 1835 to 12th November 1840*, p. 14.

7. Ibid. Also, he mentions, 'The soil and the inhabitants, if I may be allowed the expression, always react on each other. A sober, industrious race of inhabitants, for example, will have a greater desire to improve their country than men of a contrary character, and will also possess greater physical power to carry their desire into execution. Place such a body of men in a district overrun with noxious weeds and timber, and fast degeneration into a morass; and can there exists any rational doubt that they will clear it sooner, and longer preserve it in that improved state, than men of a different disposition? Place in a similar situation, or even in the district thus improved, a body of men who are idle and intemperate, and the immediate result will be, that the soil will deteriorate for want of proper care, the weeds will reappear, the drains will become obstructed, the edible products of earth will lessen in quantity, and diminish in their nutritive quality: the inhabitants will become unhealthy from the bad state of their grounds . . .'.

8. Ibid., p. 48.

9. He mentions once again that, 'When we reflect on the habits and customs of the natives, their long misgovernment, their religion and morals, their diet, clothing and c., and above all, their *climate*, we can be at no loss to perceive *why* they should be what they are.' Ibid. p. 52.

10. James Ranald Martin to J.P. Grant, 15 April 1838, *Appendix F: to Reports of Committee Upon The Fever Hospital and Municipal Improvements: Containing Miscellaneous Evidence and Papers,* Calcutta: Bengal Military Orphan Press, 1839, p. 378.

11. Ishita Pande, *Medicine, Race and Liberalism in British Bengal: Symptoms of Empire,* Abingdon, New York: Routledge, 2010, p. 97.

12. Ibid., p. 106.

13. *Appendix D: Evidence taken by the Second Sub-Committee upon The Fever Hospital and Municipal Improvement,* Calcutta: Bengal Military Orphan Press, 1838, pp. 11–13.

14. Patrick Joyce, *Rule of Freedom: Liberalism and the Modern City,* London: Verso, 2003, p. 14.

15. See Richard Sennett, *Flesh and Stone: Body and City in Western Civilization,* New York, London: W.W. Norton, 1994, pp. 255–354.

16. Joyce, *Rule of Freedom,* p. 65.

17. Alain Corbin, *The Foul and the Fragrant: Odor and the French social Imagination,* Cambridge, Massachusetts: Harvard University Press, 1986, p. 91.

18. For a history of the building of the new Fort William, see Kaustubh Mani Sengupta, 'The New Fort William and the Dockyard: Constructing Company's Calcutta in the Late Eighteenth Century', *Studies in History,* vol. 32, no. 2, 2016, pp. 231–56.

19. C.R. Wilson, 'The Building of the Present Fort William, Calcutta', *Calcutta Review,* July 1904, p. 374.

20. Cited in Sarmistha De and Bidisha Chakraborty, 'Maidan: The Open Space in History', *Social Scientist*, vol. 38, no. 1/2, 2010, p. 7.
21. See http://dalhousieinstitute.in/tiki-index.php?page=DI%20History, accessed 26 June 2016.
22. John Remfry, *Narrative of the Rise and Progress of the Dalhousie Institute, Calcutta*, Calcutta: W. Newman, 1904 [1872], p. 8.
23. Ibid.
24. Ibid., p. 10.
25. *Proceedings, Home Department, Public Branch*, 13 June 1861, nos. 70–72, National Archives of India, New Delhi.
26. *Proceedings, Home Department, Public Branch*, 14 November 1860, nos. 17–22, National Archives of India, New Delhi.
27. Ibid.
28. From Secretary of Dalhousie Institute John Remfry to Secretary to the Government of India W. Grey, 29 April 1861, *Proceedings, Home Department, Public Branch*, 13 June 1861, nos. 70–2, National Archives of India, New Delhi.
29. *The Building News and Engineering Journal*, 1 February 1861, p. 92.
30. Ibid.
31. Ibid.
32. From Remfry to Grey, 29 April 1861, nos. 70–2, *Proceedings, Home Department, Public Branch*, National Archives of India, New Delhi.
33. *Proceedings, Home Department, Public Branch*, 19 June 1861, no. 78; 31 July 1861, no. 148 (B); 14 August 1861, no. 63 (B).
34. *Proceedings, Home Department, Public Branch*, 21 September 1861, no. 124 (B), National Archives of India, New Delhi.
35. *Proceedings, Home Department, Public Branch*, 11 March 1862, no. 24, National Archives of India, New Delhi.
36. Remfry, *Narrative of the Rise and Progress of the Dalhousie Institute*, p. 21.
37. Joyce, *Rule of Freedom*, p. 76
38. Martin, *Notes*, p. 17.
39. Corbin, *The Foul and the Fragrant*, p. 90.
40. Ibid.
41. For a detailed discussion on these issues, see Kaustubh Mani Sengupta, 'Bazaars, Landlords and the Company Government in Late Eighteenth-century Calcutta', *The Indian Economic and Social History Review*, vol. 52, no. 2, 2015, pp. 121–46. The discussion below on Tiretta's market is based on this essay.
42. Letter from Edward Tiretta to Governor-General and Board, *Proceedings, Home Department, Public Branch*, 11 July 1782, National Archives of India, New Delhi.
43. *Proceedings, Home Department, Public Branch*, 3 April 1780, no. A, National Archives of India, New Delhi.

44. *Proceedings, Home Department, Public Branch*, 11 July 1782, National Archives of India, New Delhi.
45. Original Consultations, *Proceedings, Home Department, Public Branch*, 9 February 1778 (?), no. 13, National Archives of India, New Delhi.
46. *Proceedings, Home Department, Public Branch*, 25 March 1871, nos. 76–8, National Archives of India, New Delhi.
47. S.W. Goode, *Municipal Calcutta: Its Institutions in their Origin and Growth*, Kolkata: Kolkata Municipal Corporation, 2005 [1916], p. 289.
48. Ibid., p. 290.
49. *Proceedings, Home Department, Public Branch*, 25 February 1871, nos. 96–7 and 25 March 1871, nos. 76–78 [combined in one file], National Archives of India, New Delhi.
50. Ibid.
51. Ibid.
52. *Proceedings, Home Department, Public Branch*, 25 March 1871, nos. 76–8, National Archives of India, New Delhi.
53. Ibid.
54. Cited in Chris Furedy, 'Where you can Buy Everything under the Sun . . . Calcutta's New Market', *Capital*, 24 December 1979, pp. 4–10, see www. yorku.ca/furedy/papers/ko/3art79.doc, accessed 5 June 2018.

3

ROOFSCAPES

A Speculative History of Terraces in Colonial Calcutta

SWATI CHATTOPADHYAY

> I clearly sense the difference between those days and our present times
> when I notice that neither humans nor ghosts and spirits frequent the
> rooftops of today's dwellings.
>
> —RABINDRANATH TAGORE

Rabindranath Tagore's lament about the vanished charm of
rooftops was written in the last years of his life and indexed the
lost world of his childhood.[1] The modernity of twentieth-century
Calcutta, its crowded streets and the glare of electric lights had
banished the enchanted evenings that clung to the nineteenth-
century city. Indeed, the loss of rooftop sociality signalled a loss
of dwelling space in the city, if by dwelling we mean both a space
of inhabitation and a site of imagination that enable being in the
world.

If each generation mourns the loss of the city of its childhood—
it is as true today of Kolkata as it was three quarters of a century
ago—the changes in the culture of rooftop terrace sociality has
some historical backing. In twenty-first-century Kolkata we
only see vestiges of the practice that flourished a century ago.[2]
Rabindranath's recollection of mid- and late nineteenth-century
Calcutta is fortuitous for historians of the city, because it is during

that time, and in his extended family, that we can trace the gendered character of rooftop spaces taking on a new shape. By the 1940s that gender dynamics had been sufficiently transformed to appear as a loss of dwelling space.

Rabindranath's elaborate recollection of rooftop space, however, is also a staging. It is his search for an opening—literally and figuratively—to his boyhood days. As a child, the open space of the terrace had allowed Rabindranath to set up his own relationship with the outside world. At a time when his movement within and outside the house was restricted, the raised vantage of the rooftop terrace enabled him to see and connect to the life outside the house. The constricted movement opened up a different possibility of seeing the urban landscape. The parapet wall of the terrace rose above the child's head, so he would peer through the openings in the parapet:[3]

I could see the line of coconut palms demarcating the limits of our inner garden; through these could be seen Singir Bagan,[4] a pond in the locality, and next to the pond the cow-shed of Tara, the milk-woman, who supplied us with milk; farther still intermingled with the tree tops the range of Calcutta terraces with their various shapes, sizes and heights, reflecting the brightness of the afternoon sun and disappearing into the pale blue haze of the eastern horizon. The occasional eagle perch, raised attic stairs, stood out on those distant rooftops. . . . Overhead the searing brilliance of the sky, and from its farthest reach the shrill cry of an eagle would reach my ears and in the lane next to Singir Bagan a peddler passing by the mid-day-siesta-silent houses would give his melodic cry 'want bangles? want toys?' turning all my thoughts forlorn.[5]

Such glimpses of mid-nineteenth-century Calcutta Rabindranath might not have considered suitable for writing history. He began his reminiscence by making a distinction between a literary work and history writing:

I do not know who paints the pictures on the canvas of memory. Whoever does so, his task is to paint pictures. He does not sit brush in hand to reproduce whatever that happens in front of him. He deletes much and keeps much else in accordance with his own taste. He reduces big events to small episodes and enlarges those that are small. He hesitates not a bit to alter the sequence of events. . . . Reminiscence of one's life is not history . . . the impressions on the canvas will not suffice to furnish evidence in a court of law.[6]

The sarcasm about evidentiary status aside, his analogy between
memory and pictures deserves attention. Rabindranath pointed out
that when he sat down to look back upon his life, the past appeared
as image-impressions. These images were not endearing merely
because they were the stuff of familial affection. The memories
were enchanting because 'picture viewing has its own addiction',
and when he 'found the respite to look back' he became engrossed
in 'perusing these pictures of the past'. A subtle distance, if not
detachment, emerges between the images and the viewer in this
mode of thinking, a process that enables the impressions to be
plucked at will and woven into the fabric of a literary narrative.
His declaration—'there is nothing in these memories that deserves
to be rendered eternally memorable'—is not mere modesty, but
a mode of releasing the picture-memories from the burden of
standing as evidence, of revealing more than they possibly could
tell.[7] It also freed him from adhering to the norms of male Bengali
autobiographical writing. He could indulge in the painfully personal,
the affect of prosaic domesticity, and the utterly ordinary details of
familial relations without embarrassment or accusations of emotive
excess. As material for an (auto)biography, he considered these
images trivial—'incomplete and unnecessary'.[8]

Rabindranath's notion of history was far from naive or
reductive. In the heyday of 'scientific' history, he argued for the
need to popularize history by injecting it with the magic of good
storytelling.[9] Rabindranath's claim that this is not the stuff of
history is thus not an academic distinction but an insistence that
imagination (*kalpana*/fancy) be given free reign in reflecting upon
one's experience. His entire reminiscence may be seen as a way of
expressing how he came to acquire this habit of imagination.[10]

The tone of Rabindranath's reminiscence differs from most
others of the autobiographical genre in nineteenth- and early-
twentieth-century Bengal, irrespective of whether these are
written by Europeans or Indians, in English or in Bengali.[11] I will
nevertheless draw from these other memoirs alongside those by
Rabindranath to attempt a speculative history of rooftop terraces
in Calcutta, because I find Rabindranath's attention to the 'small
things forgotten'—despite his insistence and perhaps because of his
insistence of their historical insignificance—a compelling approach
to imagine the experience of terrace life in colonial Calcutta.[12]

I am borrowing the phrase 'small things forgotten' from James Deetz's book on colonial American archaeology in which he argued that if we want to understand cultural history, we need to pay attention to the small things that constitute the everyday life of a people. By mapping practices across different types of material culture, we can discern the logic that undergird choices made in the production of objects, be it houses, ceramics, pipe stems, gravestones, or cuts of meat. He came across the phrase in a probate inventory: those who conducted the inventory assigned a small value of a few shillings to the 'small things forgotten' in acknowledgement of their minor worth.[13] Deetz suggested that paying attention to the small things of everyday life might be the only way to access the significance of cultural practices that have not been accorded importance in the traditional narrative of history.

My attempt to link the small, scattered references to terraces in various reminiscences of colonial Calcutta with representations of physical space such as paintings, city maps, and architectural drawings is not intended to reconstruct Calcutta's erstwhile built space. There is, after all, no unmediated return to those spaces. Nor am I inclined to *fix* the memoirs to particular places. Rather, this is an exploration of the significance of the terrace in the context of Calcutta's diverse cultural pasts. Links between literary and physical space can only be speculative—the literary references help us assemble the physical spaces anew, contingently. What attaches to the sources I have gathered here are constellations of affect that deepen our understanding of how and why a built space such as the roof terrace matters at a given moment; how spaces that are ordinary become invested with extraordinary valence.

Terraces, like houses in the city, came in all sorts of sizes, and much of what I will be tracing here are stories of terraces that are indeed not dimensionally small, but they only seem to appear in narrative interstices or as backdrops, rarely emerging as sites important in their own right. Only by catching the narrative moments when they do emerge in relief can we place the myriad small references—often only snippets of information—into a larger structure of historical understanding, one that is necessarily open-ended.

That the terrace as an everyday space acquired a special quality is borne out by its repeated appearance in the literary archive: in memoirs, short stories, and novels. A space of leisure and intrigue, games and performance, of household labour, and gardens, the terrace was most of all a vantage for observation and for crafting connections. Rabindranath was sufficiently impressed with the promise of the terrace as vantage to have turned the terrace into a trope of liberation in his stories. In the memorable concluding scene of his novel, *Char Adhaya* (Four Episodes, 1934)—a love story set in the context of terrorist nationalism—the rooftop becomes the site for the declaration of romantic love that seeks to oppose the death drive of nationalism.[14] That sense of the terrace as a liberating experience, as a space of deep affect, was perhaps rooted in his own experience, articulated with great care in his two memoirs, *Jibansmriti* (1912) and *Chelebela* (1940) that will form the centerpieces of this essay.

Terrace Architecture

Rooftops and upper-floor terraces were among the few open-to-sky unprogrammed spaces in middle- and upper-class houses in eighteenth- and nineteenth-century Calcutta.[15] In other words, rooftop terraces did not have a predetermined use; they were open to multiple spatial interpretations and susceptible to improvisation as needs arose. The meaning of the roof terrace evolved between the eighteenth and nineteenth centuries to encompass a range of social practices and then waned by the end of the twentieth century, as the milieu that generated the sociality of the rooftop terrace slackened.

The practice of building flat roofs, perfectly suited for hot dry climates, should have been an anomaly in the monsoon-drenched settlements in the lower reaches of the Gangetic delta. But it was not; the houses that were built borrowed the elite legacy of Mughal north India where town houses had flat roofs. We see this trend also in precolonial towns such as Murshidadabad, Krishnanagar, and Dhaka where elite mansions of the eighteenth century adopted flat roofs as a distinct expression of a modern masonry building. Such flat roofs made sense in the climate of north India with its extreme hot dry weather followed by a short monsoon season. Often an open-sided pavilion on the roof—*barsati*—was added to enhance the experience of the roof terrace as a leisure space. The overhead shade protected from the sun and rain while allowing passage to the cooling breeze. When the temperature fell sharply in the winter months, the sunny roof terrace provided relief. Scores of Mughal and Rajput miniatures convey the importance of the terrace and the terrace pavilion as a space of pleasure.

This stylistic preference for flat roofs among the Indian population was reinforced by the Mediterranean-inspired neoclassical architecture brought to Calcutta by Europeans in the eighteenth century. As in the case of transferring vocabulary from northern India to Calcutta, an architectural form that made perfect sense in the temperate climate of the Mediterranean made little climatic sense in England, but stylistic preferences have historically little to do with climatic considerations. This overlap of formal preference ensured that terraces acquired a distinct presence in colonial Calcutta that would continue into the mid-twentieth century.

The lavish attention often paid to the design of the roof balustrade signalled the importance of the terrace line as the culminating element of the building's façade, with cornices and parapets conspicuously decorated with urns, garlands, and floral motifs. In terms of design, the Palladian-styled balustrades popularized by pattern books such as James Gibbs's *Rules For Drawing* (first published 1732) were the most common forms of parapet design of eighteenth-century and early nineteenth-century colonial buildings in Calcutta, both public and private (Figs 3.1 and 3.2). This is something the buildings of colonial Calcutta shared with many contemporary cities of the world. Variations on the Palladian urn were all the rage in the late eighteenth-century city and the importance of such a dignified roofline is demonstrated by how dutifully these were depicted by contemporary artists. The form of the Palladian balustrade, amenable to improvisation, became the standard for not only crowning buildings but for veranda railings and boundary walls.

From the mid-nineteenth century onwards, with a larger number of Bengali upper-class families settling in the city, balustrade designs of townhouses became more ornate, the terrace balustrade design being considered part of the building's façade treatment,

FIGURE 3.1: House on 11 Russell Street (Turf Club)
showing Palladian style roof balustrade, *c*.1830; © Swati Chattopadhyay

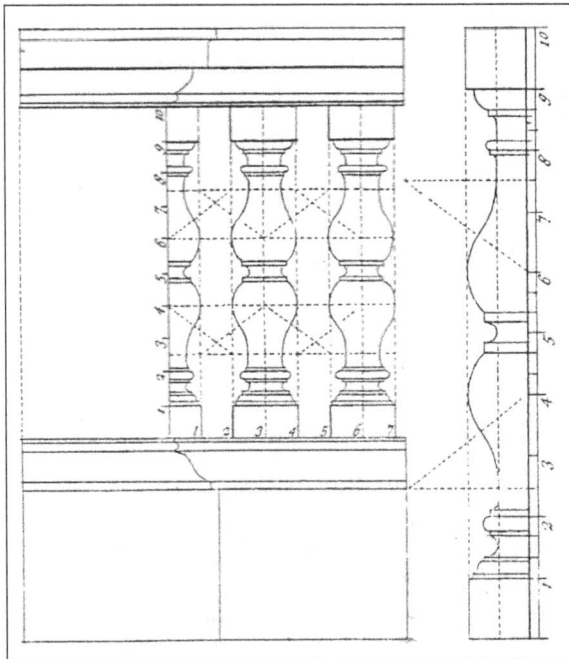

FIGURE 3.2: Drawing of balustrade from James Gibbs,
Rules for Drawing the Several Parts of Architecture, 1738

even in buildings that fronted narrow streets (Figs 3.3 and 3.4). Demonstrating affluence, these elaborately designed façades constituted a new engagement with the city's street life in which one's visual self-presentation was paramount.[16] Decorative terrace lines remained popular into the twentieth century: town houses and apartment buildings along Central Avenue (renamed Chittaranjan Avenue) (Fig. 3.5) and Southern Avenue (Fig. 3.6) built between the 1920s and 1940s testify to their continuing visual importance to the owners and builders.

FIGURE 3.3: Townhouse on 8 Masjidbari Street, late nineteenth century; © Swati Chattopadhyay

FIGURE 3.4: Townhouse near Chitpur Road, late nineteenth century;
© Swati Chattopadhyay

While some of these design traits were borrowed from foreign shores and were popular among both Indians and Europeans, in the *use* of terrace space emerged distinct cultural practices. British visitors were not familiar with the use of the rooftop terrace as a space of leisure or work, and the novelty of the practice was the subject of frequent remarks. Lady Maria Nugent, visiting Calcutta between 1811 and 1814 with her husband, Commander-in-Chief Sir George Nugent, commented on the style of houses in Garden Reach: 'many of the houses look like villas in the neighbourhood of London, only they are without chimneys, and the roofs are all terraces, where the inhabitants take air in the morning, or late in the evening.'[17] Maria Nugent lived in a house in the neighbourhood of Chowringhee, close to the open expanse of the maidan, and maintained a daily journal. From her entries we know that whenever she was unwell, which was frequent, she went to the terrace for her daily perambulation. This 'walk on the house top', as she put it, was in lieu of the usual ride on the riverside course.[18]

FIGURE 3.5: Apartments on Central Avenue, *c*.1920s;
© Swati Chattopadhyay

An astute observer of architectural preference and social mores, Colesworthy Grant, noted that in the Calcutta houses of the early nineteenth century the terrace was 'the greatest extent of ground trodden by way of exercise by the European foot'.[19] These rooftops would typically have dual access: a service stair, usually on the outside, and an inner staircase for the occupants of the house. The cool southern evening breeze in the oppressive summers of Calcutta was a luxury enjoyed by those who had the privilege of stepping

FIGURE 3.6: Two-story detached residence on Southern Avenue, *c*.1930s;
© Swati Chattopadhyay

up to a higher level in their house. Yet we have few instances from British sources where the terrace was turned into a space for meals, sociality, or a garden, all of which became the norm among Indian families.

Such raised terraces came with an added charm: terraces of two and three storied houses provided magnificent panoramic views of the city. Sometimes, real estate advertisements would make a virtue of this feature: an 1803 advertisement of an upper-story masonry house to be rented made a point of mentioning the 'commanding view of the Salt Lakes' and that miles of country could be seen from the third-floor terrace.[20] Celebratory dinners at Government House located in the administrative heart of the city often ended with fireworks in the maidan fronting Government House and the building's southern terraces (not rooftop terraces) became platforms for enjoying the show. Such viewing from the terrace incorporated the larger space of the maidan into the domain of the Governor's palace in a spectacular assertion of power.[21]

It is evident that in depicting the houses in the southern suburbs of the city, still quite close to the city centre, the amateur painters of Colesworthy Grant's time portrayed the city from rooftops. Except for two watercolours by William Clerihew who visited India between 1842 and 1845, however, there is scarcely any depiction that actually shows the rooftop itself. Most likely painted in 1843, these two images by Clerihew not only show the location from which they are drawn but are also exceptional in that they do not depict the city's monuments. One of these is a view of the river Hooghly showing the garden houses on its opposite bank. The slice of the low terrace that is the artist's vantage sets up a reciprocity with the buildings on the opposite bank of the river in Garden Reach.[22] The other painting shows a view of the city's rooftops (Fig. 3.7). In this Clerihew captured the rhythmic volumes as seen from the rooftop of a building located in the densely built centre of the city. The roofscape appears as a blurred extension of the painter's position: the sepia, pale ochre, and grey tones capture the massing effect of the masonry buildings rather than accurately define light and shade.

By the time Clerihew was visiting Calcutta, certain pictorial norms of representing Calcutta had been established. Between Thomas and William Daniell, Charles D'Oyly, James Baillie Fraser, and scores of other professional and amateur painters, the same

FIGURE 3.7: Rooftops in Calcutta, William Clerihew, 1843;
© Royal Institute of British Architects

British colonial monuments were drawn and redrawn—Government
House, Town Hall, Old Fort, Tank Square, the Mint, St. John's
Church, St. Andrew's Church, and the riotous display of boats and
ships plying the river or moored at the ghats on the river banks.
Typically sketched from boats or elephant-backs or from rooftops,
the images tried to capture the panorama and exotic pageantry of
city life or they aimed ambitiously at topographic documentation.
The grounds of Daniell's sketches and aquatints are exaggerated to
create an impression of expanse and grandeur, and the buildings
are all identified. As a result these were treated as documentary
evidence of the layout and disposition of buildings in the city by
contemporary and later commentators. Such claims to historical
validity have only been reinforced in much art historical writing in
the last three decades. Contrary to these stand Clerihew's paintings
of nameless buildings and unrecorded events. What attaches to
these is a pleasure of the visual and a claim to vantage. The only
other images of Calcutta drawn by British artists where terraces are
clearly indicated are those drawn from the terraces and the glacis of
Fort William, which no doubt was meant to be a power vantage.[23]

For Bengalis who migrated from the provinces to the city,
the rooftop space was often just as intriguing. Typically used to
rural houses with sloping roofs of tile or thatch, planned around
courtyards, the flat expanse of the roof in the urban townhouse
was a novelty that became a convenient supplement to the ground
floor courtyard of the house. In the city, the courtyard was often
considered too public, inadequate, or inconvenient for the women
of the household to conduct all their domestic chores. Indeed
the courtyard in middle-class houses was often too small for the
plethora of domestic tasks that were conducted in open-to-sky
spaces in a Bengali household.

Terraces carried many connotations in Bengali culture. The
Bengali word for terrace is *chhad*, and several qualifiers were added
to the term to designate various forms and uses of terraces. *Nyara*
(bald) *chhad* indicated terraces without balustrades and were not
meant for conventional use.[24] Eliminating the balustrade was often
a cost-saving measure. *Chiler chhad* (eagle's perch) as indicated earlier
referred to the raised attic that led to the terrace from the floor
below. The roof of the attic was typically sloped on one side in

keeping with the incline of the stairs. It was possible to climb up the slope to reach the flat rectangular crown that constituted the horizontal part of the *chiler chhad*. Further distinctions, depending on household practice, were made between the terrace above or in front of the kitchen (*ranna-gharer chhad*) and room for worship (*thakur-gharer chhad*). In the latter case, the terrace was often deliberately inaccessible to avoid stepping on top of a sacred space.

We see this kind of nomenclature in the artist Abanindranath Tagore's grandson Sumitendranath Tagore's conjectural plan of the now-destroyed house on 5 Dwarakanath Tagore Lane (Fig. 3.8). The different terraces in this house were given different names because they were assigned different functions based on adjacency and location: terrace above the car-porch (*gari-barandar chhad*) accessed by the north-facing veranda, the raised terrace above the *nachghar* (dance room), the large terrace on the fourth floor, terraces on the third floor, and the terrace in front of the kitchen. The open terrace in front of Abanindranath's eldest brother and artist Gaganendranath's room on the west was partially covered with a tiled roof, providing a shaded space on the terrace. The fourth floor terrace, the highest in the house, was the space for flying kites and the annual fireworks on Kalipuja/Diwali were set off from there. Pickles, fruit pulp, and *bori* (lentil dumpling) were dried in the square patch of sun on the terrace next to the kitchen, while the *thakur-gharer chhad* (terrace above the room for worship) was inaccessible. Similarly the multiple terraces in 6 Dwarakanath Tagore Lane in which Rabindranath grew up were designated different names in terms of their location: third floor terrace, second floor terrace, interior terrace, etc.[25]

Interiority

The house on 6 Dwarakanath Tagore Lane, originally begun in 1783, and enlarged in the first two decades of the nineteenth century, consisted of several later additions (Fig. 3.9). The most important addition was the construction of a *baithak-khana bari* (literally, meeting house) in 1823 as a separate building on the right of the main entrance to the premises (Fig. 3.10). Built by Rabindranath's grandfather Dwarakanath, this building functioned

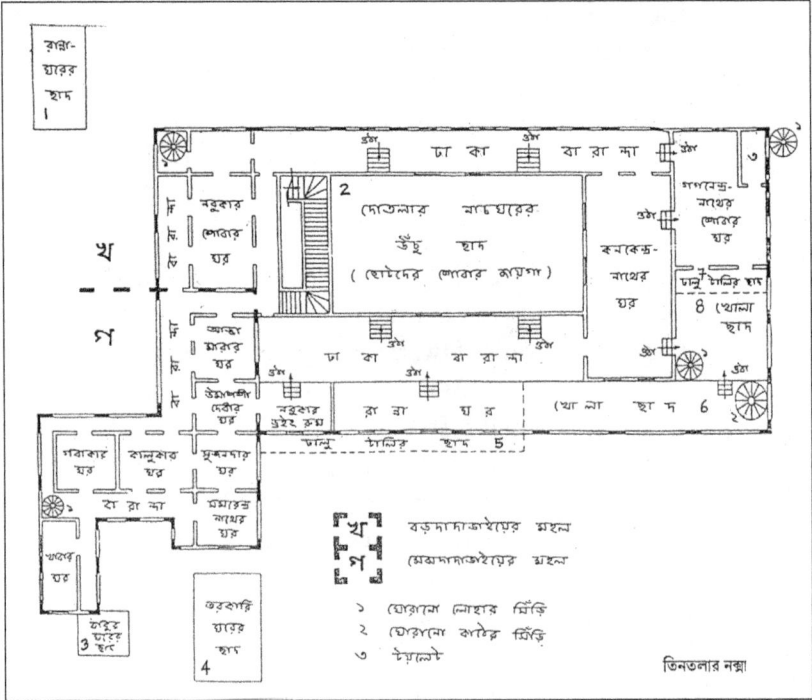

FIGURE 3.8: Conjectural Plan of 5 Dwarakanath Tagore Lane.
1. Kitchen terrace; 2. High terrace above second-floor dance room;
3. Terrace above *thakur-ghar*; 4. Terrace above room for cutting vegetables;
5. Sloped tile-roofed terrace, 6. Open terrace on the south;
7. Sloped tile-roofed terrace in front of Gaganendranath's room;
8. Open terrace on the south-east;
Source: Sumitendranath Tagore, *Thakurbarir Jana Ajana*, 1997

as Dwarakanath's office/salon/banquet house. He entertained his European acquaintances here, and when his relation with his wife Digambari Debi became strained, he moved into the *baithak-khana bari* for good.[26] After Dwarakanath's death in 1846, his eldest son, Debendranath (Rabindranath's father), inherited the main house, while the middle son, Girindranath (Abanindranath's grandfather) moved into the *baithak-khana bari*.[27] The latter had to be significantly reconfigured with the addition of courtyards and rooms to accommodate the needs and privacy of nineteenth-century Bengali domestic arrangement. The original building inherited by Debendranath received the address 6 Dwarakanath

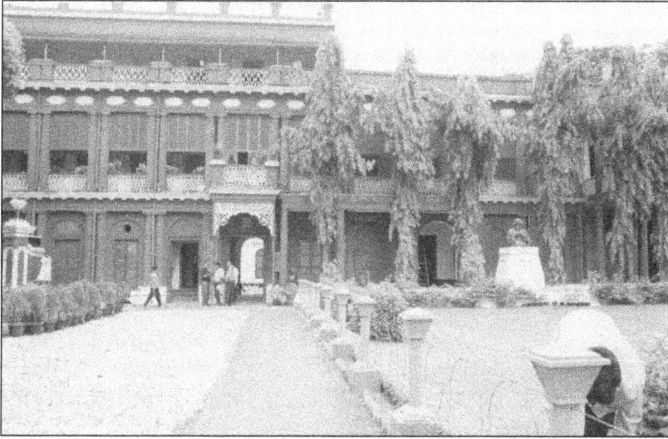

FIGURE 3.9: View of 6 Dwarakanath Tagore Lane, 2009;
© Swati Chattopadhyay

FIGURE 3.10: View of *Baithak-khana* bari in the early twentieth century;
Source: Sumitendranath Tagore, *Thakurbarir Jana Ajana*, 1997

Tagore Lane, while that inherited by Girindranath acquired the
address 5 Dwarakanath Tagore Lane (Fig. 3.11).[28] Both houses were
modified to suit the changing needs of the extended families, and
indeed three new buildings were added in the late nineteenth and
early twentieth centuries adjacent to the west and east sides of #6
(only two of these later additions are shown in Fig. 3.11).

The original house, #6, was a sprawling mansion divided
into several parts in which the distinctions between the public
apartments in front (*bahirmahal*) and the private apartments at the
back (*andarmahal*), and that between servants' space and family
space were paramount (Fig. 3.12). The latter often took the form
of a separation between the lower floor for public purposes and
services and the upper floors for the family's private apartments. The
children of the household were confined to the sphere of servants,
occasionally emerging into the peripheral space of verandas and
terraces. Only when they were a little older could they dwell in
either the outer or the inner spaces of the household commanded
by grown up men and women respectively. The gendered distinction

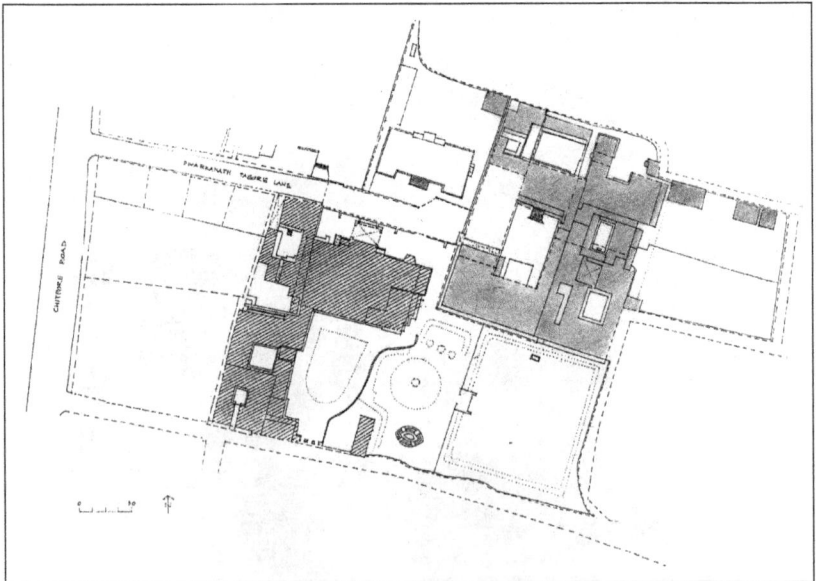

FIGURE 3.11: Site Plan of 5 and 6 Dwarakanath Tagore Lane,
based on Plan of Calcutta 1901; © Swati Chattopadhyay

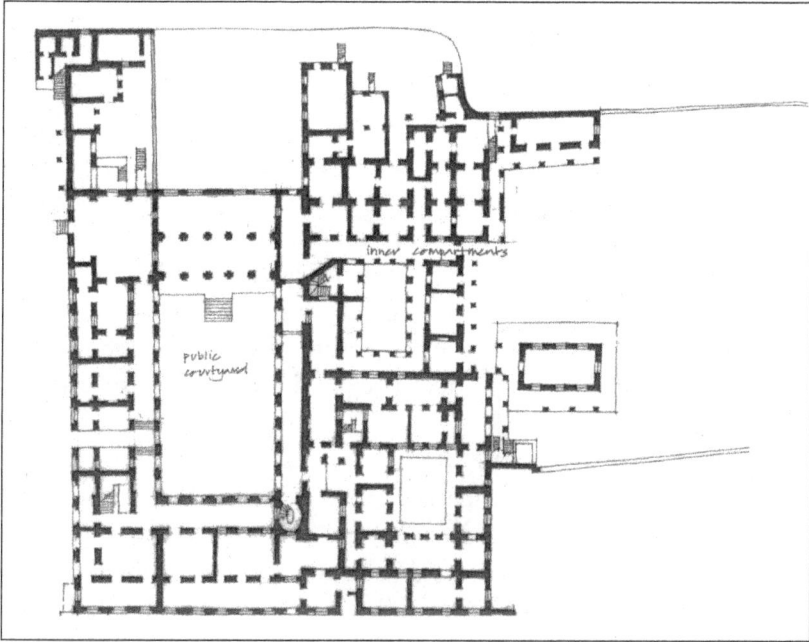

FIGURE 3.12: Ground Floor Plan of 6 Dwarakanath Tagore Lane, based on plan in the collection of Bichitra Bhavan; © Swati Chattopadhyay

between the inner compartments for the women of the family and the outer compartments for the men began to change only in the 1870s.

Rabindranath's vivid description of the interior spaces of his childhood home and specifically the terrace of the *andarmahal* focus on the many everyday domestic tasks that sustained the large extended family:

This terrace, above the private quarters of the house belonged entirely to the women. The place was well in tune with the demands of the larder. It received direct sunlight which facilitated the pickling of limes. There, the women, their brass vessels full of ground black gram, squeezed out drops of the mixture to form *bori*, while they dried their hair in the open. The female attendants would hang out the washing in the sun. Unripe mango was dried to make *amshi*, and mango juice was poured into stacked-up black-stone ornate moulds of various sizes, and left to congeal. Tender jackfruit pickle, steeped in mustard oil would mature in the sun, *keya-khoyer*, screwpine-scented catechu, was prepared with great care.[29]

Work and leisure commingled, with the hard physical labour performed by the multitude of servants that populated the household (the servant population was at least three times the number of family members). A significant amount of labour went into preparing the ingredients for the *bori* and pickles as these needed to meet the demands of a very large household: various kinds of lentils had to be soaked, ground, and mixed with spices, and piles of fruits and vegetables cut and juiced to fill earthenware and stoneware jars. Every evening the *bori* and pickles had to be brought down from the terrace and returned when the sun was up. The pickles and dumplings thus prepared were meant to last the entire year.

Rabindranath saw in the life of this terrace a whiff of village life: the terrace accommodated those activities that would be carried out in the courtyard of a rural household.[30] The lengthy labour-intensive process of food production, from husking grains in a *dhneki* and grinding grains and lentils in a quirn to preparing the daily supply of cooking spices using a grinding stone took place within the household well into the twentieth century. Until the availability of refrigerators in the twentieth century, it was imperative to utilize the daily fresh produce and dry or pickle fruits and vegetables for the off-season. Churning milk to produce butter, preparing fresh cheese and yogurt, and evaporating milk to produce sweet confections were routine household activities.

Life on these terraces ebbed and flowed with the seasons and the time of the day. Many of the household tasks were performed in keeping with propitious times of the lunar calendar. Such rituals gave significance to mundane domestic activities and became celebratory occasions for the women of the household. As communal processes, such tasks taught the women skills and familial roles. The purification rites involved in making *kasundi* (prepared mustard) and *bori* were followed dutifully into the first half of the twentieth century.[31] Young women were taught the art of preparing *bori*; shaping these dumplings such that they retained their erect form was considered an auspicious sign and preparatory for more important ritual tasks at weddings and religious events.[32]

Gaganendranath's daughter Purnima Debi has left us a precise description of the small terrace next to the *thakurghar* on the third floor of the *andarmahal* of #5 (see Fig. 3.8). This terrace did not have a railing and was specifically intended for drying foodstuff, particularly *bori* and fruits:

A wire-net-enclosed sliver of terrace; it had a lock and key. After lentil dumplings, mango pulp, tamarind and pickles were put out to sun in this terrace, the door would be locked. Mango pulp on decorated stone platters would be set out to mature in the sun. When Didima put away the dried mango pulp, *amsattwa,* she would give us the remnants from the plate: 'no more now, Didima would say; once the mango season is over, you'll get the *amsattwa*. Now eat this'.[33]

Such autobiographical details conveyed the importance conferred on these domestic tasks, and functioned to document a way of life that by the time Purnima Debi was writing had already become a thing of the past. But she could always return to that moment of postponed desire. Intended to teach the children seasonal variations in food, her grandmother Saudamini's scant gift built anticipation and created a narrative moment that gave depth to her story of the inner spaces of the Tagore mansion. Between the elaborate preparation and the regulated serving, the ordinary event became memorable.

Rabindranath's recollection of terrace life of the inner compartments of his childhood, although two generations before Purnima Debi's, echoes that very sense of lost space, a space that wove ordinary household activities with multiple strands of everyday intimacy to produce a realm of deep affect. It was as if each small insignificant act and gesture, from drying hair to pickling mangoes or reading a book (none of which in and of itself could be explained as the reason for such fond recollection), deposited a kernel of attachment on the space. Each time the act was performed, the attachment gathered depth. This is not a form of affect that is anterior to reason or action; indeed repetition and long duration seemed to have been necessary for the affect to take form and anchor itself to place. The loss that Rabindranath and Purnima Debi seemed to convey was perhaps this lost sense of duration belonging to a long-gone world.

Time in the women's world of his childhood, Rabindranath mused, moved slowly: it created an interior space untrammelled by the schedule-bound responsibilities of the outside world.

Rabindranath's mother, Sarada, spent her summer evenings on the
third floor terrace at #6 with her female companions sprawled on
fine mats laid on the terrace floor:

Their talk required no hard facts. Their only need was to while away their
time. Those days, there was no regular supply of diverse pastimes to fill the
hours of the day. The day was not a close-knit mesh, but more like a loose net
with copious gaps and openings.[34]

Rabindranath had from an early age chafed against the grid of time
that dictated the everyday lives of boys and men in the urban world
of colonial Calcutta. He was dismayed that following their morning
lessons together, he had to entertain the unpleasant prospect of
going to school, while his sister, Barnakumari, moseyed into the
house 'without a single worry'.[35] The child imagined that the inner
compartments were a space freed of compulsion—a mysterious
space of cherished interiority. Looking back upon his childhood
days, Rabindranath remarked that until he realized the 'freedom
within himself', he failed to learn anything.[36] The realization of
this freedom required a time-space to call one's own. He repeatedly
wrote of the need to fend off the encroachment of business/
busyness (anabasar) in all domains of life.[37] Time gaps (phank) and
respite from work (abasar), he insisted, were necessary for creative
pursuits and for shaping one's subjectivity.[38]

　　Terrace leisure had a slightly different connotation in the
andarmahal at #5 where Saudamini, Abanindranath's mother,
presided over evening gatherings. Saudamini, widowed at an early
age, ruled the household in #5 in a manner quite different from
#6. In the latter, Sarada was the mistress of the household and
exercised considerable control over everyday domestic matters,
but her husband Debendranath as the head of the house set the
household norms. The widowed Saudamini was second to none
in her household. The terrace next to Saudamini's room was
the 'centre' of activity in summer evenings. There, her servant
Mokshada laid out two low divans covered with fine mats, so that
a large number of people could be accommodated.[39] Important
decisions regarding family events and invitation protocols were
made here and Saudamini's three sons along with her brother-in-law
participated in the discussions. Access to Saudamini's gatherings

was restricted. Children were asked to stay away from such grown-up conversations, and the daughters-in-law did not participate directly in these decisions.[40]

It is useful to remember here that the practice of young women and housewives gathering or strolling on terraces with low parapets were considered socially unacceptable into the 1870s in both elite and middle-class houses.[41] Free movement between terraces even for the boys of the household was a privilege of age. For Abanindranath, the ability to get up on the fourth floor terrace and fly kites would signal the attainment of maturity, ranking high with the privilege of smoking.[42] As a child, when he had yet to step on this terrace, the folktales told by her maidservant in the evening brought the terrace close to him—the child would use fragments of the story to correlate the sounds he could hear from the terrace. When both sight and foot were constrained, the ear would help create a fairy tale world of its own.[43]

Private Worlds

The recollections of Rabindranath, Abanindranath, and Purnima Debi about terrace life in their households speak as much to their own aesthetic sensibilities and search for creative loci as to the ability of those relatives who managed to craft exceptional spaces from the quotidian fabric of the extended family.

When he was a child, Abanindranath's pictorial sensibility was sparked by one room in his house at #5 that stood out as an exception. On the third floor of their house, Abanindranath's aunt Kumudini Debi had created a little world of her own, combining her uniquely furnished room with the terrace in front where she kept a variety of fancy pigeons—*lakka, shiraji, mukshi*—in bamboo and wooden coops. Unlike the halls and other bedrooms in the house that were furnished after the European manner, the artwork that brightened Kumudini's room included Indian paintings from Jaipur, Bengal *pat*s that depicted mythical Hindu themes, as well as oil paintings. It brought to mind Suryamukhi's room in Bankim Chandra Chattopadhyay's novel *Bishabriksha*. Here Kumudini would spend her leisure hours, reading, crocheting, and knitting. This was the only place in the house in which the young Abanindranath could 'breathe comfortably'. At dusk Kumudini would feed the pigeons on the high-walled terrace. The sight of her aunt sitting on the terrace, swarmed by pigeons struck Abanindranath's pictorial imagination. The ample sunshine on this terrace and its raised walls also made it suitable for other purposes such as taking group portraits of the family. The novelty of family photographs taken by a European woman on this terrace cast a lasting impression on Abanindranath.[44]

For Rabindranath, the terrace became a landscape unto itself. When he was a little older and could escape from servants, he found in the terrace the time-space he yearned for: the key to his 'freedom'.[45] He recalled walking about aimlessly under a moonlit sky among the shadows cast by potted palms on the third floor terrace of the house that his sister-in-law Kadambari had arranged with great care.[46] The terrace became a sensory field into which he could insert his own desire to rupture the ordinariness of the everyday, and his own limits. Rabindranath cited two specific instances of his boyhood days in which the everyday space was catapulted to the realm of an exceptional aesthetic experience. Both of these involved the third floor terrace of the *bahirmahal*.

At #6, two sets of third floor rooms on the terrace were built—one set of rooms in the *andarmahal* and the other in the *bahirmahal*—to accommodate the expanding extended family and to more fully utilize the open environs of the terrace. Though unadorned on the inside, the tiled-roofed verandas that surrounded these light-filled airy rooms distinguished these spaces from the rest of the house. They helped create private worlds within a house full of relatives and servants.

When Rabindranath's father, Debendranath was home, visiting from his usual sojourn in the hills, he would occupy the third floor room of the *bahirmahal* and make it his private domain. In the early morning he would meditate in the adjacent south-east terrace: 'he sat still like a stone sculpture, his hands folded', Rabindranath recalled with awe.[47] When Debendranath was away, the small boy would sneak up to this now vacant closed room and while away his afternoons. He had discovered an 'oasis' on this third floor. In 1872, the Tagore household had taken advantage of the introduction of piped water supply in the city, and the water had sufficient pressure to reach the third floor bathroom. The pleasure of an indulgent impromptu secret shower thrilled him. The midday hours, when everyone else was asleep, felt like midnight to the child—'time for the child-*sannyasi* to renounce the world'. In that precious spell of loneliness, he would feel the 'thrill of high adventure, like crossing the seven seas'.[48]

Much later, when Debendranath was at an advanced age, these rooms next to the terrace were refurbished to suit Debendranath's minimalist tastes.[49] When the western balcony suffered damage during the 1905 earthquake, a set of canvas awnings—'like the sails of a ship'—were set up to protect the rooms from the sun. In consideration of his frail health, upturned earthen vessels were installed on the roof to assist passive cooling. In the last years of his life, servants would carry him to the terrace in a chair so he could conduct his morning and evening prayers, with Priyanath Shastri reciting the *mantra*s. Rabindranath was summoned to sing on these occasions.[50]

By that time the terraces in the Tagore mansions had become important sites for musical events and plays, but here too certain transformations took place in the 1870s when the terrace in #6 witnessed some formal and social changes, hastened in part due to the passing of Rabindranath's mother Sarada in 1875. Social relations between brothers-in-law and sisters-in-law, as well as between husbands and wives became more informal as household members broke gender barriers to participate in plays, edit literary magazines, and collaborate in writing songs and setting music to lyrics.

In the 1870s Rabindranath's elder brother Jyotinindranath and his wife Kadambari occupied the topmost room in the *andarmahal*. The room had a small added-on kitchen, and the tiled-roof veranda surrounding the room opened onto the terrace. Such a spatial ensemble provided the couple a private corner; it was not intended to function as a communal space characteristic of Sarada's terrace gatherings on the third floor. Kadambari had 'full possession' of her terrace.[51] Some years later the couple moved into two rooms on the third floor of the *bahirmahal* and Jyotinindranath's younger sister Swarnakumari, a writer, took up the rooms next door. This was a novel experiment in modern living within the Tagore household.

For Swarnakumari and Kadambari, this also meant claiming a time-space to nurture their talents and subjectivity.

Swarnakumari's terrace rooms in the *bahirmahal* enabled her to keep aloof from the day-to-day domestic activities that animated the *andarmahal*. Her children lived in the *andarmahal* in the care of servants, except the youngest one who stayed with Kadambari. Swarnakumari's daughter, Sarala Debi, remembered that they would play on the third floor terrace with other children of the house, but her mother in the adjacent rooms remained an 'unapproachable goddess figure', engrossed in her writing.[52]

For Kadambari, the terrace became an asset for articulating a romanticism that even a decade earlier would have been unthinkable. The new rituals of Kadambari and Jyotinindranath included hosting summer evening musical soirees on the terrace. Kadambari arranged tall potted palms on the terrace and a host of flowering shrubs completed the fragrant ensemble: 'jasmine, gardenia, tuberose, oleander, white ginger lily'. 'There was no concern', Rabindranath thought in hindsight, 'that this might hurt the structural integrity of the terrace'.[53] Since grown-up women of the household were not yet supposed to use the ground-level gardens in the west and south, this new terrace garden was a refreshing introduction to the old rooftop space. Rabindranath who was admitted to this privileged space recalled the delight of seeing the changes wrought in Kadambari's apartment now furnished in a modern style. Jyotinindranath's morning coffee was served in the shade of the attic, and Rabindranath often accompanied him in finishing the latest literary work, until ten o'clock when the sun robbed the terrace of shade and the crows started claiming their food and space.[54] The evening gatherings were more intensely aesthetic:

At the end of the day, mats and bolsters would be arranged on the terrace. On a silver dish, jasmine garlands wrapped in damp handkerchiefs would be placed; there would be a tumbler of iced water on a saucer, and in a bowl fragrant *paan* of the indigenous variety. Freshly bathed and dressed, her hair coiffed, Bouthakrun would take her place. Jyotidada would appear, a light wrap cast airily across his shoulders. He would put his bow to the violin, and I would launch into song on a high note. . . . Across the rooftops my song would carry into the sunset sky. From the far-off sea, the southern breeze would blow, and the sky would fill with stars.[55]

Such soirees at dusk became a family practice of sorts when the three spent time in the garden houses at Chandannagar and Panihati next to the Ganges, and even earlier in Shelidaha. The open expanse of the river here was a welcome substitute for the relentless line of rooftops in Calcutta. What Rabindranath remembered most about these musical evenings was the delightful harmony of the open terrace, the distant views, and the shelter of the open sky in the warm glow of early evening, all of which facilitated the writing and appreciation of music. In his memory, these various terrace experiences were knit together as a finely knit many-hued fabric.

Kadambari's sudden death in 1884 shattered this poetic haven and brought about a deep transformation in the grief-stricken twenty-four year old Rabindranath. The terrace in which he had spent evenings strolling about amid potted palms became a different exploratory site, now touched with the agony of loss. The gap in life that now appeared was fundamentally different from the time-gaps that he had so cherished. The loss arrived as a gaping hole 'in the fabric of life' unsettling the meaning of comfort that he had ascribed to the life of the *andarmahal*:

When death arrived to tear apart in an instant a portion of this closely held world, my mind was perplexed beyond measure. . . .

Alone on the roof terrace of our house, in the deep darkness of the night, I longed to see the fluttering banner on one of the spires of the netherworld, at the main entrance of which inscribed on the black stone would be a letter or a sign, and like a blind man, I groped about in search of it the entire night.[56]

Through the multiple metaphors of darkness as loss, the terrace became in his writing an affective space defined by sightlessness and inaccessibility. The haptic, auditory, and visual pleasures that had until then created the time-space of the terrace were radically reversed. He learned to cope with this loss, however, coming to the realization that this dark emptiness too could be a creative opening of sorts, preparing 'a distance necessary to perceive the world in its completeness and beauty'.[57]

Rabindranath's recollection of terrace experience, both his fond memories as well as the agony of loss, highlighted, in reverse, the routine temporality of terrace life. His terrace sojourns are remarkable because he was able to slip out of this routine and discover something enchanting, precious. It is therefore not entirely surprising that he professed to have felt a sublime self-realization during one of his strolls on the terrace in Jorasanko at dusk:

The glow of the setting sun commingled with the pale light at the end of day, making the onset of the evening especially captivating. Even the walls of the adjacent buildings appeared beautiful. I wondered whether this lifting of the veil of banality from the everyday world was merely a trick of the descending darkness. But it was definitely not so. I could see plainly that the evening had fallen inside me, I have been shrouded by it.[58]

That this feeling of transcendence did not occur amid the natural surroundings of the country or the hills, the usual favourite retreats of the elite, is noteworthy. As if an environment defined by the patently unromantic stained walls of city buildings was necessary as a banal contrast for the poet's self-revelation.

Private Space, Public Sphere

Kadambari's terrace design was an exceptional cultural and social intervention in more ways than one. In terms of design, terrace gardens were a novelty in Calcutta, and indeed the use of flowerpots and potted shrubs, large and small, was a relatively new introduction to Indian households, inspired in large measure by the practice of acquiring seedlings and immature plants in earthen pots from colonial botanic gardens.[59] Equally important, the aesthetic elaboration suggests that Kadambari and Jyotirindranath's conjugal romance needed an audience. Rabindranath was a willing participant and audience, so were close friends of the couple. The terrace garden was thus not simply a display of Kadambari's creative talent; it remained in other people's memoirs—since she did not write one herself—the inscription of her intense desire to carve out a space of her own. Much like an autobiography, the terrace garden had a confessional and testimonial aspect about it: it was already oriented towards a public. The openness of the terrace indeed allowed such aesthetic display to travel outwards catching the imagination of the rest of the extended family, and through them the larger social milieu of Calcutta at the turn of the twentieth century.

I am making a tentative distinction between two kinds of attachments or engagements that characterize much writing on city terraces. The first is an accumulation of affect around the small things of everyday domesticity. Such affect remains localized and enables the recollection of terrace life as a function of an anchored experience and correspondingly a lost household space. The second is an aesthetic elaboration that tends to subsume the myriad domestic acts to unleash the poetic imagination, travelling outwards. Kadambari's third-floor terrace garden invoked this latter mode of engagement. In so doing, Kadambari planted the germ for understanding the terrace as an open-air salon, a part of the public sphere of the city. By turning a domestic ritual into a literary event, one that competed with the all-male gatherings in the *baithak-khana* (that continued to be held on the first floors of both #5 and #6 into the twentieth century), she changed the spatial idiom of the terrace and with it the idiom of cultural events in the late nineteenth-century city. A setting for poetry readings, musical gatherings, and plays, though private affairs, the terrace-salon harboured the intersection of the private and public, one in which women could participate freely. This spatial intervention was necessary because women's access to public space was severely circumscribed. 'Respectable' women were not expected to visit the public theatre, see plays, let alone perform at a public venue in the nineteenth-century city. In elevating the household event into an aesthetic episode, she made the transition from *gharoa* (domestic) space to public sphere, a relation that would soon be mediated by an emergent Indian nationalism, making that passage smoother than it had been for Kadambari.[60]

Indeed the tradition of hosting musical events and plays on the rooftop did not end with Kadambari. Numerous plays were held on the third floor terrace of the outer compartments of #6 into the first decade of the twentieth century. Setting up a stage on the open terrace sufficed for launching a new play in front of a select gathering of family and friends. Rabindanath's son Rathindranath remarked that the terrace of the outer compartments of #6 was so large—'size of two tennis courts'—that the space was suitable for elaborate stage settings and accommodated large audiences. The centre part of the terrace was raised and acted as a 'natural' stage. Prompted by the size of the terrace, here we already see the intention to expand the audience. Tugged on one side by the increasing fame of the writers and artists in the Tagore family, and on the other by the 'democratization' initiated by the nationalist movement, the line between public and private increasingly began to be blurred. Even though contained within an elite space, these events began to shed their private, household character. Whether as sites where the literary magazine *Bharati* was launched or where *Valmiki Pratibha* was staged, there was an incipient claim to these spaces as 'public spaces', or at least as part of the city's public sphere. This was at a time when who or what constituted 'the public' as well as the appropriate form of public gatherings and felicitations remained largely unsettled.[61]

A few clarifications are in order here. First, large gatherings on rooftops were not initiated by literary or musical events. Rooftop terraces in both elite and middle-class houses served as gathering spaces for weddings and feasts, with temporary cover thrown over the open space to protect guests from the weather. Such *pandal*s on the rooftop continued to serve this function well into the twentieth century and in some cases they still do. At such times rooftop terraces shed their private quiet character to become quasi-public spaces within the house.

Second, there were other activities that conferred upon the terrace some characteristics of public space. The most popular seasonal activity that stretched the private character of the terrace was kite-flying. Flying kites, a precolonial tradition and a decidedly male activity, was a mode of getting to know one's neighbours and sharing a competitive spirit. This community camaraderie was a gendered privilege.[62] Sumitendranath in his recollection of #5 in the 1930s and early 1940s noted that on *akshay tritia* in spring the kite-flying season would commence and conclude with Viswakarma Puja in autumn. Sumitendranath remembered this seasonal sport lending not just the house but the entire neighbourhood a distinct character. The topmost terrace of the two Tagore houses were the chosen sites for unfurling the kites:

Our fourth floor terrace was huge. On one side were two tanks that supplied water to all the bathrooms in the house. We stored our kites in the shaded space underneath these tanks . . . .

You can no longer behold that sky of north Calcutta during kite season. At that time north Calcutta was an elite Indian neighbourhood. It had not shifted to south Calcutta yet. The sky was transformed in the late afternoon.

The boys from Rajen Mallick's house, Jorasanko Rajbari, and the Daw House, as well as other neighbouring houses would climb on the terrace to fly kites. The variety of colour and shapes of these kites is beyond description.[63]

The boys brought down the kites when the light faded and 'the flocks of bats' began their journey southwards at dusk. Although the passion for kite-flying cut across socio-economic class, the edge between public and private was more easily controlled in large houses such as those of the Tagores, Mullicks, and Daws. These were relatively self-contained buildings and stood out as large figures in a tightly knit and fine-grain urban fabric in the northern and central parts of the city. Most middle-class town houses shared party walls or were separated by narrow lanes. So chasing a kite took on a different meaning for boys from the middle and lower classes; it required a different facility in navigating the roofscape of the city. Middle-class houses would often have small bridges between them at the roof level so that women could move between the houses without stepping onto the street. These connectors came in handy during kite season. The continuity of such a roofscape afforded other uses as well. During the nationalist period and afterward, it was possible to move between houses undetected by the police on the street.

Finally, the rooftop terrace in town houses, large and small, served an essential function of complementing the verandas, arcades, and front porches as platforms for watching the city, of seeing the city as a public landscape. Nirad Chaudhuri wrote of his first encounter with the skyline of Calcutta when he moved to the metropolis from Kishorganj in the early twentieth century. The cityscape, studded with church spires, seen from the fourth floor terrace of a house on Serpentine Row seemed 'dream-like'. Seeing the city and the neighbourhood from the rooftop became his regular preoccupation.[64] He was not alone in this. The taboo against respectable women appearing on the public street-side verandas and terraces had eased by the first decade of the twentieth century. At the slightest intimation of a procession or demonstration, people, young and old, flocked to these street-side spaces. While in the nineteenth century religious festivities, weddings, and funerals were the main occasions for watching street processions, by the twentieth century nationalist processions and political rallies were

added to the list of spectacular events. Sisir Kumar Bose recalled
visiting his granduncle Satyendranath Dutta's house in Wellington
Square to watch nationalist processions from the rooftop terrace.[65]
Enterprising homeowners rented out their rooftops on such
occasions.

The provisional transformation of the terrace from a private to
a public space did not go uncontested. Sisir Bose narrated one such
incident involving their house in Woodburn Park in south Calcutta.
Built by his father, barrister and nationalist leader Sarat Chandra
Bose in 1928, this spacious house was designed as a modern
detached residence (Fig. 3.13). The tradition of using the veranda
for work and meals and the rooftop for exercise, prayers, and soirees,
however, retained practices from the past. Mahatma Gandhi stayed
in this house during his visits to Calcutta in 1937 and 1938. Gandhi
took his morning and evening walks on the rooftop terrace of the
house, often slept on the terrace, and his prayer meetings were held
there. Dance, *bratachari*, and music performances were organized
for such gatherings.[66] The house had two large roof terraces, of
which, the lower one above the second floor veranda, must have
been used for Gandhi's prayer meetings. The plan configuration of
the house with its curved rear and side walls created a terrace space
that could be conveniently divided into two sections, one for the
performers and one for the audience.

Mahatma Gandhi's presence in this house prompted the gathering
of immense crowds, so large that even the spacious terrace could
not accommodate all those who wanted to participate. Masses
of people crowded nearby streets and occupied the terraces and
verandas of nearby houses in the hopes of catching a glimpse of
Gandhi. On one such occasion, the force of the crowd wanting to
move past the main entrance of the house damaged the colour-glass
panels on the front door. When Sisir Bose tried to explain to those
gathered in the car porch that this was a residence, not a public
space, so it was not possible to accommodate everyone, someone
in the crowd remarked: 'Mahatma Gandhi is a public man, wherever
he stays becomes a public place.'[67] That the meeting was held on the
terrace and not in one of the interior halls of the house perhaps
encouraged such claim to access. Perhaps terraces as open-to-sky
spaces had become in the imagination of the city's residents part
of the city's public space.

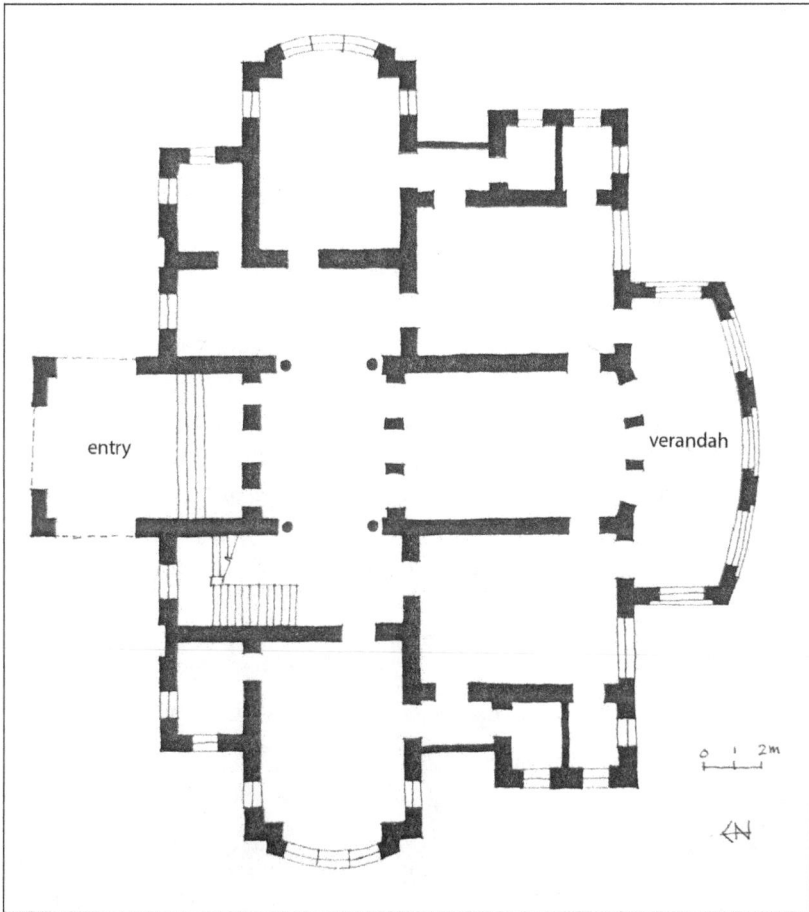

FIGURE 3.13: Plan of Bose residence, 1 Woodburn Park, Kolkata.
Based on drawing in the collection of the Kolkata Municipal Corporation.
The curved verandahs at the back and on the sides culminated on the
terrace level to produce suitable configurations for performers and
audiences; © Swati Chattopadhyay

Coda

Despite Rabindranath's mourning the loss of terrace sociality in the
first decades of the twentieth century that life did not pass away so
quickly; it lingered on into the end of the twentieth century and in
some respects it continues to brighten the lives of city residents. In
some older houses, typically single-family residences built prior to
1950, and infrequently in apartment buildings, residents continue to

use rooftop and car porch terraces as garden space (Fig. 3.14). The more recent trend of terrace gardens in luxury apartments in the city, however, remain detached from the older modes of sociality I have described. Such terrace gardens, often raised many floors, come programmed—predesigned as settings for entertainment—while the interior remains hermetically sealed as air-conditioned space.

In contrast, as an unprogrammed space, the terrace of the nineteenth- and twentieth-century city was open to seemingly endless spatial interpretations and uses. Even when small and architecturally modest, these spaces facilitated domestic chores, fostered a space of imagination, and harboured the conditions that made the experience of city-living memorable. Most of the time rooftop terraces remained vacant spaces where one could escape on a secret errand or in search of close company. The empty quality of these spaces even enabled the imagination that at nightfall, when

FIGURE 3.14: Garden in the terrace over the car porch in Ramesh Chandra Majumdar's residence, Kolkata, 2015. The house was designed in 1932, and this terrace accessed through a long verandah was directly connected to Ramesh Chandra's study and library; © Swati Chattopadhyay

the young women or servants had brought down the clothes from the clothes lines and the boys had finished flying kites, the terraces would revert to a dark roofscape inhabited by spirits![68]

If that terrace tradition and imagination is in decline, it is because of the disappearance of the social milieu that endowed these practices and spaces with significance. With the rampant demolition of mid-rise houses in the city, the urban fabric that might sustain that social life is fraying as well. Practices such as drying clothes and sunning pickles on terraces may not have vanished yet, but these activities increasingly share space with cable television antennas and satellite dishes.[69] On main streets, terrace parapets are hemmed in with commercial hoardings, giving new meaning to the notion of peering through terrace parapets. As the roofscape of the city changes and new media constructs new social geographies, it is entirely possible that a different set of ghosts and spirits will come to inhabit the terraces of the future city, allaying Rabindranath's concern about the loss of dwelling space.

Notes

1. Rabindranath Tagore, *Boyhood Days* (*Chelebela*), tr. Radha Chakravarty, New Delhi: Puffin Classics, 2007, p. 48. In the references that follow, I have indicated where I have used Radha Chakravarty's translation. When I have resorted to my own translation, I have indicated the original source in *Rabindra Rachanabali*.
2. Throughout this essay I will be using Calcutta to refer to the colonial and twentieth-century city and use Kolkata to refer to the city in the twenty-first century when its name was changed.
3. Rabindranath Tagore was at least seven years old at that time and it is likely that the parapet walls of the *andarmahal* terrace at that time were higher than the extant one.
4. Garden of the Singha family.
5. Rabindranath Tagore, 'Jibansmriti', in *Rabindra Rachanabali*, vol. 9, Calcutta: Visva-Bharati, 1994, p. 416.
6. Ibid., p. 411.
7. Ibid.
8. Ibid., p. 412.
9. For Tagore's views on history, see Dipesh Chakrabarty, *The Calling of History: Jadunath Sarkar and his Empire of Truth*, Chicago: University of Chicago Press, 2015.

10. In this connection, for an explanation of the idea of imagination in Tagore's poetry, see Dipesh Chakrabarty, 'Nation and Imagination', in *Provincializing Europe*, Princeton: Princeton University Press, 2000.

11. The notable exception being the reminiscence of his artist nephew Abanindranath Tagore, *Apankatha* (1929–30, first published in book form in 1953). For a historical discussion of Bengali autobiographies, see Partha Chatterjee, *The Nation and Its Fragments*, Princeton: Princeton University Press, 1993; and Rimli Bhattacharya, 'Introduction', in *Benodini Dasi: My Story and My Life as an Actress*, New Delhi: Kali, 1998.

12. James Deetz, *In Small Things Forgotten: The Archaeology of Early American Life*, 1977; New York: Anchor/Doubleday, repr. 1996.

13. Probate inventory is an inventory of a person's property after their death. It typically includes a list of objects in the household and/or farm/business. In the eighteenth and nineteenth centuries, this might contain an inventory of 'chattel'—household animals and slaves.

14. Rabindranath Tagore, *Char Adhyay* (Four Episodes), *Rabindra Rachanabali*, vol. 9, Calcutta: Visva-Bharati, 1994.

15. The same could be said for the provincial towns in Bengal.

16. For my discussion of the importance of the façade in Bengali elite residences, see Swati Chattopadhyay, *Representing Calcutta: Modernity, Nationalism, and the Colonial Uncanny*, London: Routledge, 2005.

17. Lady Maria Nugent, *Lady Nugent's East India Journal*, ed. Ashley L. Cohen, 1839, London: Oxford University Press, 2014, p. 55.

18. Ibid., p. 59, 63ff.

19. Colesworthy Grant, *Anglo-Indian Domestic Sketch*, Calcutta: Thacker, Spink & Co., 1862, p. 11.

20. W.S. Seton-Kerr, *Selections from Calcutta Gazettes*, vol. 3, Calcutta: Military Orphan Press, 1864, p. 567.

21. Swati Chattopadhyay, 'The Limits of "White Town"', *Representing Calcutta: Modernity, Nationalism, and the Colonial Uncanny*, London: Routledge, 2005.

22. Image in the collection of the Royal Institute of British Architects.

23. For example, William Hodges, 'A View of Calcutta taken from Fort William', 1781. Line Engraving with etching by W. Byrne from Hodges' *Travels in India*, London, 1793; Samuel Davis, 'View of Calcutta from Fort William', c. 1805, Coloured aquatint engraved by C. Duburh, 1807. See Jeremy Losty, *Calcutta City of Palaces*, London: British Library, 1990.

24. Kalyani Dutta noted that in her childhood, in the first half of the twentieth century, the *nyara chhad* was the place, among other found spaces, for school-going girls to hang out. See Kalyani Dutta, *Thor Bori Khara*, Kolkata: Thema, 1998, p. 90.

25. For a recently published good discussion and images of these terraces at #6 Dwarakanath Tagore Lane, see Suranjana Bhattacharya, *Kabi'r Abas*, vol. 1, Kolkata: Ananda Publishers, 2015.

26. The ostensible reason for their strained relationship was Digambari's objecting to Dwarakanath's relaxing the strictures of Hinduism, including serving forbidden meat and liquor to his European guests.

27. Dwarakanath's youngest son, Nagendranath, died at the age of 29, without children, and his wife Tripurasundari Debi was given property elsewhere in Calcutta.

28. These are the house numbers found in plans from the late nineteenth century. These numbers have since been changed with the addition of new administrative buildings of Rabindra Bharati University that occupy these premises at present.

29. Tagore, *Boyhood Days*, pp. 48–50. *Bori* is a dried lentil dumpling, *amshi* is dried green mango, and *khoyer* or catechu is used in preparing *paan* or betel-leaf (stuffed edible leaf).

30. For an excellent description of house chores and rituals carried out in the courtyard of a rural house, see Rani Chanda, *Amar Ma'r Bap'er Bari*, Kolkata: Visva-Bharati Granthana Vibhaga, 1977.

31. Sumitendranath Tagore's recollection of these rituals in the 1930s and early 1940s contains wonderful details. Fine-mesh trays were laid out in front of the mistress of the household (Abanindranath's wife), and she would squeeze out two large *bori* and anoint them with turmeric, vermillion, and *doob* grass as an auspicious beginning to the process. Then the other women filled in the trays with smaller dumplings, which were placed to dry on the kitchen terrace or the *thakurghar* terrace. The large *bori* were served to the mistress and master of the house as an honorific gesture and the remaining added flavour and protein to the variety of vegetable and fish dishes served year-long. Sumitendranath Tagore, *Thakurbarir Jana Ajana*, Kolkata: Mitra & Ghosh, 2001, pp. 58–9.

32. Purnima Debi, *Thakurbarir Gaganthakur*, Calcutta: Punascha, 1999, p. 68.

33. Ibid., p. 47.

34. Tagore, *Boyhood Days*, p. 48.

35. Tagore, 'Jibansmriti', p. 448.

36. Ibid., p. 458.

37. Ibid., p. 488.

38. In this context see my discussion of Rabindranath's *Strir Patra* for an elaboration of *abasar* as expressed through the protagonist Mrinal, who needed to step out of marital bonds to claim such a space. Chattopadhyay, *Representing Calcutta*, p. 250.

39. Purnima Debi, *Thakurbarir Gaganthakur*, pp. 10–11.

40. Ibid., p. 64.

41. Saudamini Debi, Debendranath's eldest daughter recalled that their neighbours complained that the young women could be *seen* on the rooftop terrace. Saudamini Debi, *Pitrismriti*; cited in Chitra Deb, *Antahpurer Antahkatha*, Kolkata: Ananda Publishers, 1992, p. 32.

42. Abanindranath Tagore, 'Apankatha', *Abanindra Rachanabali*, vol. 1, Calcutta: Prakash Bhavan, 1973, p. 12.
43. Ibid., pp. 22–3.
44. Tagore, 'Apankatha', pp. 45–7.
45. Rabindranath Tagore, 'Chelebela', *Rabindra Rachanabali*, vol. 9, p. 725.
46. Ibid., p. 466.
47. Ibid.
48. Ibid.
49. For a charming description of this see, Abanindranath Tagore, 'Gharoa', *Abanindra Rachanabali*, vol. 1, Calcutta: Prakash Bhavan, 1973, pp. 93–5.
50. Purnima Debi, *Thakurbarir Gaganthakur*, pp. 59–60. These prayer meetings could be seen and heard from the next-door terrace at #5.
51. Tagore, 'Chelebela', p. 726.
52. Sarala Debi, *Jibaner Jharapata*, Kolkata: Subarnarekha, 2007, p. 16.
53. Tagore, *Boyhood Days*, p. 63.
54. Tagore, 'Chelebela', p. 732.
55. Tagore, *Boyhood Days*, pp. 62–3.
56. Tagore, 'Jibansmriti', pp. 508–10.
57. Ibid.
58. Ibid., p. 491.
59. The botanic gardens, such as the Royal Botanic Gardens in Sibpur, used to give away seedlings and seeds on a regular basis to anyone interested in propagating flowering plants, various kinds of palms, and fruit trees, and the lists they maintained suggest it was a fashion among the city's upper-class Indians, along with both civilian and non-civilian Europeans, to acquire such plants.
60. For a discussion of the relation between public space and public sphere in colonial Calcutta see Chattopadhyay, *Representing Calcutta*.
61. For one of the controversies on the form and format of public meetings, in this case the memorial meeting held after novelist Bankim Chandra Chattopadhyay passed away in 1894, see Partha Chatterjee, 'Two Poets and Death: Civil Society in a non-Christian World', in *Questions of Modernity*, ed. Timothy Mitchell and Lila Abu-Lughod, Minneapolis: University of Minnesota Press, 2000.
62. For descriptions of pigeon and kite flying in Dhaka in the early twentieth century, see Paritosh Sen, *Jindabahar O Ananya Rachana*, Kolkata: Punascha, 2003.
63. Tagore, *Thakurbarir Jana Ajana*, pp. 75–6.
64. Nirad Chandra Chaudhuri, *Aji Hote Satabarsha Aage*, Kolkata: Mitra O Ghosh, 2000, p. 26. His various recollections of Calcutta life contain snippets of information on terraces and views from terraces. For a description of pigeon flying, see, p. 32. For the story of his infatuation with a young woman whom he saw drying clothes on the rooftop terrace next door, see Nirad Chandra Chaudhuri, *Amar Debottor Sampatti*,

Kolkata: Ananda Publishers, 2013, pp. 211–12.

65. Sisir Kumar Basu, *Basubari*, Kolkata: Ananda Publishers, 1995, p. 26.
66. Ibid., p. 74.
67. Ibid.
68. There is a long tradition of Bengali stories of resident ghosts in terraces. For some hilarious ones, see Lila Majumdar's short stories, e.g. Lila Majumdar, "Bh-bhut", *Kheror Khata*, Kolkata: Ananda Publishers, 2003.
69. I thank Bhaskar Sarkar for conversation on this point.

4

SALT LAKE

A Bridge between the Old Calcutta and the New

ANURADHA ROY

A Nowhere Land

Once upon a time, Calcutta was a rural area with a big nowhere land lying to its east: a sprawling marshy swamp or salt water lake formed by the tidal action of tributaries, distributaries, and redistributaries of the river Hooghly, that carried volumes of saline water from the Bay of Bengal through the Sundarbans and spilled it over this vast tract of land. The river Bidyadhari was the most important among these spill-channels. The marshy tract must have been in shape as early as the fifteenth or sixteenth century, though it was getting gradually reduced in size to make room for agriculture and pisciculture, which also obstructed the natural flow of the tidal rivers. What further contributed towards making the rivers moribund was the change of the course of the Hooghly and the construction of a number of canals for the purpose of navigation as well as for solving the newly emerging city's drainage problems and the disposal of its untreated sewage and rubbish. The Bidyadhari became gradually useless and by 1942 it was declared 'absolutely dead without chance of revival'. The city sewage and storm water now came to be diverted into the salt water lake, which made it highly disreputable as a source of the health hazard to the city. This is despite the fact that the Dhapa dumping ground that formed part of this marshland saw interesting experiments in sewage farming, compost manufacturing, garbage-scavenging, and fishing; ever since the 1960s.[1]

The sanitation problems of Calcutta were often attributed to the insalubrity of the wetlands lying to its east; and various projects for reclaiming it were considered by the colonial government from time to time. An improved and internal drainage system for the city was envisaged instead of using the salt water lake as Calcutta's sewage and storm water outfall. But no concrete step was taken in this direction during the colonial period.

So this marshy swamp remained a nowhere for the citizens of Calcutta, particularly its upper- and middle-class residents. Occasionally the babus would come here for picnics and bird hunting. But for them, the desolate land was basically a robber infested place which they were wary of. Indeed, the place saw frequent riots to gain possession of the *bheries* (fisheries) and the robbers were instrumental in these strifes.

And yet it is the Bengali middle-class culture that seems to have shaped this tract of land as it stands today. And the present article intends to explore how this has happened.

A Utopia Planned out of Nowhere

Independence had just arrived, accompanied by Partition. Refugees from East Bengal swelled the population of Calcutta. Dr Bidhan Chandra Roy, the then Chief Minister of West Bengal, formulated a plan to create an auxiliary township on the marshland lying on the eastern edge of Calcutta, to relieve the city of its population pressure to some extent. He also expected it to remove a major health hazard to Calcuttans. A mixture of sand and water obtained by dredging from the bed of the river Hooghly was to be pumped through a big pipeline via a number of pumping stations and deposited in the low-lying saucer-shaped salt water lake area. Indeed, the Hooghly in the west of Calcutta needed dredging to maintain the minimum draught. The idea had dawned upon Dr Roy on the banks of the Rhine during his visit to the Netherlands, with the example of Zuiderzee before his eyes.[2]

On Dr Roy's invitation, the Netherlands Engineering Consultants (NEDECO) submitted a plan in 1953, for the city extension, reclaiming an area of 3.75 sq. mi. comprising 12 *mauzas* in the northern part of the salt water lake. It intended to provide accommodation to middle class and lower-middle class families, with modest housing complexes and 3–4 *cottah* plots at a low rate (7–10 *cottah* plots were very few). Apart from residential accommodation, the township was to have offices, shops, commercial complexes, other amenities, and services. The hydraulic filling system suggested by NEDECO for reclaiming the land seemed economical and was estimated to take no more than seven years. The actual project had other components aimed at the reclamation of some other parts of the far-flung salt water lake. In 1962, after floating a global tender the government selected a Yugoslav firm Messrs Invest Import, to carry out the first part of project, i.e. the building of Salt Lake. The farm was to function under the supervision of a semi-autonomous board attached to the state government.

Thus started Calcutta's eastward extension. With the river Hooghly on the west and the salt water lake on the east, the city had hitherto developed lengthwise along the left bank of the river, i.e. from north to south. The length of the city (more than 60 km.) was disproportionate to its width (about 6 km.), which meant high costs of services such as water supply, conservancy, etc. Taking steps towards expanding the city breadthwise, i.e. towards the east was considered prudent and this was another motive behind Dr Roy's plan. The new township was to be a wonderland in the periphery of the city, free from its usual disorders and hassles such as traffic snarls and sound nuisance. It was to be largely self-contained, even though integrated into the city. The work of reclamation towards this end was formally launched on 16 April 1962. Salt Lake township was later renamed Bidhan Nagar in recognition of the role Dr Bidhan Chandra Roy had played in its creation.[3]

Longue Duree and Conjuncture Collapsing into Individual Time

Right from the onset of the year 1976—I had just stepped into my college life then—my family comprising my parents, my younger sister, and me became dwellers of Salt Lake. The history of Salt Lake, thus, largely unfolded before my eyes and it is difficult for me to externalize it as an object of study. This essay, hence, is mostly based on my personal experiences.[4]

It was a vast and desolate wilderness back then with just about a few houses scattered here and there. The cluster of casuarinas at the east end of the expanse was a treat to the eyes. They could not but make one feel in close proximity to the coastal areas of the Sundarbans. The gusty wind sweeping gently over the casuarinas, felt no short of a sea breeze flurrying by. Coming from the congested north Calcutta, we would marvel at the beautiful red and orange hues of sunrise overseeing the casuarina spread in the east as well as the scarlet blazing sunset across the horizon in the west. Adding to the mysticism of the place were jackals, our nights used to be abuzz with their howls. Now and again we even spotted some of them in broad daylight. Besides, the area was also infested with lots of snakes, especially during the rainy season, which would naturally summon the snake charmers with their enchanting flutes. During the time of the Durga Puja, the tract of land would be decked in white with a host of *kash phool* (kangrass) fluttering all around in all their splendour. From our first floor's rooftop, we could catch a distant view of the Howrah Bridge; and could hear the whistling of the train from the nearby Ultadanga railway station (later renamed Bidhan Nagar railway station), particularly during those unusually silent nights.

Taking long walks with our German Shepherd on a leash through the expanse was such a pleasure. But going beyond Tank No. 5 (these tanks are for supplying underground water to the residents) was an absolute no. We were told that this was the robber's haunt. In the wee hours of a misty, wintry morning, I did go a bit too far and lost my way. The dog was in no mood to trace the road and take me home and rather dragged me along farther off by pulling on his leash. Finally it was some random person who helped me find the right direction. Perhaps, he, was a robber! Who knows!

At that time there were quite a few families in Salt Lake that we knew of, who despite having built their houses, left the place after selling off their properties. This was because of the rumour that the surface of the marshland would gradually subside and engulf the houses. But my maternal grandfather, who happened to be a civil engineer, would always assure us: 'What about your house in

Shyampukur! Even that was built over a pond which was filled and covered.'[5]

Even if we assume this was a rumour, there were many other difficulties that made our living in Salt Lake truly challenging. First and foremost being the torture of the mosquitoes—millions of them from early in the evening. Water; high in iron content, was another source of anxiety. New water pipes in our bathroom got clogged very fast. Clothes caught yellow patches all over. Lack of shops in the locality was another problem. There was the CA Market and also the BD Market. But my mother being used to shopping in the famous old markets of Hatibagan-Maniktala area, could never find shopping satisfying in Salt Lake. Transport was also iffy. L14 and Shuttle 9 were the only two buses available during those times and even between the two, the latter was unavailable in the afternoon. We sisters faced great problems commuting to our school and college. Very soon, however, I became aware of the foot bridge route from Lake Town, traversing which led to a muddy road that would take me home.

However, having cited all our troubles, I must also say that those days of ours in Salt Lake are rather unforgettable. Staying in an almost secluded piece of land lent our house a certain mystic charm. Also the fact that each one of us in the family was very keen to make our home creatively palpable enhanced the happiness. We had stepped into this house at a time when it was in an incomplete state and the construction was still on. We poured our creativity in sketching grill designs, remodelling the furniture, etc. It was a nest carefully woven out of love and care. A sweet home for a middle-class family—just what Dr Bidhan Roy had envisioned. Almost every family that had its house built in the township back then invested similar emotions in it.

Our former house in Shyambazar, built by my paternal grandfather was also a nice and neat dwelling. But there were some incorrigible things about this house that created a whole lot of inconvenience, for us—shortage of space, perpetually flooding bathrooms, no garage, etc. The footpath in front of the house was also a cause of disturbance. It had a tubewell that emitted a weird, irritating noise every time people used it. And finding a spacious footpath (a rare thing in north Calcutta), localites would gleefully dump rubbish on it. Then there were a number of cinema halls nearby and our lane was always teeming with the cine goers' hustle-bustle. Noise of rickshaw bells and chattering of people returning after a night-show used to rob us of our much needed sleep.

It was the Naxalite movement during which my parents decided to leave the area. Politically speaking, that lane was partially taken over by the Communist Party of India (Marxist) (CPI-M) and partially by the Naxalites. Although my father used to be routinely informed by each party, 'Do remove the car, *daktarbabu* (doctor)' before every bombing session, the experience was not a pleasant one. Many a time my father had to rush to see patients on emergency calls during the night in the midst of such turmoil. This would leave my mother spending sleepless nights. Murders happened every now and then. The son of our domestic help was killed right in front of our house. The boy's bloodcurdling cry is still afresh in my memory. Another incident of hideous murder was that of Hemanta Basu, a leader of the Forward Bloc and respected by all as an absolute gentleman. Getting away from such disturbing occurrences had become a dire necessity for my parents. So the moment they won the plot in Salt Lake in a lottery, they could not think of letting go of this opportunity. The very idea of living in a nicely planned township amidst people who were expected to be educated and cultured, far away from the anarchic state of Shyampukur Street, was very reassuring for them.

When we first relocated to Salt Lake, there were only five houses within eyesight that comprised our neighbourhood. We used to fondly call ourselves the 'Pancha Pandavas'.[6] Initial insecurity due to dwelling in a new and lonely place propelled us to cling to one another. Right from exchanging food to sending fruits and vegetables from one's garden, helped foster fairly strong bonds.

In a few years, however, the character of the neighbourhood and its human bonding underwent big changes. As the place started teeming with doctors, engineers, professors, government officers, and people from myriad walks of life, it became evident that all the residents were not of the same cultural level. There were people who were into business and with very little education, prone to showing off their wealth, behaving crudely with their servants and being insensitive to neighbours. One business family near our house ceremoniously worshipped Siva, Kali, and other divinities in their house and made massive arrangements during those pujas. Microphones pointed towards our house would blare terribly loudly on such occasions. All the more irritating was being invited to all this.

We found even families with good academic credentials, and in one case, with children settled in the US, a source of culture shock too. This family lived close by. We would be compelled to listen to the same old stories of the brilliant careers of their children every now and then, sit through all the talks regarding the cars those children possessed in the US, diligently go through the photographs of those cars, and of course, lend them our car whenever they needed it. One day the lady of the house took our car to the CA market for shopping. Her youngest son (whose sole goal in life was to settle in the US like his elder siblings), and my sister were also in the car accompanied by a few other kids. It was shocking to hear that she bought her own son plenty of chocolates and toys in front of the other kids but did not bother to give them a single chocolate.

Then there were people who used to host large-scale drinking parties on a regular basis, accompanied by hideous dancing (at least in our eyes). One of them was an employee in a foreign-owned company and his money scams were well-known. However, this man became the secretary of the Block Committee within a few years; by paying thousands of rupees as subscription during Durga Puja and retained this position for many years at a stretch.

Among the neighbours some remained close to us. But the intimacy that used to be shared between five or ten families, seemed a bit forced and artificial when the number increased. Yet the hobnobbing continued for some more years. People kept inviting each other during household pujas, also during marriages or rice-eating ceremonies or birthdays or marriage anniversaries. This created a botheration for us. It felt awkward to attend these as we did not know most of these families well. But of course, there were people who used to be hurt if they were not invited on such occasions. Such celebrations constituted the core of the budding culture of the emerging middle-class Salt Lake society, where these people had a compulsive urge to show off and these were good opportunities for that. Individuals were of different types—good or bad; but collectively speaking, this seemed to be the hegemonic culture of Salt Lake.

Developing an Elite Myth

A major aspect of the hegemonic culture of the township was acquiring an elite stature. And this elitism was not just grounded in its 'modern' and 'planned' layout—gridded blocks, centralized markets, small pocket parks, wide roads, relative absence of shanties, slums, hawkers, etc.: there was much more to it. It involved the imagination and constant projection of a unique and exclusive lifestyle of the residents, which, above all, would indicate their opulence. This matched and stretched (and also somewhat twisted) the drive towards distinctiveness and exclusivity that was there in the very plan of Salt Lake. Such was the proliferation of the elitist mentality that, much before making room for stationary shops and grocery shops, it was the creation of a huge swimming pool right next to our house (sometime in the late 1970s) that seemed to be of prime importance to some of the residents. The locality, being essentially a planned residential area, the idea of swimming pool was completely out of place. But there were energetic and resourceful retired people who made it possible, so that they could continue to have an occupation and wield power even after retirement. Even those of us who were initially reluctant were talked into it eventually and I must admit that I got my first swimming lessons in that pool itself. A government college, a bank, a ladies' hostel, a number of shops, and restaurants evolved slowly around the pool. The area became highly crowded. Cars flocked our narrow lane and it became difficult to drive even our small Maruti 800 car amid these. The character of the locality completely changed.

Another step towards elitism was the establishment of a Rotary Club in Salt Lake (also in the late 1970s). The same persons who were instrumental in the construction of the pool initiated the process of founding the Rotary Club as well. They had even dragged us, i.e. my father and me, into it. We edited the magazines of the Rotary and the Rotaract clubs, respectively, for some time. It was not, however, possible for us to remain there for long, as the power strifes within that small club to acquire the president's or the secretary's position became unbearable, particularly because all this was done behind the ostentatious mask of social service.

Showcasing of swanky, plush houses, in the likes of foreign architectural buildings, was yet another trend in vogue. Blindly aping designs from books published abroad, which are not conducive to Indian climate seemed to be a sure path to gaining elite status for some people. This tradition was initiated by the architect Mr D.C. Paul and his sons. The 'White House' built by them used to be flocked by viewers coming to just take a glance at it. Soon it so happened that the other houses built by them surpassed the awe that their initial work had inspired.

So Salt Lake soon became a place for the rich, a word that was perceived as synonymous with elite amidst the localites. And they were highly pleased to have assumed this elite stature. For this they had to be okay with the unusually high market prices of goods of otherwise low quality and could not even get into bargaining. They also had to survive the immense pocket-pinch during Durga Puja without protest. My father used to say, 'How can a place which was quoted at 3000 rupees per *cottah* be a place meant for rich people! Bidhan Chandra Roy had after all laid the Salt Lake plan keeping the middle-class Bengalis in mind.' Dad, back then, could not gauge that the prices of lands in Salt Lake would soon shoot up to lakhs and crores, unofficially, thanks to the elite myth. Though no one in the township was an owner of lands (which were leased for 99 years) and legally did not have the right to sell it, though the houses were meant mainly for self-occupation, people started selling houses, even house floors; thereby naturally attracting people who were definitely rich and most of whom were not Bengalis.[7]

Beside the show of economic prowess, there came the assertion of political prowess as a mark of elitism. Chief Minister Jyoti Basu came to live in Salt Lake. His government-funded palatial mansion with tight security became the reason for pride amidst many in Salt Lake. But with his large measures of security, the roads meant for use by pedestrians grew so narrow that it posed trouble for the commoners; and the rate of accidents increased.

Along with the politicians, came their cronies from different strata of the society, many of whom were known as *buddhijibis* (intellectuals). Most of these people arrived here on the basis of a quota facility, a system of patronage wielded by politicians.

Apart from this, the creation of various important government official buildings like Sech Bhavan, Vikas Bhavan, Mayukh Bhavan, etc., shifted here from central Calcutta helped in the enhancement of the township's elite stature. So many people had to tread the corridors of power in these buildings to get their work done, regardless of right or wrong! This naturally inspired awe for the place. The giant-looking Bidyut Bhavan is one such symbol of absolute power. This building's architecture is uncouth and odd (at least to me), to say the least. However, the elite Salt Lake gradually spread over a large area in this way. Grew from sector to sector, became an administrator's area and then a notified area (from 1989), before coming under an elected municipality (1995).

Of all the five sectors of the township, it was Sector V that acted as a catalyst in promoting Salt Lake's elitism. It is an IT complex marked as a Special Economic Zone (SEZ) that started giving employment to the new techno-managerial generation of middle-class families. It proved to be a gold mine for this class. No matter what great service to humanity was rendered there, it ensured a huge sum of money to its employees. Middle-class parents of these young employees became immensely proud and elated to see their offspring earn such money that was unthinkable in their times.

Gradually, Salt Lake came to boast of Yuva Bharati Krirangan, a multipurpose stadium that is the largest of its kind in India; Nicco Park (erstwhile Jhilmil), the first amusement park in eastern India; Banabitan or Central Park, the largest park in the city after the Maidan; City Centre, a huge and uniquely designed shopping mall; INOX multiplexes; 5-star hotels; superspeciality hospitals, etc., all contributing to the township's elite status.

Becoming an Imagined Community

What grew simultaneous to the act of becoming elite was the drive to imagine the residents as a community (or communities) that would look very close-knit and practice a seemingly intimate community culture. This was another aspect of the hegemonic culture of Salt Lake. Salt Lake is divided into a number of planned spaces called 'blocks' (there are seventy-four such blocks now), and the communities centred on the residential blocks started fostering this community culture. The immediate task of these cultural communities turned out to be funding festivities. Durga Puja being the quintessential festival of the Bengalis, each block began to celebrate it with as much grandeur as possible.

Apart from being a tremendous five-day affair of lights and decoration, with songs playing on the loudspeakers, accompanied by *dhunuchi naach* (a form of dance people do during Durga Puja celebration) and *siddhi* (a special intoxicating drink): the puja is also meant to be a saree/dress competition among women. Indeed, showing off of wealth and other material successes took centre stage in this carnivalesque atmosphere. After all, being ostentatious has to be an integral part of the elite culture. Alongside, of course, there was this concept of 'Come, we are a family, Let us feast and enjoy together during the puja days!'

Eventually, within a few years, the number of families increased and quite a few fights followed which upset the community unison. Thus, the puja began to be celebrated separately by two rival committees in our block. Later, though, they reconciled. It soon became the trend to have one puja per block. Indeed, block committees seem to have been created with the sole idea of conducting Durga Puja, in mind. Bengali culture, thus, could be seen in full bloom during this festival. Later other cultural activities like *Dol* (festival of colours), Rabindra Jayanti, Republic Day, etc., were also added.

This was perhaps an attempt to temper the modern self-centred life by imagining a traditional and spontaneous kind of bond, feigning the intimate *para* (locality) culture of the old Kolkata in this case. The Salt Lake block committee is nothing but an organization pretending to be forming a community.[8] Nor is it interested in forming a modern civil society to ensure civic amenities and the basic civility in the locality. The block collectivities here indulge in culture of festivity only. Our family has never been quite comfortable with this culture and kept aloof from it.

Though we could distance ourselves from the community puja, we could not avoid the community culture that continued to be manifest in the empty plot beside our house. This is the plot which has remained vacant forever, down the years. There was this rule that once one has taken the lease of a plot, it must be built into a house within a stipulated time. This is why my parents, despite many difficulties, had laid the foundation of our house almost as soon as it was bought. Perhaps some persons were above the rule. The owner of the plot next to our house had bought three plots in Salt Lake for his three sons. He had built a house on one and kept the other two plots untouched. After his demise, the sons fought for the plot beside our house and the fight reached the court. Probably the case still lies at the court unresolved, while we have to endure the flavour of popular culture of our locality through this plot. It became the dumping ground for the localites and living became difficult for us. After a point, a vat was set up nearby where rubbish could be dumped. But even that was not of much help, as there was more garbage outside the vat than within it. It was sometime later that the municipality came up with a trash car that still comes whistling every morning to collect the garbage. We were stunned to see that even after this the plot remained a favourite among the localites. It was not only a dumping ground, but also a public toilet.

The periphery of the plot was lined with rubbish while the interior was highly dense with trees and bushes. Sometimes its thickness seemed enough for a tiger or a lion to hide. Parthenium shrubs, a known trigger of asthma, also filled the area. Cleaning was sometimes done and pandals erected when there was a marriage ceremony in the locality. But we had to pay for this dearly when post-celebration the leftover stale food items emitted such terrible smell that for days we felt sick. We just could not figure out how people could feast in a place which remained a garbage dumping ground for most of the time! Our family, of our own accord, used to get the ground cleaned two to three times a year. Whenever passers-by noticed us supervising the cleansing act, they stopped to comment, 'Oh! There must be a marriage happening in their house.' The concept of getting rid of filth and rubbish only for the sake of keeping your area neat and tidy just did not register with this class of elite people. Well, this was how we grew to learn quite a bit about the culture of the Bengali elite *bhadralok* of a township much hyped for its pollution-free environment and aesthetically pleasing appearance.

A Dehistoricizing and Dehumanizing Process
to Create an Urban Utopia

Sketched above is how the long-term and medium-term history of the area became an intimate history of an individual's life. But where did the long-term and medium-term history go? We, residents of Salt Lake, did not bother about this history and made it vanish quite effectively. The land was used as a blank slate to construct the dream township of Dr Bidhan Roy. It was planned and settled as a utopia not only by negating the history of the larger metropolis in which it was embedded, but also by denying its own innate history. The large number of people who used to live and earn their living here, through fishing and other occupations, were simply made invisible in the urge to create this urban utopia. Some arrangements were made for them, which were not, however, adequate. The Duttabad colony was established in the 1950s as a resettlement site for families displaced by the reclamation of Salt Lake. Most of them were fisher–folk who can trace back their family history in this area several hundred years. Later when the Salt Lake Stadium was constructed, many displaced families of Duttabad were rehabilitated in Sukanta Nagar. The slums of Duttabad, Sukanta Nagar, Srikrishna Pally, Naya Patty, Keshtopur, etc., surround Salt Lake; technically they are under the same administrative and police jurisdictions as Salt Lake; though Salt Lake is out of bounds to these people.

And yet these slums and the 'posh' Salt Lake are location wise and economics wise interdependent. There is a clear economic relationship between the middle-class babus of Salt Lake and the people of these slums who constitute a big section of Salt Lake's informal labour market as domestic helps, street vendors, rickshaw-pullers, construction workers, etc. Yet they were almost totally excluded from the township's infrastructure from the very beginning. Their overcrowded slums are marked by poor housing conditions, illegal electricity hook-up, inadequate water supply, lack of drainage, and frequent flooding, existing side by side with the sanitized, formal, and master-planned space of Salt Lake. They live without any security or legal protection. The underprivileged Sukanta Nagar in Sector IV, for example, lies close to Nicco Park and the Nalban Boating Complex. The children of Sukanta Nagar are not entitled entry into these exclusive places and are often run over by the speeding cars of the babus. From time to time the government seeks to evict these people to ensure 'development' and enhance the quality of middle-class life. But such plans cannot be carried out beyond a certain point, not only because of the resistance these people put up but also because their labour is a key determinant of the sophisticated urbanization process launched in the area.

Indeed, this is the broad trend of urban planning and management, that was pioneered by Salt Lake and that can be seen everywhere today. Riches and poverty, formality and informality co-constitute the broad urban fabric. Poverty and informality in social and economic life is an overwhelming and enduring reality, yet they are excluded from the planning of urban development.[9] Andrew Rumbach, whose research focuses on Salt Lake to understand the intersections of urbanization and the environmental risk, highlights in his work the spatial divide between Salt Lake proper and the surrounding slums, as having profound implications for disaster risk.[10] Due to the uneven geographies of risk and resilience, the slum people appear to be on the 'brink of civic disaster' all the time, whatever may be the cause of that disaster—a rise in cyclonic storm intensity or more frequent and severe heat waves due to the global climate change, outbreak of vector-borne diseases or breaking out of fire. This area being a low-lying floodplain, these slums get submerged whenever there is heavy rain—a plight, the formally planned township of Salt Lake with underground sewer lines, drainage canals, and elevated pumping stations usually escapes.[11] Rumbach argues that earlier the problem with Calcutta was lack of planning, nowadays it is sheer bad planning. I would just add that while the slum people are more vulnerable in this regard, the middle-class residents run some risk too, for the poor living condition of those labouring people cast a dark shadow on the middle-class localities—in terms of spread of disease, occurrence of thefts and robberies, and so on. But of course, we residents of Salt Lake, who usually do not care even about rubbish heaps, open manholes or carcasses of dead dogs right in front of our houses, could not care less about such problems generated by the slums which are present nearby and yet remain invisible to us.

It so happens that the building of Salt Lake was just the beginning of Calcutta's eastward expansion. An insatiable appetite for land, mainly for the purpose of promotion of real estate, pushed the process further. The Eastern Metropolitan Bypass was inaugurated in the 1980s connecting the north and south of the city and this was a further boost to the creation of a jungle of concrete on the ruins of the east Calcutta wetlands. As a result, today the bypass serves as one of the main roads of the city rather than a bypass. Land-sharks are reigning supreme in the area. This has disturbed the ecological balance, the price of which is being paid by the entire city of Calcutta.

This has done grievous harm to the flora and fauna of the region. The fish farms and agricultural farms that had provided the city with a natural pollution treatment system in the pre-reclamation days have disappeared. A number of *bheries* are gone, thus adversely affecting fishermen and other employees and also resulting in a shortfall in the supply of fresh fish to the markets of this city of fish-loving Bengalis.

It has also been argued that such a city extension has affected the drainage of Calcutta which has a natural slope towards east and which is consequently no longer available for the disposal of storm water and sewage. During the monsoon in particular, Calcutta's drains are choked and large areas get waterlogged adding much to the health hazards of the residents.

Also, this area that had acted as the world's largest natural urban waste recycling system since the 1860s and thus been called the city's 'kidney': is at the mercy of real estate promoters today and this threatens the entire city with the prospect of 'renal failure'.[12] And it was not only the city's kidney, but also its 'lungs for purification of Calcutta's air' that has stopped being so.[13] There has been an alarming decrease in the oxygen content in the air of Calcutta as a result. The average wind speed of the city has also decreased thereby affecting its public health.[14]

The process has also hindered the development of Calcutta's hinterland that lies in the north-west. The logical and natural development, it is argued, should have been in the direction of Kalyani and Haringhata and in select stretches of the western bank of the Hooghly. Indeed, Kalyani was another dream project of Dr

Roy launched in the 1950s, but being about 50 km. from Calcutta and given the Calcutta-centric mentality of the Bengali *bhadralok*, could not achieve much success.

Salt Lake itself suffers from several infrastructural problems, drinking water being a major one. The township has 15 deep-sunk tube wells as the source of water supply. But underground water–levels dwindled very fast, threatening to make the township another Fatehpur Sikri. The master plan had proposed that water should be supplied from Palta-Tala which, however, is in the area of Calcutta Municipal Corporation. The technical problem of jurisdiction stood in the way of the materialization of this plan for many years. Proposals were mooted at one point of time for merger of Bidhan Nagar administration with Kolkata Municipal Corporation. Ultimately the hurdles were overcome and Salt Lake was connected with Palta-Tala without merger of municipalities. But water still remains a critical problem in the township with its burgeoning population.[15]

From Nowhere to Erewhon

Full of anomalies in its plan in geographical and environmental terms and also in the way it developed in social and cultural terms, the nowhere land of Salt Lake became an *Erewhon* rather than a utopia. This essay, however, is not so much an ecological or economic study, nor a study of inter-class tensions. It is rather a take on the culture of the middle-class residents of the Salt Lake, which, facilitated by the official plans and policies, has overwhelmingly shaped many other aspects of the township. The point I am trying to make is that the political economy of urban development is not just about official planning or governance, more fundamentally it is about people's culture. In the case of Salt Lake, it is the peculiar Bengali *bhadralok* culture full of aberrations and contradictions. The *bhadralok* sought to dehistoricize the place, but could not help carrying their own history into the township. In this section, I would try to further analyse what I have already observed about the culture of Salt Lake, a comparatively recent incarnation of the Bengali *bhadralok* society.

Economically speaking, all the *bhadralok* (literally gentleman), basically a self-styled class, never belonged to the same level. Right

from a zamindar to a petty clerk, all fell under the category of
bhadralok.[16] This is why social scientists classify the *bhadralok* as a
'status group' rather than a class. Right from the nineteenth century,
people tried to construct their *bhadralok* self-identity mainly in
terms of education and culture, distinguishing themselves on the
one hand from the filthy rich babus who used to patronize a vulgar
ostentatious sort of culture (though sometimes babu and *bhadralok*
are regarded as synonymous terms) and from the low-class and
low-caste *chhotolok* on the other. Till the 1960s and 1970s, the term
seemed to stand for a person characterized by refined taste and
discernible knowledge. Yet affluence has always somehow dictated
the culture quotient for the so called *bhadralok*. Today social scientists
tell us that the economic motive and the economic consequence of
bhadralok education and culture have always remained important.[17]
Perhaps this is true to an extent. We have always been familiar with
the saying, 'Education can make one afford to ride horses and
cars'—a very materialistic take, I must say. And along with cars, if a
person can afford to build a house, then should it not be considered
a superb achievement? If this is accompanied by education, well
and good. But how does education really matter, when it boils down
to how wealthy one is? Moreover, nowadays it is not mandatory to
be educated and land a job like in colonial days (though even today,
the service sector is the most important source of our income and
if that helps one earn in dollars and euros, that is the most coveted
thing). Today there are so many other means of making money,
various small and big businesses including chit funds, and most
importantly, real estate. For a long time historians regretted that the
bhadralok was an unproductive class. What we have today is quite a
productive one. But, it cannot but be noticed that even though the
Bengali middle class has undergone a whole lot of transformation
in terms of composition, structure, cultural environment, etc., since
the nineteenth century, nevertheless they still seem to carry some
remains of their heritage in terms of mentality.

The coming-of-age scenario of Salt Lake is a fascinating
example of the culture of the evolving *bhadralok*. My observation
in this matter is as follows. From the very beginning, one definitive
element for a person to be at one with the Salt Lake society was
being a *bariwala* (owner of a house)—be it a big palatial one wrapped

in marble or a small ordinary one. Just having a house would set one in the league. Many housing complexes started cropping up soon after, aiding people in making their way into that league. Of course, there had to be differences between flat culture and house culture. And there was a strong sense of hierarchy too.[18] But being the owner of a residence was the unanimously proclaimed identity of the first generation Salt Lake dwellers and was pivotal to the process of identity formation, all the more so because nobody knew much about the other's background. It perhaps happens in all new townships that mere acquaintanceship is compensated with a lot of advertisements. It happened in Salt Lake too. Very quickly, however, one got to know about the scandals of one's new neighbours through rumours. Someone was rumoured to have murdered his brother to get hold of property, while someone had disowned his parents, left them in some ghetto and shifted here.

Also, in many cases, the house was not merely a place to live or a 'sweet home' for them, but a source of income as well. Bengali *bhadralok* always banked in some way or the other on a piece of land, either as an intermediate tenure-holder or as a zamindar. Even a petty clerk was known to own a plot back in his village. Land was a symbol of both wealth and status. The colonial middle class did not have the option of business and thus always had an eye over landed properties to sustain a living. Hence, while erecting a mansion in Kolkata in the early colonial period, the affluent always constructed slums around it, to let out. In this way they would make money through rent and it would be a great mode of mental satisfaction for them. Indeed, this was the characteristic difference between Calcutta's White Town and Black Town, according to a historian of Kolkata. The latter nurtured the culture of stuffing places with people. Tidy, sparsely populated residential areas were never desired.[19] Salt Lake seemed to be upholding that very characteristic feature of Calcutta's *bhadralok*. Moreover, among the residents of the township there were many who were from East Bengal. Having lost their land and dwellings there and having gone through years of adversity, they had come to live in Salt Lake. Many of them naturally wanted to become landlords with tenants around, and so the tendency to rent. And there was no dearth of potential tenants looking out for house owners so as to get a few rooms in an elite place like Salt Lake. The owner of the house just behind our house had a ceremonious house warming party one day. The house was put on display for all his relatives and friends. And from the very next day we found various kinds of tenants peopling the house. Every floor was rented separately. Some of the tenants lived with family, while some were business firms on rent. Gradually renting houses to commercial concerns became a trend in Salt Lake. These were rented mostly to non-Bengalis, Marwaris in particular, as this ensured more money (because they were in business) and less trouble (because they were minorities). In later years, illegal selling of houses and floors became common too and again the buyers were mostly wealthy non-Bengalis.

Now coming back to the question of culture. Culture is a manifestation of social values or rather serves as the reflection of the society one lives in. First, being boastful (subtly, if not openly) about one's riches became a part of our Salt Lake culture, as that is how the *bhadralok* society had evolved to be. Of course, a house is a sure manifestation of one's riches, but one needs to follow it up with other things. So much so that this culture of opulent flamboyance effected a retreat to the babu culture that the *bhadralok* had once despised and discarded. Frantic wastage of money through various forms had become the raging fashion. Of course money was no more spent on courtesans or getting cats and dogs married, but then we had so many other forms of extravaganza. Why shouldn't one enjoy them thus making others jealous? And the ambitions of the jealous ones result in unfulfilled dreams being thrust upon their children. These children succumbing to the parental pressure, in due course of time abandon their parents leaving them to rot in dejection (and there are sentimental films made on such topics of despair and stuff, reflecting the changing middle-class scenario, of which Salt Lake is a typical example). Nowadays there are no more Pyarichand Mitras or Hutom Pyanchas to criticize the mindless and tasteless greed of the middle class.[20] Not even the pieces that we have come across in our childhood reading, criticizing the insensitive and mean-minded propertied people (moreover, glorifying poverty) are seen today.

Second, culture, for these middle-class people, being a public display involving as much pomp and show as possible, is usually not a personal grooming affair, nor a definition of personhood. Hence, some of the most intense private moments of one's life can easily be brought before the public eye by this middle class for ostentatious display. The merrymaking that we often see in the neighbourhood not only on happy occasions like wedding but also for *shraddha* ceremonies (obsequies) on the death of a family member is a sure indicator.

The third and strangest aspect of the middle-class culture is to litter the 'outside'. Besides being the place of their gaudy public performance of culture, the 'outside' is also the place for dumping rubbish for them. Indeed, very perplexing are the characteristics of our 'outside'. Sociologists and historians have been busy fathoming this complex nature of our 'outside'. They are contrasting our habit of hurling trash from the window with the hygienic and disciplined 'outside' of the bourgeois civic culture in the West.[21] They explain this in terms of the retarded development of capitalist economy and culture in our Third World. But the thing is that Salt Lake is not a place of economically and socially backward peasants or workers. Residents are rather an elite class of people. Maybe everybody is not really 'bourgeois' from the economic point of view, but it is a fact that most of them aspire to be so. Nonetheless these very people continue to throw rubbish anywhere and everywhere. Our family is still experiencing this thriving culture through the continuous dumping of trash on the vacant plot next to our house, and this has actually instilled a deep sense of alienation in us. After all, a dumping ground has to be a place outside and not inside. This in its turn has made us a set of outsiders within.

I would state once again that I am only talking about the hegemonic collective culture of Salt Lake. Not everybody in this township is so insensitive and uncouth. Some of them are decent people with social sensibility. And of course, Salt Lake also has people who, by their very status, fall outside the ambit of this hegemonic culture—people who are not in the league of house owners, e.g. the tenants. Indeed, we bonded well with a few good-hearted tenant families in our neighbourhood (including a Marwari family). But unfortunately they were not in the good books of the self-proclaimed leaders of the locality and had to vacate and shift due to a forced ruckus created by their landlords and other neighbours. Also, labourers who being economically weak, are in any case the 'other' in Salt Lake society. The trend of housing such labouring families in garages as guards and domestic help became common. It was a bit upsetting for hassle-free living and of course went against the avowed exclusivity of the township and the occasional drive of the municipality to keep it free from informal encroachments of shanties, hawkers, etc. But the house owners did not find this contradictory, even though they were very conscious about the 'otherness' of such people (the latter's exclusion from the township's cultural activities like Durga Puja is sure proof). Otherness on the basis of religion or caste is apparently not very important in Salt Lake. However, I was witness to an incident of casteism that once took place amidst the merrymaking of Durga Puja in our block. A few die-hard religious ladies, being upper- and middle-caste themselves, resented the participation of a shudra neighbour (that is a low-caste woman) in the puja rites. How dare she help in the work of chopping and cutting of fruits that are meant to be offered to the goddess! And when a Bangladeshi Muslim friend of mine came here for medical treatment and I went room-hunting for her, the intolerant narrow-minded side of the Salt Lake residents was revealed to me very clearly once again. Otherwise keen to rent, they suddenly seemed very reluctant when it came to letting a room to a Muslim.

Barring a few exceptions, Salt Lake's elite society looked somewhat like this: no one bothered to take care of the lady who was all alone and ran high fever next door. No one showed a little bit of concern for an aged cancer patient in the neighbourhood, hence loudspeakers could blare shamelessly next to his window. Having fireworks piercing the air creating terrible noise and almost causing heart attacks during Kali Puja became normal (this was initiated by the Bengalis themselves and not the Marwaris, who joined later and took it to a new height). Residents of Salt Lake are too sophisticated to stand up to such insane activities. Then there were flourishing activities like digging the ground right in front of somebody's main gate to make a channel for a telephone wire and then leaving the ground as it is without covering up the crater post-installation. Sometimes by mistake while mending TV cables someone would damage a neighbour's telephone line, but they do not even have the decency to come up and at least apologize. And I say all this from bitter personal experiences.

If this was the kind of mentality this class of people possessed towards immediate neighbours, then it is barely possible that they could have greater social sensibility instilled in them. Eventually the area grew infested with thieves and robbers. Illegal activities became widespread. Police officers rented houses to terrorists, a respectable professor's house became the breeding ground for an illegal prostitution business, and a reputed doctor got involved in child trafficking. A great shock for us was learning that a neighbour—a housewife often seen going to drop her son to school—had been arrested as she was part of a gang involved in stealing motorbikes. She used to surreptitiously hide those stolen bikes in a bushy vacant plot. Both the lady and the plot left us awestruck—some other plot of land could beat the plot beside our house then!

Salt Lake also gets a sudden swarm of school/college-going boys and girls bunking classes to cosy up with their partners, some of them in a drunken state, in the nooks and corners of the roads. No one cares. Rich kids drive expensive cars rashly without indicators, breaking traffic rules, running over pedestrians. No one comes forward to help the victim (if anyone did, one could safely assume that they were not a Salt Lake inhabitant, it was either someone among the construction labourers or a domestic help from Keshtopur or Duttabad). As if this is not enough, there is also a section of elite society whose sons were into eve-teasing and computer-hacking business. (Thankfully many of these Salt Lake children are settled abroad, thus sparing the inhabitants.)

The more we witnessed all such nuisances, the more we missed our previous dwelling. The 'para' culture in our Shyampukur Street unlike Salt Lake, was far better, far more humane. My mother recollected the incident of a neighbour, a total alcoholic, who was never seen to come home without drinking. But the same man slapped a bunch of young boys when they tried misbehaving with my mother on the road. He also escorted my mother home safely. Then, one day, at about the age of two or three, I had a terrible bout of hiccups. Dad was not home and mother was crying helplessly in the veranda on seeing my plight. A lady from the neighbourhood, whom Ma hardly knew, surreptitiously came from behind and slopped my back with a sudden force. It worked wonders and terminated my hiccups. From that day she became a mother to my mother and I lovingly called her 'thamu', i.e. grandma.

We had left Shyampukur to free ourselves from the chaotic living there and to avoid the foul smell from the manhandled garbage. But the place we moved to hoping to be relieved from all this, proved no better. It had most of the previous problems associated with north Calcutta, and to top it all, lacked the humanity that people of Shyampukur possessed. But so far as I know, even Shyampukur has transformed a lot since then with the coming of new people having different tastes and values.

Salt Lake: A Bridge between the Old Calcutta and the New

From the 1990s, with the launching of the neoliberal economics and politics, Salt Lake jumped on to the bandwagon of 'development', and for the last fifteen years or so, this development has hit the fourth gear. It is advancing at a speed with which the elite kids drive their cars in this township. Within a short span of time Salt Lake saw itself amidst an array of elaborate, posh shopping malls, delectable restaurants, and a host of other entertainment centres— all promising a feel-good and global lifestyle. The township today is a major site for commercial and residential real estate speculation and investment, with old buildings being demolished and new ones coming up everywhere. The vacant plots, however, remain full of garbage. The footpath is hardly available for the pedestrian to use. Either the residents have their garden covering the footpath or have their trash dumped all over it. State-of-the-art private hospitals are there for the *bhadralok* to receive expensive medical treatment (and finally, to die on a ventilator), but the only government hospital is in a shabby state (after all, only the labouring people go there!) Though jewellery shops and the like abound, the daily needs markets are not up to the mark. But of course, such markets are being replaced by big shopping malls these days. The attempt to replace the BD Market by a multi-storeyed shopping mall has, however, been resisted by the local residents who want to safeguard the residential environment. It was towards the end of the Left Front regime. The residents' objection was dismissed by the then municipality chairman saying, 'Why don't you all sell your houses and leave the place? You guys are not fit for a place like Salt Lake!' But ultimately, the residents could hold their own.

It feels good to know that the people of Salt Lake are beginning to put up resistance. In 2000, the Left Front had hired hooligans armed with guns and bombs to win the FD block re-poll and thus emerge victorious to capture the municipality. Residents felt bad, but there was hardly any protest. In 2015, widespread incidents of violence marked the civic polls in Salt Lake, instigated by the ruling party that has been in control of the area since 2010. But this time the citizens were vocal in protest. Organizations like the Householders' Association and the Welfare Association are said to have been working on the basis of such broader social concerns for many years, which seems commendable, considering the culture of absolute social insensibility we have seen nurtured by Salt Lake residents in general, for many years. Having said that, somehow I am of the opinion that there still lies a basic difference in this respect between Bengali *bhadralok* of yesteryears and those of Salt Lake today. According to some Marxist scholars, the fact that the *bhadralok* of nineteenth-century Bengal did not belong to any distinct class, made them easily assume the role of liberal bourgeois on different social and political issues. Though their protests were not very radical, they were pretty active in various civil rights movements, thus seeking to build a civil society. This mentality is rarely manifest in Salt Lake. Leave aside broad social issues, even guarding one's own rights in the locality itself is a rare happening here. The age of the majority of the residents may be partially responsible for this. With their children mostly settled abroad or at least outside the state, the Salt Lake residents are too old and infirm to protest.

With the real estate enterprise accelerating, Salt Lake today continues to remain as an area under construction. Stone chips, sand, cement, and marble cutters occupy the streets. Amidst a whole lot of din rising from machines, hustle bustle of labourers, and marble dust adversely affecting our lungs: we carry on with our lives. We have grown accustomed to it. Or rather it seems practical to make peace with this way of things. What else can one do? And it should also be noted that new dwellings are no longer 'sweet homes' where the family members invest their love and creativity. They are just taken over from the real estate promoters in exchange of hefty sums of money. In any case, these are not houses, but apartments resembling beehives, howsoever expensive they may be.

The change of guard since 2010 has definitely brought some changes in the makeover of Salt Lake. For example, the park in our block that lay as a jungle for years has been cleaned for children to play and older people to stroll. But nothing beyond this has changed. Even the small lane leading to the park remains lined with stinking garbage. Actually it is not politics, but society that should be probed to understand the character of the township. Development or *unnayan* (literally 'going up') has been going on as unabated, though this gives some of us acrophobia. And of course, this *unnayan*—basically carried out through renting and construction—continues with the permission of the municipality itself. Indeed, the new regime has legalized all the illegal transfers. Why not? After all, this will earn the government some revenue. So who would bother about the common man's problems caused by uncontrolled business and construction activities? The municipality does not bother, nor does the secretary of the block committee. Both the police and the municipality argue that this is not under their jurisdiction. Even appeals to the Department of Environment do not help. Seeing all our appeals turn futile, we decided to talk to the troublemakers directly. It was then that we discovered they were not out and out bad people.

There is a dance training centre in the house behind ours that trains students in Bollywood dance. Classes begin early in the morning. Our day thus starts with the ridiculously loud and jarring music reverberating with '1-2-3-4' beats. At times, it becomes unbearable and I would walk up to the dance master and request him to lower the volume, explaining 'I am a teacher and am finding it difficult to prepare for my class'. This would work for a little while as the dance teacher would respond courteously and reduce the volume. But it would recur a few days later. Then again my job is to go and repeat the same request. The last time when I went with my plea, I found there was a new dance teacher. This one was a little arrogant. So quite sternly I said, 'You see, this is Salt Lake, a respectable residential area! This is not Rajarhat New Town!' This seemed to have worked at that moment. He did consider lowering the volume for a few days. But later I wondered if I had said the right thing. Hasn't the Rajarhat project been born out of Salt Lake itself? Isn't it but a product of our very own selfish motives, vulgar greed and reckless aspiration for 'development'?

Rajarhat New Town, another fast-growing planned satellite township, is actually an extension of Salt Lake.[22] Planned towards the end of the Left Front regime, huge acres of cultivable lands and water bodies of the villages Rajarhat and Bhangar were taken over to materialize this project. The mode of overthrowing original inhabitants, many of whom were farmers, continued in full swing there with the help of hooligans. Rajarhat was very much in the news at one point of time as an instance of the highly insensitive and tension-generating urban planning and management that has resulted from a bizarre 'developmental imagination' and become the overwhelming reality of Calcutta in recent times. Towards the end of the Left Front's rule, it did create quite a ripple of protest. But ultimately this could not deter the developmental dream of the middle class centring on the budding township with its upscale gated residential complexes and commercial and entertainment centres. Indeed, Rajarhat New Town has gone a step ahead of Salt Lake in achieving its developmental goals.

These are some of the features of Rajarhat as highlighted by Ishita Dey, Ranabir Samaddar, and Suhit K. Sen.[23] First, the problem of the eastward growth of Calcutta eating away the wetlands and thus causing ecological disruption; second, the virtuality of capital and reality of the primitive mode of accumulation (eviction, threat, coercion, murder, gun-running, etc.) coexisting, and showing the contradictions of global capital; third, the displacement and loss of livelihood for many to create a utopia for the upper and upper-middle classes; fourth, the dismemberment of the public into private segments—hence, there is no real public space or scope of public action for the residents. No civil society is possible. Fifth, there is no authentic private too—the private has almost lost out to a culture of consumption, flaunting of wealth, and commodification. There is no real private and sharing of the pleasure of privacy.

In this essay, I have tried to show that the roots of all this were already there in Salt Lake, with which the process of Calcutta's eastward growth started. It is Salt Lake that launched the process of ecological and social disruption leading to a fractured urbanism that we see all around us today. Unlike historians of Rajarhat, I do

not view this as a complete break from the earlier history of the
middle class. I have argued that all this is partly rooted in the age-
old tradition of the Bengali middle class, some of whose innate
tendencies got magnified in Salt Lake and then got further magnified
in Rajarhat, thanks to new social and economic developments. Thus,
Salt Lake is a sort of bridge between the old middle-class Calcutta
and Rajarhat that has been called 'beyond Kolkata' by its historians.
It is a bridge in the temporal, physical, cultural, and metaphorical
sense.

Indeed, Bidhannagar Municipal Corporation (BMC) has
been reconstituted in 2015, after merging erstwhile Bidhannagar
Municipality, Rajarhat-Gopalpur Municipality, and parts of
Mahisbathan-II Gram Panchayat. The BMC is constituted by 41
wards, while earlier it had only 23 wards (later increased to 25).
Also, the Bidhannagar Police Commissionerate has jurisdiction
on not only Salt Lake, but also the Airport, Rajarhat, Gopalpur,
Baguihati, Keshtopur, and Lake Town. This has put a seal on
the all-pervasiveness of the process of urbanization in this area
and shows how villages, slums, standalone middle-class houses,
sophisticated gated communities, etc., are all integrated in one and
the same process of 'development', though on differential terms.
The idea that this is the most natural way to shape the social order
is thus being made part of everyone's common sense and even the
non-beneficiaries and sufferers are sought to be co-opted into the
process, though how far such efforts will be successful remains to
be seen.

The nexus between the middle class and the neoliberal
economy and politics in the projects of mega-urbanity in post-
liberalization India can be shown with reference to a number of
cities. Although sponsored by realtors, big business, and the state:
middle-class aspirations and interests in general play a big role in
the process too. And everywhere it takes place in the name of the
grandiose ideology of development, which is seemingly neutral
but actually full of contradictions and exclusions that it tries to
conceal by creating a 'world class' and complacent ambience and
more often than not by forging an artificial community feeling in
some way or other. New towns promoting 'bypass urbanism'[24]—
often built on the edges of existing cities—are a key feature of

such contemporary urban growth. Salt Lake that was planned as a middle-class township on the edge of Calcutta and came into existence quite some time before the neoliberal age helps us to historicize this process of exponential urban growth on the global economic stage and creation of 'bourgeois utopias'.

Salt Lake (at least its old part) still perhaps looks somewhat less mega and overall different from many other parts of the city running after mega-urbanity. A major part of it still consists of residential blocks with small standalone houses. But as the essay has shown, these houses are on the way to being demolished and replaced with more pompous, multi-storeyed apartment houses (though still not more than four storied in most cases). Mega-urbanity has indeed entered the township in several big and small ways. Apparently it may look like a self-devouring process for the Bengali middle class, as very rich people are fast outnumbering ordinary middle-class people in Salt Lake, and most of them are non-Bengali businessmen. But globalization is surely closing off whatever distinctness was once there in the culture of middle-class Bengalis who used to brag about their education and cultural sensibility and looked down upon such non-Bengalis as crude mammon-worshippers. Indeed, it seems that their cultural claim was always superficial and hypocritical. This essay has sought to show that what is happening in Salt Lake today has its roots in various mental and behavioural complexes of the Bengali middle class itself. And the not-so-rich Bengali residents, whether they remain in Salt Lake or migrate after selling their houses to outsiders at fabulous prices, are no less a part of the ambitious and globalizing middle class and vying with each other to participate in the process.

Alongside underlining the historical rootedness of the process of today's mega-urbanity, the present essay has also probed its culture-specific character. Needless to say, today's mega-urban growth is unfolding in different ways in different settings, driven by different cultures. The specific culture of Salt Lake middle class may look somewhat different from the middle-class cultures of the big cities in other regions of India. For example, in some other cities of India, the middle classes are filling the ideological vacuum in their life by embracing the ideology of the Hindu Right. Salt Lake's (or for that matter, Bengal's) middle class apparently looks

different in this respect. We cannot, however, say that the danger is
not lurking around. It is significant that though the BJP candidate
of the Barasat constituency for the Lok Sabha elections of 2014,
lost to the Trinamool candidate, he did win the Salt Lake segment
of the constituency. This is another indication of the cultural
levelling that is taking place today across different regional middle-
class groups of India.[25]

Notes

1. For this section and the next, I am immensely indebted to Haraprasad
   Chattopadhyaya, *From Marsh to Township East of Calcutta: A Tale of Salt
   Water Lake and Salt Lake Township*, Calcutta: K.P. Bagchi, 1990. It is a
   Department of History, University of Calcutta monograph.
2. Zuiderzee was a shallow bay of the North Sea in the north-west of the
   Netherlands, a large part of which was reclaimed as land by means of
   drainage and dikes.
3. Andrew Rumbach (Assistant Professor of Planning and Design at
   the University of Colorado, Denver) broadly interested in urban
   sustainability and community resilience; and particularly in the uneven
   geographies of environmental risks in cities, did his doctoral work
   focusing on Salt Lake for which he was awarded a Ph.D. on 'City
   and Regional Planning' in 2011 by Cornell University. I have found
   this work very helpful. Also important is his article 'Do New Towns
   Increase Disaster Risk? Evidence from Kolkata, India', in *Habitat
   International*, vol. 43, 2014, pp. 117–24). I will use his unpublished Ph.D.
   dissertation as well as this article later in the present essay. Here I
   would particularly like to mention another article by Rumbach titled,
   'At the Roots of Disaster: Planning and Uneven Geography of Risk
   in Kolkata' (published online in *Journal of Urban Affairs*, n.d., where he
   argues that Salt Lake was envisioned by Dr Roy as a home to both poor
   and middle-class Bengalis and was to achieve an inclusive and integrated
   growth according to the ideology of Nehruvian socialism, which was
   influential at that time, though later it developed as an exclusive suburb
   for upper- and middle-class people only. Rumbach says that it was
   Toskovic, the young planner hired to design the township, who was
   responsible for this departure from the original intention. In any case,
   that Salt Lake grew as an exclusive township for middle-class people
   (though in different economic positions) from the very beginning is a
   historical fact.
   I have, however, a problem with one of the points Rumbach makes

in this regard. He says, 'In Toscovic's original master plan, the ratio allocated for middle-class, multi-family apartment buildings and high-income, single family structures was approximately 70-to-30. Today the ratio is nearly reversed, with the majority of plots containing detached houses rather than multi-family units or apartment blocks.' My experience, however, is just the opposite. In the early years, Salt Lake saw building of mostly detached and standalone houses as middle-class homes with some apartment complexes like Vidyasagar, Laboni, Boisakhi, etc., here and there. Demolishing the standalone houses to construct big apartment houses, each apartment of which is meant for only upper-middle class and very rich people to buy, is a rather recent phenomenon. Maybe, as Toskovic's plan deviated from Dr Roy's original vision, the executors of Toskovic's plan in their turn deviated from it. I am grateful to Dr Rumbach for providing me with all his above-mentioned works.

4. There is also another reason for this. As I intend to explain the evolution of Salt Lake from the earliest to the present times largely in terms of middle-class culture, my personal experience as a long-time resident of the township should prove most valuable in this exercise. Even concrete happenings that are reflections of this culture—like murky changes in the original land-use designations of plots or illicit transactions of lease holds, often through the complicity of the municipal and state governments and dubious political patronage—are difficult to prove with documented 'hard evidence'. Rumbach, too, has mostly used memories of the residents to make such points in his 'At the Roots of Disaster'.

5. Indeed *pukur* means pond.

6. 'Pancha Pandavas' of the *Mahabharata* fame are said to be the first 'civilized' persons from north India who stepped into the godforsaken eastern part of the country for the first time.

7. In 2012, municipal authorities estimated that 35 per cent of residential plots in the township had been illegally sold or transferred since their original allotment, says Rumbach in 'At the Roots of Disaster', and as Dr Rumbach pointed out by way of commenting on my essay—'the legalization and regularization process that happened a few years back, and the sheer number of houses and plots that paid the fee to be regularized, is evidence of those illegal transactions that so many residents I interviewed described.'

8. There is a major sociological theory contributed by the German sociologist and philosopher Ferdinand Tönnies, in which the two concepts *Gemeinschaft* and *Gesellschaft* categorize social ties into two dichotomous sociological types, defining each other. The *gesellschaft* is basically the outcome of a process in which traditional intimacy amongst people starts taking a backseat and planned communities begin

to be imagined as a mark of sociability in place of that age-old intimacy. On the other hand, a community based on the 'primordial' bond and real intimacy with each other is called *gemeinschaft*. However, a *gesellschaft* often steals the poetry of primordiality from the *gemeinschaft*, i.e. it feigns a profound intimate bonding. See Ferdinand Tonnies, *Gemeinschaft und Gesellschaft*, Leipzig: Fues's Verlag, 1887. For an English translation of the 8th edition, see, Charles P. Loomis, *Fundamental Concepts of Sociology (Gemeinschaft und Gesellschaft)*, New York: American Book Co., 1940. However, Salt Lake's Block Committee is not even a *gesellschaft*, it is an artificially constituted organization feigning to be forming a community.

9. In this connection, Rumbach points out that many planned parts of Salt Lake are themselves unplanned, illegal and informal ('At the Roots of Disaster'). He cites Ananya Roy's thesis that the key axis of inequality in Southern cities is not between the formal and informal but within informal production of space itself, that informality itself is a flexible concept and an expression of class and political power. So while middle-class and elite informality is overlooked, that on the part of the poor is criminalized and targeted by the state. (Ananya Roy, *City Requiem, Calcutta: Gender and the Politics of Poverty*, Minneapolis: University of Minnesota Press, 2003).

10. Rumbach, 'Do New Towns Increase Disaster Risk?'.

11. Though during a major flood in 1978, even the artificially elevated Salt Lake was submerged under water.

12. Samantak Das, 'Calcutta's Wetlands and Urban Waste Management', *The Telegraph*, 15 February 2017. This is happening despite Ramsar status granted to the area.

13. Asok Mitra, 'Calcutta's Backyard', part II, *The Statesman*, 24 January 1984; cited in Chattopadhyaya, *From Marsh to Township East of Calcutta*, p. 112.

14. Debashis Mitra, 'Starved of Oxygen', *The Statesman*, 28 November 1988, cited in Chattopadhyaya, *From Marsh to Township East of Calcutta*, p. 120.

15. 2,76,000 in 2011 and currently more than 3,00,000.

16. Sumit Sarkar, 'Conclusion', in *The Swadeshi Movement in Bengal 1903-1908*, New Delhi: People's Publishing House, 1973.

17. Tithi Bhattacharya, *Sentinels of Culture: Class, Education, and the Colonial Intellectual in Bengal (1848–85)*, New York: Oxford University Press, 2005.

18. In the 1970s and 1980s, flats were rather looked down upon. Today, with their prices sky-rocketing, they are most prestigious and sought after.

19. Pradip Sinha, *Calcutta in Urban History*, Calcutta: Firma KLM, 1978.

20. *Alaler Gharer Dulal* (1857), a novel written by Pyarichand Mitra under the pseudonym Tekchand Thakur and *Hutom Pyanchar Naksha* (1862) in the nature of burlesque written by Kaliprasanna Singha under the pseudonym Hutom Pyancha are famous sarcastic takes on the ways of the Bengali middle-classes of the nineteenth century.

21. Dipesh Chakraborty, 'Of Garbage, Modernity and the Citizen's Gaze', in *Habitations of Modernity: Essays in the Wake of Subaltern Studies*, Chicago: The University of Chicago Press, 2002.

22. A high-tech township, Rajarhat New Town has won a slot in the Indian 'Smart cities' competition. But the smartest thing about it is perhaps the flourishing 'syndicate raj' that controls the supply of building materials there, often indulging in murders and riots. 'Syndicate' is an extortion racket that runs in areas where real estate is witnessing a boom. Unemployed men backed by the ruling party use the clout and threat of violence to force contractors into buying inferior building materials from them at a premium. The trend had started under the erstwhile Left Front rule and continues under the present Trinamool regime.

23. Ishita Dey, Ranabir Samaddar, Suhit K. Sen, *Beyond Kolkata: Rajarhat and the Dystopia of Urban Imagination (Cities and the Urban Imperative)*, New Delhi: Routledge India, 2013.

24. S. Chakravorty, 'From Colonial to Global City? The far from complete spatial transformation of Calcutta', in *The Urban Geography Reader* (Routledge Urban Reader Series), ed. N.R. Fyfe and J.T. Kenny, New York: Routledge, 2005. The phrase 'bypass urbanism' means seeking to create new zones of exclusivity where urban elites having exited the core cities can maintain a comfortable distance from the labouring class and enjoy amenities of the metropolis and its informal labour force. This has been cited in Rumbach, 'Do New Towns Increase Disaster Risk?'.

25. For a good example of the contemporary neoliberal urbanism one may look up Mona G. Mehta, 'Ahmedabad: The Middle-Class Megacity', *South Asian History and Culture*, vol. 7, no. 2, 2016, pp. 191–207. The author shows how the middle class has successfully mediated its aspirations and interests vis-à-vis the broader agenda of neoliberal urbanism and played a big role in the remaking of Ahmedabad as a megacity; also how the process has been shaped partly by the local culture, which involves an inclination towards Hindutva. The importance of Ahmedabad lies in the fact that it was the face of the 'Gujarat model development' that was showcased to the rest of the country as a model worthy of emulation during the parliamentary elections in 2014.

5

FROM *PARA* SHOPS TO MALLS

The Ecology of
Retail in Contemporary Calcutta

SUKANYA MITRA

In this essay I seek to examine the ecology of retail in Calcutta in the contemporary period by exploring the evolution of the sites and modes of consumption. The use of the term 'ecology' in relation to retail is not new. Ecology is a term used in the natural sciences in order to signify the relationship between organisms and their relationship to the environment. When the term ecology is used in relation to retail it seeks to describe the experience of retail in relation to a particular environment; in other words, the different types of shopping experiences that one tends to come across depending on the changing nature of the surroundings. The theory of natural selection is often used to describe the evolution of retail in both advanced Western cities as well as those located in the so-called Third World in order to show how older sites of consumption give place to newer ones and how and why the latter emerge in their place. This essay, while studying consumption ecology, asks whether an analogy of natural selection borrowed from the study of ecosystems is applicable to the retail scene in a city like Calcutta. The essay also tries to understand how physical settings affect human behaviour and whether the built environment acts as an active agent in the culture of consumption. In order to do so it identifies some dominant building typologies in the history of consumption in Calcutta and tries to unearth the linkages between physical space and urban culture, if any.

Calcutta's history of retail has a unique trajectory and has witnessed different phases of development. From the *haats* and bazaars of old Calcutta to the *para* (neighbourhood) shops to New Market and air-conditioned market (AC Market) in the 1950s and 60s and the malls-cum-entertainment complexes of contemporary times, shopping has evolved over the decades and so have the sites of consumption. Amidst all these developments what has remained constant are hawkers, even though the latter has also undergone a number of changes. From mobile to static, hawking activity in the city has only increased over the decades due to several reasons. How does hawking create an alternative/parallel culture of consumption in the city and what is its relation to other forms of shopping within closed spaces such as in malls and other shopping complexes? This essay will try to address these issues while tracing the ecology/landscape of retail in the city.

Calcutta's Retail Scene

To begin with, let me delineate the different types of retail institutions in the city in order to provide a somewhat clear idea about its retail culture. The retail scene in Calcutta is extremely varied and complex. While the *para* shops are the smallest retail units in the city catering to almost all daily household needs, the bazaars such as the Maniktala bazaar in north Calcutta or Lake Market in the south have a very old history. These markets are usually congested and often internally divided into areas according to the products sold. For example, the Maniktala bazaar has an area within it that sells only fish while potato sellers are confined to a separate place; vegetables and fruit sellers are gathered elsewhere and household items have their own place—all within the market area. Therefore, one needs to enter the place and let the sellers know about the specific item one needs in order to be guided to that place. Even broomsticks are sold at a specific location within the market which has several entrances and can be accessed from many sides. A similar retail environment can be discerned in the case of Lake Market even though many of its shops spill onto the streets. There are also areas in the city lined by shops selling specific items. For instance, the book shops in College Street or the jewellery shops in Bowbazar give these areas a specific character. Similarly the Burrabazar area is home to the biggest wholesale market in the city selling a variety of products including textiles, electronic goods, and spices. The 'variety stores' in Hatibagan introduced a new concept into the retail scene—that of selling several types of products in a single shop. Another kind of shop is the large departmental store, whose history can be traced back to the Kamalalaya Stores in Dharmatala as well as perhaps to the Whiteway Laidlaw store in Chowringhee. The Dakshinapan Shopping Complex, which came up in south Calcutta sometime in the 1980s, inaugurated a different shopping experience to the middle classes in the city, providing them with the choicest handloom and handicrafts from all over the subcontinent. The New Market on Lindsay Street in central Calcutta, built by the British in the late nineteenth century, continues to thrive amidst changing times, attracting a huge customer base so much so that hawkers consider sitting outside it as one of the best means to sell their wares—as a result of which driving to the New Market is often a nightmare.

The hawkers, of course, have been omnipresent throughout the city for years providing an alternative shopping milieu to Calcuttans, attracting them as well as inviting their censure in equal measure for occupying large amounts of pavement space and adding to the aleatory chaos of the city. The contemporary shopping mall can thus be viewed as an addition to a heterogeneous and varied retail scene dotting the cityscape. Even within them one notices a definite hierarchy. For example, the Big Bazar retail chain caters to a less affluent section of the middle class as can be discerned from the prices of the goods sold to the quality of material from which the clothes are made. Again, a close observation will reveal that the malls attract different sections of people depending upon their location. The Mani Square Mall in the Maniktala area attracts a different group of people than say, the Quest Mall in Ballygunge or Forum Mall on Elgin Road. This hierarchical nature of consumption sites is a reflection of the social inequalities of Calcutta and is a feature that must be kept in mind as we probe further into this study.

Shopping Malls in India and Abroad:
Different Perspectives

When the first shopping mall in Calcutta, the Forum Mall, opened its doors in March 2003, it was welcomed with much fanfare. Although it was located in Bhowanipore (Elgin Road to be precise), which is situated quite far away from my house in north Calcutta, I remember making my way there with some of my friends to watch a movie in the multiplex located inside the mall, for the first time in my life. It was a new experience for all of us because unlike watching movies in standalone theatres, movie watching in this case was a part of the total 'mall experience' which included shopping (window shopping as well as actual buying), eating out, and generally spending time with friends and family in a different kind of setting. We were pleasantly surprised at the ambience and comfort of the theatre, the wide screen, good sound system, and other infrastructural innovations. Movie watching had undergone a sea-change.

After the movie we decided to take a walk and look around the mall. After all it was the first time that any of us had visited a mall in Calcutta. I still remember feeling quite lost amidst the different types of clothes, shoes, bags, cosmetics, etc., not to mention the glitzy surroundings and the names of brands we had never heard of before. That was my first encounter with the contemporary shopping mall. Within a period of six or seven years Calcutta became a witness to the construction of a number of such mall-cum-entertainment complexes in various parts of the city—the City Centre in Salt Lake, an upscale neighbourhood in north-east Calcutta; the Mani Square Mall along the Eastern Metropolitan bypass; the City Centre 2 in New Town Rajarhat; the Gariahat Mall in Ballygunge; and finally the biggest of them all, the South City Mall on Prince Anwar Shah Road, an area in the extreme south of Calcutta in 2008.[1] The Quest Mall in Ballygunge and the Acropolis Mall on the Eastern Metropolitan bypass have been the most recent additions to the list having opened their doors in 2013 and 2015, respectively. The Acropolis Mall is in fact a joint venture of the Merlin Group and the Kolkata Municipal Development Corporation (KMDA) indicating the importance the government attaches to such ventures. This is perhaps linked to the discourse of development and globalization, which considers the building of malls to be an integral part of new-age cities.

The opening of each of these malls-cum-entertainment complexes created headlines and witnessed a fair amount of excitement amongst middle-class citizens. A lot of the buzz resulted from the fact that the malls offered a new experience of consumption to visitors with their fully air-conditioned interiors, escalators connecting the different levels, well-staffed shops selling international designer ware, English-speaking young men and women helping the shoppers to make their choices, clean toilets, sleekly designed passageways, and the availability of a multiple range of products from food, clothes, stationery, groceries, books, electronics, and everything else you can think of—all under one roof. Most importantly, these consumption sites provided a space where one could spend time with one's family or friends, i.e. these spaces were designed as places to 'hang-out' and not only to shop in.

The literature on contemporary shopping malls, both within and outside India, have portrayed them as spaces which are opposed to and existing outside of everyday life.[2] The late twentieth-century megamall, according to scholars, expresses a spatial unity and temporal stability that contrasts with the dynamic and discontinuous, fragmented and segregated reality beyond its bounds.[3] In terms of scale, 'megamalls' like the Mall of America in Minnesota, USA, represent almost a 'city within a city' and are designed in such a way that customers driving up to the entrance in their cars can be totally oblivious to their surroundings.[4] In other words, malls epitomized the late twentieth-century trend of turning away from public streets towards a model of alternative urbanity.[5] Shopping malls are one of the spatial products of globalization, which are structured for consumption and movement and not for communication and reflection.[6] They also represent the increased privatization of 'public space' and the rise of a form of citizenship based on consumerism.[7] Malls are a part of the geography of commodity production and consumption and their built environment are spectacularly designed to lure visitors and make them stay on for long intervals inside the premises so that they indulge in impulsive buying. Their postmodern architecture with extensive use of glass and spatial organization confuses exterior-interior divisions. They are designed in the form of spectacles in order to bedazzle and overwhelm the visitors.

According to postmodernists, in the contemporary societal condition, where consumption dominates production and the symbolic often subverts the material order, the distinction between reality and illusion has become problematic or is entirely done away with. Hence, in Guy Debord's *Society of the Spectacle*, everything that was directly lived has receded into a representation that is commodified or bureaucratically administered and is cleaner, safer, and preferable to reality.[8] On the other hand, in Jean Baudrillard's society of the simulacrum, the real has been replaced irrevocably by the illusion, and the world is not just *represented* in the form of commodified images but it *consists* of such images. The image has a more substantive effect than reality—it is hyperreal.[9] Debord says that in contemporary society the spectacle, which is capital accumulated to the point that it becomes images,[10] has spread itself so far that it now permeates all reality.[11] Therefore, the spectacle is not only preferable to reality; the latter cannot escape the former since it has become all pervasive. The spectacle has integrated itself into reality to the same extent as it is describing the reality, and the reality is reconstructed by the spectacle while simultaneously being described by it.[12] The contemporary shopping mall represents the economic and political capacity of speculative capital to create an entire built environment and a total cultural experience that often blurs the distinction between the real and the illusory.

The malls in the west are not just shopping centres but are worlds unto themselves. In North American cities shopping malls are heralded as the new town squares.[13] They are often built in the suburbs or downtown areas and by distance or design, they are located away from the older parts of these areas such as the Carousel Center Mall in Syracuse, New York.[14] By virtue of their scale, form, and design, the shopping malls in the west appear to be public spaces even though they are exclusionary in practice catering largely to the needs of the white middle class.[15] They provide the imaginary of urban streets with street lamps, street signs, benches, and shrubbery. They are sensitive to the needs of the shopper and provide rest areas and facilities for the handicapped, elderly, and shoppers with children, such as diaper changing stations.[16] Other facilities such as gift wrapping and shipping, coat checking, valet parking, strollers, electric shopping carts, lockers, customer service centres, videotext information kiosks may be available for a fee. Malls can host post offices, satellite municipal halls, automated government services and public libraries, and space is sometimes provided for public meetings and religious services. They stage fashion shows, education exhibits, and music recitals. Many malls open their doors early for mall-walking and some have public exercise stations with health and fitness programmes sponsored by the YMCAs and the American Heart Association. The Middlesboro Mall in Middlesboro and the Kentucky and Sunland Park Mall in El Paso, Texas, provide adult literacy classes while university courses are offered by Governors State University, University Park, Illinois, offering twenty-eight classes at Orland Park Place Mall in Chicago.[17] Clearly, the malls in America are almost megacities and not just megamalls.

In India, the American style shopping malls began to be built from 1999 onwards with the Crossroads Mall in Bombay being the first. The scale and range of facilities of Indian malls cannot be compared with the American megamalls, however. In Calcutta a number of malls have been built with a range of public services on offer such as ATMs, infant-care facilities, touchscreen kiosks, car parking, drinking water facility, and first-aid. They are designed mostly as shopping-cum-entertainment spaces with particular attention on children since almost all malls have separate kids' sections with a variety of games on offer. Special activities for children are organized on holidays and special occasions to attract them. The malls are also seen as spaces that cater to the needs of rich NRIs or business executives who need not travel to other areas of the city for their daily needs. Therefore, the five-star hotel in Rajarhat, Swissotel, has been built with a mall, the City Centre 2, in Action Area II, located just minutes away from the airport. The promotional material of the mall talks about a pluralist architectural vocabulary promising to provide the feel of a mall coexisting with a bazaar.[18] It promises a feeling of being in the 'open' without realizing that it is a tropical summer day outside. There is a sense of seamless wandering as a result of the absence of dead ends within the mall. Facilities include shops, films, business conference areas and lounges, and spaces to hold marriage parties and to relax. Health food and spa, tourism and window-shopping are also available. One is tempted to ask whether the malls in Calcutta are as integrated into the lifestyles of the people as the ones abroad. In order to answer this, one needs to keep in mind the nature of Calcutta's middle class.

Calcutta's Middle Class and their Varied Modes of Consumption

Much has been written about the 'new Indian middle class' in the context of globalization and the development of a new economy in India. If we consider their physical presence in Calcutta, one has to admit that it is lesser than in many other 'happening' cities of India such as Delhi, Bombay, Bangalore or Hyderabad. The reasons for this are many, lack of large-scale industries and jobs being the most important. This means that the number of very rich people in the city cannot be compared to other cities of India even though the average income of a large section of the middle class in the city has certainly increased as compared to the pre-globalized era. The Calcutta middle class is a complex heterogeneous entity with varied responses to the practices of consumption. Even within the middle class there are several layers based on an uneven distribution of income. To the more affluent sections of the middle class, the mall culture has become a part of their lives but for the lower strata of the same middle class, it remains more of an illusion, outside everyday reality.

Malls are often seen as being detrimental to the functioning of small shops and traders and are often visualized as a threat to the street vendors and the practice of street trading.[19] In fact in Calcutta as well as in other parts of India, there have been protests by broad coalitions of shop owners, traders, and hawkers against allowing multinational brands such as Walmart, Tesco, Reliance Fresh, Subhiksha, More, and others from retailing in the country.[20] Members of the Gariahat Indira Hawkers' Union under the banner of the Hawker Sangram Committee (HSC) in Calcutta organized protests against the opening of the Spencer's Mall in Gariahat in 2008 and agreed to its functioning only after the RPG group, which owns the mall, the Calcutta Municipal Corporation (CMC), and the HSC came to an agreement that there will be no similarity in terms of quality and prices of goods offered by the mall and the hawkers.[21] Organized retail is widely seen to be a threat to street trading.

While street vending and the space of the marketplace both in India and abroad are seen as a natural and spontaneous evolution and open to all, shopping malls are specially designed retail environments with controlled entry and exit points and are imagined to be artificial in their growth and functioning.[22] Even though entry into the malls is free, the design of the built structure, security check at the entry points and the clean, sanitized environment make it an exclusive and exclusionary space. The concept of natural markets is integral to street vending. A natural market is a phenomenon in which 'the growth of a commercial activity, especially street vending happens naturally around the unplanned/planned areas of public congregation'.[23] It is in some ways a continuation of the concept of the oriental bazaar. The shopping malls on the other hand are synthetic and portrayed as symbols of the changing environment of the cities in which they are built and are meant to be harbingers of change. This is equally true in the case of the suburbs of America[24] and the Hornsby area in Australia[25] as it is for Bombay[26] and for Calcutta.

In the case of the latter, these are seen as symbols of a new and resurgent city which had set its sights on becoming a 'global' and 'happening' place. They are perceived to be image boosters that have created a positive buzz about the city and on the surrounding locality. The Forum Mall was credited with turning its neighbourhood from a quiet residential area into an 'upmarket' shopping destination according to Rahul Saraf, the chairman of the SAPL group, which built it.[27] The reverse is also true as in the case of South City Mall, which was built keeping in mind the large number of residential complexes that were constructed around the area (apart from the South City residential towers consisting of 1,600 flats built by the mall owners themselves), which provided a regular clientele for the mall.[28]

Malls have also been studied as sites of work along with call centres, BPOs, the IT sector, and the like who employ a significant number of the youth. Nandini Gooptu's case study of young workers in organized retail in shopping malls in Calcutta shows the malls as providing a new context of work for the shaping of neoliberal subjectivities. These new workplaces are playing a decisive part in crafting suitable workers and citizens in consonance with the needs of the market and of neoliberal governmentality for self-governing citizens and self-driven, pliant workers.[29] These studies project malls as significations of the entrepreneurial mode of urban development characterizing contemporary urbanism and place a lot of importance on the ability of the built environment in shaping the social, economic, and cultural practices of cities.

The question that I wish to raise here is that of the relation between built environment and urban culture and to what extent the former influences the latter. In this connection, culture needs to be understood in two broad aspects—one related to working in the mall and the other related to consumption. Even though Gooptu's work can be categorized as a study of the political economy of consumption, she places a lot of importance on the impact of the environment of shopping malls in generating a particular culture of work and subjectivity—that of enterprise. Jonathan Shapiro Anjaria, on the other hand, questions the assumption that the very design of shopping malls necessarily brings about changes in the practices of consumption in a city. He argues that the mall is a rich site of practices that have emerged from, while still continuing to affect the bigger landscape of which it is a part, rather than being a metonymy of larger political and social changes.[30] Now, while Gooptu's focus is on the young boys and girls who are employed as staff in these malls, Anjaria is speaking about the consumers who visit the malls. Hence, the relationship of these two groups with the built environment of the malls might vary in terms of the latter's impact on their respective activities, namely that of work and consumption. Since my own focus in this essay is on the consumers and their relation to the physical space of consumption, I would agree with Anjaria's contention that the malls are a part of the bigger landscape of the city and continue to affect the latter. In other words, it is not something that exists completely in isolation as it may seem at first glance. If we think of the malls as part of the landscape of Calcutta, we can certainly view them as a part of the same concept of development and urbanization as gated complexes or theme parks. Together they are a part of the new landscape that is being created keeping in mind the needs and aspirations of the 'new middle class'. The malls are a part of the process of the reordering of space that has characterized the growth of the city from the 1990s onwards and their specific structure and environment have definitely facilitated a new culture of consumption in the city. In this sense it is nothing new since the same process is a part of contemporary culture in the other big cities of India as well. What is distinctive in the case of Calcutta is how the people who visit these malls make meanings of these spaces through their uses and practice.

Making Meanings:
The Built Form and its Uses

In this section, I propose to make a study of the built form of certain selected malls in Calcutta and along with an exploration of the consumption practices of a group of citizens, I hope to make sense of what Anjaria has called the meaning of the mall and how citizens respond to its built environment. I also propose to understand whether the practices of shopping in malls and on pavements are mutually contradictory, and to what extent the latter is threatened by the former. In addition to my own experience of visiting the malls, I use data from newspapers and websites as well as promotional material in order to understand the popular discourses surrounding the malls and the ways in which perceptions about social spaces and practices are created.

I still remember the first day I visited South City Mall sometime in early 2009. I had gone to listen to a lecture in Jadavpur University and decided to visit the mall out of sheer curiosity. The first thing I remember was that auto drivers from the Rabindra Sarobar metro station refused to go to the university and instead all of them asked me whether I would like to be dropped off at South City. I was quite appalled because autos provided the most convenient mode of transport to reach the university. On probing the reason for their refusal, I was told that since the distance from the metro station to the mall was less than the distance to the university and the number

of passengers visiting the mall was more, it was more profitable for
them to run a shorter distance at the same price. I therefore had
no other way but to get down at South City and walk all the way to
the campus. However, before going to the university I decided to
step into the mall. It was 11 a.m. and I received a further jolt when
I made my way into the huge atrium. Since it was a weekday I had
expected the footfall to be less but I was not prepared to walk into
an almost empty mall. As I made my way through the interiors,
the huge mall spread across a million square feet welcomed me
with its shiny interiors, wide passageways, and sliding elevators. I
decided to spend time looking around and the sheer size continued
to overwhelm me. As I went from one shop to the other, I began to
see people slowly entering the mall. A large number of them were
young boys and girls who seemed to have skipped school/college
to have a good time. Most of them were not buying anything but
just hanging out with their friends. After having some snacks in
the food court on the top floor of the mall, I glided down one of
the elevators and decided to speak to a lady and a gentleman who
seemed engrossed in window shopping. I asked them whether they
were planning to buy anything in particular and they told me that
they had no plans to do so. In reply to my query as to why they
had come here, the lady, Tultul Goswami, a housewife aged thirty-
eight years and a resident of Behala, said, 'My daughter is taking
her exams in a school nearby and since I stay far away from here
and I have to spend nearly two hours waiting to take her home,
I thought of coming to the mall to while away my time. It is air-
conditioned and I can move around comfortably.' Pointing to the
gentleman she continued, 'He is my brother-in-law and he has come
to accompany me. Neither of us has come here to buy anything. We
never buy things from malls . . . they are too expensive. We like the
environment and like to take a look around, but when it comes to
buying we prefer our *para* shops. They are much more reasonable
you know.' [31]

I nodded my head in agreement and asked the gentleman what
he thought about the mall. He introduced himself as Biswanath
Choudhury, aged 50 years and working in the service sector. He
also said that he never went for shopping in malls and preferred
small shops which were affordable. However, he liked the South

FIGURE 5.1: South City Mall in Calcutta

City Mall and felt that more such malls should come up in the city.
'Even though we may not buy from malls I feel they should be built.
They are good for the city's image.'[32] In other words, the mall is an
integral part of the perception about the city. It is an image booster,
a spectacle and not just a marketplace.

The attitude of the visitors to the mall makes it clear that the
ways in which customers appropriate the space of the mall and
attach meanings to it belies any straightforward explanation. It also
shows the success as well as the limitations of the mall experience.
Calcutta malls are places where some kind of intermixing between
classes does take place albeit, to a limited extent. They are not
simply fortresses to which only people with credit cards and high-
end mobiles obtain entry. Even though they may not constitute the
dominant number, sections of the lower middle class also go there,
especially the Mani Square Mall, the South City Mall, and the City
Centre Mall in Rajarhat due to their location in areas with mixed
populations. To them the mall is a space where they can spend
some time in cool and comfortable surroundings among dazzling
spectacles and do some window shopping free of cost. As Anjaria

has pointed out, the actual physical space of the malls is consumed by people in ways that are different from how they are originally intended to be and it is the people who endow the mall with new meanings. On another visit, as I loitered inside the South City Mall, I noticed that the food court became extremely crowded between 2 p.m. and 4 p.m. and by evening the mall was quite full. I found large families making their way through the plush interiors and quite a number of children were to be seen during the evening.

My experience at the other malls that I have chosen to study here have been more or less the same with some differences. The Salt Lake City Centre Mall is located in DC Block, Sector 1, and needs closer scrutiny since its architecture makes it stand out from

FIGURE 5.2: City Centre Salt Lake, Calcutta

the rest of the malls in the city. It is said to be the most 'un-mall-like-mall' in the city. Designed by the celebrated architect Charles Correa, it is an island property measuring around 6.5 acres with a road on all four sides. The mall's website claims that the opening of the mall in June 2004 changed its surroundings completely.

According to the website, before the mall was built, the entire area was plagued by a near-complete lack of lifestyle and retail infrastructure. The mall helped change the complexion of Salt Lake.[33] However, such claims must be viewed with a high degree of scepticism since Salt Lake was built as a planned township with markets in each block catering to the basic needs of the people. At the same time, it is true that a mall like City Centre not only caters to the needs of a particular locality but also attracts people from all over the city. In this sense it can be said that despite the presence of local markets, a mall like City Centre does add to the image of a neighbourhood on the one hand, while on the other many citizens also complain about the decline of its tranquillity and quietude.

Unlike other conventional malls with their enclosed spaces, the City Centre Mall offered to its customers 'a street feel without the street'.[34] Inside the premises stalls selling street food such as *bhelpuri*, *jhalmuri*, and ice-cream can be seen along with tea-shops at the corners. The absence of a boundary wall surrounding the mall area creates an openness so that it does not feel like a gated complex. The intention of the builders seems to be to encourage people to actually consume the space of the mall along with the commodities on display. In other words, the architecture of the mall makes it *a site to be consumed apart from its function of being a site of consumption.* While in the case of the South City Mall the peoples' consumption of its space was unintentional, in the case of City Centre, the mall was deliberately constructed to enable its consumption.

Unlike the malls abroad whose interiors are designed according to particular themes such as the Ibn Battuta Mall in Dubai[35] or the Mall of America in Minnesota, USA.[36] In order to lend rootedness and authenticity to a structure otherwise symbolizing artificiality and placeless-ness,[37] malls in India are more or less uniformly designed with exceptions such as the City Centre Mall in Salt Lake, Calcutta. One of the criticisms against malls is that they have independent and indifferent interiors insulating the visitors from the possible inconveniences of the surroundings by producing its own climate, history, and geography. Time-travel and exploitation of nostalgia are techniques that are often used by the architects in designing malls whether in America[38] or in Dubai[39] and these spaces are often built as idealized representations of the past or distant public spaces. The Salt Lake City Centre Mall is designed to evoke nostalgia through a celebration of the heritage of the city like its vanishing trams and its tradition of '*adda*'.[40] It provides consumers with the illusion that though they are within a cosmopolitan environment, they actually remain rooted within the locality. In other words, the dichotomy or opposition between the local and global, open and closed spaces, familiar and unknown, private and public are sought to be overcome within a single premise even though they cannot be overcome so easily in reality.

The Kolkata Store in City Centre, Salt Lake, is a horse-drawn tram car dating back to 1880. It evokes a sense of nostalgia and symbolizes the celebration of heritage along with the spirit of *adda*, which is captured in the designing of the 'kund' area—a huge multi-stepped plaza with a central water body and a fountain that may be lit up at sundown. It is a place where people and especially youngsters can just sit and chat or even observe their surroundings, which in the words of Correa is a 'marvelous tradition which has always been essential to life in the great city of Calcutta'.[41] The City Centre is promoted by its makers as Calcutta's first 'integrated and unconventional hangout' where shopping is not the primary but is the secondary activity.[42] Spread across 4.5 acres of commercial and entertainment spaces, it consists of the mall, the plaza blocks, the Cineplex, the Tower, and the Residency apart from the 'kund' area. Hailed as an icon of change for a city that became 'happening' all at once, the mall claims to be characterized by 'inclusiveness', 'uniqueness', and 'diversity'—qualities which are seen as lacking in other malls. It also claims to have successfully erased the 'upmarket' and 'mid-market' divide.[43] Most of these claims are based on the design of the urban form that is said to accommodate the smallest '*dukaans*',[44] along with glamorous boutiques and large departmental stores.

The feeling of the street is said to be further accentuated by special kiosks such as henna stalls, *bhelpuri, jhalmuri*,[45] ice-cream,

FIGURE 5.3: The Tramcar in City Centre

and corn stalls along with coffee shops placed at pivotal locations
to provide opportunities to rest under wide-spreading trees and
take in the surroundings. In other words, the City Centre claims
to achieve a 'harmonious presence of the bazaar and the mall'[46]
within its premises. My own experience within the mall suggests
that although the design and layout of the mall indeed make it
stand out and the 'kund' area does provide a perfect hang-out zone
for youngsters, the claims of providing a street experience in the
absence of actual streets and the attempts to capture the spirit of
adda in Kolkata do not really work. My observation is that unlike
in South City, Mani Square or City Centre 2 most people who
visit this mall are affluent and a smaller number of casual visitors

belonging to the lower middle class come here. In contrast to my experience in South City, the City Centre Mall is filled with people even in the morning. It is also a favourite with the young people who work in the IT sector or live in Salt Lake. In fact the built form of the mall may be a clever attempt to counter the criticisms that are otherwise made of them by providing an illusion of the smoothening of socio-economic differences. The attempts made to celebrate the heritage and traditions of the city are ways to counter the feelings of alienation from one's own roots inside the otherwise cosmopolitan environment of the mall.

A detailed study of the architecture of the malls is beyond the scope of this essay. However, one must elaborate a bit on the architecture of one like Quest Mall in Ballygunge if only to compare it with City Centre I. The entrance façade itself makes it stand out with its asymmetrical design meant to represent variety. Made of glass, with solar lighting, it is a glitzy entrance of a high-end shopping destination. The glossy and closed interiors housing high fashion and lifestyle brands immediately create an environment different from that of City Centre Salt Lake even though they both have their attractions and uniqueness. Therefore, the importance of the form of these shopping-cum-entertainment complexes cannot be undermined in influencing and enticing consumers. Studies show that shopping in such an environment has a definite influence on the psychology and behavioural pattern of consumers who indulge in impulse buying as a part of 'retail therapy'; often in order to overcome depression and other psychological problems.

A brief look at the historical context of shopping in Calcutta will show that before the advent of the American style shopping malls beginning with the Forum Mall in 2003, popular shopping destinations for the middle and upper middle class citizens in the city were the New Market, the AC Market, the Vardaan Market, Metro Plaza, etc. Until the 1950s and 1960s large departmental stores like Whiteway and Laidlaw catered to the demands of the elite. However, the new malls do not simply entice people to shop. They are complete family destinations where there is something on offer for each member of the family. Although Anjaria has emphasized that the so-called neoliberal globalization is not the first time that Bombay has witnessed the circulation of 'global' commodities or the radical structural transformations of everyday life in the city,[47] I would argue in the context of Calcutta, that the 'newness' of experience is something which cannot be completely undermined even though a narrative of total rupture with the past may not be feasible. However, I do agree with Anjaria's other contention that the coming of the mall does not necessarily negate other forms of trade and consumption such as street vending.[48] This is what I shall explore in the following section.

Consumption Practices

Over the years, the arrival of multinational retail in India has faced a lot of organized opposition from coalitions of petty traders, shopkeepers, and hawkers alike. Malls with their cleaner, safer, and sanitized interiors and the ability to offer a vast range of goods under the same roof; along with facilities such as ample parking space, food courts, and multiplexes; are perceived to be a threat to the small traders, shopkeepers, and street vendors. Significantly, as my study of the Operation Hawker drive in 1975 shows,[49] at that time, the hawkers were perceived as a threat to the business of big shop-owners as a result of which the 'Mina Bazaar' on Russell Street never took off. In recent years it has been the protests of street vendors against organized retail that has attracted countrywide attention. Scholars too have highlighted the antagonistic relationship between shopping malls and street vending/traditional markets. However, a closer look at the ground reality suggests that street vending, at least in Calcutta, is surviving well and media reports often suggest that street shopping and traditional markets like New Market often score over malls in luring away potential buyers particularly during special occasions such as Durga Puja.[50] Thus, the threat perception dominating discourses relating to street vending and shopping malls is a simplistic way of understanding the situation. A diversity of narratives surrounds the mall and a study of the consumption practices of people reveal the intersection between life on the street and in the malls.

On a hot Tuesday afternoon I was sitting and talking to some hawkers in Hatibagan, an area in northern Calcutta when I noticed that the area had a mall called Citimart which was located just opposite the place where I was chatting with the hawkers. Although not upscale like the South City Mall or the City Centre, it is quite popular among residents of the locality. I noticed a lady along with a little girl coming out of the mall with a couple of bags and bargaining with one of the hawkers selling towels on the pavement. I asked her as to why she chose to bargain with a hawker when she could easily have bought a towel from Citimart. The lady whose name was Smriti Poddar (42 years, housewife) smiled and said that she had enquired about towels in Citimart but had not been satisfied with their quality. So she preferred to buy it from the hawker who, according to her, had offered a better bargain. To my question on whether she preferred malls or buying from pavement hawkers, she said that she liked both and bought from both depending on where she got a better deal. Though she hardly visited malls like City Centre she did shop at the Big Bazar outlets apart from places like Citimart and very often picked up a few things from the hawkers on her way back home.[51] Listening to her, Amal Saha (52 years), a hawker selling bags for the past 30 years, told me that he too knew of customers who visited Big Bazaar but bought from pavement hawkers as well. According to him and a few other hawkers like Ratan Kundu (44 years, sold bags) and Lohitranjan Haldar (58 years, sold ladies garments) who had overheard our conversation, the existence of Citimart and Big Bazar had not led to a decline in the sales of hawkers in the area. Customers who went to these malls either never bought from the pavements or else they bought from both places depending on the quality and the prices of the goods.[52]

Take the case of Manju Raha (84 years, widow). A resident of Rainey Park in Ballygunge, she lives alone while her son and daughter live abroad. Her domestic help does the daily grocery shopping for her. While she prefers buying fish from the Park Circus market, she visits the Spencer's Mall in Gariahat to shop for her clothes and other necessities. To my surprise she told me that when she was younger she loved picking up knick-knacks from the Gariahat footpath, her favourite being costume jewellery.[53] During the Puja season serpentine queues greet shoppers on the pavements of Bidhan Sarani in north Calcutta as well as Gariahat in the south where there is scarcely any space to walk. Personal interaction with customers and availability of traditional materials help the street markets steal a march over malls. According to a customer malls scored for everyday stuff but there was no alternative to the sari stock at Gariahat.[54] According to Man Mohan Bagree, the vice-president (commercial and marketing) of South City Mall, marketing strategies and target audience of malls and traditional markets are totally different and the new generation prefers malls because of its variety.[55] However, to people like Suchismita Mitra (23 years and working in the hospitality industry), malls display many pieces of a single variety and do not excite her when it comes to buying fashionable clothes. She prefers to buy eatables and everyday items from malls like Food Bazar and Spencer's instead.[56] As one media report stated that barring the almost negligible sale of vegetables in the new hypermarkets such as Big Bazaar, one could see how integral street markets were for the social and economic functioning of the city.[57] One of the reasons behind the continued proliferation of hawkers and their ability to survive despite the presence of malls is the lack of 'establishment cost' which allows them to offer good quality products at lower prices. Malls need huge infrastructure to run efficiently and so they have to spend more and need to make enough profits. Hence, they are unable to lower the prices of their products. Hawkers do not have to bear any such responsibility. The ability to satisfy the customers at low cost is the secret behind the hawkers' success in attracting them, feels Shaktiman Ghosh.[58] Therefore, mixed and discriminate shopping practices are an important reason for the continuation of street vending in Calcutta even after the advent of shopping malls.

The middle class's attitude towards hawkers is highly ambiguous. On the one hand they cry foul over the filth and dirt created by the hawkers and claim that footpaths are meant for walking. On the other hand, the same middle-class citizens buy cheap food from the hawkers and feel they offer a good bargain. The situation in Rajarhat is a case in point. Numerous hawkers can be found on the pavements opposite DLF IT Park in Action Area I in the New Town. Moreover, in the absence of a proper community market, hawkers run a makeshift one on the pavements adjacent to New Town police station and opposite Reliance Fresh, an organized retail brand.[59] The food stalls mainly cater to employees of the corporate sector and operate round the clock. According to Rupali Shaw, who sells momos in front of DLF gate no. 3, 'Since there are no economical eateries, people flock to our stalls. On a good day, we earn up to Rs 1000.'[60] Hawkers are not only surviving the competition from malls, they are doing quite well, thanks to their clients belonging to rather lower levels of the middle class. Pavement trading and street trading are therefore a necessary part of the city. Since Calcutta consists of price-conscious consumers who may initially be bedazzled by glitzy malls but will ultimately opt for a good bargain, malls and supermarkets will not be able to easily replace street trading and traditional markets. Unlike megamalls in America, where all kinds of services including banking, insurance, and such other daily necessities are available, malls in India and more so in Calcutta concentrate on providing entertainment apart from shopping. Hence, as of now one can safely argue that unless something drastic happens in the near future, street trading will continue to flourish and be a regular feature of the life of the city of Calcutta, even though malls do satisfy the needs of an aspiring middle class with money in their hands.

I wish to conclude this section by stating that my study of the malls in Calcutta and the consumption practices of the city reveal that built environments and urban forms do have an impact on the way people behave. However, the modes of behaviour and practices of the urban life of the cities also add their own meanings to urban forms which may be at variance with the meanings which the builders wished to impart to them.

Conclusion

In this essay I have made a small attempt to understand the meaning of the mall with an emphasis on the built form and how malls seem to have different meanings for different people. Adopting an ethnographic approach I attempted to show that not only do built environments have the ability to influence people, but the latter too actively consume the space of the built forms and add meanings to them. I argued that although I agree with Anjaria that malls are a rich site of practices that have emerged from the larger urban landscape of which they are a part, at the same time I cannot deny the affective impact of the urban forms on their surroundings. Finally, through a discussion of the consumption practices of the citizens of Calcutta I have tried to show that despite the presence

of malls and large retail stores, street vendors are and will continue
to survive in the city.

Jane Jacobs in her work on American cities proposed to counter
the myth of the city with the reality of cities, i.e. how cities work in
real life.[61] According to her, 'One principle emerges ubiquitously . . .
this ubiquitous principle is the need of cities for a most intricate
and close-grained diversity of uses that give each other constant
mutual support, both economically and socially . . . unsuccessful
city areas are areas which lack this kind of intricate mutual
support.'[62] In her book, Jacobs argues that a properly functioning
sidewalk is a deterrent against crime. A busy sidewalk, used day
and night by people on their way to work, home or leisure, checks
crime. Meanwhile, proprietors and neighbours, situated close to
the ground, provide 'eyes upon the street', a citizen surveillance
system that builds trust, not destroys it.[63] This conception of the
city supports the various uses of city space by different groups of
people. It goes against the homogenization of the city space and
makes the contention that it is essentially a divided space. As my
study has shown, the coexistence of *para* shops, street vending, and
luxurious malls indicate that the local may not always be in conflict
with the global, just as sideways and alleys can coexist with the
highways and flyovers. Therefore, the ecology of retail in Calcutta
throws up multiple narratives of the uses of space, which challenges
the notions of homogeneity usually associated with discourses on
urbanization and development.

Notes

1. I have purposely chosen to discuss those malls which are shopping-cum-
   entertainment complexes and are not just meant for shopping. I have
   omitted specialized malls that sell mostly one kind of product and
   where the customers' activity is restricted to shopping only—E-Mall in
   Chittaranjan Avenue that sells only electronic goods or the Spencer's
   Mall in Gariahat that specializes in groceries and household gadgets or
   Home Town Mall in Rajarhat that sells household items.
2. See, John Goss, 'Once-Upon-A-Time in the Commodity World: An
   Unofficial Guide to Mall of America', *Annals of the Association of
   American Geographers*, vol. 89, no. 1, 1999, pp. 45–75; and John Goss,

'The Magic of the Mall: An Analysis of Form, Function and Meaning in the Contemporary Retail Built Environment', *Annals of the Association of American Geographers*, vol. 83, no. 1, 1993, pp. 18–47; and Deborah Karasov and Judith A. Martin, 'The Mall of them All', *Design Quarterly*, no. 159, Spring 1993, pp. 18–27. For Indian malls, see, Malcolm Voyce, 'Shopping Malls in India: New Social Dividing Practices', *Economic and Political Weekly*, vol. 42, no. 22, 2–8 June 2007, pp. 2055–62; and Anuradha Kalhan, 'Impact of Malls on Small Shops and Traders', *Economic and Political Weekly*, vol. 42, no. 22, 2–8 June 2007, pp. 2063–8, among others.

3. Goss, 'Once-Upon-A-Time in the Commodity World', p. 45.
4. Ibid.; and Karasov and Martin, 'The Mall of them All'.
5. Karasov and Martin, 'The Mall of them All', p. 27.
6. Malcolm Voyce, 'Shopping Malls in Australia: The End of Public Space and the Rise of Consumerist Citizenship?', *Journal of Sociology*, vol. 42, no. 3, 2006, pp. 269–87.
7. Ibid.
8. Guy Debord, *Society of the Spectacle*, tr. Ken Knabb, UK: Aldgate Press, 1996.
9. J. Baudrillard, *Simulations*, New York: Semioxete, 1983.
10. Debord, *Society of the Spectacle*, p. 17.
11. Guy Debord, *Comments on the Society of the Spectacle*, tr. Malcolm Imrie, London & New York: Verso, 1998, p. 9.
12. Ibid.
13. Lynn A. Staeheli and Don Mitchell, 'Community in American Shopping Malls', *Urban Studies*, vol. 43, nos. 5/6, May 2006, pp. 977–92.
14. Ibid.
15. Goss, 'The Magic of the Mall', p. 25.
16. Ibid., p. 26.
17. Ibid.
18. See newtown.citycentremalls.in/swissotel-kolkata.aspx, accessed 1 May 2018.
19. See Kalhan, 'Impact of Malls'.
20. See www.news.oneindia.in, accessed 1 May 2018.
21. *Indian Express*, Calcutta, 8 July 2008.
22. Although entry is free in the shopping malls in India, the presence of guards and the process of security check might intimidate and keep certain sections of the population at a distance.
23. *Integration of Street Vendors in the City Development Plan-Nallaspora-Vasai-Virar Sub-region, Final Report*, Yuva, November 2005, p. 3.
24. Goss, 'The Magic of the Mall'.
25. Voyce, 'Shopping Malls in Australia'.
26. Jonathan Shapiro Anjaria, *Unruly Streets: Everyday Practices and Promises of Globality in Mumbai*, Umi Dissertation Publishing, September 2008.

27. *The Telegraph*, Calcutta, 23 July 2008.
28. See www.southcitymall.com, accessed 1 May 2018.
29. Nandini Gooptu, 'Neoliberal Subjectivity, Enterprise Culture and New Workplaces: Organized Retail and Shopping Malls in India', *Economic and Political Weekly*, vol. 44, no. 22, 30 May–5 June 2009, pp. 45–54.
30. Anjaria, *Unruly Streets*, p. 189.
31. Interview by author, March 2009.
32. Ibid.
33. See www.saltlakecitycentre.com, accessed 1 May 2018.
34. Ibid.
35. Upon entering the Ibn Battuta Mall, consumers are exposed to a series of representations that conjure some of the places that the fourteenth century explorer Ibn Battuta claimed to have visited such as Andalusia, Tunisia, Egypt, Persia, India, and China. See, Gokce Gunel, 'A Flying Man, A Scuttled Ship, and A Timekeeping Device: Reflections on Ibn Battuta Mall', *Public Culture*, vol. 23, no. 3 (65), Fall 2011, pp. 541–9.
36. Goss, 'Once-Upon-A-Time'.
37. Ibid., p. 425.
38. Ibid.
39. Gunel, 'A Flying Man'.
40. A place of an informal get-together in which everything from high culture to neighbourhood gossip is discussed and debated upon. It is an important feature of life in Calcutta.
41. Charles Correa, www.saltlakecitycentre.com, accessed 1 May 2018.
42. Ibid.
43. See www.saltlakecitycentre.com, accessed 1 May 2018.
44. Small shops.
45. Names of street food in Calcutta.
46. See www.saltlakecitycentre.com, accessed 1 May 2018.
47. Anjaria, *Unruly Streets*, p. 198.
48. Ibid., p. 169.
49. Sukanya Mitra, 'Reconfiguration of Space: A Study of Postcolonial Calcutta from 1950s to 2000', chapter 3: 'Street Vendors and the Space of the Everyday', unpublished thesis, 2013.
50. 'Markets Mirror Malls in Festive Frenzy', *The Telegraph*, Calcutta, 21 September 2009.
51. Interviewed by author, April 2010.
52. Amal Saha, Ratan Kundu and Lohitranjan Haldar spoke to the author in March–April 2010.
53. Interviewed by the author, June 2010.
54. *The Telegraph*, Calcutta, 21 September 2009.
55. Ibid.
56. Interviewed by author, February 2010.
57. *The Telegraph*, Calcutta, 22 April 2010.

58. Interviewed by author, April 2010.
59. *The Telegraph*, Calcutta, 22 June 2012.
60. Ibid.
61. Jane Jacobs, *The Death and Life of Great American Cities*, New York: Vintage Books, 1961.
62. Ibid., p. 14.
63. Ibid., pp. 20–2.

6

NEVER MIND THE CROWS IN CALCUTTA

Alka Saraogi

As we turn to the left on the wide arterial street known as Sarat Bose Road in Calcutta, now called Kolkata, from the cul-de-sac of our house, a whiff of frying *besan* (gram flour) assails our noses every morning. It is the Gujarati shop making its popular breakfast snack from the western part of India, the *ganthia*. Already there are buyers returning from their morning walk at nearby Minto Park, which has failed to overthrow its colonial name, officially replaced by the Martyr Bhagat Singh who was hanged by the British at the tender age of twenty-one.

History sticks. Just as eating habits from western India have stuck to people who have made Calcutta their home for many generations. But what is this horde of crows pouncing at? Their flapping blackness and relentless cawing could make a soundtrack for some eerie movie.

Well, the crows are eating *ganthia* too and vying with each other to eat more of the delicacy! Feeding the crows is supposed to ward off the negative impact or ire of Shani (planet Saturn) in the horoscope of a person. The trading communities from Gujarat and Rajasthan surely need more luck and a benevolent Shani to survive the recent meltdowns in the world economy. But it has always been a Marwari tradition to feed the crows and the *cheel* (eagle). Even in the calendar, there is a special day dedicated to this ritual of feeding the crows. Sweet *pakoras* (small round dumplings) are made at home for this custom.

The majority of the population in this part of the large municipal area known as Bhowanipore consists now of the business communities from western and north-western India—the Gujaratis from Gujarat and the Marwaris from Rajasthan—though it was once a typical Bengali locality. During the Gujarati Jain festive season in the monsoon, it is common to spot men and boys draped in a silk dhoti and silk shawl, all unstitched clothes, walking to the nearby Gujarati temple in the morning. In the spring season, after the festival of Holi, huge crowds of Marwari women draped in bright red tie-and-dye Rajasthani saris can be seen at the Goddess Sheetla's temple, queuing up with offerings of food prepared on the previous day.

Bhowanipore has always been a predominantly Bengali area since the affluent and educated migrants from East Bengal settled here in the 1850s, far away from the north Calcutta Bengali stronghold. The Durga Puja of the illustrious Mitra family in Bhowanipore, the main religious festival of the Bengalis, goes back to more than 150 years. Many Englishmen too built their bungalows with customary gardens in the backyard. Bhowanipore was adjacent to the Maratha ditch that encircled the old Calcutta, which when filled up later came to be known as the Lower Circular Road. Their institutions like Bhowanipore Congregational Church began its first service in 1843 and St. John's Diocesan school for girls was founded in 1894. The Bhowanipore cemetery is the resting place for hundreds of British war veterans from the First and Second World Wars.

At the beginning of the twentieth century, people from Punjab and Gujarat started settling here too, arriving to share the bounties offered by the seat of the British Raj. After the British left, parts of Bhowanipore slowly took the look of a mini Gujarat. The Gujaratis were always willing to pay more than the normal rates per square feet to live in this area in south Kolkata, away from the congested localities in the north of the city. The same pattern continues till date. Their temples are here, their hospitals and educational institutions are here and of course, their eateries are here with their vegetarian cuisine.

The twenty-first century has brought a totally new makeover to this locality, which still has many of the old Bengali families settled here from yore. The cityscape of Kolkata, as it took on its pre-British old name again, had been changing at an accelerated pace since the liberalization of the economy and more so, since the astronomical rise in real estate prices at the beginning of this century. There is not a lane in this area of Bhowanipore, where small houses owned by the local Bengalis are not being torn down for modern apartments mostly bought by the Gujaratis and the Marwaris. 'Oh! This too is gone,'—is the general reaction when another house starts getting dismantled.

The Bengalis, now with a bigger bank account usually shift to the outskirts of the city and get perhaps more space, as the city spreads horizontally. The old Bhowanipore neighbourhoods of the bygone era imbibing a harmony in architecture with their usual wooden window shutters, are now dotted with mismatched modern apartment houses with their aluminium glazed windows. The peaceful neighbourhoods are assailed by ever-increasing cars honking to make way, as also by the cawing crows outnumbering the sparrows, the common mynahs and the pigeons. The land-sharks keep looking at the remaining specimens of old houses of another era, trying to gauge when and how they can be vacated. There are advertisements in the newspapers by construction companies offering to build and offering a new partnership to lure the owners sitting on their gold mines.

Kolkata had always been a cosmopolitan city with a black town for the natives in the north, a white town for the British in the south and a grey zone in the middle with the Parsees, Chinese, Jews, Anglo-Indians, Armenians, Greeks, and Italians and various sects of Muslims like Ismailis and Bohras. Today's Kolkata has not changed its cosmopolitan nature, for more than half the populace of the city is non-Bengali, hailing from other states of India. Bhowanipore still retains its typically Bengali local market 'Jadu Babu Bazaar' for grocery, fresh fruits, and vegetables and typical sweetmeat shops like Balaram Mullick, not to forget the roads and lanes named after Bengali stalwarts like Ashutosh Mukherjee, the Netaji Bose family, and the Mitras. But it is metamorphosing into an area that caters more to the tastes and lifestyles of the business communities with a perceptively larger disposable income.

Jadu Babu Bazaar sells fruits and vegetables not only of the local or Indian variety, but from all over the world. You can buy an American apple, a kiwi from New Zealand, as well as a rambutan from Malaysia, there. The prices for local produce are usually higher than at similar markets in nearby Ballygunge or Beckbagan and so is the quality. The century old sweet shop Balaram Mullick has started selling chocolate and black forest flavours of *sandesh* and other modified sweetmeats along with its traditional fare of sweets made from cottage cheese and jaggery. Several coffee joints, franchises of international brands, cafes, and fashion boutiques have sprung up in almost every other bylane. Flower and gift shops, and beauty salons have replaced small roadside eateries catering to the suburban customers commuting to the city. Recently, massage parlours or Thai spas have sprung up everywhere. The juggernaut of globalization is fast changing the looks of the locality. One can suddenly wake up to a swanky ice cream parlour with a 'toughened' glass facade, as if produced by the same magic wand that turned a pumpkin to a chariot for Cinderella.

The high-rises have taken over the main roads in the periphery of Bhowanipore, usurping the huge space of the garden houses of the British. In the winding bylanes, small apartments jostle to gain your attention amidst the remaining small Bengali houses with moth-eaten wooden shutters and peeling faded paint. Small banyan and peepal plants grow out of the nooks and crannies of these old structures at times. Yet history does find a way of surviving the ferocious beast of development. There are a few relics that stand out with fresh paint and a facelift. These have been converted into luxury boutiques or Montessori schools or some other lucrative business. At times history also remains intact because the property cannot be sold off due to some legal tangle or if the owners are too laidback or nostalgic to move ahead with the times. But these are not tagged as heritage properties and hence will be brought down eventually for lack of any public sense of history or aesthetics in people motivated only by the one dimensional idea of profit.

Seventeen years ago, my family had shifted to a cluster of eight row houses in Bhowanipore, each of them joined to others on both sides by an adjoining room. It was more like a multistorey building lying on its side. We had the advantage of having a small patch of garden in the front and a roof on each of the eight houses. The row of houses being in a small cul-de-sac off the busy Sarat Bose Road, offered us the surprise of greenery all around and freedom from the noise and din of the perpetual traffic. It was like living far from the madding crowd! Not only this, the view from my bedroom was a window to history. There stood a British made one-storeyed bungalow with a porch and winding wooden staircases and a huge overgrown lush green garden. So much so that it was like the marshy jungle Calcutta must once have been, prior to the British coming in.

After a couple of years, we were dismayed to hear that a nine-storey high-rise was coming to replace the old bungalow and the jungle. 'But surely that is illegal', we approached the local councillor, 'how can they build so high in a narrow lane?' 'You can, if you are near the main road and within 75 metres', we were told. The builders had bought the adjacent plot too to circumvent the rule and showed them as one property. In this way, they were just within the distance allowed to build high enough to block our southern sun in winter and cool winds in summer. The greenery turned into a concrete jungle and the street noise reached us through the cars parked in there.

Rules can be bent easily in Kolkata, or for that matter, anywhere and everywhere in India. For some it entails huge profits, but for many it is purely a matter of survival. As Bhowanipore becomes more and more upmarket, catering to the demands made by an increasingly consumcrist society and gets the first shopping mall— Forum—what is left for those who are at the lower rung of the hierarchy? There is a huge chunk of people who need affordable food as they commute to Calcutta every day for various kinds of jobs from the suburbs. To cater to their needs, the roadside eateries have spilled on to pavements along with their cooking stoves and utensils serving all kinds of cuisines from all over the world.

This is the street land of Kolkata, the largest unauthorized bazaar one can ever find in a metropolis. The pavements are no longer for walking, they have been taken over for cooking and serving food. You can see daily wage earners sitting on their haunches eating steamed rice and fish curry in steel plates, though you can also find executives in crisp business shirts eating on the streets in disposable plates. Street food is 'the great leveller', as this is what a shop claims on its hoarding. There are tea sellers where you can find people in swank cars thronging for tea in the mornings and sitting in plastic chairs in a circle on the pavements. There is a *bhelpuri*-wala, making a popular snack from puffed rice, in front of our house. Every evening there is a traffic jam because of parked cars coming to eat *bhelpuri*. Calcutta crows too, from several generations, have fed on the leftovers at street food junctions and small eateries and still have a merry feast throughout the day.

Kolkata, despite this eclectic mix of the old and the new, of the pedestrian and the elitist, of the regional and the pan-Indian, remains the most humane face of a metropolis. It is easy to survive here on a minimum wage because it is not only food, but rentals, transport, and medical facilities that are cheaper here than in any other metropolis in India. Recently, a young writer-translator known to me had shifted to Delhi with a much higher salary, but within a year he was back to his old job in Kolkata. He said that he had more money to buy food in Kolkata than in Delhi, even with the higher salary. Kolkata, it seems, has a survival plan for the lower middle class and even the ones below the poverty line. It accommodates everyone and is tolerant of all, as it has always been ever since its inception; to people from all over the world, to large communities from all over India; to the exodus of refugees from Bangladesh, to even crows who get their share to survive and thrive. Every evening, one can see two or three dozens of them sitting around the parapets of houses discussing gravely, the changes around and their survival strategy.

As we are about to enter our cul-de-sac from the increasingly noisy Sarat Bose Road after a morning walk at Minto Park, we are greeted by the smiling barber setting up his shop on the pavement at the entrance of our lane. He is handicapped due to some spinal injury. His hand-driven cycle-rickshaw is safely parked on the pavement. He's just let out his colourful pet cock who rides pillion with him every morning and evening to explore the world around. He smiles and shakes his head, when asked if the handsome bird is not in danger of being run over by the increased traffic in our once upon a time quiet lane. To think, is it a bad joke or an intended irony that the nine-floor high intruder has been named 'Classica', while it dislodged a classic structure! The barber's face is serene as he looks at the bird prancing around, just like in the evenings when he plays his melodious flute before wrapping up his shop, which comprises of two flat stones to sit on and a bit of a plastic shield tied to four low wooden posts to work as an awning. He is the true face of Kolkata, one can feel. Marred yet unbeatable. Feisty yet an artist by soul!

The City in Time:
The Eventful Twentieth Century
and Beyond

7

IMPRESSION OF SHIPS

Calcutta during the 1910s

SUCHETANA CHATTOPADHYAY

'The ship we could see no longer;
It was far too dark o'erhead.'

——HEINRICH HEINE, *Homeward Bound*

Introduction

In the second decade of the twentieth century, the impression
of ships left their mark on Calcutta.[1] Though the city had lost its
dubious distinction as the administrative capital of colonial India
in the course of 1911–12, the flow of capital continued as before.
Calcutta's role remained unchanged as the conduit of the imperial
drain and surplus extraction from the interiors; and as one of the
major links in the imperium's chain stretching across semi-colonial
and colonial port-cities from Shanghai to Alexandria. The traffic
of workers and commodities made it one of the pre-eminent ports
in the map of the empire. During and immediately after the First
World War, ships sailing from, arriving or expected to anchor in the
Calcutta Docks, spread anxiety and excitement. Certain neglected
'structures of feeling'[2] were embedded in the popular mood and
the exercise of crisis-ridden authority by the imperial state; they
were conveyed in the receptions and perceptions of ships and the
related role of Calcutta as a cosmopolitan port city. By drawing
on colonial sources and deploying them against their grain, an

attempt is made in this essay to decipher the pressure points and conjunctures, with specific social and political dimensions, that shaped the contradictory responses to ships, and the related flow of people, ideas and actions, at a time of turbulence.

The transitions in the city's colonial metropolitan status marked the decade. An apocalyptic mood descended on Calcutta during the First World War. The conversion of social life from a colonial-civilian to a colonial-martial mode, generated a sense of imminent catastrophe. The war-time conditions in the city were located within a wider imperial canvas: the extraordinary drain of resources in the form of money, men, and material from South Asia by the British state which contributed directly to a sharp decline in the living standards of ordinary people; the support extended by the mainstream nationalist leaders to the war-effort in the hope of securing India's autonomy within the altered post-war political geography of the British Empire; the aim of different revolutionary groups to subvert and overthrow the temporarily beleaguered political order; and the strategy of the colonial government to hold on to the subcontinent through heightened repression.[3]

Embedded urban inequality was magnified by the war. Those at the middle and the bottom of the social hierarchy were hit by spiralling food prices and house rent in the absence of any government control; a regional 'cloth' famine raged and assumed severe proportions from 1916 onwards as supply of manufactured products from England dried up; death from infectious diseases climbed upward and took a heavy toll, especially in the Indian neighbourhoods and slum quarters. In contrast, urban remodelling and war profits further improved the lives of those at the top, especially the custodians of colonial capital.[4] The unequal distribution of material benefits, organized through a convergence of race and class was reinforced by the war-time privations and intensified the gulf separating the colonizers from the colonized. The micro-enclaves of prosperity among the Indian rich also highlighted the division existing within the colonized subject populations, the social chasm of class that could not be bridged by a shared subordination to the imperial state and colonial capital.

How did rumours circulating in the public sphere, war-time profit-seeking by colonial capital, the strategies of imperial surveillance, the policing of the cityscape, forecasts of doom and aspirations for momentous changes become entangled in the impression of ships? Though ships were sometimes but not always the direct catalysts, the way they were perceived fused with and contributed to these currents.

Imaginary Ships

Fantastic German vessels, pouring destruction upon the city by air and water, overwhelmed the popular imagination during the early months of First World War. European officials, voices representing colonial capital and the colonized subjects waited for this possibility with varying degrees of fear, dejection, thrill, and excitement. At the beginning of the war, the wider material, social, and political tensions in the city were registered on a day-to-day basis. Despite repeated declarations of loyalty to the British Empire by associations and individuals, the popular mood in the city was often interpreted as 'informally pro-German', or at least expectant of British defeat. This volatile undercurrent grew because of war-induced material hardship and was a source of recurring anxiety to the colonial authorities. Stray incidents, making their way into police records, vividly painted such a scenario. On an August evening in 1914, thousands of 'natives' were caught star-gazing in the Maidan (the open space at the centre of the city) and the streets; they had mistaken a terrestrial body, glittering in the sky as a German airship, sent to pulverize the imperial order. The European police official recording the incident was struck by the crowd's 'credulity' behind the 'solemn' glances: 'In reality it was Venus seen through a small cloud. The planet is at present exceedingly bright, being at the furthest visible eastern distance from the sun, and after sunset for a short time is the most brilliant object in the sky.'

Away from the music of the spheres, floating rumours related losses of sea-going vessels in the maelstrom of war as signals of an impending collapse of British power. Clerks of Messrs Mackinnon Mackenzie, a Scottish business firm with a large share in the shipping trade, allegedly spun an imaginary tale, and it was repeated by their friends working for the Bengal Chamber of Commerce and Industry, that the majority of the company's ships—twenty-two out of forty—requisitioned for the war, had been sunk by the German navy. They also spoke of the deaths of 20,000 Indian troops being carried in these vessels. They held 'that the steamship *Golkonda*, one of the remaining ships and one of the finest owned by Messrs Mackinnon Mackenzie, was lost sight of and that no news of her whereabouts was forthcoming, and she was believed to be missing'. They thought the Indian troops already dispatched overseas will not fight alongside the Allied forces. The clerks insisted their European employers, the *sahibs*, had forbidden them to divulge any news related to the war and threatened them with dismissal.[5]

These popular perceptions, emerging from the novelty of German air-raids in Western Europe, whose 'slender foundations' the authorities were at pains to refute, gave way to a full-blown panic. This was triggered by the sudden arrival of the German cruiser *Emden* in the Bay of Bengal. The belief in the unshakeable hold of the largest empire on the capital over the eastern seas, cultivated since the eighteenth century, came to be abruptly challenged by an unexpected rival. The enemy ship's appearance interrupted the calm confidence of the British colonizers. *Emden* quickly became known for its stealth. The ship appeared unnoticed in the mouth of the river Hooghly on 15 September and destroyed five English vessels coming down from Calcutta.[6] On the night of 22 September, it shelled the storage tanks of the Burma Oil Company and the storage batteries in the Madras Docks.[7] During the early months of the War, *Emden* destabilized sea-routes, commerce and mail-connections between the British, French, and Dutch colonial empires in Eastern Asia.[8]

Shipping in Calcutta was directly disrupted by the *Emden* effect. Rising unemployment among casual labourers at the dock[9] was accompanied by the refusal of many passengers to embark at the port. On a November afternoon, S.S. Egypt arrived with 117 passengers at the Khidirpur Dock. More than 500 passengers were on board when the boat left London; the majority, 'suffering, apparently, from what may be termed "Emden Fever"'-got off at Bombay'. The ship sailed surreptitiously, 'from Colombo to Calcutta in two and a half days, hugging the coast, the whole of the way lights extinguished'.[10] The ship *City of Marseilles* reached Outram Ghat on a late November afternoon from Liverpool. A large crowd had gathered to receive the ship, 'which carried about 196 passengers for Calcutta'. The vessel had stopped at Naples, Port Said, Suez, Aden, and Colombo and met 'friendly war-ships at various points'. Its course had been slightly altered 'in order to avoid an encounter with the *Emden*'.[11]

European opinion-makers regarded the ship as a source of menace and danger, as an agent of devastation in the realm of profit-making and capital accumulation. Losses were anticipated and bemoaned. *Emden*'s rapid success in destroying British capital assets was seen as 'so monotonously frequent' that 'its possible depredations' were 'taken into account as a normal business risk in times of war'. A sense of doom invaded the jute trade, and the related depiction of merchant ships and maritime commerce:

Transactions in jute and gunnies continue in a spirit of fatalism. Contracts are concluded, and ships are loaded. Those ships may reach their destination, or they may reach the sea floor. But that is a matter which concerns Fate and the acceptors of insurance. Risks are borne by the insurance companies, by Lloyds and by the Home Government. The loss to commerce rests in the enhanced insurance rates and the stagnation due to uncertainty.[12]

As the ship retreated further eastwards and its threatening presence from the immediate vicinity of Calcutta was removed, *Emden* became a source of thrilling entertainment and drama to the European public in the city. The ship was observed from a distance as a chameleon with the ability to deceive 'watchful' Japanese vessels:

One of the most interesting stories of the *Emden* which has as yet reached us (says the *Pioneer*) comes from Penang via Rangoon and possibly has lost nothing in the telling from the distance it has travelled. It has described how this 'De Wet of the Seas' originally escaped . . . in the guise of a British man-of-war. First the ship was painted the correct shade while the engineers rigged up a dummy funnel.

To complete the deception, and with an audacity which takes one's breath away, the crew of the *Emden* raised three hearty British cheers, and though they were probably given with something of a foreign accent the Japanese could hardly be expected to detect it. *Si non e vero, ben trovato.*[13]

While the ship was being vested with an aura of mythical invincibility, common people in Calcutta were gripped by an apocalyptic vision. From 16 September, the day after *Emden* had raided and sunk the British steamers, the colonial officials noted that panic-driven rumours were gaining ground. Words were spreading that the government was planning to transplant its seat of power to the interiors of Bengal by shifting from Calcutta to Dhaka, German cruisers were about to invade Calcutta, and the German navy had greater strength in the waters of Eastern Asia. Many contemplated an escape from the city with their families.[14] The final flight of the colonizers was visualized at a time when they had already removed their central administrative headquarters to New Delhi. In the face of a concentrated German offensive, British authority was seen as a force of imperialism-in-retreat, ready to abandon the city to its doom. A social disaster of unknown magnitude was imagined, induced by the exit of the colonial masters and the erasure of the civic infrastructure by the invading German forces. Yet, the anticipated annihilation of the city and colonial capital did not materialize.

The *Emden* effect wore off with the destruction of the ship. The Captain was feted as a war-hero in enemy uniform. He and his vessel instantly assumed a place within imperial military folklore associated with codes of 'gentlemanly' honour and enterprise, specific to the self-image of white male 'master-races' in colonial settings:

The elfin audacity displayed by the *Emden*, and the ingenuity and success with which her commander followed out the plans suggested to him by an exceptionally vivid imagination, first aroused the amusement and then the admiration even of those who were, strictly speaking his unwilling victims. It may be confidently affirmed, however, that all this would have failed to make Captain Van Muller a hero in British eyes but for the generous treatment which he invariably extended to his prisoners. To a world which had begun to doubt whether any German was capable of displaying such qualities he has proved that a German officer can behave like a gentleman.[15]

Emden also became a symbol of subversion and noble conduct among cross-class, multilingual, and different religious segments of the Indian urban population. *Al Hilal*, an Urdu pan-Islamist weekly edited by Maulana Abul Kalam Azad, declared in September that *Emden*, sunk by a Russian ship, had resurrected itself and wreaked havoc. At a mosque, some Muslims were overheard discussing the vessel with admiration; they claimed its German crew had treated captured Muslim lascars 'very well' even though the latter were fighting for a British victory. In northern neighbourhoods of Calcutta, 'large objectionable placards' in Bengali announced: 'Bharat Samudre abar Emden' (*Emden* returns to Indian Ocean) in red letters. They had been posted to advertise the services of a *kaviraj*; this was explained in smaller print below the attention-grabbing exercise. The police, instead of customers, distinctly un-amused by the trick, visited Bejoya Press owned by Ramesh Chandra Choudhury, a 'well-known' *bhadralok* nationalist 'suspect' from Sylhet; he was 'brought' before high-ranking officials and interrogated on his intentions for publishing the material.[16]

The spectre of German invasion remained unrealized. It nestled, for a while, in the imagination of the colonizers and their subjects. It was observed, on behalf of colonial capital, that 'consuming countries are now in the position that they must have jute or gunnies, as the case may be; so business is proceeding in spite of the *Emden's* successful deception'.[17] With the continuation of the super-profitable jute trade, which initially suffered from the vanishing of the continental market, particularly in Germany and Austria-Hungary,[18] the anxiety of European proprietors subsided. The colonized subjects also realized that the colonizers were not yet ready to leave the city. Their sense of dread and dissent against colonial authority at a time of rising hardship was expressed through other outlets. However, war-time watch on the river by the colonial authorities persisted, as did the rumours surrounding the vessels arriving from the East. Soon, the imaginary and distant battle-ships, charting the sky and the sea, were replaced by the ships of sedition.

Vessels of Sedition

The *Emden* effect was followed, accompanied and replaced by the 'Ghadar' effect. Ships carrying Sikh and Punjabi migrant labourers returning from the Americas sharply increased the anxieties of the colonial authorities during late 1914 and early 1915. Haunted by a spectre of return, the colonial state openly advocated iron-fisted repression and intensified surveillance. These strategies had an opposite impact on the urban milieu, stimulating rumours, cross-class protests and solidarities, resistance, and diasporic activism from below.

Even before *Komagata Maru*, a ship carrying mostly Punjabi labourers who had been turned away on racist grounds by the Canadian authorities, reached the shores of Bengal, the colonial state apparatus was making arrangements. The police authorities secretly planned to imprison the most vocal passengers at the moment of arrival and send the rest by a special train to Punjab. They also decided that the ship must not reach Calcutta. *Komagata Maru* had already attracted public attention. If it was allowed to sail into the port city, a large and volatile crowd could gather to welcome the ship and its passengers; this was to be prevented.[19] The government's priority was to 'neutralize' those arriving with the intention of stirring up 'trouble'; having been forcibly turned away from Vancouver and refused entry at Singapore, the passengers were perceived as dangerous and capable of rising against the colonial order in India. More importantly, they could inconvenience and embarrass the State at a time of war, when it was banking on the loyalty of Indians and the resources of the subcontinent. By launching a potentially popular public campaign against imperial racism, they could disrupt the war-effort. The colonial authorities suppressed a telegram from the passengers to their sympathizers in Punjab and Bengal. The message which never arrived had urged Indian nationalist leaders to receive the ship at the Calcutta Port, followed by a movement to force the government to investigate the circumstances leading to its return. A note between the concerned provincial governments observed:

The Lieutenant Governor (of Punjab) thinks it advisable, in the present crisis, to prevent the arrival of these men from being used as the occasion for a recrudescence of the agitation with regard to Indian emigration in the British colonies, and he therefore proposes to take action under Ordinance No V of 1914, dated the 5 Sept 1914, to procure their return to their homes immediately on landing.

Paradoxically, the majority of the ship's passengers were described in confidential correspondence as 'harmless', 'destitute', and disinclined to follow 'the leader of the expedition',[20] the implicit assumption being they would be easier to control.[21]

The colonial administration in India, in close touch with the authorities in British Columbia, British diplomatic missions in Japan, and the police-forces in British-controlled port cities of

China and South-East Asia such as Hong Kong and Singapore was monitoring the passage of the ship. On 27 September a deceptively calm telegram reached the authorities in Simla from Calcutta: 'KM met today by Bengal and Punjab officers as arranged. All satisfactory so far.' The next communication was a long one for a telegram and sent on 30 September. The version given, followed by an official communiqué to the press which formed the master narrative of all official accounts, was later held up by the *Report of the Komagata Maru Committee of Inquiry*; they exonerated the government over the massacre of 21 passengers on the night of 29 September. The police officials on the ground, while making statements, repeatedly declared they had remained passive in the face of 'insolence'. They also freely admitted to being prepared to use force and mobilize troops from Fort William and elsewhere while the passengers, despite their suspicions, were peaceful; they had put up with colonial authority, including searches. They had obeyed the orders to turn back from the road to Calcutta and remain herded in the railway station at Budge Budge. The officers acknowledged having underestimated the ability of the emigrants to close ranks and defend Gurdit Singh, the organizer of the voyage, when they realized the British authorities had special plans for him. David Petrie, a high-ranking police officer who was present at Budge Budge, reported the mood of resistance soon after the incident. As far as he was concerned, alongside the rest of the colonial bureaucracy, the battle line was already drawn:

Most of the Sikhs, too, were men who had been abroad in the colonies and elsewhere-Hong Kong, Shanghai, Manila, and so on. It is a matter of common experience that Indians too often return from abroad with the tainted political views and diminished respect for their white rulers . . . it is difficult to avoid the conclusion that . . . defiance of authority must have led, sooner or later, to the same result.[22]

Following the resistance of *Komagata Maru*, all ships sailing from America and the Far East, especially those carrying Sikh labourers, came to be closely watched. The migrants were subjected to a combination of imperial control over the 'lesser races' and a planned offensive from above. In November 1914, Central Intelligence sent clear instructions to the Intelligence Branch officials of Bengal to conduct rigorous enquiries on the 'particulars of all boats that have arrived in Calcutta subsequent to the Komagata Maru, with Indians from the Far East, stating briefly what sort of people the passengers were'. He was keen to know 'how they were dealt with'.

Racial stereotyping merged with a fear of class war from below. The great majority on board these ships were labourers. Other passengers comprised watchmen, tailors, students, policemen, and deportees from North America. Being poor, Sikh deck passengers were regarded as potential carriers of the 'Ghadar tendency' and became special targets of surveillance. The numbers of those arriving were recorded before they arrived, with active cooperation from the shipping companies. These enterprises were subordinated to the monopolistic 'Managing Agency' houses, commercial pillars of British colonial capital in Asia. Apart from Mackinnon Mackenzie, Jardine Skinner, and Andrew Yule were the two other large British business firms which controlled the shipping traffic in the docks of South Bengal from Calcutta. They were the official agents, respectively, of British India, Indo-China, and Nippon Yusen Kaisha lines which transported travellers to various destinations between eastern India and the American West Coast.

The vessels were stopped in the docks on the river Hooghly, south of Calcutta. All passengers had their belongings searched thoroughly, under the watchful gaze of experienced Intelligence officers of the Bengal Police. Tins, pails, boxes, and baskets of food, comprising the meagre worldly possessions of the returning emigrants were inspected by customs officers to determine if 'false bottoms' existed. Those with prior political records were imprisoned under 'Ingress into India Ordinance' and the rest speedily deported to Ludhiana by a special train under armed escort from Howrah Railway Station where they were subjected to further screening. The process ensured that the passengers, while travelling through Calcutta's immediate neighbouring regions, will be unable to enter the city.[23] In mid-October, *Nam Sang* reached the docks at Diamond Harbour near Calcutta. The commander and First Officer complained of the insolent, abusive, and violent conduct of the Punjabi migrants; they alleged that the migrants had terrorized white passengers, chased the ship's crew, and tried to prevent the rescue of a European woman who had gone overboard.[24] Three Sikhs were arrested from the ship as principal ring-leaders after being pointed out by the First Officer. *Foo Sang* also arrived around the same time; she carried proscribed leaflets. Three Sikhs were arrested, including a 'seditious' bookbinder from Singapore who was previously employed in the government press and used his skills against his masters.[25] A month after *Komagata Maru*'s arrival, *Tosa Maru* anchored with Sikh passengers from North America and East Asia. They 'openly' talked of rebellion.[26] Captain Dallas-Smith, Assistant Commandant, Dacca Military Police Battalion, who was put in charge of accompanying the passengers under armed escort by train, complained of inadequate food and water provisions which inflamed the feelings of the passengers. Unhappiness with the lack of support he received from his superiors, the 'indefiniteness of the instructions' which prevented an application of 'overwhelming' force, having to deploy diplomacy and good humour in the face of abusive conduct and 'wild talk' from those below him, left their mark on his report. He observed the 'attitude' of the migrants had 'left no doubt as to the frame of mind in which they were returning to their country' and during the railway journey they were an 'unceasing cause of anxiety'. *On Sang* came in early January 1915, carrying soldiers of the Indian Army who were on sick leave, 'distressed' seamen, some businessmen and labourers. Over 170 Punjabi migrants, mostly from Canada and the US, were on board. Two passengers, described as 'dangerous characters', were detained. The rest, with the exception of those allowed an 'extension of stay' in Calcutta, were promptly dispatched by a waiting train to Punjab, 'quietly and expeditiously'.[27] Once the 'special train' was in motion, the polite and compliant demeanour of some of the passengers underwent abrupt transformation. Occupants of one of the carriages shouted 'Bande Mataram', 'called it to one another, to the Bengali railway men, and to a small knot of European police officers who were on duty at the time of departure'. A man made a gesture of 'hatred and contempt', throwing something with open hands at the officers, interpreted as 'I throw dust on your head'.[28] In the closely observed ships and upon embarkation, the migrants responded to imperial authority through everyday acts of fleeting and transient subversion. The police authorities congratulated themselves upon their smooth control over the rebels. Nevertheless, the spectre of 'defiance' by the returning emigrant, tainted by subversive views cultivated abroad, continued to visit them.

In the streets of the metropolis, rumours with a distinct anti-state edge, circulated through public conversations. Immediately after the confrontation at Budge Budge, the British authorities were accused of having shot and killed unarmed women and children travelling on *Komagata Maru*, of British soldiers having opened fire on a Sikh regiment that had mutinied after reaching the shores of India.[29] After the shooting at Budge Budge, a group of loyalist Punjabis gathered at Burra Sikh Sangat, located on Harrison Road, a busy thoroughfare in north Calcutta. Prompted by the government, they were keen to display their confidence in the British Crown. Condemning the passengers of *Komagata Maru* as rioters and seditionists, they pledged unshakable support to the war-effort. A high-ranking British police official was forced to admit that a mood of scepticism hung in the air: 'I am given to understand that many of the Sikhs did not wholly associate themselves with the resolutions passed, saying that the meeting was an official one. They keenly desire an impartial enquiry into the matter with non-official members from their own community.'[30]

Those arrested after the massacre, recorded their ill-treatment and exhaustion. They were brought to Calcutta not under the circumstances they could have chosen and incarcerated at Alipur Central Jail. They represented the suppressed voices from *Komagata Maru*. Their statements, written down in police stations and prison-cells, offered counter-claims of abuse, clashing with the narratives of events furnished by their captors. The interned travellers recounted their exhausting journey through a nightmarish and unfamiliar topography of terror. After escaping from the Budge Budge railway station, as 'fugitives', they had been chased and shot at by the troops. They had crossed rivers, trekked through marshes, fields and roads, hidden in forests, begged for alms, and sought asylum in the nearby villages, adjoining districts, suburbs, and neighbourhoods of Calcutta. Tara Singh claimed of having received help from an unknown Bengali gentleman while escaping on foot; his anonymous benefactor had warned him that the British could hang him if he was captured, gave him money, provided clothes and disguise. Surain Singh, later convicted under the Arms Act of 1878, also spoke of local assistance and of being beaten by the constable who arrested him.[31] Amir Mohammad Khan, a close aide of Gurdit Singh and secretary of the passenger's committee, was interned as one of the chief 'trouble-makers' for an unspecified period of time. He complained of rapid loss of weight in jail and of being condemned without trial 'in violation of all laws divine and human'.[32]

Outside, certain open and secret connections between local critics of colonial policies and Punjabi dissenters were being forged. This was already evident from early 1914 when *Komagata Maru* sailed to Canada and was forced to turn back. Several Calcutta-based Bengali and English language newspapers and periodicals, run by Hindu and Muslim intellectuals from Bengal, discussed Canada's anti-immigrant laws, the racism of the imperial authorities, and the loss of livelihood in India under British rule which had contributed to mass migration. After the Budge Budge incident, some of them 'deplored' the state action. They argued that the passengers should have been allowed to reach Calcutta, those being held without trial were harmless and deserved freedom, and that the Sikhs returning from abroad and the community living in Calcutta and its suburbs were being harassed and persecuted.[33]

While middle-class expressions of civil rights were registered in the colonial public sphere, a cross-class underground network was also developing in the city. The secret society networks of middle-class Bengali Hindus were strategically stepping beyond their elite confines to establish links with 'Ghadar' and pan-Islamist revolutionaries. This was a part of a wider programme to get arms from Germany and spread rebellion in the ranks of colonial troops from Lahore to Calcutta to Singapore; this history has been recorded.[34] Certain local dimensions were also at work. The strategy to procure guns and money by underground cells, discernible from 1913, rose sharply in a climate of war. The revolutionaries took advantage of the Sikh presence among service sector workers and the increase in the volume of motor vehicles in the streets. In 1915, several taxi-cab robberies, including the 'Garden Reach dacoity' in February and the 'Corporation Street dacoity' in December, were executed with the help of Sikh drivers. On the afternoon of 12 February 1915, when three employees of Bird & Company, a British managing agency house in Calcutta, were transporting a cash amount of Rs.18,000 in a *ticca ghari* (horse-drawn carriage) to the South Union Mill, they were stopped by armed Bengalis travelling in a taxi. The four young men forced the occupants of the carriage to hand over the money; the robbers then rapidly left the scene of crime, 'throwing out the chauffeur as they drove off'. The chauffeur, a Sikh employee of the Indian Motor Taxi Company, turned out to be an accomplice. On the evening of 2 December 1915, five armed Bengali young men also arrived in a motor car and looted gold and silver ornaments from a pawn-broker's shop at Corporation Street. Since the robbery took place in the heart of Calcutta, several people witnessed the deed. None of them offered any clue as to the direction taken by the fleeing perpetrators. This car was also traced back to the fleet of Indian Motor Taxi Company. Chait Singh, an employee, was arrested on suspicion of being the 'actual' driver. The refusal of the complainant and eyewitnesses to identify the revolutionary robbers, made the 'detection of the case' impossible. Ultimately, the 'suspected participants' were dealt with 'in other ways' under the Defence of India Act.[35]

The interconnections between Ghadar influence, Sikh workers, and the militant nationalists became the theme of a panic-stricken enquiry by the police:

It is not merely the occasional use of Sikh taxi-cab drivers for political *dakaities* that is disturbing but the likelihood of organised use being made on a bigger scale of the Sikh drivers, should any big disturbance break out in Calcutta. From what one hears there seems little doubt but that many drivers speak Bengali and are on close terms of intimacy with members of the Revolutionary Party.[36]

The revolutionary underground subordinated the identity of the Sikh drivers as workers to that of nationhood while depending on the labour they performed in the urban milieu. The Sikh rebels in turn found an organized channel of subverting British authority through the revolutionary network. So far, their relationship with the city had been confined by the entwined conditions of migration and livelihood. The nationalist revolutionary milieu connected them, for the first time, with planned political action. Chait Singh, a resident of the city for nine years, was described as 'a man of Ghadar sympathies'. He was depicted as a 'fanatical' former colonial soldier who was 'full of grievances' against the British Empire. His revolutionary colleagues belonging to *Jugantar* bailed

him out. To celebrate his release, they participated in elaborate
'feasts'. In Bhowanipore, a mixed multilingual neighbourhood
where they had met and interacted, sheep were slaughtered to cook
curry and liquor was consumed. These convivial gatherings where
Sikh drivers and Bengali babus rubbed shoulders, displayed the
forging of an anti-colonial social alliance and friendship among
young men that temporarily dissolved class, caste, linguistic, and
regional barriers. The celebrations were short-lived. Chait Singh
was arrested for a second time, with his Bengali friends and
jailed indefinitely under repressive war-time regulations. He had
developed a following among fellow cab drivers who initially tried
to cover his tracks.[37] Dewan Singh, a door-keeper of the Howrah
Gurudwara, was imprisoned for asking soldiers of the 16th Rajputs,
an infantry unit deployed against the *Komagata Maru* passengers
and stationed at Fort William, to rebel. For sixteen years, Dewan
Singh had lived in Bengal. By his own admission, he had worked
as a semi-permanent ticket-inspector in the railways. He tendered
his resignation 'because he refused to arrest respectable people'
for trespasses. He had also 'quarrelled with his superiors'. He was
suspected of having connections with *Komagata Maru* passengers;
these suspicions were strengthened when Sher Singh, his nephew,
was arrested in possession of Ghadar leaflets, supposedly carried
by the ship's passengers and deposited at the Howrah Gurudwara.
A man of fifty, Dewan Singh was criminalized in police reports
as an 'undesirable character' known to the local police as a *pukka
budmas* (seasoned evil-doer). It was alleged he had begun his career
in Punjab as a 'bazaar dancing boy', a derisive euphemism for a male
child prostitute.[38] In contrast, Bhupendra Kumar Datta, a Bengali
revolutionary belonging to *Jugantar*, who shared jail space with
him in Calcutta, described Dewan Singh as a kind and courageous
veteran warrior who made new political prisoners feel at home
in a prison environment. Dewan Singh was apparently 'incensed'
when younger revolutionaries contemplated going on hunger strike
to protest prisoners' abuse but were in favour of excluding older
political inmates. When he and other elderly prisoners insisted on
fasting, the idea of boycotting food was hastily given up. Datta
also remembered having met Chait Singh there. Unlike the British
officials who saw him as a secretive figure exuding quiet menace

and ferocity, Datta saw him as a 'tall man' with a 'heart-felt, open smile'.[39]

The Sikh members of the revolutionary underground were rounded up by 1916, alongside the local host network. The colonial authorities were satisfied that the arrests and searches would suitably intimidate the Sikh migrant workers of Calcutta, Howrah and the suburbs and permanently deter them from engaging in movements opposing the state.[40] This was not to be. In the upsurge against capital and empire in the years following the First World War, a section of Sikh workers, while aligning leftward, consciously focused on the memory of the ship which had symbolically propelled the migrants towards participation in local politics.

The horizon of the post-war political landscape in Calcutta and its surroundings was extended and altered by anti-colonial mass movements, labour activism and the emergence of the Left. This was also the period when migrations from Punjab and the size of the Sikh labour-force increased. To the Sikh migrants who joined post-war strike-waves and formed unions in the 1920s and early 1930s, an unofficial commemoration of the *Komagata Maru*'s voyage became inseparable from contemporary resistance to the domination of colonial capital. They engaged with, worked upon, and simultaneously moved beyond the boundaries of nationalism by focusing on a self-aware identity of class, based on organized action. This understanding was linked with the lived experiences of migration and imperial exploitation, the components of a diasporic identity that had come to the forefront during the voyage of *Komagata Maru* and underlined the actions of Sikh revolutionaries in a war-time city.

Floating Revolution and Counter-Revolution

The 'Ghadar' effect had exposed the imperium's fear of a social uprising from below. Following the Bolshevik Revolution of 1917, the *Emden* and Ghadar effects were substituted by the 'Bolshevik' effect. The latter unfolded against the backdrop of Germany's defeat and the Russian civil war: the final collapse of Germany and the Allied intervention in the former Russian Empire to destroy the newly formed workers' state. As the war drew to a close and popular grievances against the colonial state were uncorked in the city, the fear of 'Bolshevism' at the top and stray expressions of support for the Bolshevik government at the level of colonial society could be noticed. These impulses and imperial strategies to curb a possible 'Bolshevik' penetration from 'outside' became tied with the arrival of ships carrying Russian sailors, counter-revolutionary crew, and suspected Bolshevik activists. The colonial state used the war-time and post-war surveillance measures to watch the vessels reaching the port which consisted of 'Pro-Bolshevik' sailors, passengers, and literature. The phobic perceptions of water and of population and labour transfer underlined the actions of the state.

In March 1918, in accordance with communications sent from Bombay, the officers and crew of the Russian vessels *S.S. Eduard Barry* and *S.S. Baikal* were detained upon arrival in Calcutta under war-time security acts. The following month, the Marine Department of the colonial government cancelled the internment orders on the officers involved, but the sailors accompanying them remained incarcerated.[41] While the sailors were seen as potential mutineers from below, preferential treatment as natural social allies could be extended to the officer class. Two years later, when the White Russian ship *Ural* landed in the docks, it was welcomed and refuelled. The 300 cadets and officers, half of whom were exiles from the Petrograd Soviet, were described as 'Kolchak's men'. *The Englishman*, a newspaper catering to the European community in the city, observed in light tones, that a section of this cheerful young crew was seen playing music and entertaining ladies in their saloons. Unable to conceal the uncertainties facing the counter-revolutionary forces, the report also described the ship as old, battered, and rusty. Loaded with ammunition by the British forces at Vladivostok, it had sailed through allied Japanese waters and the British colonial ports of Hong Kong and Singapore, stopping for coal at Calcutta on its way to Alexandria. Its final destination was unknown.[42]

No attempt was spared to keep the port, city, and region free of the 'Bolshevik menace', as the deportation of Frank Bilboa and John Burtovich demonstrated. Respectively of Spanish and Russian origin, Bilboa and Burtovich arrived in 1919 on a British merchant vessel, the *S.S. Boverie*, with a mixed crew 'of all nations'. They had previously participated in strikes led by the Industrial Workers of the World at Broken Hill, New South Wales in early 1918, and after having been sentenced to six months in jail were detained until November as the Australian authorities pondered ways to get rid of the pair. After months in prison they were served with deportation orders to Chile, but the Chilean government refused to receive them, having taken anti-radical measures of its own. According to a statement of the ship's officers, they had tried without success to put the men on other steamers belonging to the same shipping line, and had already separated them from the rest of the crew to prevent the spread of revolutionary ideas. The statement branded the two youths as 'well known bad characters' placed on their vessel by the Australian authorities, and complained that the ship had been refused entry at every port because of them. The Deputy Commissioner of the Port Police consequently arrested the two under the war-time Defence of India Act, for allegedly carrying on Bolshevik propaganda, and given the 'impossibility of allowing them to remain at large in India'.

Following interrogations and an examination of their papers, the colonial authorities readily concluded that they were in close touch with Bolshevism and confirmed the statement of the ship's officers that they were 'dangerous and a menace to the ship'. The papers nevertheless showed anarchist and anti-authoritarian links rather than any clear 'Bolshevik' position, reflecting the wide interpretation made of the term at this point. They were kept at Alipur Central Jail, a familiar destination of political prisoners in the city, though the authorities pressed for their transfer to the Ahmadnagar military internment camp since it contained 'prisoners of this type of Bolshevists'. Ultimately, in August, Balboa was put on a ship sailing for Port Said, and Burtovich on one sailing for Shanghai, from which the British authorities intended to deport him to White Russia. Apparently Burtovich resisted this course of action, getting off the ship at Singapore. After their deportation, the trail of the two strikers faded from official reports.[43] The circumstances of their arrival and departure nevertheless suggest that local authorities in the port cities of the colonial and semi-colonial world were becoming increasingly vigilant regarding the 'Bolshevik Menace'. The network of surveillance against political dissidents already existed, but was expanded at this point to look out for Bolshevism and so-called Bolshevik agents travelling by sea.

The volume of reports on Bolshevik agents increased in 1920 since the imperial authorities specifically asked for them. Through guidelines sent in 1919, closely following instructions from London, on a potential 'ingress' of 'Bolshevik agents' and literature into India, the specific parameters of anti-Bolshevik surveillance, based on racial stereotyping of suspects, were being set.[44] To keep up with the demand, reports drawing on the experiential and mythic and bordering on the curious and the fantastic were supplied by local intelligence agents. Random impressions were rarefied into facts of interest. Slices of daily life, isolated from other mundane aspects, became staples of political policing. They enveloped police accounts in a haze of rumours and stereotypes. Versions of events and descriptions of individuals were concocted and embroidered.

Individual cases indicated these developments. Harry S. Durkee, holder of US and Russian passports, allegedly a Bolshevik agent with 'somewhat Jewish features', arrived and left through the Calcutta port. A report was also prepared on the non-existence of an Esperanto Club, tipped as centres of Bolshevik internationalist intrigue in port-cities such as Shanghai.[45] Tan Pei Yun was a Chinese actor who played the role of a clown and stopped the dramatic performance early to deliver a subversive anarchic-Bolshevik lecture. He was expected to land in Calcutta, and sow mischief among its large Chinese community, having travelled through British-controlled Kuala Lumpur with his troupe. His arrival was never recorded.[46] Ele Levy Menashe, arriving by a passenger ship from Rangoon, was also suspected to be a Jewish-Bolshevik agent, but instructions on him arrived too late and his luggage remained unsearched when he left again for Bombay.[47] In 1920, even if Left literature originating from the Third International was scarcely noticed, the publications of the newly formed Communist Party of Great Britain were banned before they could reach India by ship.[48]

Although neither coherent nor organized, the sympathy for Bolshevism was interpreted by the colonial authorities as a potential social tendency for turning leftward. As the Russian civil war was fought concurrently with the launching of anti-colonial mass movements and a strike-wave in and around Calcutta, solidarity towards Bolshevism increased and filtered down the social scale.

In this climate, Bolshevism entered an urban dreamscape and found sympathy among those engaged with the world of workers. One intelligence report described a meeting held in 1920 in the industrial suburb of Kankinara. A young Hindu speaker, whose precise identity could not be established, had delivered a 'fiery' speech. According to the police he was either a troublemaking outsider from Punjab or Allahabad working for the Bengal Khilafat Committee, or an unemployed Calcutta clerk. The speaker allegedly told the assembled Muslim factory-hands, who formed the majority in the area, that if the people of the country knew what Bolshevism meant, they would welcome it with open arms. The English, he pronounced in a millenarian vain, trembled at the very name, because they were conscious of their sin; the Bolsheviks had destroyed Tsarist authoritarianism which had ruled Russia the way the British controlled India. In praise of their growing strength, he declared the Bolsheviks were about to take Germany where the Kaiser's tyranny has collapsed. They had extended a helping hand to the Amir of Afghanistan so that the latter did not have to bow to the British Empire. Soon they would open a united front with Turkey. He urged his Muslim brethren to see the coming together of Muslim powers and Bolshevism as a sign of the future decimation of colonial rule. According to the police agent present, the speech was 'highly seditious and . . . delivered in the strongest terms'.

The mood of a section of the crowd, armed for the first time against forces of colonial surveillance, was consequently reported as a source of worry:

> . . . a little after the 'Panditji' began speaking, some Muhammadans moved about among the audience with canes in their hands and when enquiries were made as to what they were after they said that they were in search of 'khapia police' meaning the CID. They were purposely sent to be assured if any CID officer was taking notes, for they knew that the Pandit would deliver a fiery speech.[49]

In 1920, *Mohammadi*, a weekly Bengali-Muslim newspaper, observed that the Bolshevik menace was a myth created by the government and the Bolsheviks were not sending agents to organize labour strikes in and around the city; the workers themselves were rising against hunger and exploitation.[50] When the left emerged in Calcutta during the early 1920s, from the experiences of the labour upsurge and receptions of Marxism and Leninism following the Bolshevik Revolution, the state lost no time in projecting its central figure, Muzaffar Ahmad, a former Muslim cultural activist and Bengali journalist, as 'a Bolshevik agent' recruited by M.N. Roy on behalf of the Communist Third International. He was suspected of using his links with sailors and their union to communicate with the Comintern.[51] The myth of a Bolshevik outsider could be transformed and effectively utilized as a practical strategy to suppress individual activists and miniscule collectives, the local responses to an internationalist current.

Conclusion:
'Who can Curb the Lordless Waters?'[52]

In the course of a single decade, state authority was imposed upon and transferred by successive projections of ships and passengers, passing through Calcutta and its immediate environs, as threats to the very survival of a waterborne empire. Britannia still ruled the seas but without the heights of confidence reached in the previous century. The colonial government was deeply disturbed by the prospect of a German attack, a Ghadar-influenced insurrection and the Bolshevik 'menace'. The fear of German invasion was combined with a panic-driven response to the return of radical labourers. These were followed by the spectre of communism. Often, the perceived threats were exaggerated to expand surveillance and justify xenophobic ideas and their practical applications. The spectres formed different components of a colonial climate of concentrated repression overpowering the city. Official perceptions hovered between mythic demonization of opposition and prosaic strategies to preserve the British Empire. From the perspective of the colonizers, the urban terrain was a disturbed zone where unmanageable forces of dissent, opposition, and resistance lurked. Being a cosmopolitan port city, Calcutta's official value to the imperium was repeatedly emphasized. At the same time, the city was projected as open to contaminations by alien forces and activities, rooted in the outside world. The ships were seen as physical carriers of enemies with mutating features and subversive ideas against whom impenetrable barriers had to be erected.

This position, in turn, bred contra-positions: support for those classified and labelled as 'enemies' anxieties underpinning social existence in the city that could turn against the ruling authority and hopes of freedom from colonized conditions among the various class-segments of the subject populations. The changes that encompassed the journey of Calcutta from a capital city to a provincial capital during the First World War and the immediate upheavals of the post-war period were on display at the popular level through stray emotions, developing ideas, and concrete strategies; they made their way into the colonial public and submerged spheres as rumour, sensationalism, curiosity, panic, end-of-the-world dread, indistinct anti-authoritarian hopes and expectations, fractured confrontations with authority, and organized anti-imperialist resistance from below. This essay has attempted to understand some of these tendencies; their diffusions in Calcutta of the 1910s converged with the impression of ships.

Notes

1. The city of Kolkata is being denoted as 'Calcutta', a colonial nomenclature. A recent article traces the mystery of 'Kalikata' becoming Calcutta in English to commodity fetish. The author suggests the East India Company officials adopted the name 'Calcutta' to invest Bengal cotton exports in the European market with the aura of the more well-known and highly prized cotton from Calicut. The earliest English East India Company document recording the transfer of zamindari rights over three villages, and dating back to the late seventeenth century, refers to 'Kalikata'. See, Jaladhar Mallick, 'Kalikata ingrejite CALCUTTA hoawar rahashyo' (The mystery of 'Kalikata' becoming Calcutta in English), *Ganashakti*, Special Autumn Number, B 1421, 2014, pp. 302–4. For delighted and enthusiastic references to ships in early twentieth century Calcutta and Bengal, see, Nirad C. Chaudhuri, *The Autobiography of an Unknown Indian*, Oakland: University of California Press, 1968, pp. 110, 286, 293.
2. Raymond Williams, *Marxism and Literature*, Oxford: Oxford University Press, 1977, pp. 128–35.
3. Sumit Sarkar, *Modern India 1885-1947*, Delhi: Macmillan, 1983, pp. 147–9.
4. For a social interpretation of urban politics in early twentieth century Calcutta, see, Rajat Ray, *Urban Roots of Indian Nationalism, Pressure*

Groups and Conflict of Interests in Calcutta City Politics, 1875-1939*, Delhi: Vikas, 1979. A treatment of the war-time material conditions, including price-rise, cloth-shortage, and social protests in Bengal can be found in Upendra Narayan Chakravorty, *Indian Nationalism and the First World War (1914-1918)*, Calcutta: Progressive Publishers, 1997.

5. *Weekly Reports of Intelligence Branch, Bengal Police 1914.*
6. Hugh Johnston, *The Voyage of the Komagata Maru: The Sikh Challenge to Canada's Colour Bar*, Vancouver: University of British Columbia Press, 2014, p. 148.
7. Randall J. Metscher, 'Emden', in *The European Powers in the First World War: An Encyclopedia*, ed. Spencer C. Tucker, New York: Routledge, 2013, pp. 239–40.
8. Cornelis Dijk, *The Netherlands Indies and the Great War 1914-1918*, Leiden: KITLV Press, 2007, p. 183.
9. Johnston, *The Voyage of the Komagata Maru*, p. 149.
10. *The Statesman*, 7 November 1914.
11. *The Statesman*, 21 November 1914.
12. *The Statesman*, 6 November 1914.
13. Ibid.
14. *Weekly Reports of Intelligence Branch, Bengal Police 1914.*
15. *The Statesman*, 19 November 1914.
16. *Weekly Reports of Intelligence Branch, Bengal Police 1914 and 1915.*
17. *The Statesman*, 6 November 1914.
18. Amiya Kumar Bagchi, *Private Investment in India 1900-1939*, Cambridge: Cambridge University Press, 1972, pp. 275–6.
19. Political reports, Home Department, Government of Bengal, West Bengal State Archives (WBSA), 322/14.
20. Home (Political) WBSA, 322/14.
21. Colonial control exercised upon the Sikh passengers of Komagata Maru after they had landed has been analysed by Darshan S. Tatla. See, Darshan S. Tatla, 'Introduction', in *Voyage of Komagata Maru or India's Slavery Abroad*, ed. Baba Gurdit Singh, Chandigarh: Unistar/Punjab Centre for Migration Studies, 2007, p. 20.
22. Home (Political) WBSA, 322/14.
23. IB (Intelligence Branch of the Bengal Police), 1105/14 (57/14); Home (Political) WBSA, 322/14.
24. *Weekly Reports of Intelligence Branch, Bengal Police 1914.*
25. IB, 1105/14 (57/14).
26. Chakravorty, *Indian Nationalism and the First World War*, p. 113.
27. IB, 1105/14 (57/14).
28. *Weekly Reports of Intelligence Branch, Bengal Police 1915.*
29. Home (Political) WBSA, 322/14.
30. *Weekly Reports of Intelligence Branch, Bengal Police 1914.*
31. Home (Political) WBSA, 322/14.

32. Home (Political) WBSA, 26/15 (64-68).
33. *Report on Native Newspapers of Bengal 1914.*
34. Sarkar, *Modern* India, pp. 147–8.
35. *Annual Report on the Police Administration of the Town of Calcutta and its Suburbs for the year 1915* (1916).
36. IB, 454/1916 (13/16).
37. IB, 664/16 (50/16); IB, 454/1916 (13/16).
38. IB, 454/1916 (13/16).
39. Bhupendra Kumar Datta, *Biplaber Padachinha* (Footprints of Revolution), Calcutta, Sahitya Sansad, 1999, pp. 35, 42.
40. IB, 664/16 (50/16); IB, 454/1916 (13/16); IB, 689/19.
41. Home (Political) WBSA, 142/1918.
42. IB, 80/1920 (112/20).
43. Home (Political) WBSA, 281/ 1919.
44. Home (Political) WBSA, 405/1919.
45. IB, 80/1920 (112/20).
46. L/P&S/10/887(1229/1920). 'P&S' files originate from Indian Political Intelligence records stored in the British Library, London.
47. IB, 15/1920 (350/1920).
48. IB, 38/1921 (130/21).
49. IB, 80/1920 (112/20).
50. IB, 117/20.
51. Suchetana Chattopadhyay, *An Early Communist: Muzaffar Ahmad in Calcutta 1913-1929*, Delhi: Tulika, 2011, p. 117.
52. Heinrich Heine, *Poems and Ballads of Heinrich Heine*, tr. Emma Lazarus, New York: R. Worthington, 1881, p. 69.

8

MAKING AND REMAKING CASTE AND LABOUR

Calcutta Municipal Methars *and their Strikes in 1928*

Tanika Sarkar

This essay dwells on the caste-class ramifications of being *Methars* in colonial Calcutta: workers who cleaned private and public privies, streets, and underground drains. I first underline some puzzles about their work and social designation, and then briefly discuss aspects of corporation politics and modern sanitary reforms that influenced their lives, although surprisingly few sources—archival or vernacular—observed their living and working conditions. I conclude with two strikes by corporation *Methars* and sweepers in 1928, when they came of age as political agents, forged in the crossfire between nationalist corporation authorities and communist trade unionists.

I

Methar is the name tag for scavengers. They belonged to the larger category of municipal scavengers, along with sweepers, coolies,

*An early and different version came out as "'Dirty Work, Filthy Caste": Calcutta Scavengers in the 1920s', in *Working Lives, Worker Militancy: The Politics of Labour in Colonial India*, ed. Ravi Ahuja, Delhi: Tulika, 2013. I am very grateful to Sukanya Mitra and Anirban Bandyopadhyay who helped the research at that stage.

and Muddafarash, or men who cremated corpses. The 1928 strikes, however, involved *Methars* and sweepers alone. All four categories were untouchables, segregated from society by dreadful pollution taboos—the *Methars*, especially so. We begin, therefore, with a definitional puzzle: is *Methar* an occupational or a caste category? Does untouchability derive from a ritually 'degraded' caste or from the work they do? Mahatma Gandhi ascribed it to work: if they carried excreta on handcarts, he suggested, instead of on their heads, untouchability would disappear.[1] They were widely percieved, however, in caste and pollution terms. A 1703 account of the East India Company describes them as 'hollocrores':[2] a corruption of *halalkhore*, a common name for untouchable workers.

Censuses relegate scavengers to Dom and Hadi castes: lowest of the low, even among untouchables—*hadir haal*, or the condition of Hadis being a conventional Bengali description of absolute wretchedness. They traditionally removed human and animal waste from village homes and roads.[3] Contemporary Bengali records, on the other hand, call them Dhangars.[4] The term, according to several nineteenth- and early twentieth-century sources, was originally applied to Kol Adivasis from the Chhotanagpur region. An 1844 painting of Calcutta scavengers by Colesworthy Grant shows them in attire that was typically worn by the Kols. Early nineteenth-century missionaries travelled with Calcutta scavengers to their Chhotanagpur villages to set up their missions.[5]

We can reconstruct a temporal sequence for the formation of *Methar*-scavengers by connecting recurrent deposits of different workers into the city over time. The three villages that constituted early Calcutta would have been served by local Dom and Hadi *Methars*. As the city grew with an enormous building spree in the eighteenth century, and continued to expand till the mid-twentieth century, demand for nightsoil removal also grew exponentially. An influx of migrant labourers from Chhotonagpur then joined the work, sometime in the early nineteenth century. Censuses, as well as contemporary Bengali dictionaries, call *Methars* forest-dwelling *junglee*, *ashabhya*, and *anarya* people: uncivilized, beyond, and below the Hindu caste order.[6]

Most probably, Adivasis were first imported to clear forests and drain marshes—they were widely renowned for such skills—that abounded in early Calcutta. The city was slowly carved out from deep wilderness, till the mid-nineteenth century, and also well beyond. Before the construction of Fort William, the Maidan—later a stretch of landscaped nature where sahibs and memsahibs rode in the evening—was a 'tiger infested jungle'. Fort servants were terrified of crossing it at night when tigers and dacoits lay in wait.[7] Till 1835, Chowringhee, later the epitome of colonial luxury, was 'a complete jungle, interspersed with huts and small pieces of grazing land'.[8]

Once tree felling and marsh draining slackened, they would turn to other urban occupations and, since the tribal people were definitionally outcastes, waste removal would be a reasonable option. Afterwards, waves of north Indian migrant labourers poured into Calcutta in the late nineteenth century, and many joined the ranks of Dhangars/Doms/*Methars* as they turned to manual scavenging. But till at least the 1860s, tribals predominated '. . . Dhangars and other hill tribes who do such important though dirty work in the drainage of Calcutta . . .'[9]

Some scavengers were a few notches above them. One Bala Chamar tried to block the strike of 1928.[10] Chamars, an untouchable tanner caste, were ritually somewhat superior to Doms or Hadis. H.H. Risley, in 1891, also described *Methars* as 'a sub caste of Hadis who remove nightsoil' as well as as 'a section of Maghaya Kumhars . . . of the Dharkar subcaste of Doms'. The latter were untouchable potters who were ranked above nightsoil cleaners. For them scavenging had led to downward caste mobility. A very small segment was Muslim. In the 1891 Census, they constituted 1,232 out of a total of 15,375 sweepers and scavengers, and in 1911, they were 1,539 of a total of 15,381. The 1911 Census also shows the sudden appearance of sixteen Christian scavengers.[11] In the 1911 Census, women Methranis numbered 1,889 as against 7,210 men.[12]

Clearly, they came from multiple sources, drawn from a bottom pool of destitute, outcast, tribal and non-Hindu labour. Once slotted within the occupation, they became a distinct untouchable caste on their own, lower than any of its orignal components.

The very sight of them was profoundly repugnant to upper caste corporation ratepayers. Bishnunath Motilal, a Bengali gentleman, wrote to municipal authorities in great horror in 1837, that nowadays

*Methar*s can even be seen on the roads 'at all times of the day'. The sight, he complained, turns the stomach of well-born Bengalis, especially after they had enjoyed a good meal.[13] A short story by Rabindranath Tagore, written in 1928, sometime during the strikes, is a tale about an elderly *Methar* and his small grandson who are returning from work, freshly bathed and cleanly dressed. As they pass a crowd of temple-goers and inadvertantly brush against them, their telltale broom and pail give away their caste and pious pilgrims pounce on them to lynch. The husband of an ardent Gandhian activist wants to rescue them but she is adamant: 'Even if they were Hadis or Doms, we could have done it. But they are *Methar*s.'[14]

The city badly wanted to excise them from its sight. But, it also needed them, equally badly, to tackle their intimate daily needs: excreta and waste production. In 1864, the rapidly growing colonial capital was producing 200 tons of nightsoil every day and the volume grew relentlessly with urban expansion.[15] The anomaly indicates a perpetual social dilemma of how to extract labour, and yet excise the labourer from one's social horizons.

In 1928, however, the urban public saw them primarily as a labour force and caste was not invoked in public discourse except indirectly, since no other caste would do their work. Communists did not mention it at all, except once. On 4 March 1928, on the first day of their first strike, Muzaffar Ahmad addressed them in a public speech as 'Dear *Methar*, Dom and Dhangar brothers'.[16]

II

A second puzzle relates to their status as workers: were they primarily domestic workers, since even as Calcutta Corporation employees they continued to clean private privies? Or were they public servants? Let us take up the former point first. Household based master-servant relationships are the first and most enduring school where generations learn to produce and reproduce caste and class. In that small, enclosed space, the maintenance of purity-pollution is exceptionally complex and delicate. Till at least the middle or late decades of the twentieth century, brahman cooks— called *thakur* (the lord) if they were men, and *bamundidi* or *bamun meye* (elder sister or daughter) if they were women—were the most privileged domestic servants, merging easily into the larger kinship network of their masters. *Methars* occupied the opposite pole.[17] The distance between the two may be measured by the status of their workplaces: the kitchen being a repository of maximal purity, cooking, ideally, was the brahman's task—whereas the latrine was the dirtiest and most polluted domestic space. Older Calcutta residential buildings usually had a winding iron staircase that connected with the outermost room, the latrine, on every floor from outside. This ensured that their cleaners would not enter other rooms. Homes without this useful appurtenance did allow *Methars* inside, but only after ensuring that nobody came within touching distance. Amiya Samanta, now a retired Bengali police official, recalls how he was severely chastised by family and neighbours because he had handed over the *Methar*'s salary to him instead of throwing down the cash on the ground to be picked up. Even if their hands did not actually touch, he was contaminated by the horizontal spatial connection.

The Corporation pulled them into the municipal workforce from the 1870s, though they continued to clean private latrines. They straddled, therefore, the home and the street, the private and the public, they were domestic servants as well as government employees. Nandini Gooptu, discussing untouchable municipal labourers in Uttar Pradesh towns, thinks that being government employees, however meanly paid, did bring them a measure of self esteem.[18] We have seen how persistently their pollution stigma chased *Methars* in streets and in homes. Nonetheless, institutionalization as public servants, and a corporate identity as urban workforce, did gradually introduce a sense of collective strength, even before unions appeared. Strikes, significantly, began only after they became employees of the Corporation. As domestic servants, caste was their manifest identity. Now a class identity began to form. Strikes added a third dimension: it made them union men and women.

Unlike factory labour, however, their work was peripatetic, they moved from house to house, street to street, drain to drain. Unlike factory workers, again, they lived around the wards they cleaned. Their salaries varied according to the rates their domestic employees paid to the Corporation.[19] Above all, a very significant difference lay in the way their strikes impacted the city. While factory workers affected only their immediate employers when they struck work,

*Methar*s alone brought the entire city to a complete standstill when they went on strike. Their degraded caste then gave them invaluable bargaining power. During a warime strike of 1940, rumours were floated that the Corporation would replace *Methar*s with civic guards, recruited from the middle classes. Immediately, guards' recruitment plunged, even though the posts were coveted ones.[20] It was work that announced itself as such only when it ceased.

III

From 1703, hollocrores were first employed to clean European quarters and streets in the White Town, and from 1760, they were supervised by the Director of Conservancy. It provided four bullock carts for European and two for Indian quarters for garbage cleaning. By 1802, more carts were added and two depots housed them. *Methar*s took out garbage from homes to load into municipal boats at Nightsoil Ghat near the old Mint at night. Boats dumped the lot into the Hooghly River. But most waste was simply abandoned into the nearest ditch, pond or gutter: notwithstanding the cholera epidemic of 1770, when more than 70,000 Calcutta residents—many of them Europeans—died and piles of human and animal carcasses rotted on the roads,[21] and despite Wellesley's Minute of 1803 that underlined the dangers of such a disposal system.[22]

Before John Straw's theory of waterborne cholera gained ground in the 1850s,[23] sanitary measures were negligible—as, indeed, they were in British towns and cities of those times. James Chevers, a renowned European doctor in Calcutta, complained that Indians and Europeans alike were innocent of basic sanitary precautions. He described, in profuse and visceral detail, the filth and stench in the overcrowded native quarters which made Calcutta 'nasty and pestilential'. In fact, its very location was to blame, he said, the city being so close to the 'nastiest river, next to the Thames, that the world has ever seen', and to the 'vast salt lagoon' that were the Salt Lakes. Miasma rendered the city 'this Dismal Swamp, this Slough of Despond'.[24] European indifference was ascribed to the fact that most of them were transients in the city.[25] Contemporary Bengalis confirmed the horrors. A biography of Ishwar Chandra

Vidyasagar described the open ditches that lined city streets when he first came to Calcutta. They overflowed with faeces and garbage, rotting and stinking, producing quite spectacular stomach ailments for Vidyasagar and his brothers which, too, are described in graphic detail.[26]

Once epidemics were medically connected with waterborne infections, city fathers had to act. Many ponds—easy receptacles for filth—were filled up and roadside open drains were paved over, hiding what floated underneath. In the 1870s, grandiose sewage pipe construction for waste disposal and clean-water supply were underatken by Chief Sanitary Engineer Clark. Around 38 mi. of brick sewers and 3 mi. of pipe sewers were soon laid down, and massive funds raised to provide piped supply of clean water. Garbage was now taken out through municipal depots, pumping stations, and waste treatment centres to the Salt Lakes, about 3 mi. away from the city, and connected by Bidyadhari River to the Sundernbans: until the early twentieth century, when the river became moribund, creating yet another crisis of waste disposal.[27] This was a time when, under a new electoral system, Indian corporators joined the ranks of civic authorities. Many were nationalist Congressmen.[28]

Underground drainage largely replaced the dry trenching system. Predictably running from south to north—first serving European residents and then moving to the Indian quarters—a network of pipes covered the city by the 1890s. The Jorasanko residence of the Tagore family, for instance, had access to piped water by the 1870s.[29] From the early twentieth century, middle-class homes were connected with drains through the new flushing system, though manual nightsoil collection was legally abolished only in the 1980s.[30] The Bengali *bhadralok* saluted the new innovations. A poem, published in 1874 in *Basantak*, a satirical magazine, and otherwise critical of the Corporation, welcomed the miracle: 'All the shit of the city is fed into these drains . . ./Unseen by human eyes', though it also chafed at the extra burden of taxes this imposed on ratepayers.[31] The class divide definitely became far more critical than the much discussed racial one. It was the urban poor who were hopelessly left out of the loop of urban development.

Improvements continued, ushering in a corporation-driven, small-scale technological and entrepreneurial revolution: something

seldom noticed or studied. By the 1920s, improved sanitation and
water supply reached most well-off residents, Indian and European.
They stimulated small industrial units, all capitalized in India, and
most owned by Calcutta-based Indian entrepreneurs. The 1935
Calcutta Municipal Gazette carried pages of illustrated ads of new
sanitary gadgets: covered pans, pull flush commodes, motorized
municipal refuse disposal lorries, etc. There were pictures too, of
'revolutionary' drainage and sewer building material.[32]

Municipal conservancy, then, provided a field for Indian private
capital investment and profits, a local labour market, minor capital
goods production, as well as a new civic and patriotic pride, for
this went along with an expansion in municipal franchise and the
capture of the Corporation by the electoral wing of Congress
nationalists—the Swarajists. A Bengal Iron Company advertisement
proudly proclaimed that it used 'Indian material, Indian labour'.[33]
Nationalist corporation authorities were careful to invite tenders
from patriotic Indian businessmen who liberally added to their vote
bank and coffers. In 1924, Subhas Chandra Bose, CEO under Mayor
C.R. Das, accepted a tender from a firm of Bengali contractors
and builders for the hugely lucrative Palta Water Works Extension
Scheme. The firm, in return, deposited a hefty donation into
Swarajist election funds. Indian godown owners gratefully funded
the Bengal Congress in exchange for favours by the Swarajist
dominated corporation.[34]

Elected Indian representatives to the Corporation came from
the most privileged upper caste urban gentry ranks in the late
nineteenth century, even though a few low caste Suvarnavaniks
also found their way into it, on account of their great wealth.
In the 1920s, somewhat less exalted professional middle-class
men—gradually even a few women—joined their ranks. But the
caste profile remained unchanged.[35] In 1924, the candidature of
Birendranath Sasmal, a well-known Mahishya nationalist from an
upwardly mobile 'clean' shudra caste, for the post of CEO, was
blocked by Chittaranjan Das and Bose.[36]

The gulf between Corporation employers and *Methars*, therefore,
could not have been greater. At the same time, since their rivals
were Europeans, Indian nationalists were, perhaps, just a bit more
accountable to Indian labour. This created a peculiar tension

between their two identities: as upper caste, propertied public employers who were remarkably parsimonious and insensitive to low caste, working class needs and as leaders of a mass movement who proclaimed themselves the real guardians of Indian people. In the first strike, the Corporation was under nationalist control and in the second strike Swarajists were out of power. There were remarkable differences in the press reportage in the two phases.

IV

In the age of urban improvement, nothing changed for those who loaded buckets of filth with their hands and carried nightsoil on their heads to take them to municipal dumps. When corporation trucks carried garbage to the Dhapa Square Mile landfill in eastern Calcutta, foetid waste, 'sickly smelling', was spread out every day with bare human hands to raise the ground level.[37] Huts of the urban poor were set right on damp earth without any elevation at all. Walls were wet mud and roofs were thin piles of straw. Damp dripped from the very pores of houses, entirely unventilated, lying next to what the Fever Hospital Committee described as 'pits of stagnant water often made close to the doors'. Municipal garbage carts found slum lanes too narrow to enter, and scavengers could not afford to pay nightsoil and garbage cleaners.[38] Public latrines were very few. Human waste, consequently, festered on their doorstep. It is ironical that what they removed from the city took permanent residence where scavengers were forced to live.[39]

Slums had a curious three-tiered structure. Landowners rented out land to house owners who built huts and rented them out to poor tenants. Responsibilities circulated endlessly and inconclusively among them. Land and houseowners had no interest in improvement as the space where scavengers lived was considered contaminated and would never see a better class of tenants. Scavengers could not pay a higher rent. Landowners, being men of substance, had much clout in corporation politics, and they disobeyed sanitary regulations with impunity. If, goaded by epidemics, the Corporation stepped up pressure, and they simply demolished the huts and rented out or sold the vacated land to rich residential housing developers, public institutions or commercial establishments. In 1875, the zoological gardens, with their extensive gardens and beautiful buildings, were built on land 'cleared' by the government who threw out the local poor. So were the Presidency and Medical Colleges.[40] Europeans and Indians alike preferred slum clearance as the 'cheapest option' for urban health and beautification.[41]

Large-scale land acquisition and evictions marked the last years of the nineteenth century and the early years of the next one. The Corporation connived at displacements in the name of a sanitary crisis that officials attributed to the 'defecating habits' of the poor:[42] 'people who apparently delight in filth and dirt'.[43] A vicious circle formed: bustee demolitions were undertaken in the name of the filthy habits of the poor, which put the entire city at risk. The displaced were then forced into even more congested and insanitary surroundings—for which, again, they were blamed. Urban development, as always, conducted through dispossession carried very dark connotations for the urban poor.

If this was the general fate of the urban poor, scavengers fared much worse. In a novel set in the 1940s, Samaresh Basu, himself then a trade unionist, describes a Communist unionist who stumbles upon a slum of *Methars* who cleaned latrines for jute workers. Used to the working-class squalor, he is still stunned by the depths of their povery that illustrates a stark form of 'bare life'—one where beasts and humans may exchange identities.[44]

In 1878, Calcutta had a total of 39,756 listed houses. Only 5,400 were connected with sewers and 11,496 houses made private arrangements to remove their waste. The Corporation employed 1,100 scavengers to clean the rest and who also cleaned underground drains and the 68 public toilets in the city. *Methars* also removed the vast deposits of animal excreta from the streets, most of the transport being animal driven till well into the twentieth century. In 1900, the Corporation admitted that improvement schemes, whether for water supply or for drainage, have benefitted the urban rich alone.[45]

The monthly pay of scavengers in the 1870s varied between 8 *annas* for cleaning houses that paid an annual corporation tax of Rs.50 and Rs.8 for those who cleaned houses paying Rs.5,000 per year.[46] In 1928, the Communists prepared a monthly budget for the average Corporation scavenger: their pay was between Rs.10

and Rs.14. Those who worked a double shift had higher wages. In these 50 years, wages had, indeed, gone up but prices of essential goods went up far more. Their monthly expenditure came to more than Rs.12: payments for rice, lentils, and oil for food, drinks, and soap—the last two essential items, given the nature of their work—fuel, rent, and interest on loans, and bribes to Sardars or middlemen who recruited them and decided on leave and re-employement. No surplus was left for medicine or education for children or for old age and accidents: for none of which their employers made any provisions. They lived in slums without electricity, ventilation or water supply; paid exorbitantly high rents; had no leave entitlement nor death benefit for the family even when death occurred through corporation negligence. They cleaned undergound drains, clogged with noxious fumes, and many drowned and died of suffocation as they worked without protective gear, gloves or masks.[47] Interestingly, neither Communists nor anyone else observed the precise nature of their work.

The Corporation was forced by the strikes to set up a special committee in 1933 to investigate, for the first time, scavenger conditions. They found that wages had remained at the same level. About 2,000 *Methars* lived in corporation barracks while the vast majority rented a single unventilated 25 sq. ft. hovel per person, which barely had room for a string cot. Sometimes they were as small as 13 sq. ft. where a whole family lived and cooked. It recommended aprons for *Methars*, maternity leave for Methrani women, a winter blanket for outdoor scavengers, and a raincoat for gully pit 'boys' who cleaned drains. They also suggested cheap stores with provision for credit. They found it deplorable that their rooms adjoined corporation bullock stables that water supply was extremely meagre, and one latrine did for 60 people.[48] Though Swarajist nationalists waxed proud that they had set up four corporation schools, scavenger children obviously found no entry there. In 1946, K.P. Chattopadhyay, Corporation Education Officer, suggested in despair that Christian missionaries should be invited to teach them. The invisibility of *Methars* was compounded by the Corporation that did not maintain service records and treated them as casual, daily wage workers even if they had spent a lifetime at the work.[49]

There was no concern at all about their safety, and there is none
to this day. In 1907, a *Methar* drowned while cleaning a manhole,
and Nafar Kundu, a middle-class youth, died as he tried to save
him. Satyandra Nath Datta, an eminent poet, dedicated a poem
to Kundu and the Bengal Lt. Governor had a memorial built for
him.[50] No one mentioned the *Methar* who had died, nor was a
count maintained for such deaths—nor safety devices provided.
The incident, however, made Datta write yet another poem on the
Methar, celebrating his selfless dedication to the cause of urban
survival and denouncing the stigma that attaches to him. 'Who calls
you untouchable, my friend/purity itself follows you . . .'.[51] The
moral elevation—remarkable, really, when untouchability was still
to enter elite public discourses as a problem—was conditional on his
continued selfless service. Later, Tagore translated it in English for
the *Modern Review*, and it was also published in the *Calcutta Municipal
Gazette*. Significantly, the gazette published it during a brief strike
in 1924 as proof of municipal and middle-class sensitivity to their
services in a gesture of appeasement.

All this bears an interesting parallel with British sanitary
developments in the mid-nineteenth century. Edwin Chadwick's
celebrated report on the state of sanitation in Britain in the 1840s
had attributed diseases and epidemics to the way in which the urban
poor 'chose' to foul their surroundings. A slew of underground
drains—universally seen as the panacea to urban disease—was
immediately organized. Scholars have pointed out that both
diagnosis and prescribed cure short circuited a medical alternative
that had focussed, instead, on structural problems in the living and
working conditions of the urban poor: low wages, unhealthy and
meagre diet, and cramped, unventilated, accident prone factory
space.[52] Colonial Calcutta, likewise, ignored the working and living
conditions of city cleaners. It built drains for others instead.

V

Calcutta municipal politics constituted a highly competitive arena
from the 1870s as Congress nationalists tried to snatch control
over civic space from European residents and state officials. The
Corporation, therefore, provided an important site for a nascent

nationalist governance—especially its class interests and labour policy. In fact, relations between scavengers and nationalists had long been strained. In October 1907, at the height of the Swadeshi movement—Bengal's first anti-colonial mass upsurge—large numbers of '*Methar*s, dhangars, sweepers, etc.' set upon nationalists at Beadon Square, beat them up, and robbed them as they preached the swadeshi message.[53] Nationalists alleged that the government had incited them. Be that as it may, decades of neglect and contempt had without a doubt built up a sense of deep alienation and anger against the nationalists. In April 1928, during the Howrah scavengers' strike, a Swarajist Municipal Councillor was 'set upon and assaulted' by workers.[54]

This changed, briefly, in 1928, when Bose mobilized urban workers for protest demonstrations against the Simon Commission. He waxed eloquent about the 'umbilical cord' between labour and nationalism. Almost 4,000 scavengers joined the demonstrations in January, even though their union did not support Congress nationalism.[55] This shows their autonomy in political decision making, and also the pull of popular, militant nationalism that stirred an otherwise indifferent urban poor at a peak time of protest. It also knitted them into the city public, albeit for a transient and exceptional moment—an unusual and heady experience for them.

Communist party cadres and its mass fronts—Workers' and Peasants' Parties—tried to unionize scavengers from 1927. Muzaffar Ahmad was a towering figure and the Workers and Peasants Party (WPP) provided a small but extremely efficient cadre base. I want to avoid the pitfall that marks the studies of Indian Communists: a focus on international networks, or on intra-party factions or on iconic leaders who, seemingly, breathed life into an inert mass of passive workers. Strikes, which the Communists undoubtedly led, should move into several simultaneous and interrelated histories.

Founded in 1925, the miniscule party did become something of a spectre that haunted the empire. It faced five conspiracy cases in the first decade of its life and Intelligence Bureau reports were voluminous and continuous. Directed by the Communist International, it was, at this time, about to distance itself from Congress nationalism and pursue a different kind of anti-imperialsm, founded on working-class activism led by the vanguard party. It intended to lead an all-India general strike as a prelude to revolution. Strikes were, therefore, its primary and abiding concern.

In the late twenties, however, the party was still at the crossroads.[56] The Communist International line of allying with bourgeoise nationalists in a multi-class alliance against colonialism continued but it was about to mutate into an independent Left anti-imperialism. The disastrous fate of the Kuomintang-Communist unity in China in 1927 made the multi-class bloc a chimera. A letter from the Scavengers' Union to the All India Trade Union Congress observed that Swarajists sponsored police brutalities against scavengers on strike. This revealed that 'there is a tendency to mobilize nationalist sentiments against us in a Fascist manner'. Nevertheless, the party would not yet oppose Swarajists on class lines since that would disrupt the multi-class bloc. So natioanlists were, for the time being, opposed on the ground of their weak anti-imperialism.[57] The 1928 strikes stregthened the new ideological imperative.[58]

A very tiny group of very young men—no women among them—Communists were certainly exceptionally efficient labour organizers. But they were by no means the first to mobilize scavengers. There were lone independent labour leaders too. Some of them were women, both Hindu and Muslim, from privileged backgrounds. In the 1910s, Begum Rokeya Sakhawat Hussein encouraged young women from upper-class Muslim families to visit the slums for welfare work. Santoshkumari Gupta worked among jute labourers in the early 1920s. In the thirties, Begum Sakina, a remarkable woman of aristocratic Iranian descent, and Maitreyi Bose, a doctor, would form non-Communist scavenger unions.[59]

Prabhabati Dasgupta was born into a rich nationalist family, who owned the Calcutta Chemicals. As a young Ph.D. scholar, then freshly returned from the US, she had met M.N. Roy at Berlin who encouraged her to work in the labour belt. She visited scavengers in their slums over a long time after their working hours, drinking tea and snacking at their small shops—thereby, recklessly flouting caste taboos of commensality. She exchanged rough badinage with the men, flagrantly violating gender and class taboos about respectable feminine conduct. Though scavengers were at first suspicious, their reserve eventually melted into acceptance and they began to call her their mother: *dhangar ma.*[60] This was the most common cultural code for coming close to a young woman without the pitfall of possible sexual overtones complicating the closeness.

This route to cultivating personal closeness with social 'Others' opened up an alternative kind of labour activism which Communists, in contrast, undertook with a more straitlaced economistic mobilization. Prabhabati continued to cross impregnable thresholds. During the first strike, she was apparently involved in a brawl with 'low born' strike-breakers in a public place. That was doing the unthinkable as the scuffle, too, is a form of physical intimacy with the untouchable. Public aggression, moreover, was totally intolerable in a woman. She faced appropriate penalty—to spend a night in police custody: something that no woman of her social status had been subject to at that time. But her class and gender provided some cushioning, and prominent women nationalists held a protest meeting about this, led by Basanti Debi, widow of C.R. Das. Great indignation was expressed. That was absent when scavengers were brutally flogged and arrested in their hundreds or when Ahmad was arrested the same day. On one occasion, an arrested scavenger was released on a bail of Rs.100 that was somehow paid by the WPP—an impossibly big sum for the very poor worker and a cash starved union.[61]

How do we look at these extraordinary women who crossed several insuperable social frontiers and challenged their gender, class, and caste norms far more transgressively than did other contemporary nationalist women activists or suffragists from women's organizations? They possessed a powerful sense of social and class justice. One that did not follow a party line but was no less determined and passionate for it. Communists, at that time, had no women activists at all, and women's organizations rarely reached beyond middle-class associational politics, except as philanthropic gestures. But I would also partly link their extraordinary travel across social spaces to an inter-war phase in middle-class gender history in Calcutta when a youthful *avant garde* experimented with daring lifestyle changes, and regarded it as an adventurous personal journey into a prohibited world and its inherited prescriptions for propriety, rather than view it in terms of political ideology alone. These women formed a part of second wave 'New Women' who now outstripped the parameters set by educated and professional women of the late nineteenth–early twentieth century in many ways.

Arya Samaj ascetics like Swami Kumaranand and Vishwanand also worked in the union. Asking them to form a union in February 1928, Kumarananda told the sweepers and *Methar*s that Russian workers had dethroned the Czar and now ruled the country themselves.[62]

*Methar*s, however, did develop earlier contacts with the wider world which persisted till the 1920s. Contemporary hagiographies indicate that Vaisnav proselytisers had worked at moral reform—especially anti-alcoholism—in Dom-Hadi slums from the time of the Calcutta plague epidemic of 1893. Caste or class was not mentioned but devotional musical sessions and processions as antidote to epidemic were organized and musical instruments and devotional literature distributed among Dom singers. Prabhu Jagatbandhu and Atulchandra Champati 'converted a few' Doms and Hadis in the 1910s. Contrary to traditional taboos, they allowed them to join the processions and Hari Sabhas as singers. Vaisnav musical processions frequently disrupted mosques with their loud music and this was a source of major communal tension in the twenties.

Muslim community leaders worked among north Indian labourers and tried to address their grievances. Tablighis, on the other hand, spread news of anti-cow slaughter riots from Uttar Pradesh and Bihar to raise Muslim political temper.[63] In the 1926 riots, they armed corporation Jamadars—labour contractors—into militant bands. Though Bose did try to induct some Muslims as Swarajist candidates, he got nowhere, and Hindu corporators used a markedly communal rhetoric in elections. Nationalists hardly ever tried to distance themselves from the Hindu Sabha propaganda.

Unions, in very sharp contrast, were multi-community. They were able to develop a different route to mass militancy, remarkably soon after the devastating riots where scavengers played a considerable role.[64]

The All Bengal Scavengers' Union was formed in 1927. Prabhabati, the first to open up contacts with scavengers, was its president, and Dharani Kanta Goswami from WPP, its secretary. Organizers came mostly from the WPP. Their cordial working relationship with Prabhabati, in sharp contrast to their bitter rivalry in the jute belt strikes at the same time, was completely overturned in 1935 when communists warned scavengers against her possible encroachments among them. They said that she had been unduly adventurist in 1928 and had incited workers to go on a futile strike. Not only did they castigate the non-Communist rival, but they also, implicitly, overwrote their own remarkable work in 1928 by calling the strike a pointless one.[65]

VI

But *Methars* had not waited for middle-class leaders to set out on their path of militant protests. Earlier, privately hired *Methars* collected waste from individual homes, which allowed them some bargaining power. But an Act of 1863 centralized cleaning operations under Corporation tolla *Methars*. It fixed wages and put scavengers under Sardars licensed by the municipality. With a rapid municipalization of nightsoil services in the 1870s, they lost their earlier leeway, and in 1877, they struck work in protest. They spread rumours among municipal sweepers who turned up for work that they would be eventually packed off to the West Indies by corporation authorities as indentured coolies. They also sent off emissaries to district municipalities to spread the strike. This was their first public appearance in the history of Calcutta.[66]

There was a brief second strike in May 1924, again before the emergence of unions. Mayor C.R. Das, stalwart Congress leader, met them and offered them a lot of facilities along with a wage rise. All proved to be empty promises but the nationalist press made much of Das' magnanimity in meeting *Methars*. *Methars*, themselves, would have seen it as a victory for collective protest. For the first time in corporation history, the Mayor himself—undisputed leader of the Bengal Congress, moreover—was forced to come face to face with people the municipality and the Congress had ignored all along, and talk to them in a conciliatory manner.[67] Press reportage, inevitable, given the unprecedented encounter made *Methars* important public figures.

Union building efforts of Prabhabati and the WPP fell, thus, on fertile ground as the efficacy of the strike weapon had already been driven home. Nonetheless, the strikes of 1928, fully unionized and extraordinrily well-organized, set the real endurance test for both scavengers and the city. Both learned what each had been doing, and could do to one another. It was the critical moment in *Methar* class consciousness as 1928 was followed by a steady spate of strikes for the rest of the colonial period, despite frequent defeats or half defeats in 1933, 1935, 1940 (two successive ones in March and August), 1943, and 1945.[68] We may say that 1928 initiated a parallel life for *Methar*s: one that was the 'Other' of their degraded, forgotten, everyday existence.

As the 1928 strikes entered the second phase, clearly demonstrating their staying power, *The Statesman* made a perceptive observation. In 1924, when scavengers had spontaneously downed tools without a union, they presented grievances. In 1928, they made 'demands' instead.[69] The shift in vocabulary suggests a leap. The earlier strike had shown desperate militancy. In 1928, the union brought them self-confidence. It provided legal counselling, raised regular subscriptions—one day's salary per month—and solicited funds from the Bengal and the All India Trade Union federations. Scavengers expressed solidarity with the ongoing Lillooah Railway workshop strikes. Acting as an umbrella that unified multiple unions, the WPP also organized solidarity messages from very diverse unions for them: Kankinara Labour, Bengal Jute Workers', Chengail Jute Workers', Tramwaymen's, Press Employees' , BNR Labour, Seamen's, Marwari Association, Port Trust Marine Workers', EIR Labour, Howrah Metal Workers, Bauria Jute Workers', and even Corporation Teachers'. All of a sudden, scavengers were woven into a fabric of city, province, and national level working class identity.[70]

The Union also introduced scavengers to news of global strikes and to foreign communists like Philip Spratt who worked in their slums.[71] It dizzyingly expanded their points of self-identification, and it also presented them with a vision of a different and highly militant world: the presumed magnitude of this brave new world was an invitation to join it with their own militancy. Their speeches and pamphlets brought in news of scavengers' strikes in other places in Bengal and India, of other strikes in the country, of strikes all over the world, and finally, of the Soviet Union that was described as a Workers' Raj. All were interconnected in a series of concentric rings, the Soviet Union forming the overarching outer one. The rings were strategically crafted: as if all strikes were happening simutaneously in the present, and all were on a winning streak. The British General Strike of 1926, which had actually been defeated already, was included among them and the defeat went unmentioned.

The Soviet Union was the point of culmination in the teleology of working class militancy which started with a single strike, rolled onto a general national strike, and then became a global revolution. The utopic mythology of the Soviet Union as paradise on earth was invaluable to cement their conviction in the inevitable success and eventual revolutionary end of each strike, however small or localized. It helped *Methar*s to see themselves on a world stage, as part of an international historical and moral mission.

The news had a pedagogic function. It gave workers instant and short lessons in world history and geography, both founded on strikes. The pedagogy, however, was simple, and the Marxist dialectic about class and class struggle or about capitalist production methods and relations were absent from it. The Soviet Union was characterized as a place of perpetual plenitude, permanent work and dignity.

Communists ignored their caste completely as caste did not play any role at all in their historical or social understanding, nor in their ideological discourse. Nor did they bring them basic education of any other sort, though Aghore Sen, a non-Communist unionist in Dacca, did run a school for scavengers before Congress municipal councillors shut it down.[72] But the WPP-scavenger relationship had to be forged under great difficulties. Their contact was transient, formed on the eve of a strike, and never outlasting it. There was no time, really, for changing the mental or cultural horizons of workers with a long term programme of patient reforms. Right after the 1928 strikes, a big chunk of communists, including Ahmad, would be incarcerated under the Meerut Conspiracy Case charges, denuding the WPP leadership considerably.

But strikes themselves, as we saw, were a school for workers: one where they learnt the art, meaning and possibilities of strikes. Actually, workers and leaders learnt the lessons together as their leaders were, at the time, complete novices at their job.

The small pool of activists also simultaneously managed several strikes at the same time among other workers in railway workshops, oil and rice mills, in the huge jute belt and also among scavengers in Mymensingh, Dacca, and nearby Howrah. They travelled right across Bengal all the time. When the first Calcutta strikes broke out, the leadership was caught unawares as they were busy with a massive strike in another district among railway workshop labourers: scavengers just came and informed them that they had declared a strike.[73] When strikes erupted again in June, the union was once more unprepared. On 1 July, Prabhabati informed the press that Gowkhana *Methars* had declared strike 'absolutely without our knowledge'.[74] It seems that workers made up their minds about several important decisions without taking the union in their confidence. In both cases, the union entered the strike scene post facto and managed the consequences of the initial action.

No communist leader ever described his momentous first encounter with scavengers: or its caste/class consequences on himself and on the workers, the texture of the individual lives that opened up before them, the initial difficulties in setting up the conversations. Unionism seems to have been rather bureaucratically managed and focussed on a precise end, despite the risks and the repression which both workers and leaders faced together, though in unequal proportion. Workers are curiously faceless figures in Ahmad's autobiography, for instance, suggesting a rather instrumentalist approach towards the revolutionary class.[75] Strikes not only framed communist contact with workers, they were its sole content.

How did scavengers experience the strikes? They left no records. But we can know what they heard from the union leaflets, like the *Tariq Ki Talab* circulating from February, and another red leaflet signed by Dharani Goswami in June[76]—and from the speeches of union leaders at public meetings. As a way of sustaining strikes, masculinity was frequently invoked though many were Methranis, equally militant.[77] Hindustani was the standard language for both pamphlets and speeches: strident, declamatory, reiterative. Intelligence Bureau and police informers collected or transcribed them assiduously and translated them in several languages. They commented profusely on all their aspects. During the first strike,

Intelligence officers were delighted by the ringing and 'outspoken condemnation' of nationalists.[78]

These words were mainly produced by middle class leaders but their popularity makes them something like a consensual discourse, producing a shared imaginary: something like the 'controlling narrative' that Patrick Joyce had in mind.[79] Their reiteration would have installed the messages as an ineffable, integral part of working class consciousness, even though workers did not author them.

VII

There were two strikes, one between 4 and 9 March, involving 9,000–10,000 scavengers and another between 25 June and 5 July, involving 3,000 scavengers. The first strike happened when the Corporation was under Swarajist rule and J.N. Sengupta was Mayor. But subterranean rivalries between him and Bose made the latter's *Forward* comment rather gleefully on the many failures on the part of the authorities.[80]

The middle classes soon realized that though scavengers had reported their obvious difficulties to the Corporation, the latter had ignored them altogether. The strike was, therefore, more the responsibility of Corporation authorities. Strike reportage was often fairly sympathetic to workers and highly critical of the Corporation, even though they faced enormous problems from the workers' strike action. As soon as the first strike began, Mr Daud, an opposition councillor, asked the CEO if he had replied to the representations from the union. A.C. Bannerjee, from the ruling group, told him to shut up as his questions 'may add to our difficulties', a sentence that was repeated in response to many other questions regarding basic information about workers' conditions.[81]

Workers got their views across with ease. The union held its meeting in the most public of spots—the Maidan, abutting on the Sahib Para, but also an area crossed by office workers returning home after work from the Dalhousie Square. Their speeches left no one in any doubt about scavenger miseries and the rightness of their demands.

The urban public became increasingly irate and nervous as garbage piled up dangerously and stench became unbearable with the onset of hot weather in March and of monsoon rains in June–July. Epidemics were predicted. Nationalists tried to persuade the high caste youth in different neighbourhoods to prove their patriotism by sweeping the streets: their appeal found little purchase and it was, in any case, a very limited effort as mere sweeping touched only the surface of the piles of garbage. In any case, the critical work of the *Methar*s, nightsoil removal, remained untouched and that constituted the most palpable sanitary danger. Eventually, Sengupta was forced to negotiate with workers' representatives and the delegation included a few Hindu and Muslim workers. They agreed on a Re.1 monthly wage increase, release of all arrested workers and restoration of pay for the strike period. The agreement remained entirely on paper till workers went on another round of strike in June.[82]

Congress-Swarajists were at a loss about how to deal with the strikes. On one hand, their nationalism did not teach them to bridge the social gulf. Gandhi's Harijan welfare programme lay in the future, as yet. Their own labour perspective as administrators was elitist and disciplinarian. On the other hand, the success of their rival WPP in an important mass constituency called for some damage control exercises. They were also under great public pressure, too, as the city reeled under a sanitary breakdown.

They cracked down very hard on strikers. Hundreds of workers were beaten up mercilessly as they sat on pickets. They were threatened, blacklegs were promised the skies, and scavengers were excluded from local cheap price shops and credit, and worst of all, water supply and public latrines were closed to men and women on strike. Notwithstanding such constraints, strikes were highly resolute. Even better off scavengers who cleaned homes of Europeans, ignored blandishments of preferred treatment and joined the pickets. When Sardars or jobbers were approached to provide an alternative labour supply, they confessed that they just could not find the men.[83] In the June–July strike, when Swarajists lost control and officials could count on government support to import blacklegs in bulk from distant locations, they still could not find a large enough supply to replace men and women on strike.

The Intelligence Bureau now began to fear that the strikes 'will also in all probability add very greatly to the prestige of the Bengal

Communists, who have been regarded up to the present as men of straw.'[84] It seemed that the nationalist menace would be replaced by an even deadlier one.

VIII

During the seventeen days of the two strikes, the fundamental importance of *Methar*-scavengers to Calcutta life became manifest in several ways. Most immediately, as garbage choked the city and the entire urban public appealed to the Corporation to negotiate with them. Second, their meetings occupied prominent public spaces: Deshbandhu Park, the largest public space in north Calcutta and the Maidan—the largest, most beautiful and well kept green in the entire city, a pleasure ground of the rich and the sahib.

The spatial strategy was significant. First, as we saw, it ensured that they had a multi-class audience as various categories of employees returned from work when their meetings began in late afternoon. The sanitary crisis had affected the entire public who would, therefore, eagerly listen in and hear the full version from the union side. Second, this ensured that the city was told exactly how crucial was this despised labour form to their survival and health. For the first time, it fully registered *Methars* and street sweepers as essential constituents of urban life. Third, for the first time too, scavengers, especially *Methars*—kept at a shuddering distance and not even looked at—now actually addressed them from the podium. Even before the strike began, they addressed the meetings, side by side with other leaders.[85] Strikes gave them a public voice.

Scavengers had, at the most, bargained for a bit of wage increase, Re.1 per month, and non-victimization. The second strike ensured that an enquiry committee would look into their grievances though it yielded no practical remedy. Public memory proved remarkably short and the city was happy to forget them as soon as things returned to normal. They failed in 1928 and they failed in later years too. The Corporation played its delaying tactics very well. When both combatants were worn out by strikes, it would offer to investigate scavenger claims and promise non-victimization. That would end the strike and then the authorities dragged their feet till another strike threatened. They had the resources to ride out the storm every time. But *Methars* did not. If their untouchable work gave them strength to hold out for some time, it also ensured that they would not find alternative sources of employment because of caste stgma.

Yet, strikes were also a moment out of time: creating a 'new normal', for a few days. They served a different purpose: less tangible and rarely discussed, but very important to consider, nontheless. They were more a liminal intercession, interrupting the structures of everyday, and creating a sense of festive communitas that, in the strange year of 1928, seemed to encompass the entire world. The experience of becoming unhidden, public, of swelling into the heart of the city, of occupying what was previously non-touchable, was something that stood apart from their quotidian lives of work and degradation or from the prosaic and limited demands they set to the authorities as bargaining points.

Their leaders had advised them to tell the authorities: 'Ask our anjuman (union): we know nothing'.[86] Nonetheless, belying this passive image, they spoke in public and they spoke in accents of their own. An Intelligence Bureau report on a meeting observed that a 'stout methrani' sat next to the main speaker and it was because of her vigorous interventions from the podium that workers finally decided to continue the strike. Ram Nagina, a very vocal worker, advised scavengers to use violence without hesitation if they were attacked.[87] Women were visble and loudly audible on days of strike, though they were not incorporated in unions, nor were their special problems—lack of creche and maternity leave, for instance—given room in the otherwise rather ambitious union charter.

There was an old tradition behind women's words of protest— words that came out of another liminal occasion: ritual inversion ceremonies when urban subalterns took out public processions, loudly making fun of urban bosses. An early twentieth century song by a Methrani of the Calcutta Corporation is worth citing at length, being a most rare eruption that has been recorded. Its words too, were composed by her: women being, as always, adept at oral compositions. The song reveals their sense of professional and collective strength, their absolute irreverence towards their masters, their audacious mockery of a world that denigrates them. It is a song where the world is turned upside down.

My name is Hari Methrani
I am the grandma of the municipality
If anyone accuses us of being abusive
We quit work in unison
Our caste is well bonded.
But the Babus are different
They shamelessly lick the half eaten plates of Sahibs
. . . And then they retort 'Don't' touch us, methrani
. . . Oh we will wed Brahmin priests.

They raunchily mock their babu employers who shun them in public as untouchables, all the while licking the boots of another set of untouchables, the sahibs.[88] They also seem quite confident of their sexual prowess and the secret lust of brahmans for untouchable bodies. It has been dated loosely as a composition from the early twentieth century. It does seem to exude the confidence that arises out of strikes: so, it could date from the end twenties, in all probability. Their public degradation and their absolute distance from caste determined rules of respectability gave them a stridency and an earthy boldness that was both linguistic and political.

We have referred to the way caste stigma ensured *Methars'* monopoly over an essential urban work that became critical when the work stopped. Their work also gave them a rather unique kind of threat that they—and only they—could flourish with great efficacy in strikes. During the Howrah scavengers' strike in April 1928, they drove away Anglo Indian sergeants by upending pots of excreta upon their heads, thus turning their signs of degraded caste and work into a weapon of offence. Sergeants fled, tearing off their uniforms and vowing never to return. The example inspired a middle class activist, Sachinadan Chatterjee, who advised them to drench the police in nightsoil when they came to arrest them.[89] Often they blocked traffic by heaping filthy refuse on streets and tramlines, helped, by 'street urchins' or homeless children. It was difficult to remove the blockages as few would touch the rubbish.[90] At long last, the untouchable matter they worked with could be proudly, usefully, even joyfully claimed and displayed as their very own.

The strike was both an affirmation of their working class identity, now translated as a source of strength. It was also a brief but real transcendence. For those two weeks, they were no longer scavengers and *Methar*s, they were a new and different people: people on strike. In a world that was on strike. And strikes that were, surely, going to change the world.

Notes

1. *Collected Works of Mahatma Gandhi*, vols. 54–55, Ahmedabad: Navajivan Prakashan, March–April 1933, pp. 185–6.
2. P. Thankappan Nair, 'Civic and Public Services in Old Calcutta', in *Calcutta: The Living City*, vol. 1, ed. Sukanta Chaudhuri, Calcutta: Oxford University Press, 1990, p. 220.
3. P.J. Marshall, 'The Company and the Coolies: Labour in Early Calcutta', in *The Urban Experience: Calcutta—Essays in Honour of Professor Nisith R. Ray*, ed. Pradip Sinha, Calcutta: Riddhi-India, 1987, p. 26; A.E. Porter, ed., *Report on the Census of India*, vol. VI, pts. 1 and 2, Central Public Branch, West Bengal State Archives, Kolkata, 1933, p. 112; H.H. Risley, *The Tribes and Castes of Bengal: Ethnographic Glossary*, vol. 2, Calcutta: Bengal Secretariat Press, 1891, p. 92; and Subol Chandra Mitra, *Saral Bangla Abhidhan*, Calcutta: New Bengal Press, 1909, p. 1280.
4. Haricharan Bandyopadhyay, *Bangiya Shabdakosh*, vol. 1, Delhi: Sahitya Akademi, repr. 1966, p. 1115.
5. Marshall, 'The Company and the Coolies'. I am grateful to Dr Sangeeta Dasgupta for bringing the painting to my notice and pointing out the topknot and the belt which she identified as Kol dressing; and to Dr Uday Chandra for the information about missionaries.
6. Mitra, *Saral Bangla Abhidhan*, p. 1280; and Bandyopadhyay, *Bangiya Shabdakosh*.
7. Lt. Col. H.A. Newell, *Calcutta: The First Capital of British India*, Calcutta: Caledonian Printing Company, 1916 (?), p. 424.
8. James Ranald Martin, *Notes on the Medical Topography of Calcutta*, Calcutta: Bengal Military Orphan Press, 1837, p. 9.
9. Anonymous, *Five Hundred Questions On the Condition of the Natives of India: A Paper Read Before the Royal Asiatic Society, London, June 19, 1865*, London: Truber & Co., 1865, p. 1.
10. *Amrita Bazar Patrika*, 27 June 1928.
11. H.F.J.T Maguire, *Report on the Census of Calcutta*, Calcutta: Bengal Secretariat Press, 1891, pp. 198–9; and L.S.S. O'Malley, *Report on the Census of India*, vol. VI, pts. 1 and 2, Calcutta: Bengal Secretariat Press, 1913, p. 112.
12. *Census of India*, 1911, vol. 6, pt. 1, Calcutta: Bengal Secretariat Press, 1912, pp. 15–72.

13. S.W. Goode, *Municipal Calcutta: Its Institutions in their Origins and Growth*, Calcutta: Corporation Publications, Edinburgh, 1916, p. 168.

14. Rabindranath Tagore, 'Samskar', May 1928, in *Galpaguchha*, Calcutta: Visva-Bharati Publications, 1401, pp. 646–9.

15. Nair, 'Civic and Public Services in Old Calcutta', p. 228.

16. Report of Muzaffar Ahmad's speech in Meerut Conspiracy Case Proceedings (MCCP), P 193-40(T), National Archives of India, New Delhi.

17. On colonial servants, see, Swapna M. Banerjee, *Men, Women and Domestics: Articulating Middle Class Identity in Colonial Bengal*, Delhi: Oxford University Press, 2004.

18. Nandini Gooptu, *The Politics of the Urban Poor in Early Twentieth Century India*, UK: Cambridge University Press, 2001.

19. Maitreyi Bardhan Ray, *Calcutta Slums: Public Policy in Perspective*, Calcutta: Minerva Press, 1994, p. 7.

20. I owe this information to Ishan Mukhopadhyay who has submitted a Ph.D. dissertation on wartime developments in Bengal at the University of Cambridge.

21. Martin, *Notes on the Medical Topography of Calcutta*, p. 9.

22. Goode, *Municipal Calcutta*, pp. 1–13.

23. Mark Harrison, *Public Health in British India: Anglo Indian Preventive Medicine, 1859–1914*, Cambridge: Cambridge University Press, 1994, p. 3.

24. Norman Chevers, *Lecture on Sanitary Position and Obligations of the Inhabitants of Calcutta*, Calcutta: R.C. Lepage and Co., 1853.

25. Baron Dowleans, 'Calcutta in 1860', *The Calcutta Review*, vol. 34, no. 68, 1860, p. 96.

26. Subol Chandra Mitra, *Ishwar Chandra Vidyasagar: A Story of His Life and Work*, Calcutta: New Calcutta Press, 1902, p. 55.

27. On the history of the river, which gradually died of siltage in the early twentieth century, see Haraprasad Chattopadhya, *From Marsh to Township East of Calcutta: A Tale of Salt Water Lakes and Salt Lake Township*, Calcutta: K.P. Bagchi, 1990; Christine Furedy, 'From Waste Land to Waste Not Land: The Role of the Salt Lakes, East, in Waste Treatment and Recycling', in *The Urban Experience: Calcutta—Essays in Honour of Professor Nisith R. Ray*, ed. Pradip Sinha, Calcutta: Riddhi-India, 1987, p. 147.

28. For an excellent history of the fate of the elective system, see Rajat Kanta Ray, *Urban Roots of Indian Nationalism: Pressure Groups and Conflicts of Interests in Calcutta City Politics*, Delhi: Vikas, 1979.

29. Rabindranath Tagore describes the pleasures of bathing under a shower in a second floor bathroom in his childhood—around the early 1870s. See *Jibansmriti, Rabindra Rachanabali,* vol. 10, Centenary Edition, Calcutta: Visva-Bharati Publications, 1961, p. 12.

30. Nair, 'Civic and Public Services in Old Calcutta', p. 228.

31. Republished in Chandy Lahiri, ed., *Basantak*, 2nd year, Calcutta: New Age Publishers, 1874, p. 182.
32. *Calcutta Municipal Gazette*, Silver Jubilee number, Calcutta, 1935, p. 98.
33. Ibid.
34. Ray, *Urban Roots of Indian Nationalism*, p. 166.
35. Ibid.
36. I am grateful to Neha Chatterjee for bringing this to my notice.
37. The only eyewitness account that I found of the grisly manual scavenging comes from a nineteenth-century English tourist, see, Edmund Mitchell, *Thacker's Guide Book to Calcutta: Its Highways and Bye Paths*, Calcutta: Thacker, Spink and Co., 1890, p. 206.
38. Dowleans, 'Calcutta in 1860', pp. 10–11.
39. Martin, *Notes on the Medical Topography of Calcutta*, p. 21.
40. W. Newman, *A Handbook to Calcutta, Historical and Descriptive*, Calcutta: Newman and Co., 1875, p. 58.
41. For living arrangements of the urban poor, see the excellent account of Maitryei Bardhan Ray, *Calcutta Slums*, pp. 12–13.
42. Martin, *Notes on the Medical Topography of Calcutta*.
43. Dowleans, 'Calcutta in 1860', p. 9.
44. Samaresh Bose, *Jug Jug Jiye*, Calcutta: Ananda Publishers, 1985, pp. 291–2.
45. 'Memorandum of the Army Sanitary Commission, 1878', in *Parliamentary Papers, East India, 1878-9,* India Office, British Library, pp. 176–80.
46. Ibid.
47. Meerut Conspiracy Case Proceedings: Prosecution Exhibits, pp. 545–8 (10).
48. K.P. Chattopadhyay and Gautamshankar Ray, eds., *Municipal Labour in Calcutta*, Calcutta, 1947.
49. Ibid., p. 12.
50. Radharaman Mitra, *Kalikata Darpan*, pt. 1, Calcutta: Subarnarekha, 1980, p. 119.
51. Satyandra Nath Datta, 'Nafar Kundu "and" *Methar*', in *Kuhu O Keka*, 1907; reproduced in *Kabita Sangraha*, Calcutta: Bangiya Sahitya Akademi, 1988, p. 180.
52. Edwin Chadwick, *Report on the Sanitary Condition of the Labouring Population of Great Britain...*, London: W. Clowes and Sons, 1843; Christopher Hamlin, *Public Health and Social Justice in the Age of Chadwick: Britain, 1800-1854*, Cambridge: Cambridge University Press, 1998.
53. Sumit Sarkar, 'Conditions and Nature of Subaltern Militancy: Bengal from Swadeshi to Non Cooperation', in *Subaltern Studies*, vol. 3, ed. R. Guha, Delhi: Oxford University Press, 1984.
54. IB, Report on the Political Situation and Labour Unrest for Seven Days Ending 18 April 1928.
55. Tanika Sarkar, '1928–1929', in *Bengal, 1928-1834: The Politics of Protest*, Delhi: Oxford University Press, 1987.

56. See, Frederick Petersson, 'The "Colonial Conference" and Dilemma of the Comintern's Colonial Work', in *Communist Histories*, vol. 1, ed. Vijay Prashad, Delhi: Leftword, 2016.

57. Meerut Conspiracy Case Proceedings: Correspondence related to Scavengers.

58. On Indian communist activism, see, Gautam Chattopadhyay, *Communism and Bengal's Freedom Movement*, Bombay: People's Publishing House, 1970; Sumit Sarkar, '1928–1937: Nationalist Advance and Economic Depression', in *Modern India, 1885-1947*, London: Macmillan, 1983. On Bengal communists, see Sarkar, '1928–1929'. On the early life of Muzaffar Ahmad, see, Suchetana Chattopadhyay, *An Early Communist: Muzaffar Ahmad in Calcutta, 1913-1929*, New Delhi: Tulika, 2011.

59. Manju Chattopadhyay has pioneerd research on such figures. See, Manju Chattopadhyay, *The Trail-Blazing Women Trade Unionists of India*, Delhi: All India Trade Union Congress, 1995.

60. See, Sarkar, '1928–1929'. Also see, Manju Chattopadhyay, 'Kolkatai Dhangar Dharmaghat Ebong Prabhabati Dasgupta O Sakina Begum', in *Itihas Anusandhan*, vol. 2, ed. Gautam Chattopadhyay, Calcutta: K.P. Bagchi & Co., 1982; transcript of interview with Prabhabati, Oral History Section, Nehru Memorial Museum & Library, 24 April 1968, New Delhi.

61. *Forward*, 26 July 1928.

62. IB, Weekly Reports on the Political Situation in Bengal, week ending 22 February 1928. Kumaranda's speech at Calcutta Maidan.

63. Kenneth McPherson, *The Muslim Microcosm: Calcutta, 1918 to 1935*, Wiesbaden: Franz Steiner Verlag, 1974, p. 72.

64. Parimalbandhu Das, *Prabhu Jagatbandhu*, Calcutta: Sri Jagatbandhu Harililamela Karyalay, 1913. (I am grateful to Santanu Dey for this.) Also see McPherson, *The Muslim Microcosm*, pp. 82–97.

65. IB, File No. 90 of 1928: Fortnightly Reports on the Political Situation in Bengal, 1928-39–First half of July 1935.

66. Goode, *Municipal Calcutta*, pp. 162–7.

67. *The Statesman*, 26 June 1928, recalled the 1924 events. Many of their grievances like bribes exacted by Sardars were repeated in 1928.

68. Chattopadhyay and Ray, *Municipal Labour*, pp. 8–9.

69. *The Statesman*, Calcutta, 26 June 1928.

70. *Amrita Bazar Patrika*, 3 July 1928.

71. Meerut Conspiracy Case Proceedings: Correspondence related to Scavengers.

72. IB, File No. 448/28, Confidential, No. 606/50-25, 2 February 1928.

73. Sarkar, '1928–1929'.

74. *Amrita Bazar Patrika*, 26 June 1928.

75. Ahmad, *Myself and the Communist Party of India, 1920–1929*, vol. 2, Calcutta: National Book Agency, 1970.

76. IB, Weekly Report on Political Situation… week ending 29 February and week ending 23 May 1928.

77. IB, Weekly Reports between May and July 1928.

78. Ibid., week ending 18 April 1928.

79. Joyce, *Visions of the People: Industrial England and the Question of Class, 1840-1914*, UK: Cambridge University Press, 1991, pp. 329–35.

80. I have culled strike details from the *Forward*, *Ananda Bazar Patrika*, and IB files for March to July 1928.

81. *Amrita Bazar Patrika*, 2 March 1928.

82. See especially, *Amrita Bazar Patrika*, March to July 1928.

83. IB, Weekly Reports, March to July 1928.

84. Ibid., week ending 4 April 1928.

85. Ibid., week ending 1 February 1928.

86. Sarkar, '1928–1929'.

87. Meerut Conspiracy Case Proceedings: Bengal and Bihar Speeches, P 1926(T).

88. Collected by Tinkari Sur, in his *Teensho Bochhorer Kolkata*; cited in Anindita Ghosh, *Claiming the City: Protest, Crime and Scandals in Colonial Calcutta*, Delhi: Oxford University Press, 2016, p. 94.

89. IB, Weekly Report, week ending 18 April 1928.

90. *Amrita Bazar Patrika*, 9 March 1928.

9

RETHINKING URBAN HEALTH

Calcutta in the Turbulent 1940s

SRILATA CHATTERJEE, RITWIKA BISWAS
AND AVIRUP SINHA

Introduction

The city is becoming increasingly important in historical research
to understand social evolution and cultural change. Concepts like
'urban modernity' in trying to analyse the modernization process
of urban society and economy have added a new dimension to
the study of the city as a symbol of modernity, development,
and progress. Historians have not failed to focus on the study of
the Indian cities both in their precolonial and colonial existence
to scale the extent of change that marked urban life in India.
These studies emphasize varied aspects of urbanity, ranging from
demographic patterns, economic and social life to urban politics
and public culture. In comparison, historical research on urban
health, sanitation, and medical culture have drawn little attention.
Partho Datta's work on the city of Calcutta has focused on the
connection between urban planning and incidence of disease. He
shows how epidemic disease and climatic concerns influenced
town planning and improvement of Calcutta.[1] That there was 'an
intimate connection between colonial planning and concerns rising
from health and hygiene especially—threat of epidemics' is evident
from the reports and observations of the Indian Medical Service
(IMS) doctors serving in the city's hospitals. Control of disease

became the new trend of governance and urban planning became essential to ensure public health. In this essay, we aim to focus on how the broader political and economic issues affected health and hygiene in an urban locality. Calcutta, which represents a unique example of urban development in a colonial setting, has been selected as a case study and the period of study will be between 1939 and 1950, a politically stormy decade. Health, generally viewed as a social and cultural construct, is mediated by greater political and economic factors, and great events like the Second World War, Bengal Famine of 1942, communal violence and Partition of India, and the refugee problem in post-Partition period can affect the broader public health condition of a city like Calcutta. This essay analyses how on account of the Second World War and Bengal Famine, a large number of people flocked to Calcutta from *muffasils* in search of food and livelihood and how this had not only impacted the broader public health condition of Calcutta but also changed the attitude of the varied social and occupational groups living in the city towards matters related to health and medicine. In the post-Independence period, a major threat to the public health condition of Calcutta was the refugee problem. They were forced to live in extremely unhygienic conditions and the refugee camps and colonies became a source of diseases like cholera. The urban environment of Calcutta underwent a major change in the decades that saw the transition of power and the birth of a nation. New dimensions were thus added to the health determinants in urban Calcutta, directly reflecting the impact of political and economic changes on issues related to urban health and hygiene, especially of the multitude of urban poor and the middle class living in the city. The essay is divided into three sections. While the first section provides an understanding of the broader public health issues in the nineteenth- and early twentieth-century Calcutta, the next two focus on the decades of the 40s and 50s of the twentieth century, when the city was experiencing massive changes.

I

Calcutta developed from a riverine rural settlement into an urban metropolis after the British settled here and made Kalikata the centre of colonial commercial and political activities. Calcutta, along with Madras and Bombay, has been described as 'essentially European cities in conception, design and primary functions, but transplanted on an alien Asian soil'.[2] The early European towns that developed in India lacked in urban planning and architectural design. In the case of Calcutta too, urban development was primarily guided by defence and commercial concerns. As a consequence, politically and strategically, Calcutta was ideal for an administrative and commercial capital. James Ranald Martin, a Scottish doctor in the IMS associated with the Native General Hospital (NGH) in Calcutta, acknowledged the importance of the city as a British capital and opined:

Nowhere has the activity and enterprise of British commerce been better displayed than in the rapid rise of this capital. . . . Previous to 1756 Calcutta was in short but a trading factory—a valuable one to be sure, yet affording little promise of its future greatness. Soon after the re-occupation of Calcutta by the British an extraordinary impulse seems to have been given that within forty years, and notwithstanding all the disadvantages of position, it became a city numbering five hundred thousand individuals, a degree of prosperity unparalleled perhaps in any other quarter of the world.[3]

However, what became a cause of great concern for the European settlers of the city was Calcutta's insalubrious climate. The choice of Calcutta by Job Charnock as a site for the British factory was regarded as unfortunate for 'he could not have chosen a more unhealthful place on the entire river'.[4] The salt water lake, situated 3 mi. to the north-east of Calcutta, was seen as the main source of pure drinking water that caused yearly mortality of the Europeans.[5] Hence it was with an eye to protect European health that sanitation and municipal planning began in the city. Situated on the left bank of river Hooghly, Calcutta in the early nineteenth century occupied a space of 4.5 mi. stretching from Chitpore in the north to Khidirpur in the south and 1.5 mi. in the east-west direction from the river bank to the Circular Road.[6] The suburbs of Chitpore, Simlah, in the north and in the south the clusters of villages stretching from Ballygunge, Bhowanipore, Alipore to Behala, was the peripheral region surrounding Calcutta. The pattern of settlement in Calcutta characteristic of the early colonial cities created a spatial segregation of European Town in the south and the

'Native' or Black Town in the north. The British settlement around the citadel of Fort William depicted an urban growth resembling a European fort city. The region was dominated by important public buildings, the most spectacular being the fort. This was Dihi Kalikata, which protected the British settlement naturally from outside attack. In comparison, the 'Black Town' inhabited by the local people represented a swarming conglomeration of settlements centring around a network of bazaars and brisk trading activities in congested streets. The physiological segregation of space into white and black as the English settlers gradually withdrew from Sutanati to Kalikata, and the concentration of the locals in Sutanati also created specific identities for the two parts of the same city and this psychological barrier was difficult to overcome.

As the urban area in Calcutta began to expand, there was greater social and occupational interactions between the Europeans and the local people, increasing the risk of disease. The anxiety in the bureaucratic circle for the health of the white population in the city provided the incentive for a wider public health policy. This led to the implementation of sanitary and municipal regulations by the colonial state. The process began from 1794 with the formation of the Committee of Justices of Peace. By early nineteenth century, concerns about improving the condition of the city with regard to health and sanitation found a place for the first time in the official exchanges. In 1803, Lord Wellesley declared: 'The increasing extent and population of Calcutta, the capital of the British Empire in India and the seat of Supreme authority requires the serious attention of the Government. It is now become absolutely necessary to provide permanent means of promoting the health, comfort and convenience of the numerous inhabitants of this town.'[7] Wellesley's Minute on Calcutta, it has been argued, revealed 'that although Calcutta had become the capital its rapid growth as the most important entrepot in eastern India without adequate planning had played havoc with its civic services'.[8] His keenness in the creation of an imperial capital aesthetically beautiful and also clean, healthy, safe, and convenient symbolized the new notion of modern town planning that was reiterated throughout the nineteenth century.[9] Such concerns led to the creation of the Lottery Committee. This initiated an era of municipal sanitation through organized committees and public subscription, thus transplanting, in the opinion of S.W. Goode, the English institutional model onto Indian soil.[10]

In the late eighteenth and early nineteenth centuries, new theories of medical geography had an influence on the European settlers in the tropics, which involved finding the causal relation between environment, climate, and disease. The medico-climatic discourse that began to take shape from this time attributed the dynamism and progress of the Europeans as well as their racial superiority to the cooler climate of the temperate zone and identified the tropical lands with natural fecundity and rapid decay. Diseases in the tropics were associated closely with the hot and humid climate and the miasma or putrid vapour from decaying organic matters.[11] Much of this knowledge was constructed by the doctors in the IMS who, on the one hand, brought up the issue of European acclimatization to the diverse local conditions and, on the other hand, created an urgency among the medical practitioners to find the natural locus of the tropical diseases among the local population. A special knowledge about the medical topography of the tropical lands also proved professionally beneficial to the European practitioners of the IMS in securing their position within the medical hierarchy. The IMS doctors acted as negotiators inducing the early colonial state to take some interest in matters other than military and politics. Due to their initiative, hospitals and dispensaries for local people were established in the city. The NGH was established in 1792 as a surgical hospital to treat accident cases. The hospital began in a rented house of the Fowjdar (Commander of the Army) of Chitpore. It was financially aided by charity coming initially from the Europeans and later the Indian elite.[12] Although intended as a surgical hospital, it was forced to treat patients with varied ailments. The need for a fever hospital to manage the growing incidence of fever epidemic in the city led to the formation of the committee for the establishment of the Fever Hospital and municipal improvement of the town of Calcutta and its suburbs in 1836. The committee was formed at the independent initiative of the governors of the NGH, especially Martin, through a public meeting held in the Town Hall. It also involved the indigenous elite as members. Dwarakanath Tagore, Rustomji Cowasji, Radhamadhab Banerjee, Ramcomul Sen, and Muttylal Seal were invited to join the committee because 'it was thought right in the first instance to rely on them'.[13] As hospitals emerged as the new forms of civic philanthropy for the Indian elite towards the poor, these local elite contributed large sums of money and land for the construction of hospitals and dispensaries in the city.[14]

The Fever Hospital Committee marked a turning point in the history of organized healthcare and public health policy. By deliberating on the need for a policy of institutional healthcare that would incorporate under the public domain the 'native' population of the town, it paved the way for the establishment of purpose-built hospitals for in-house treatment of patients. This culminated in the foundation of the Medical College Hospital in 1854 providing the much needed institutional space through which Western medicine would reach the city's inhabitants. The college hospital was attached with the Medical College founded in 1835 to combine medical teaching with clinical observation for the benefit of the students. By the end of the nineteenth century, multiple systems of institutional medical care ranging from hospitals to scattered dispensaries came into being as a part of the social process of Calcutta's urbanization and experiment in spatial management.

The change of power from the Company to the Crown marked the beginning of a new era in municipal and sanitary administration in urban areas. The Calcutta Municipal Act, 1863 created provisions for the formation of the Calcutta Municipal Corporation (CMC) under the Justices of the Peace of Bengal, Bihar, and Orissa.[15] In 1864, Calcutta had its first Health Officer to supervise surface conservancy. This was also the year when registration of births and deaths became mandatory with the appointment of six Registrars. CMC was reconstituted in 1876 with new responsibilities. The original drainage scheme was completed and regular supply of filtered and unfiltered water to the inhabitants helped improve urban living. *Cikitsa Sammilani*, a Bengali medical journal published from Bengal, wrote a long article on cholera in Calcutta and tap water to spread awareness about the use of filtered water to prevent cholera. In places where tap water was not available, incidence of cholera was high. Quoting from the report of the Cholera Commission which came to India in 1883, the article pointed out that 'Whatever germs may be the cause of Cholera, it is clear that drinking dirty and unclean water is the real cause of Cholera and that there is no doubt that use of clean and filtered water is the only way to remain safe from attacks of Cholera.'[16]

In accordance with the recommendations of the Sanitary Commission, the Department of Public Health had to be cautious that 'sanitary arrangements should harmonize as much as possible with the system of work in England'.[17] As far as possible, the English model of sanitary reform was transplanted into the colonies with improvisations to blend with the social and cultural values of the subject population. But the diligence that was necessary to develop sanitary administration and welfare works was lacking, which slowed down the process of development. Even in the capital city the public works staff was inadequate. In 1900, Calcutta was ravaged by the plague epidemic. The colonial government introduced stringent plague control measures to control the disease, clearly establishing the centrality of the body as the site of plague contagion. The body of colonized people and their habitats became the object of state intervention. Yet the state could hardly function in preventing contagion without social consent. In Bengal, the government took care to collaborate with the Western educated elite, especially in urban Calcutta, and it was with the society's consent that isolation hospitals, and temporary caste and community hospitals were built as domains to segregate the diseased bodies from their natural locus of disease.[18] Quarantine rules were implemented to search for the diseased body in public places like rail platforms, dockyards, etc. Once again social and religious practices like pilgrimage involving movement of people and their congregation in a place came under the scanner of state regulations. Legislative regulations and sanitary policing became the norm for disease control. With greater decentralization introduced by the Government of India Act of 1919, medical administration and public health became a concern of the provincial legislatures and local self-government. By this time, Indian participation in the local bodies through the electoral process had been ensured. In 1923, the Calcutta Municipal Act had imposed upon Calcutta a definite sanitary regulation, and the CMC was given wide powers in matters of health and sanitation. But such measures of sanitary control hardly changed the situation as the report of the Sanitary Reorganization Committee of 1920 clearly mentioned that: 'The growth of sanitation was sickly and stunted in the uncongenial climate of Bengal with its dense population, their apathy and immobility of custom, overpowering forces of nature and above all cramping paucity of funds.'[19]

II

In this section our focus of discussion would be to analyse the implications of urban public health conditions in the city of Calcutta and its hinterland between 1939 and 1950. It is important to summarize the emerging health problems of urbanization and the interrelated mix of threats to urban health among which epidemic and chronic diseases proved to be most fatal in affecting urban health. The discussion would try to address three main points: how different diseases affected the general urban health scenario; what measures the civic authorities and the government adopted to combat such diseases; and the nature of social impact of the outbreak of the diseases and their remedial measures. Through case studies of several infectious diseases, some of which often tended to disrupt the normal civic life, this essay tries to explore the inherent links among the trend of disease epidemiology, the broader environmental, economic, and technological factors like water supply, sanitation, and the political discourse of urban health.

Among the infectious epidemic diseases, cholera, smallpox, and malaria caused maximum damage to general health of the people and affected the overall civic condition of Calcutta. Before 1817, with the exception of sporadic outbreaks in some of India's coastal cities, cholera seemed to have been confined to deltaic Bengal, where it was endemic. However, the situation changed dramatically in the monsoon season of the mentioned year. In that year, cholera spread to various parts of India and from the subcontinent it gradually spread to various parts of the world. Calcutta did not escape from the ravage caused by cholera. In 1817, the disease first visited the city and since then the cholera epidemic repeatedly attacked Calcutta as well as Bengal after short intervals. The situation worsened with a staggering death toll of 2,173; 2,402; and 3,880 in 1943–4; 1948–9; and 1950–1, respectively, in the area under the CMC.[20] This high incidence of cholera in the city in the decades of 40s and early 50s, however, coincided with a series of political and economic catastrophes like the Second World War, Bengal Famine of 1942–4, and the Partition of India in 1947 and the refugee influx. The relation between the health crisis and the general crisis of the metropolitan life cannot escape the historian's gaze of enquiry.

The cholera issue precipitated a whole range of debates on public health in British India. The causes of the outbreak of the disease became a matter of great controversy.[21] In the mid-nineteenth century the most dominant view was that cholera was essentially a local disease. However, J. Snow's waterborne theory was also gaining ground in India and Britain simultaneously. Mark Harrison showed how in India the debate over cholera was intertwined with the issues of internal and maritime quarantine, the questions of government finance and the wider debate on the idea of governance, and the roles and responsibilities of the colonial state.[22] He also showed how the response of the Indian government to the cholera epidemic was shaped by many inherent contradictions and compulsions of British rule in India. On the one hand, the protection of the Europeans, particularly their troops, necessitated some degree of intervention in the lives of the indigenous people but any such action carried with it the risk of civil unrest. The government's fiscal policy was another factor in its reluctance to meet the demands of public health.[23] With the decentralization of sanitation and health, provincial governments and municipalities were entrusted with the sole responsibility of maintaining health and hygiene in their respective localities. In the face of chronic financial scarcity, provincial governments and municipalities often neglected the health and sanitation issues. In this situation, to hide its own inefficiency the colonial State often preferred to put the blame on the 'natives' for the outbreak of cholera. *Busties* (slums) for example, were identified as the breeding ground of diseases. It was often alleged that Hindu religious gatherings and the lack of a sense of hygiene among Indians were important causes of the disease. This view was dominant in the official circles even in the last phase of the colonial rule. While reporting the cause of the cholera outbreak, the Health Officer of Calcutta in his annual report for the year 1943–4 observed that:

. . . a good deal of cholera in Calcutta is water-borne. The heavy incidence of the disease among Hindus whose religion enjoins bathing in the river Hooghly and Adi Ganga (Tolly's Nullah) corroborates this view. In suburban wards, the use of contaminated tank water frequently causes local explosive outbreaks. The use of unfiltered water for domestic purposes, particularly during summer months, when the supply of filtered water is insufficient, is responsible for many cases of cholera. Many cases of infection occur owing to ignorance and carelessness of those nursing the numerous cases treated at home. Contamination of foodstuffs, especially cold drinks of the road side petty shops, by dust and flies is another source of infection.[24]

The government, however, took some preventive measures to combat the disease. Disinfection of sources of water supply, tanks, wells, river-ghats (quays), and houses was carried out. The CMC organized lectures, distributed leaflets, and published press declarations to make people aware about preventive measures to combat cholera, but the success rate during the colonial period and in the initial years after Independence was minimal. This was on account of the fact that the sanitary policy of the colonial government was largely a failure and the problem of the availability of safe drinking water continued to remain in the city till the end of colonial rule and in the years immediately after.

Smallpox was another threat to the public health condition in India. From the beginning of colonial rule, it remained a cause of concern for colonial administrators. Smallpox took a huge number of lives in the period of our study, with the peak years being 1940–1, 1943–4, 1944–5, 1947–8, and 1950–1. The deaths caused by it in the area under the CMC in the mentioned years were 3,860; 3,374; 8,325; 5,341; and 9,332, respectively.[25] To eradicate smallpox several measures were taken from the early years of colonial rule. Sanjoy Bhattacharya, Harrison, and Michael Worboys in their recently edited volume showed how a combination of several factors determined the public health policy in general and smallpox eradication measures in particular, during the British Raj.[26] First, the desire to cut administrative costs affected the broader health measures of the colonial regime and health became an issue of great neglect. Second, the 'fractured' structure of the British Raj also affected broader health issues. Finally, smallpox policies were influenced by the attitude of those being targeted for vaccination and/or those claiming to speak for them at different points of time.[27]

Certain general measures were taken to combat the disease. In Calcutta, for example, the medical practitioners were obliged under Section 435 of the Calcutta Municipal Act, 1923, to notify the Health Officer of every case of smallpox of which he became cognizant during the course of his practice. Under Section 438, he could also order the removal of a smallpox patient to a hospital, subject to the approval of the CEO.[28] Legislations with regard to compulsory vaccination promulgated first with the Bengal Act V of 1880 and subsequent laws failed to control the spread of the disease. The failure can be explained in various ways. Besides the administrative and political constraints, social beliefs also posed an important hindrance, e.g. the fear among people that vaccination provoked the displeasure of Goddess Sitala who would destroy them by visiting with smallpox in a deadly form. Such rumours were widely prevalent. In 1941, the Health Officer of Calcutta regretted that in spite of repeated requests from the press, a fair percentage of the people in the city did not vaccinate themselves against smallpox.[29] It was only from the early 1950s that an increase in the number of vaccination cases could be quantified. For example in 1945–6, 22,522 people vaccinated themselves. The figure increased to 1,28,103 in 1954–5.[30] Finally, on 23 April 1977, India was officially declared free from the smallpox epidemic.[31]

Another great threat to the public health condition of India throughout the colonial rule was malaria and Calcutta was an important centre of it. The strategy of malaria control raises questions about whether vector eradication as suggested by Ronald Ross was the most effective measure of control or it was necessary to give greater attention to the human factor.[32] C.A Bentley emphasized on the human factor listing three such factors responsible for malaria outbreak as tropical aggregation of labour, non-immune immigration, and 'factors of residual infection'.[33] However, from the second decade of the twentieth century, environmental changes due to development and nutritional deficiency were also being taken into consideration by the Malariologists as causes for the increasing vulnerability to malarial fever. However, in Bengal the vector control measure remained most widely accepted. Lt. Col. A.C. Chatterji, the Director of Public Health in Bengal, while delivering a lecture at the University of Calcutta, referred to a variety of breeding places of mosquitoes such as tanks, *dobas* (pools), ditches, drains, railway and roadside borrow pits, decaying rivers, slow running streams, rice fields, marshy lands, rivers, *beels* (lake-like wetlands with static water), stray collections of water, tree holes, broken pots and tins, storage and flushing cisterns, etc.[34] Lack of systematic pisciculture and indiscriminate killing of fishes led to a decrease of fish, particularly of those that ate up mosquito larva and became another cause of malaria.

Malaria left a deep impact on the urban health of Calcutta. In the period of our study, the highest number of death by malaria in the area under the CMC happened in 1943–4 and 1944-–5 when 3,026 and 3,523 people died, respectively.[35] The Health Officer of Calcutta in his annual report for the year 1944–5 related this to the Second World War and migration from the war zones in South-East Asia. This report mentioned that after 1940–1, signs of the malaria epidemic became evident in the city, as a large number of malaria-affected evacuees came from Burma and took shelter in this city. The evacuation from Burma that happened in the context of the Japanese air raids during the Second World War led to a population exodus through malaria-prone regions to reach India. Another cause was the visit of the destitute from malaria-affected villages because of the Bengal Famine of 1943–4.[36] Thus, non-immune immigration incurred by political and economic crises was considered a major cause of sudden increase in the incidence of the disease. Along with that, the shortage of quinine in the war years also caused a huge number of deaths by malaria between 1943 and 1945.[37]

To combat malaria, several anti-malaria as well as anti-mosquito campaigns were taken. For example, in Calcutta, the CMC appointed temporary staff as 'mosquito brigades' in 1909 to work for six months. Meanwhile, in 1921, the government undertook a systematic survey and control measures in the environs of Calcutta.[38] Maps were prepared showing in minute detail the breeding places of *anopheles* mosquito. These surveys revealed that sporadic breeding grounds were located in Salt Lake and in villages bordering it. From that time steps were taken to control mosquitoes in Salt Lake and the surrounding areas. At the same time, the authorities of the Bengal Nagpur Railway, the Eastern Bengal Railway, the Eastern India

Railway, and the Kalighat-Falta Railway, also undertook mosquito control measures. The men who were recruited for malaria control were appointed permanently in 1917, but for some reason these posts were abolished in 1923.[39] The CMC again recruited temporary staff to combat mosquitoes in 1927. Such temporary arrangements tended to hinder the progress of the work.

In July 1940, the government of Bengal gave permission to the CMC to construct mosquito-proof cisterns and reserve tanks.[40] This proved effective in fighting malaria. In 1950–1, a representative of the central government met the Health Officer to discuss the ways and means to reduce mosquitoes in the port areas of Calcutta. The Health Officer suggested that a separate organization under the control of the Port Health Officer should be set up for the purpose of the operation involving the inspection of the ships and the boats floating on the river Hooghly and lying on the docks.[41] The proposal that was accepted later in 1956–7 was intended to keep a check on the spread of contagion through commerce.[42] Sanitary control of trade and the port areas to control malarial spread or spread of contagious disease, however, failed to ensure adequate protection for the obvious reason that such controls were abused for economic and political reasons.[43] Meanwhile, in April 1953 the central and state governments launched a nationwide anti-malaria programme. Though this programme was launched for the rural areas of West Bengal, the Health Officer of the CMC negotiated with public health authorities of West Bengal to get some assistance for the programme, which included supply of chemical and equipment for controlling malaria in the border areas of Calcutta. However, the attempt was not successful.[44]

Much of the efforts at vector control measures in the city were undertaken by the CMC on its own with some support from the government. The mosquito control department of the CMC performed various activities to control the breeding of mosquitoes and to combat malaria, dengue, and other mosquito-borne diseases. They made people aware through demonstrations, distributing leaflets, etc., about what measures should be adopted to combat malaria and what steps should be taken by a malaria patient. Other activities included survey of the breeding place of *Anopheles sundaious*; cleansing of tanks, *dobas*, ditches, etc.; application of chemical larvicide in the breeding places of mosquitoes; and watching the fever cases being treated at the local dispensaries.[45] During the Second World War, the use of DDT (Dichlorodiphenyl Trichloroethane) introduced by the American army stationed in the region became the main method of controlling malaria. Eventually, malaria was almost eradicated in India and Sri Lanka.[46] In the year 1965–6, only three persons died of malaria in the area under the CMC.[47]

Non-epidemic infectious and chronic diseases were also important factors of urban ill-health. The impact of non-epidemic disease on the urban health of Calcutta and government policies related to these diseases can best be understood by the case study of tuberculosis. Tuberculosis, known by its various names— consumption, Phthisis or even white plague—was as old as human civilization but the nature of its causation remained unknown till Robert Koch's discovery of the tuberculosis bacillus in the nineteenth century. India was not free from the disease although the extent of its spread could be identified in India only in early twentieth century when tuberculosis had already declined in Western societies.

The nature of tuberculosis remained one of the most debated and contested issues that affected the treatment process and measures to combat the menace.[48] In mid-sixteenth century, Hyeronymus Fracastorius, a Florentine physician, built up the theory of contagion of tuberculosis and it received sufficient acceptance in Europe. However, the British attitude on this issue remained conservative and as late as late nineteenth and early twentieth century in British medical discourse the dominant view was that the tuberculosis was not a contagious disease. For example, Dr Benjamin Rush (1808) and Sir Thomas Watson (1836), the two leading physicians of Britain, did not believe in the contagious nature of tuberculosis and this opinion remained dominant among English physicians even after Koch established the germ theory of disease.[49] However, a small section of the British physicians accepted the contagious nature of the disease from early twentieth century onwards. The resolution passed at the general meeting of the British Congress on Tuberculosis for the Prevention of Consumption, on 27 July 1901 recorded, 'tuberculosis sputum is the main agent for the conveyance of the virus of tuberculosis from man to man and that indiscriminate spitting should therefore be suppressed'.[50]

The existing contradictions on this issue gave the colonial government an excuse for not acting to prevent this disease. In spite of repeated requests from the British Congress on tuberculosis, the British government in India showed a strange reluctance to take any concrete measure to combat the disease. To hide its inefficiency the colonial government often put the blame on the sufferers. Unhygienic habits and customs, poverty, bad housing conditions, and congestions and overcrowding were identified as responsible factors for the spread of this disease. For example, the Health Officer of Calcutta in his annual report of 1946–7 mentioned that:

. . . the causes of tuberculosis in Calcutta may be briefly summarized as— (i) poverty, under-nourishment, the struggle for existence under adverse conditions, etc., (ii) ignorance and carelessness resulting in indiscriminate expectoration of sputum loaded with bacilli all over the places, (iii) the purdah system, (iv) bad housing—a dark, damp, ill-ventilated room in the heart of the city, (v) the restaurants and tea shops where cups and cupboards are not properly cleansed, (vi) hotels and messes where the utensils for taking food are not properly washed.[51]

Tuberculosis was a great threat to the public health condition of Calcutta in the mid-twentieth century (Table 9.1).[52] The data in itself shows that mortality rate by tubercular infection was quite high in the decades of the 40s and 50s in comparison to deaths by other diseases in the metropolis.

The first concrete step to combat tuberculosis by the Bengal government was taken up as late as 1939 when it sanctioned surveys to be conducted at Serampur and Barisal to calculate the extent of morbidity and mortality from the disease.[53] The result of the surveys indicated a high incidence of infection and disease. Anti-tuberculosis measures by the government also involved adopting a policy of bringing tuberculosis employees of the government within the perview of proper treatment and it was decided to send all suspected cases of tuberculosis in the employment of government of Bengal to the Presidency or civil surgeon concerned who, if necessary, was to refer the case to the nearest hospital, where proper facilities were available for thorough examination of the chest.[54]

TABLE 9.1: Percentage of Deaths by Tuberculosis
in Calcutta (1939–51)

Year	Total number of death by Tuberculosis	Percentage of total death by Tuberculosis*
1939–42	9,390	9.63
1942–5	7,899	5.72
1945–8	9,035	7.51
1948–51	9,515	6.40

Note: *Total number of dead by tuberculosis in year (I) ÷ Total number of dead of year (I) × 100 = percentage of deaths by tuberculosis.

Apart from the government, private initiatives were also taken to combat the disease and in this field the Tuberculosis Association of Bengal, which was started in 1929, played a vital role. Lectures in English and Bengali were delivered in the slum areas of Calcutta, in the local parks to small congregations of residents of the localities, educational institutions, clubs, etc. In Calcutta and its suburbs the association became an active agent making people aware of tuberculosis, informing and guiding them as to what steps should be taken to combat the disease. The association was thus able to create community participation in the control and eradication of the disease. The Association maintained a team of 'Home Visitors', who worked at the clinics, visited patients in their homes, and gave instructions to the patients and their relations about how to avoid the spread of the disease. Dispensaries supervised by junior doctors helped identify and treat tuberculosis patients and by 1947, there were eight such dispensaries in Calcutta.[55] Other notable non-official organizations involved in the task of combating tuberculosis were the King George Thanksgiving Anti-Tuberculosis Fund and Jadavpur Tuberculosis Hospital.[56] Both the colonial government and the postcolonial West Bengal government adopted an indifferent attitude towards preventive measures with regard to tuberculosis. The CMC also failed to develop any concrete measure to combat the disease. It is undeniable that 'the tuberculosis problem in Bengal was immense but the measures taken by the Government to combat the disease were inadequate and callous'.[57]

This discussion shows how various diseases affected broader public health conditions of Calcutta. Colonial government paid little heed to health related issues, often ascribing the cause of the disease to social habits of the 'native' population—their condition of living and prevailing religious-cultural dogmas. Eradication of diseases like malaria through the use of DDT during the Second World War and smallpox through vaccination clearly indicated that the techno-centric approach to public health was gaining primacy especially in dealing with urban health. Exigencies of the Second World War forced the colonial government to take up measures of malaria control. In post-Independence period too, in the newly created state of West Bengal, public health issues were relegated to the background. In consequence, organization of healthcare and disease control continued to challenge the government and their activities as urban diasporas to cities like Calcutta began to create environmental, economic, political, and social risk factors for urban health.

III

A new approach to public health is to understand and acknowledge that social, institutional, economic, and political structures play a determining role in health related issues. Such approach as pointed out by Paul R. Greenough 'emphasizes on disparities rather than commonalities across the whole population'.[58] In this section, discussions would revolve around the various factors that acted as predictors of Calcutta's health status. To understand how Calcutta's urban health and hygiene related issues were influenced by these factors between 1939 and 1950, we will break the discussion under two broad heads. However, it is essential to understand that such divisions are inextricably interlinked.

Political Determinants: Impact of the Second World War, Bengal Famine, and Communal Riots on Calcutta's Urban Health

Calcutta entered a turbulent decade in the 1940s. The outbreak of the Second World War in 1939 and the declaration of India as a party to it in favour of Britain by the British colonial authority severely strained the relationship between the British government in India and Indian nationalists. The subsequent outburst of anti-colonial sentiment in the form of the Quit India Movement in 1942 created a political restlessness affecting the regular urban life of Calcutta. The fear of Japanese air attacks and the incidents of bombing causing the death of large number of poor labourers in the Kidderpore Dock and adjoining area in the air raid on 5 December 1943 disrupted the normalcy of civil life.[59] The normal civic life faced a total breakdown with the outbreak of famine in 1943, which was alleged to be a product of the evil nexus between the indigenous hoarders, British capitalists, and the colonial state rather than the outcome of a natural calamity. The severe scarcity of the basic necessities of life like food, cloth, fuel, etc., drastically deteriorated the quality of life and made a ghastly increase of mortality rate (Plate 9.1). The large scale migration of starving people from villages, who overcrowded the streets and footpaths of the city in a desperate search for sources of living, upset the social and economic balance of city life.

A relation between the Second World War, Bengal Famine, and the urban health of Calcutta can be directly inferred from the official records of the period. The Health Officer of Calcutta in his annual report for the year 1943–4 admitted that an important cause of the high mortality rate was due to the coming of a large number of famine affected destitute in the city, who died either due to starvation or a group of diseases caused on account of privation and malnutrition.[60] Greenough showed how starvation due to famine forced people to eat many things which normally did not form part of a Bengali diet.[61] Starved people began to eat leaves and creepers, snails and crustaceans, and various polluted, rotten, and discarded food items. In Calcutta, destitute:

. . . took to caste-off skins of vegetables and to rotten fruits. They collected the former from the streets and the latter from near about the fruit stalls in the markets. The receptacles of street garbage were regularly haunted... those receptacles in front of or near big hotels, boarding houses or eating establishments were regularly watched. . . . This was a common site in the city. . . .[62]

Acute starvation and eating of perished and non-eatable items made famine stricken people easy prey of several diseases and even caused their death.

PLATE 9.1: Bengal Famine: A starving child stuffing himself
with strained water from boiled rice
Source: http://www.oldindianphotos.in/2009/12/bengal-famine-of-1943-
part-2, accessed 14 June 2016

Disposal of corpses also became a problematic issue in the city. Deaths caused by Japanese air attacks or due to the famine put an extra burden on the colonial state. Janam Mukherjee narrates the pathetic condition of corpse disposal in Bengal during this time and in his words: 'Some famine corpses had been retained in constructive possessions of the state, others had been turned over to religious organizations for removal, and still others had been unceremoniously tossed into rivers and canals. Many others remained untouched where they had fallen and become a feast for wild dogs and vultures.'[63] Corpses filled up hospitals and morgues and an extremely unhygienic situation was created because of it.

The Second World War having been over, Calcutta was plunged into a new calamity in the form of communal riots. A communal tension that was swelling between the Hindus and Muslims for the last few decades assumed a serious proportion with the adoption of Pakistan proposal by the Muslim League in 1940. When the negotiations were going on in the post-Second World War period between the Indian political parties and the colonial state regarding the transfer of power, the Muslim League pushed a 'direct action' plan to achieve its demand of a separate state for the Indian Muslims. The Great Calcutta Killings of August 1946 and subsequent communal riots was a direct outcome of this. Fratricidal conflicts not only created a psychological trauma but also affected the physical health and hygiene of the urban centre. An official estimated that four thousands died and ten thousands were injured.[64] Contemporary newspapers were replete with shocking descriptions of mass murders of Calcutta inhabitants. *Hindustan Standard* reported:

Reports received from hospitals, relief organizations, rescue parties, Ambulance and Red Cross services show that no fewer than 2,000 persons lost their lives in this freezy of mob violence. The figure of persons injured stood well over 8,000. According to a Government spokesman expressing his personal opinion to a Press conference yesterday the total figures of deaths could be placed at 500 while the number of injured stood near 3,300.[65]

Corpse disposal became a great problem and dead bodies were cremated in open pyres in the middle of the city endangering the environment (Plate 9.2).

A direct outcome of the communal issue was the Partition of India at the time of Independence in 1947 and the refugee problem. The influx of millions of refugees from East Pakistan to West Bengal that had started from 1946 after the riots in Noakhali and continued for several decades affected all spheres of life in the eastern region in the newly created nation-state of India. The rehabilitation of the refugees, which was a three staged process, raised a lot of social, economic, and political questions. The refugees generally first gathered at Sealdah Station. They stayed

PLATE 9.2: The Great Calcutta Killings, 1946: Corpses lying among
pieces of wood in preparation for cremation after bloody rioting
Source: http://www.oldindianphotos.in/2011/01/calcutta-communal-
riot-or-great.html, accessed 12 June 2016

there for a few days and then were sent to different camps. Living
in camps might run for several months and even more than a year.
Finally, they were placed in colonies with a plot of residential land
and another plot of land for earning livelihood either through
agricultural or other means. However, in none of these three stages
the means of life were adequate for the sustenance of a healthy life.
Refugees who flocked to Sealdah were forced to live in an extremely
unhealthy environment. Basic facilities that were available at the
station collapsed on account of overcrowding. As a result, refugees
were forced to live in an environment in which there was no proper
arrangement for drinking water, latrines were not cleaned and
were not in a usable condition. On account of living in such an
unhealthy and unhygienic environment refugees became an easy
prey for several diseases. For example, on 22 July 1950 five refugees
including four children and a ninety-year-old man, died here on
account of various diseases, which include two cholera cases.[66]

From the station a section of refugees were ported to several government camps. In camps too the refugees faced miserable conditions. There was no private space for them. Military barracks, Nissen huts, and jute godowns were often converted into refugee camps and thousands of refugees were dumped into these camps. The space provided was so scanty that it could hardly accommodate the families and there was not even space for all members of a family to sit.

Health of the camp-dwellers deteriorated on account of living in such a pathetic condition. Refugees of the Ranaghat Cooper's Camp while sharing their experience to Shri Dalmia, who had visited that camp along with Mr N.C. Chatterjee, Mr P.K. Roy, and a group of relief workers on 8 August 1950, said:

> . . . in the Camp they lived on a bare diet of *dal* (lentil) and *bhat* (rice) which keeps their body and soul together but takes their children slowly towards death. Even in Cooper's Camp, considered being the best of its kind run by the Central Government, death claimed a toll of 300 children in the month of July alone. In the female ward of the Camp hospital, an infant-patient Nemai, Registered as No. 1807, seemed to have harboured in his young body all the diseases from which children in the Camp generally suffer. He has been in the Camp for the last one and a half month during which he has suffered in turn from dysentery, swelling of body, itching of the body, scabies, enlarged liver and a generally run-down state of health.[67]

The miserable condition of the refugees was often alleged to be the outcome of the inadequacy of government assistance and a generally indifferent attitude of the government to the refugees. These uprooted people entered the Indian nation-state in search of their homeland but their expectations were belied as they were treated like unwanted intruders. The central government was alleged to be discriminatory in dealing with the refugees from East Pakistan to West Bengal vis-à-vis those coming from West Pakistan to Punjab. As regards the allocation of funds for the relief and rehabilitation of the refugees, the state of West Bengal was severely discriminated. The measures taken by the government of West Bengal were also inadequate and often showing lack of proper concern for that wretched lot. The utter disillusionment gradually turned a large section of the refugees against Congress rule. In this situation there began an alternative political mobilization in which the leftists (the Communist Party and its allies) played a prominent role. The refugees at their own initiative built up camp committees which were brought under a central committee called the United Front Refugee Council (UFRC) in 1950. This council as the main mouthpiece of the refugees took up a whole range of issues covering from the demand of citizenship rights of these uprooted people to their healthy and hygienic living conditions in the camps. The non-Congress political parties, especially the communists, without displaying their political banner sided with this day-today struggle of the refugees for achieving a standard civic life, and thus gradually won the confidence of these alienated people to draw their discontent in a channel of opposition politics against Congress rule.[68]

The process was intensified with the third phase of rehabilitation of the refugees from camps to several colonies. Here also the inadequacy of the government measures was apparent. The government sponsored colonies were both insufficient in number as well as in their arrangement for providing a healthy residential zone with the provisions for earning livelihood. So much so, that in some cases the refugees who were sent for settlement in government colonies had to desert. In such a situation a self-initiative of the refugees was launched as an alternative arrangement for rehabilitation through forcible capture of fallow lands most of which were occupied by the landowners by violating the land ceiling Acts and Regulations. The Communist Party played a prominent role in the process. Not only the party activists participated in the process but the party also justified the programme by questioning the legitimacy of landlordism. The long-standing stance of the party that landlordism should be abolished to ensure the right of the tillers to land got a fresh cause of legitimacy on the issue of rehabilitation of the refugees. The failure of the government to procure land to make proper and adequate arrangement for the refugees was attributed to the alliance of the Congress party with landlords.[69] The indifference and hostility of the Congress government to the refugees was thus interpreted in a language of class.

Large number of squatter colonies were established in Calcutta and its suburban areas like Dum-Dum, Tollygunge, Jadavpur, Kasba,

Behala, Garfa, and Santoshpur. These colonies often suffered from an inadequate supply of drinking water, insanitary arrangements, overcrowding, and overall unhealthy and unhygienic environment. The result was that these colonies became a source of various diseases. In a contemporary newspaper report it was stated that:

Lakhs of East Bengal refugees, who have come over to West Bengal and erected hutments and set up colonies around Calcutta on their own initiative and without any Government help, have to fight appalling poverty on the one hand and epidemic disease on the other. Of all the problems they have now to face, inadequacy of medical aid is the most pressing one. . . . The medical officer-in-charge of the squads in his latest report says that deficiency diseases such as night blindness, rickets, nutritional oedema are most prevalent in all the colonies. Besides, a large number of cases of dysentery, influenza, kala-azar, malaria, and typhoid are being treated by them [doctors] daily. He also says that he is getting five to six cases of tuberculosis daily and he apprehends that this number will go on rising if Government continues to remain indifferent to the problem of the refugees as they are now, and the public health of Bengal will in no time be at stake.[70]

From the above narrative it is clear that refugee colonies were identified as disease zones that would ruin public health of the city and affect its civic life. The refugee population was deprived of basic medical facilities. Improper sanitation and supply of unhygienic water remained the main cause of various diseases. Both the central and state government did little to ameliorate the situation and take any concrete step to combat medical problems of the refugees.

Thus, it is clear that refugee influx prominently affected broader public health condition of Calcutta. Sekhar Bandyopadhyay showed how the problem of refugee influx along with other problems, such as an inadequate supply of filtered water, unhealthy condition in slum areas, etc., posed a serious threat to broader public health condition of the city.[71] An epidemic outbreak of cholera was reported in Calcutta in January–February 1948 and smallpox was already causing havoc in the city. Between 3 January and 8 May 1948, 1,326 people died of cholera and 4,861 of smallpox.[72] The Director of Health Services diagnosed that the situation did not improve on account of an inadequate supply of pure and filtered water, unprecedented urban crowding caused by the refugee influx, unhealthy conditions in slum areas, and uncontrolled sale of unclean and unwholesome food on the streets of Calcutta.[73]

Once again in the absence of governmental cooperation the refugees relied upon self-initiative to ensure the conditions of a healthy civic life. Construction of roads, sewerage system, dispensaries along with schools, libraries by the meagre financial savings and ardent manual labour of the refugees became the hallmark of the colonies to maintain the physical and social health of these uprooted people.[74] This effort, however small and insufficient, added a new dimension to the pattern of urban development, and made the issue of health and hygiene a crucial point for triggering of an alternative idea of governance.

Environmental, Economic, and Social Determinants: Influence of Urban Environment on Urban Health and Hygiene Related Issues

Case studies of important diseases between 1939 and 1950 revealed that urban environment profoundly influenced broader issues of urban health and hygiene. An important environmental risk factor includes the water supply system. Calcutta's water supply system largely depends on the Hooghly River. Numerous tanks and surface-wells are also important sources of water supply. The mechanical arrangement of filtered water supply began in 1820 when a small pumping station was constructed at Chandpal Ghat and service was extended to the white town covering portions of the areas of Old Court House Street, Dhurrumtollah, Chowringhee, Park Street, Lal Bazar, and Bowbazar.[75] A new pumping station at Palta was constructed in 1888 and in 1891; a new station was built in Bhowanipore for the supply of water to the southern part of the city.[76] The supply of water for drinking and other purposes reached the people of Calcutta through this system from the late nineteenth century until after Independence.

Initially the CMC took the target of providing 30 gallons of filtered water per person per day. However, because of increase of population of the city, it needed to revise its plan. In 1919, an expert engineer, S. St. George Moore advised the CMC to terminate the supply of unfiltered water and achieve the projected target of 80 gallons of filtered water per person per day.[77] The CMC accepted this proposal with some modifications. It decided that supply of unfiltered water would be continued but at the same time, supply of filtered water would be maintained at 70 gallons per day per person.[78] However, even by early 60s the CMC could not reach its target.[79] Thus, many homes had to meet their requirements from the municipal supplies of water from the roadside taps or tube wells. The supply of filtered water was not only insufficient, its quality also deteriorated substantially. When Palta site was chosen in 1865, the salinity of the river water from Hooghly was not at all harmful, but towards 1930s, this salinity increased rapidly. It rose to 380 parts per million gallons whereas the accepted human tolerance level for drinking is 250 parts.[80] Due to the insufficient flow of the river, mainly during the summer months, the saline content reached an incredible 2,480 parts per million gallons in 1959.[81]

Scarcity of safe water for drinking forced a large section of people in the city to drink water from tanks, wells, and tube wells, which were often unsafe. This polluted water, which often contained cholera germs as well as germs of several waterborne diseases, was used for cleaning and boiling food stuff or washing utensils. This led to the spread of waterborne diseases like cholera, diarrhoea, etc.

Solid waste disposal system was another important risk factor that affected urban health and hygiene issues. The first attempt to provide Calcutta with an effective drainage system was made by Mr Clarke, a municipal engineer, who proposed a scheme of sewage disposal through five main sewer lines along with branches and sub-branches and to consider Salt Lake as an outfall region and this scheme was eventually accepted by the government in 1859 with some modifications.[82] In the nineteenth and twentieth century the sewer system gradually extended to the greater part of the city. Still, as per the report of the Chief Engineer of the CMC, in 1950–1 one-third of the total area of the city had no sewerage system.[83]

A proper sanitary arrangement did not prevail in all wards of the city. The condition of the sewerage system of the Maniktala, Cossipur-Chitpur areas was in its worst state possible. P.C. Mitra in his representation before the Investigation Commission of 1948–9, mentioned that in the added areas (which include Maniktala, Cossipur-Chitpur areas), the hand flushed privies, and open drains are becoming horrible nuisance. The excreta from the privies discharged openly on drains. The dustbins were not regularly cleaned.[84] The commission itself admitted in 1948–9 that, in these areas there was no proper system of underground drainage.[85] The condition of Bowbazar and Burra Bazar areas was not different. Bowbazar remained notorious for its overcrowding and insanitary arrangements. The Marwari Chamber of Commerce, on 30 April 1941, passed a resolution appealing to the CMC concerns about the condition of ward 7 (in Burra Bazar area) where the heaps of dirt remained accumulated at the street corner.[86]

Apart from improper sewerage system, other problems prevented proper drainage of sewer water. Primary among such issues related with city's sewerage system was the problem of silt deposit. According to the Executive Engineer of the CMC, in 1948–9 total accumulation of silt in various drains of the city was 2,088,000 cu. ft., of which existing Corporation staff could remove only 7,50,000 cu. ft. per year.[87] Existence of service privies in various parts of the city also posed a challenge to city's sewerage system. These existed in great numbers in Cossipur-Chitpur, Maniktala, and Tollygunge areas. Dumping of organic and inorganic waste become a problematic issue for the CMC. Absence of an environmentally safe and isolated dumping ground provoked the CMC to dump garbage in the outskirts of the city's eastern fringe. The locality was known as Dhapa inhabited by migrant labourers working in the nearby leather factories, peasants and urban poor dependent on various occupations.[88] The land fill site endangered the health of numerous poor people living in adjoining areas of Dhapa. It was encouraged by the local government to use the site for 'garbage farming'. Now this region is one of the major suppliers of green vegetables to Calcutta's various markets.

Conclusion

Calcutta was a quintessence of a colonial city and its process of urbanization was determined to a large extent by imperial economic and political criteria. From the nineteenth century onwards Calcutta was experiencing a social and cultural transformation that was derived as much from the Western thoughts and practices as from its own indigenous culture. Calcutta was definitely crucial to the colonial rulers as the epicentre of the empire they were trying to build up. It was, however, as pointed out by Sumit Sarkar, equally crucial for the middle class of Bengal in the nineteenth and twentieth centuries to ensure the emergence of *Bhadralok* as a distinctive formation.[89] Calcutta's public health issues were not delinked from this social transformation and spatial growth that was changing the character of city. In the emerging public sphere, health of the 'public' became a cause of major concern for both the colonial rulers and the educated middle class but for different reasons. While the former was anxious to protect European health, the latter was relating public health and Western medicine with modernity and development. A national space was created for Western medicine and public health where the *bhadralok* were debating ideas of 'national health'. By twentieth century, Calcutta became the centre for new bacteriological research in tropical medicine and the process of institutionalization to organize health also began to take shape.

But urban health in Calcutta posed a great challenge for both the colonial government and after Independence the indigenous state government. Beyond the medical and the biological factors, social, political, and economic issues became powerful in influencing health and longevity and also government policies with regard to public health. Disease control, sanitary management, housing, supply of potable water, system of waste disposal reflected lack of planning and awareness that continued from the colonial to the postcolonial period. Yet, there was a silver lining that health and medicine along with other political issues also precipitated broader sociocultural reaction expressed in the cultural media forum. The famine affected destitute became a subject of creative art and it was used to build up broader sociocultural protest, on the one hand against degrading social norms and values, and, on the other hand, it was used for broader political gains. Bijan Bhattacharya's *Navanna* acquired an iconic status in popular protests led by actors of the Indian Peoples Theatre Association.[90]

In the post-Independence period also health inequality and the apathetic attitude of the state towards health has raised protests movements in Calcutta at different times. The issue acquired greatest intensity as well as a new dimension on the question of refugee rehabilitation. The negligence of the refugee health appeared as a part of the economic deprivation and social degradation of the refugees and a generally apathetic attitude towards them. Naturally, when the refugees became serious political critics of the government, health issue as an integral part of sustainable living contributed to their political discourse and criticism of governance. Protest agitations on health issues continued, especially the deteriorating conditions of the hospitals and breakdown of the government healthcare system. It reached a climax when protest movements from among the junior doctors across the state from the late 70s and early 80s of twentieth century raised slogans 'health is not a matter of charity, right to health is my fundamental right', and it is with that demand that Calcutta looks to a future of equitable distribution of healthcare and equal health rights for all.

Notes

1. Partho Datta, *Planning the City: Urbanization and Reform in Calcutta, c.1800–c.1940*, New Delhi: Tulika, 2012.
2. Pratik Chakrabarti, *Materials and Medicine: Trade, Conquest and Therapeutics in the Eighteenth Century*, Manchester: Manchester University Press, 2010, p. 92.
3. James Ranald Martin, *Notes on the Medical Topography of Calcutta*, Calcutta: Bengal Military Orphan Press, 1837, p. 9.
4. Alexander Hamilton, 'A New Account of the East Indies'; cited in, P.T. Nair, *Calcutta in the 18th Century: Impressions of Travellers*, Calcutta: Firma KLM, 1984, pp. 4–5.
5. Ibid.
6. Martin, *Notes on the Medical Topography of Calcutta*, p. 17.
7. Minutes of the Governor-General Marquis of Wellesley on the Importance of Calcutta, 16 June 1803, *Report of the Fever Hospital Committee*, Appendix F, p. 301 (West Bengal State Archives).
8. Datta, *Planning the City*, p. 18.
9. Ibid., p. 19. See also, Dipesh Chakrabarty, 'Open Space/Public Space: Garbage, Modernity and India', *South Asia: Journal of South Asian Studies*, vol. 14, no. 1, 1991, pp. 16–28.
10. S.W. Goode, *Municipal Calcutta: Its Institutions in their Origin and Growth, Calcutta*, Calcutta: Corporation of Calcutta, 1916, p. 10.
11. John Clarke, *Observations on the Diseases on Long Voyages to Hot Countries and Particularly on those Which Prevail in the East Indies, 1773*; cited in Mark Harrison, *Climates and Constitution: Health, Race and British Imperialism in India, 1600-1850*, New Delhi: Oxford University Press, 1999, p. 63.

12. *Report of the Fever Hospital Committee.*

13. Ibid.

14. Muttylall Seal, a wealthy businessman had donated a piece of land near Medical College for the construction of the Fever Hospital. See, Narendranath Laha, *Subarnabanik Katha O Kirti*, vol. 1, Calcutta: Oriental Press Limited, 1910, p. 29.

15. Kabita Ray, *History of Public Health: Colonial Bengal 1921-1947*, Calcutta: K.P. Bagchi, 1998, pp. 17–18.

16. *Kalikatar Cholera o Kaler Jal* ('Cholera in Calcutta and Tap Water'), *Cikitsa Sammilani*, vol. 5, BS 1295, p. 155.

17. Cited in, Roy, *History of Public Health.*

18. Report on Plague in Calcutta 1898, 1899–1900 up to 30 June 1900–1, W.R. Bright National Library, Calcutta.

19. *Report of the Sanitary Reorganisation Committee;* cited in, Ray, *History of Public Health*, p. 9.

20. Reports on the Municipal Administration of Calcutta (RMAC) for the year 1951–2, vol. 1, pt. III: Health Officer's Report, Calcutta Corporation, p. 80. (National Library, Kolkata.)

21. For much of the nineteenth century, most European and American physicians believed cholera was a locally produced miasmatic disease—an illness brought about by direct exposure to the products of filth and decay. J. Johnson, J. Fayrer, R. Martine and many others believed in this notion. According to them, the disease was caused by the operation of the climate on the soil, which provides right condition for the germination of the cholera 'seed'. It was a common assumption that those who were engaged in morally and physically intemperate behaviour, or who had inferior cultural practices were more likely to get cholera, when exposed to these miasmas and environmental conditions. Observations that the poor, who lived in densely populated urban slums, suffered from cholera in greater numbers than the rich, who were much differently housed, were used as evidence for this assertion. There were also other theories on the causes of the outbreak of cholera. For example, J. Kennedy believed that the disease was caused by contagion. Finally, J. Snow put forward the theory that cholera was a water-borne disease. In the end Snow's theory ultimately proved valid; cited in, Mark Harrison, *Public Health in British India: Anglo-Indian Preventive Medicine, 1859-1914*, New Delhi: Cambridge University Press, 1994, p. 99.

22. Ibid., p. 100.

23. Ibid., p. 116.

24. RMAC, 1943–4, p. 11.

25. RMAC, 1951–2, p. 80.

26. For details see, Sanjoy Bhattacharya et al., eds., *Fractured States: Smallpox, Public Health and Vaccination Policy in British India, 1800-1947*, Hyderabad: Orient Longman, 2005, pp. 6–7.

27. Ibid.
28. Ray, *History of Public Health.* p. 59.
29. Ibid., p. 157.
30. Ibid., p. 159.
31. Ibid., p. 163.
32. Kohei Wakimura, 'Malaria Control, Rural Health and Urban Health: Social Determinants of Health from the Perspective of Socio-Economic History', in *Social Determinants of Health Assessing Theory, Policy and Practice*, ed. Sanjay Bhattacharya et al., New Delhi: Orient BlackSwan, 2010, p. 67.
33. Sir R. Christopher and Charles A. Bently, 'The Human Factor: An Extension of Our Knowledge Regarding the Epidemiology of Malaria Disease', in *Transactions of Bombay Medical Congress*, ed. W.E. Jennings, 1909; cited in, Wakimura, 'Malaria Control, Rural Health and Urban Health', p. 67.
34. *Ananda Bazar Patrika*, 16 March 1937, p. 12; cited in, Ray, *History of Public Health*, p. 99.
35. RMAC, 1951–2, p. 80.
36. RMAC, 1944–5, p. 16.
37. M.U. Ahmad, *Report of the Health Officer of Calcutta (RHOC)* for the year 1943–4, Calcutta: Corporation Press, p. 2. (National Library, Kolkata.)
38. Ray, *History of Public Health*, p. 106.
39. Ibid.
40. RMAC, 1940–1, p. 47.
41. RMAC, 1951–2, p. 61.
42. RMAC, 1955–6, p. 59.
43. Mark Harrison, *Contagion: How Commerce Has Spread Disease*, New Haven: Yale University Press, 2012, p. xiii.
44. RMAC, 1953–4, p. 59.
45. RMAC, 1959–60, p. 59.
46. Wakimura, 'Malaria Control, Rural Health and Urban Health', p. 70.
47. RMAC, 1965–6, p. 2.
48. To know in detail about the debate on contagious nature of tuberculosis, see, Bikramaditya Kumar Choudhary, 'Colonial Policies and Spread of Tuberculosis: An Enquiry in British India (1890-1940)', *Journal of Health and Development*, vol. 4, nos. 1–4, 2008; Bikramaditya Kumar Choudhary, 'Vulnerability of Women to Bacillus: Myths and Reality in India, 1890–1950', in *Medical Encounters in British India*, ed. Deepak Kumar and Raj Sekhar Basu, New Delhi: Oxford University Press, 2013, pp. 68–70.
49. Choudhary, 'Vulnerability of Women to Bacillus', p. 69.
50. Home/Medical—A/No. 96-103/ October 1901, NAI [National Archives of India], New Delhi. Also cited in, Choudhry, 'Colonial Policies and Spread of Tuberculosis'.
51. *RHOC*, 1946–7, p. 21.

52. RMAC, 1951–2, p. 80.
53. Ray, *History of Public Health*, p. 76.
54. File No. Medl 3c-9 of 1942, proceedings B67-70, September 1944: also cited in, Ray, *History of Public Health,* p. 78.
55. *Bengal Public Health Report*, 1929–47.
56. For a detail account, see, Ray, *History of Public Health*, pp. 81–5.
57. Ibid., p. 84.
58. Paul Greenough, 'Asian Intra-household Survival Logics: The "Shen Te" and "Shui Ta" Options', in *History of the Social Determinants of Health: Global Histories, Contemporary Debates*, ed. Harold J. Cook et al., Hyderabad: Orient BlackSwan, 2009, p. 27.
59. Janam Mukherjee, 'Japan Attacks', in *Calcutta: The Stormy Decades*, ed. Tanika Sarkar and Sekhar Bandyopadhyay, New Delhi: Social Science Press, 2015, pp. 99–101.
60. *RHOC*, 1943–4, p. 1.
61. Paul R. Greenough, *Prosperity and Misery in Modern Bengal: The Famine of 1943–1944*, New York: Oxford University Press, 1982, pp. 231–2.
62. Tarakchandra Das, *Bengal Famine (1943) as Revealed in a Survey of the Destitutes in Calcutta*, Calcutta: University of Calcutta, 1949, p. 8; recalled in, Greenough, *Prosperity and Misery in Modern Bengal.*
63. Mukherjee, 'Japan Attacks', p. 108.
64. 5/46/46-Poll (I) NAI, Porter, Home Dept., India to Private Secy., 30 October 1946, para 3; R/3/2/56, IOR, F. No. 8, Coll-No. IB, IOR; cited in, Suranjan Das, *Communal Riots in Bengal 1905–1947*, New Delhi: Oxford University Press, 1991, p. 171.
65. Hindustan Standard [Reel No. 044], 20 August 1946, National Library, Kolkata.
66. 'More Refugees Die At Sealdah', *The Times of India*, 24 July 1950, p. 9.
67. 'Refugee Children's Plight: Shri Dalmia Visits Calcutta Camps', *The Times of India*, 9 August 1950, p. 1.
68. Anil Sinha, *Pashchimbange Udbastu Upanibesh*, Kolkata: Book Club, 1995; and Saroj Chakrabarti, *With Dr. B.C. Roy and Other Chief Ministers (A Record up to 1962)*, Kolkata, 1974.
69. Sinha, *Pashchimbange Udbastu Upanibesh.*
70. 'Epidemics in Refugee Colonies in Calcutta: Dalmia Relief Committee's Humane Work', *The Times of India*, 16 June 1950, p. 7.
71. Sekhar Bandyopadhyay, *Decolonization in South Asia: Meanings of Freedom in Post-independence West Bengal, 1947-52*, London: Routledge, 2009, pp. 31–2.
72. Ibid., p. 31.
73. Ibid.
74. Indubaran Ganguly, *Colonysmriti*, vol. I (1948–54), Kolkata: Ganguly, 1997.

75. Ray, *History of Public Health*, p. 229.
76. Ibid.
77. Manimanjari Mitra, *Calcutta in the 20th Century: An Urban Disaster*, Calcutta: Asiatic Book Agency, 1990, p. 184.
78. Ibid.
79. Ibid., p. 185.
80. See, Calcutta Metropolitan Planning Organization: Basic Development Plan, 1966; cited in, Mitra, *Calcutta in the 20th Century*, p. 187.
81. Ibid., pp. 187–8.
82. Ibid., p. 189.
83. Calcutta Corporation Investigation Commission (CCIC) Reports, 1948–9, p. 124; cited in, Mitra, *Calcutta in the 20th Century*, pp. 189–90.
84. CCIC, 1948–9, Final Report, vol. II, pt. II, 326 (Memorandum no. 172); cited in, Mitra, *Calcutta in the 20th Century*, p. 191.
85. Ibid.
86. Indian Chamber of Commerce, Annual Report, 1941, p. 203; cited in, Mitra, *Calcutta in 20th Century*, p. 192.
87. CCIC, 1948–9; cited in, Mitra, *Calcutta in the 20th Century*, p. 193.
88. 'On the 5th of December, 1870, by a conveyance the Secretary of State of India in Council conveyed about 200 Bighas of land commonly known as Dhapa to the Justice of Peace for the town of Calcutta for conservancy of the City of Calcutta. In or about 1880 the said Dhapa Dumping Ground was thereafter leased out to Bhabanath Sen, the predecessor-in-interest of the Sens, the respondent to the present appeal, in consideration of the lessees agreeing to pay the rent partly in cash and partly by doing work of unloading refuse wagons at their own costs and expenses. Since thereafter the Sens and their predecessors-in-interest were holding a substantial portion of the said Dhapa land popularly known as "Dhapa Square Mile" as lessees under the Corporation of Calcutta. On the 29th of July, 1909, the lease was renewed for a further period of 22 years. On the 12th of February, 1954 the West Bengal Estates Acquisition Act, 1953 came into force. Thereafter notice was served by the State of West Bengal on the Corporation of Calcutta and the Sens alleging that the said Dhapa land had been vested in the State of West Bengal under the said Act and as such all rents due from and payable by the occupiers of the land should be paid to the State of West Bengal. In 1959 this notice was challenged by the Sens and the Corporation of Calcutta in two separate applications under Article 226 of the Constitution, being C.R. Nos. 1027 and 1132 of 1959 in the Calcutta High Court'; The Corporation Of Calcutta And . . . vs Dhirendra Nath Sen And Ors. on 16 March 1973, see https://indiankanoon.org/doc/4321/, accessed 12 June 2016.

89. Sumit Sarkar, 'The City Imagined: Calcutta of the Nineteenth and the Early Twentieth Centuries', in *Writing Social History*, New Delhi: Oxford University Press, 1997, p. 170.

90. Avirup Sinha, 'Urban Development, Public Health, Sanitation: A Case Study of Calcutta and its Neighbourhood between 1939 and 1966', unpublished M.Phil. thesis, University of Calcutta, 2016.

10

KOLKATA DURING THE NAXALITE MOVEMENT, 1965–1972

From the Pen of a Participant-Observer

AMIT BHATTACHARYYA

The date was 20 November 1974. I was standing at the Ghaspani bus stand under district Kohima in Nagaland to take a bus to return to Dimapur. The road connects Kohima with Dimapur. On one side of the road, there is a camp of the Assam Rifles armed forces and on both sides there are villages on the hills. I had spent the last night in the country house of Thehiele Angami in Medziphema village on top of the hill. I noticed a fat police officer of the nearby Ghaspani police station approaching me with a constable. I was taken to the police station popularly known as *phanri* (camp) and then taken by a police jeep to Dimapur police station and pushed inside the lock up. I was arrested under the Maintenance of Internal Security Act (MISA) on the charges of being an 'extremist' and also of meeting members of the Naga Federal Government, a political organization declared unlawful by the Government of India. A new phase in my life began—in prison. Although I was influenced by the Naxalite ideology after I joined Presidency College as a History student, I do not claim to have done much political activism. However, my days in prison were truly a turning point in my life and when I look back at those stormy days, I consider myself fortunate. The following account is based partly on my personal experiences of the movement and partly on those of many others. I have quoted sources whenever needed; when it is not given, that should be considered to be based on my own experience.

The Naxalite/Maoist movement in India is one of the longest surviving Communist revolutionary movements in the history of the world. Born in 1967 in a village called Naxalbari, it has been able to withstand State brutality and rise like a phoenix from the ashes time and again. The fact that this movement has been continuing for five decades and goes on developing implies the existence of some deep-rooted socio-economic needs that the existing system has failed to satisfy. Today, every protest is being identified with 'Maoism', every dissident voice is being branded by the powers-that-be and sections of the corporate media as 'Maoist'. 'Shob Protibadi Maobadi hote Baadhyo' (All protesters are bound to be Maoists), thus sang Kabir Suman in one of his memorable songs. 'Maoism' in India has, for good or bad, been identified with the fight for dignity, justice, and human values. In this essay, I propose to deal with the period 1965–72 with the focus mainly, not totally, on the city of Kolkata in West Bengal.

Let us begin by narrating very briefly what happened in Naxalbari. Naxalbari is the name of a village in the Darjeeling district of north Bengal. The area that went by that name covers three to four police stations lying in the foothills of the Himalayas where tea plantations abound. There Charu Mazumdar, following the path charted by Mao Tse-tung, organized the tea-plantation workers and peasants against feudal forces; they formed peasant committees and revolted against the 'revisionist' Communist Party of India (Marxist) leadership who had renounced the path of armed revolution and accepted the parliamentary path as the only path leading to socialism. Eight articles—known as the 'Eight Documents'—that he wrote during 1965–7 formed the ideological basis of the Naxalbari movement. On 24 May 1967, a large police force, under the newly-formed United Front West Bengal government led by CPI(M), CPI, Bangla Congress, and others, tried to enter a village fighting for its rights. The peasants resisted with bows and arrows. A police officer was hit by arrows to which he succumbed later. The other policemen went back only to return the next day, i.e. 25 May with more men. They fired on a gathering of women when the menfolk were away and killed eleven persons, including eight women and two babies. The rebellion was crushed within a short time in the place of its birth. However, the message spread far and wide and raised waves of struggle—both in ideological and practical fields—throughout the country. That is how the Naxalbari movement—also known as Terai movement—began.

The Naxalbari movement sought to answer certain crucial questions regarding the strategy of the Indian revolution. It upheld the Marxist theory that 'force is the midwife of the old society pregnant with a new one'. It rejected the peaceful, parliamentary path to socialism and exposed the revisionist theory of 'peaceful transition' that had dominated the Indian communist movement. Second, guided by Mao Tse-tung thought, Charu Mazumdar held that the Indian revolution would be a protracted one. Because of uneven development—economic, social, and political—power could not be seized through urban insurrections, but only through protracted people's war, by creating liberated bases in the countryside where objective and subjective conditions were more favourable than elsewhere and by gradually expanding those bases towards the seizure of power throughout the country. Third, he also emphasized the role of the peasantry in the Indian revolution, the main content of which would be agrarian revolution, and pointed out that under the leadership of the working class the peasantry would be the main force of the revolution. He also stressed that the petty bourgeois intelligentsia could play a revolutionary role by integrating themselves with the toiling masses.

I propose to deal with the ground reality of Kolkata in the late 1960s and early 1970s in the following stages:

Pre-Naxalbari Phase

Immediately before and during the Naxalbari revolt, waves of anti-establishment struggle lashed West Bengal. The waves began rising early in 1966 and swelled to an unprecedented height in 1970–1 and then began to recede. Without belittling the role of the revolutionaries in colonial India, one can assert that West Bengal had never before seen such tempestuous struggles and has not seen since—it was like storming the gates of heaven with death-defying heroism and self-sacrifice.

The year 1966 witnessed acute food scarcity everywhere, while hoarders and black marketeers and political patrons waxed fat out of the toil and suffering of the masses. The rationing system collapsed everywhere and scarcity of food led to the spiralling of prices. Added to these was the failure of land reforms, all leading to an explosive situation. What began as economic struggles turned swiftly into political ones. Many sections of the people, workers and peasants, youth and students, office employees, teachers, and others were drawn into the struggles. Strikes and even general strikes and *hartals* (shutdowns), attacks on government offices, factories, schools and colleges, laboratories, and clashes with the police and the military were regular features in Kolkata and elsewhere. Released from prison on the crest of a food movement, in February and March 1966, the CPI(M) leaders helped the Congress government to bring people's rebellion under control. While mouthing militant slogans, they sought to divert all the accumulated anger of the people along a safe channel—the battle for the ballot box, due to take place in 1967. In early 1967, a United Front ministry comprising CPI(M), CPI, Bangla Congress, etc., came to power by replacing the Congress ministry.

The United Front ministry stepped into the shoes of the Congress government early in 1967. But people's struggles in both rural and urban areas continued to move forward. Between March and September 1967, according to one report, 1,20,000 workers lost their jobs in West Bengal and 269 mills and factories were under lockout.[1] When strikes as weapons became blunt, workers invented a new weapon—that of *gherao*—to enforce their demands. Baton charges by the police and even firings on demonstrating workers were frequent. Side by side, youth and students waged militant movements in support of their sectional demands as also over national issues. In November 1967, the United Front ministry was replaced by the Congress ministry and the new government arrested and imprisoned 5,000 political workers including Charu Mazumdar.

The food movement of 1966 in Kolkata and suburbs was a watershed that brought large sections of youth and students under the banner of Bangiya Pradeshik Chhatra Federation (Bengal Provincial Students' Federation/BPSF), a students' organization affiliated to the CPI(M). It was a period of intellectual awakening among the middle-class intelligentsia. Several pertinent questions were raised from the students and youth. What is revolution? Is the CPI(M) a revolutionary party? Do they deceive the people? What was the nature of the India-China War of 1962 from which the CPI got split up and the CPI(M) was born? What was the role of the CPI and the CPI(M) in the people's struggles? Why was the CPI split up into two parties? Was it due to ideological differences, or to personal enmity or organizational reasons? What was the character of the Chinese revolution? Many of those student activists were still attached to the CPI(M). Some among them were Saibal Mitra, Nirmal Brahmachari, Asim Chatterjee, Ranabir Samaddar, Biplab Halim, Azizul Haque, Dipanjan Roy Choudhury, Utpalendu Chakraborty, Koushik Banerjee, Ashu Mazumdar, and Ranajoy Karlekar.

The young generation was influenced by new dramas that were being enacted by various cultural troupes. One of those creations was the play *Kallol* (Sound of the Waves) made by the actor-director, Utpal Dutt based on the mutiny of the Royal Indian Navy in 1946 in Bombay. The set design, bringing a whole warship on stage, and the stunning lighting by Tapas Sen was something never seen before. *Kallol* conveyed the message that freedom won by non-violence was a sham; what was real was the bloodshed by martyrs like Rani of Jhansi, Kshudiram, Bhagat Singh, Surya Sen, and Subhas Chandra Bose and his Indian National Army. The play depicted the tale of the warship Khyber, where the mutiny had taken place and how its sailors had shed blood. The message was that the days of rebellion were not over; like Sardul, the leader of the mutiny whose role was played by Sekhar Chattopadhyay, there would be more revolutionaries in the days to come who would burst into flames. To Abhijit Das, an engineering student of Jadavpur University, the violent revelation of a repressive state shattered the conventional image of a free country and *Kallol* 'inspired a sense of restlessness within us—something needed to be done about a society that had failed us'.[2]

Questions such as these were discussed not only within BPSF but among individuals as also other groups such as *Chinta* (Thoughts) and literary forums such as *Nandan*, *Parichay*, etc. Other intellectuals such as teachers, artists, singers, dramatists, and young writers also joined. Among others who joined were also workers. Workers from the industrial zones of Behala, Taratala, and Dum Dum in Kolkata proper as also greater Kolkata and Uttarpara in district Hooghly, Durgapur, Asansol, and Chittaranjan in district Burdwan took part in those discussions.[3] Contact was established with various drama groups spread over Kolkata and other districts of West Bengal to which such leading personalities as Utpal Dutt, Nirmal Ghosh, Sekhar Chattopadhyaya, Siraj Choudhury, and Kali Roy Choudhury, among others, were attached. Many old practices and ideas were questioned. The CPI(M) leadership was discredited; too much concentration on trade union activities, devoid of any preparation for underground political activity towards the seizure of political power after the overthrow of the existing exploitative system, was branded as 'revisionism'. What was the class character of the Indian bourgeoisie? Was it 'national', or 'comprador'? Considerable brainstorming was done over such questions. Among those who began to think in terms of a revolutionary transformation of the Indian society there were two distinct strands. One group thought in terms of a Socialist Revolution along the Soviet path (known as 'SR group'), while the other thought in terms of a People's Democratic Revolution (known as 'PDR group') or New Democratic Revolution that advocated the Chinese path of in agrarian revolution, although none of these groups, in that formative period, had any clear conception of the stages, composition of leadership and the main forces of the revolution.

In the course of mutual exchange of ideas over several issues, the point that came up again and again was the presence of a group in north Bengal that believed in Mao Tse-tung's ideology and the Chinese path of agrarian revolution in India. That group was a group of Communist activists who were members of the CPI(M) and were led by Charu Mazumdar. Mazumdar, even before Naxalbari, became known as a theoretician and dialectical-materialist. There was an open cultural group in Siliguri town in north Bengal known as 'Katha O Kalam' (The Speech and the Pen) with which Charu Mazumdar himself was associated. The CPI(M) leadership were very critical about the presence of an anti-Party clique within the organization and branded it as 'extremist', 'ultra-revolutionary'.

They were, not surprisingly, quite malicious towards Mazumdar.

There was from then on a regular flow of Chinese publications in the Kolkata market—periodicals, Mao's writings, and other books were available in select book shops such as Radical Book Club and New Book Centre in the College Street area of central Kolkata. In Kolkata and elsewhere, radical students carried on ideological struggles among fellow students against the 'revisionist' practices of the CPI and the CPI(M). They started publishing a magazine, *Chhatra Fouz* (Student Army) as their mouthpiece from about the end of 1966. They also played an important role in the food movement in West Bengal in 1966. An All India Students Committee for Struggle was formed. In Kolkata, another group of students known as 'Presidency Consolidation', reacting violently against certain steps taken by the Presidency College authority, also emerged.

What is evident is that during that pre-Naxalbari formative period of intellectual and political ferment, a certain unity in thinking had been developing among parts of the new generation of intellectuals, youth, students, and working people in Kolkata, Siliguri, and elsewhere. The spark, however, was ignited not in the city, but in the village. It was the spark at Naxalbari that was hailed as a 'spring thunder' by the Communist Party of China and ushered in a long, protracted, and unfinished battle for a revolutionary transformation of India in the days to come.

Post-Naxalbari Phase (1967–April 1969)

Thus, when 'a peal of Spring Thunder crashed over' Naxalbari, the new radical youth in other parts of West Bengal could realize that it was a handiwork of people believing in the same path. One leaflet known as 'Lal Leaflet' (Red Leaflet) issued on behalf of the Siliguri Subdivision Committee was widely circulated in Kolkata. Wallings hailing the Naxalbari peasant struggle such as 'Naxalbari Zindabad' (Long Live Naxalbari) in the name of the CPI(M) decorated the walls of the city. As there was till then no forum, slogans were given in that early phase in the name of the CPI(M).

Some of the Communist revolutionaries outside the Darjeeling district responded immediately to the call of Naxalbari, the call of an armed agrarian revolution. One of the first responses to the call came from Sushital Roy Choudhuri, a member of the West Bengal State Committee of the CPI(M), who went to Siliguri and had discussions with Charu Mazumdar. After his return, a new forum, the Naxalbari O Krishak Sangram Sahayak Committee (Committee in Aid of Naxalbari and Peasant Struggles) was formed on 14 June 1967 at a Convention held in Rammohan Library Hall in north Kolkata. Promode Sengupta was elected president of the committee, Sushital Roy Chowdhary and Satyananda Bhattacharya were vice presidents and Parimal Dasgupta the secretary.[4] This committee tried to rally public opinion in support of the Naxalbari struggle and to propagate the politics of an armed agrarian revolution. It organized mass rallies in many parts of the city of Kolkata, held a workers' convention and a food convention when there was an acute scarcity of food; it carried on extensive propaganda against the policies of the United Front government and the repression let loose by it against the people in Naxalbari.

The first public meeting of the Sahayak Committee, in all probability, was held in Beliaghata Bhatiakhana Field in east Kolkata on 8 July 1967. It was addressed by Sushital Roy Chowdhary, Parimal Dasgupta, Saibal Mitra, and others.[5] It was followed by a central gathering in support of Naxalbari and peasant struggle in Subodh Mallick Square in central Kolkata on 18 July.[6] A cultural forum called 'Kolkata Juva O Gana-Shilpi Sanstha' (Kolkata Youth and People's Artists' Forum) presented a drama as part of the solidarity programme. Incidentally, this was the first of a series of cultural performances that were to take place in many parts of the city and beyond.[7] Later on, branches of the Sahayak Committee were set up in other areas too.

On 11 November 1967, a big rally was held on the Shahid Minar Maidan in Kolkata under the auspices of the Sahayak Committee. The last of the speakers was the ailing Charu Mazumdar who spoke only a few words. In November 1967, the members of the Sahayak Committee met and formed the All India Coordination Committee of Revolutionaries (AICCR) in the CPI(M) which was renamed All India Coordination Committee of Communist Revolutionaries (AICCCR) in May 1968.

Who responded to the call of revolution and joined the new stream? First to respond and join were sections of the radical elements within the CPI(M) who were totally frustrated with the policy of the CPI(M) realizing that the new party born in 1964 was no different from the CPI. Committee after committee, and sometimes members of different CPI(M) committees in West Bengal as also in other states joined the revolutionary forces. Besides these, those among the new youth and students, who did not have any previous political background, also joined the cause. They had a considerable following and their number grew by leaps and bounds due to intensification of socio-economic crisis and the intellectual ferment.

Meetings and processions in solidarity with the people's struggles in countries such as Vietnam also formed important aspects of the youth struggles in the months following the Naxalbari uprising. On the occasion of the Vietnam Day on 20 July, youth and students of four central student organizations took out a big procession covering parts of central Kolkata, demonstrated in front of the American Embassy and burnt an effigy of US President Lindon B. Johnson. At important road junctions, there were public speeches. Among those who made speeches were Nirmal Brahmachari, Nemai Karan, Ashim Chatterjee, and Amal Sanyal. On the same day, members of a local club Agnibina, demonstrated in front of the American Institute of Indian Studies and with the help of a bamboo ladder blackened the placard of the American centre and pasted a poster of Ho Chi-Minh on it. On the road, in front of the said building, they put a giant flag of the Liberation Army of Vietnam.[8]

After Naxalbari, activists from Calcutta went to north Bengal to meet Charu Mazumdar, to get acquainted with him and to know what that historic movement was all about. Among those who got influenced was Utpal Dutt, the well-known director-cum-artist and intellectual. On his return to Kolkata, he met many people and expressed his respectful admiration for Mazumdar. Saibal Mitra, a student leader of that time, also did the same thing after returning from north Bengal. Bhaskar Nandy, a student leader from north at Bengal, came to Kolkata, spoke in different meetings and explained how Charu Mazumdar was different from other leaders. Charu Mazumdar was very much present in Calcutta then. A legend was thus born.

Efflorescence of Creativity

A new culture was born too. The Naxalite movement did away with old ideas and at the same time gave birth to new ideas. Those new ideas were manifested through various cultural mediums, such as songs, poems, dramas, short stories, novels, articles, historical studies, etc. Individual singers composed and sang songs that left a deep impression among people. The names of Dilip Bagchi, Shantanu Ghosh, and Ajit Pandey come readily to one's mind. Dilip Bagchi, a student of North Bengal University, Siliguri, wrote and composed an iconic song on 25 May 1967. The text read as follows:

> *O Naxal! Naxal! . . . Naxalbari!*
> *O Naxalbari Mother!*
> *From wounds on your breast,*
> *The blood that has been shed*
> *Peasants cry from their chest*
> *With Flags coloured Red!*[9]

After Naxalbari, Shantanu Ghosh composed a song and Ajit Pandey sang it. The song carried a historic import, influencing hundreds people. Its lyrics ran thus:

> *Tarai kande re,*
> *kande amar hiya,*
> *Naxalbarir mati kande Saptakanyar lagiya*
>
> (Terai cries,
> so does my heart,
> the soil of Naxalbari cries for her seven daughters)

The legend is that after listening to the song, Charu Mazumdar remarked, 'The peasants of Naxalbari have been crying for generations. But now, they have risen up from slumber; they are roaring.' So Shantanu Ghosh added new lines to it and Ajit Pandey sang:

> *Tarai garje re,*
> *garje amar hiya,*
> *Naxalbarir krishak garje kshamatar lagiya*[10]
>
> (Terai is roaring,
> so does my heart,
> the peasants of Naxalbari are now roaring for power).

Shantanu Ghosh was a good actor and associated with the theatre group of Utpal Dutt. There were other leading personalities in the field of music such as Suresh Biswas, Dilip Bagchi, Paresh Dhar, Bidyut Bhoumik, Koushik Bandyopadhyay, Siuli Guha, Ajoy Das, Meghnad. The present writer can recollect a line from one song by Suresh Biswas:

Moder haal dhorechhen Chairman,
danre Charu Mazumdar,
biplab tarani-boithha bai-o[11]

(The Chairman is sitting at the helm and steering the boat of Revolution, Charu Mazumdar is rowing it. Come let's all scull the oars).

A large number of poems were also penned along with a considerable number of plays written and staged. One can mention Utpal Dutt's *Teer* (Arrow) which was the first drama written and played on the Naxalbari peasant movement. There were many others such as Jochhon Dastidar's *Jibaner Joygane*, Indrajit Sen's productions based on various Peking Operas such as *Red Lantern*, *On the Docks*, *Shachiapang*, etc., Kali Prasad Roy Choudhury's dramas on peasant revolts such as *Azaan*,[12] Nirmal Ghosh's plays on 'going-to-the-village', to name only a few. Tapan Das, a student of the Bengali Department in Presidency College, wrote a number of plays under the pen name of 'Amal Roy'.

Those plays were performed on the stage under the banners of different drama groups which included Little Theatre Group, *Shilpi*-mon, Rupantari, Uttari Group Theatre, Lok-sanskriti Sangha, Mashaal, Sagnik, Hughli Gana-shilpi Sanstha, Bharatiya Gana-sanskriti Sangha, Bingsha Shatabdi, Katha O Kalam of Siliguri, etc. Charu Mazumdar himself was associated with Katha O Kalam. He, besides doing political activities, also taught dancing and was himself a good singer.[13]

Another aspect of the cultural awakening was the writing of short stories. We have, among many others, Utpalendu Chakraborty's 'Gram-e Chalo' (Go to the Village), Jayanta Joardar's 'Ebhabei Egoy' and also stories by Brajen Mazumdar, Siddhartha Saha, Srijan Sen, and Dipen Bandyopadhyay; the themes being sacrifice of martyrs, police repression, etc.[14] Such stories, songs, poems, articles, and reports of struggles were published in periodicals which came to be known as 'Little Magazines'. In course of time it was around these little magazines that small cultural forums made their appearance. These magazines had a pronounced radical character, were critical of state policies, and championed people's cause. It was this approach that made them popular. *Chinta, Deshabrati, Dakshin Desh, Liberation, Kalpurush, Aneek, Aabad, Krantikal, Bhitti, Chhatra Fouz, Saraswat, Katha O Kalam, Ghatana Prabaha,* and *Frontier* were among many that made their existence felt, in varying degrees, among the intellectuals, youth and students.

Let us consider just one issue of *Kalpurush* as an example. It contained ten articles and editorials.[15] The first one (editorial) captioned 'Struggle in Terai' hails the Naxalbari struggle and expresses solidarity with it. The second one entitled 'Turning the Pages of History', deals with the grave food crisis in West Bengal due to hoarding by black-marketeers and asserts that there is actually no remedy unless the present system is overthrown and a basic transformation in land relations is undertaken through an agrarian revolution. There is an article on the peasant movement for the seizure of land in Sonarpur in district 24-Parganas. Another article is on a critique of economic reforms in the Soviet Union.

Another magazine that reflected the new thoughts of the time is *Aneek*. One of its issues contained a selection of seventy-five poems and nine stories that had been published in its different numbers over the past ten years.[16] Its poems included 'Itihas-er Dak' (The Call of History) by Amit Roy Choudhury which is a call to arms along the path charted by Telangana, Kakdwip, and Naxalbari. Indu Saha in his poem 'Basanta Bidroha Ane' (The Spring Heralds Rebellion) highlights the poverty and suffering of the people and ridicules Indian Independence, CPI and CPI(M) brands of 'revisionism' and the pro-American role of the Indian ruling classes. Kamalesh Sen's 'Apni Bagher Bachha' (You are a Tiger Cub) is a satirical poem with the 'revisionists' as targets of attack. Dronacharya Ghosh's 'Amar Muktir Dak' (A Call to Liberation) conveys his dream of revolution among the workers and peasants. Nabarun Bhattacharya in his *Ei Mrityu Upatyaka Amar Desh Noy* (This Valley of Death is not my Country) assails the timidity of the middle class intellectuals in the face of state terror and vows that his poems will crash, like a flame, on the land from Terai to Sundarban.

Birendra Chatttopadhyay's 'Swadeshprem-er Dipto Mahimay' (In the Blazing Glory of Patriotism) ridicules the brutal face of the Indian ruling classes. Manoranjan Biswas in his 'Khunir Buk' (The Chest of the Killer) depicts the people's struggle in a rural setting and acclaims the people's heroes. Samir Roy in his 'Lal Santras Chai' (We want Red Terror) critiques revisionist practices and upholds Red Terror. Srijan Sen in his poem 'Thana Garod Theke: Ma-ke' (Letter to mother from the Police Lock-up) relates the gory details of police torture in the lock-up after arrest. It also upholds the high spirits of the revolutionaries and assures the mother that no degree of torture and intimidation would make them submit to the enemy. In the same number there are some short stories based on similar themes and showing similar spirit.

Those who wrote stories, sang songs, composed poems or were associated with different cultural forums were not just cultural workers. Some of them got involved in political work and went to the villages to integrate with the peasantry. To them, literature and other arts were tools for social change. To them, 'Art for art's sake' was meaningless. On the contrary, art seemed a weapon in the hands of the struggling people, to bring about social change. That was the spirit of the time. By then the word 'Naxalite' had been introduced into the English vocabulary and like 'Viet Kong' and 'Al Fatah' stood for justice.

Urban Movements

A number of radicals were arrested for their political beliefs and charged with sedition and other offences. In prison, they carried on hunger strikes demanding the status of political prisoner and other rights. Outside, movements had been initiated by the Communist revolutionaries for the release of political prisoners. On 15 August—the day of Indian Independence—while the CPI(M) hoisted the tri-colour flag in their party headquarters to celebrate the day and the Congressmen held meetings in the Maidan, the radicals organized a protest procession demanding the release of political prisoners. The slogans that they raised all through the 7–8 km. long path from Deshbandhu Park in north Kolkata to Dum Dum Jail were quite significant: 'Desh abhi tak bhukha hay, Yeh Azaadi jhuta hay' (As long as the people of the country are hungry, this independence is sham); 'Shashak shrenir duti front: Congress O Jukta Front' (The ruling classes have two fronts: Congress and United Front); 'Manush Jodi banchte chao, Naxalbarir path nao' (People, if you want to live, follow the path of Naxalbari); 'Biswa jure dichhe nara, Mao Tse-tung-er Chintadhara' (The whole world reverberates with the thoughts of Mao Tse-tung); 'Naxalbarir Lal Agun dike dike chhorie dao' (Spread the Red Fire of Naxalbari far and wide). Members of various workers unions joined the spirited procession at several points on the way. At the jail gate, the 'Abhijan' cultural group sang the International and the prisoners from inside also joined the chorus.[17] Many such militant processions raising similar demands took place in other places as well.

The year 1968 witnessed a series of the struggles of workers, office employees, and others against the government of the ruling classes. Almost four million central government employees, including postal, railway, and telecommunication workers, went on a token strike on 19 September 1968 all over India. About 1,20,000 workers were retrenched in West Bengal between March and September 1967.[18] The CPI(M) and the CPI leadership tried all means to paralyse the militant activities of the working class. Jyoti Basu, the then Deputy Chief Minister of the United Front government, remarked: 'We do not want strikes and lock-out. We seek an amicable settlement.'[19]

The all-round socio-economic crisis also hit the educated middle class hard. The number of applications from the educated unemployed in the live registers of the employment exchanges in India increased from 1,63,000 in 1953 to 9,17,000 by the end of 1966.[20] There were thousands more who did not care to register as they did not hope to get any job through the exchanges.

By then, an anti-imperialist mood gripped the people. When Robert McNamara, the then president of the World Bank, a former US Defence Secretary, condemned by people as the 'butcher of the Vietnamese people', landed at Kolkata on 21 November 1968, a mammoth anti-imperialist demonstration greeted him. There were massive protest demonstrations called by the Kolkata District Coordination Committee of the AICCCR, among others. Participants came from several colleges like Presidency, Bangabashi, Maulana Abul Kalam Azad, Gurudas, Vidyasagar, City,

Surendranath, St. Paul's, Scottish Church, Hooghly Mohsin, and St. Xavier's, all of them part of what was known as the 'Presidency Consolidation'. Anti-McNamara demonstrations in other places of the world had begun at the airports where he landed. As BPSF had already decided to demonstrate at the Kolkata airport, the radicals decided to march from the Calcutta University campus to the American Consulate on Chowringhee for a demonstration. The demonstration was held under the banner of 'Students and Youth Struggle Committee'. Some of the slogans that rented the air were as follows: 'Down with McNamara, the Yankee dog'; 'Long Live Chairman Mao'; 'Burn McNamara to death in the Red Flames of Naxalbari'; 'Red Salute to Nguyen Van Trois',[21] and many others. Scared, the West Bengal government airlifted him from the airport to the Kolkata Maidan, a place that was only a few yards away from the Governor's house, where he was staying.[22]

One of the main contributions of the Naxalbari leadership was the call given to the youth and students to go to the villages to integrate with peasants. Such calls were given time and again by Charu Mazumdar through his writings addressed mainly to the new generation, as the movement progressed. On 13 April 1969, a few days before the Communist Party of India (Marxist-Leninist) was formed, a convention of revolutionary students was held in south Kolkata. That was the first-ever state-level convention led by the AICCCR held in Kolkata. Delegates who spoke in the convention highlighted the need to organize youth and students in the towns and villages along revolutionary political lines, study Chairman Mao's thoughts and get involved in the class struggle immediately. As a follow-up to the convention, a public meeting was held next day at Subodh Mallik Square followed by a procession towards the Soviet Consulate and the American Information Center and demonstrations in front of both the centres.[23]

From the Formation of the CPI(ML)
in April 1969 to 1972

The CPI(ML) was formed on 22 April 1969 at a hotel in central Kolkata at a meeting of the AICCCR. After the formation of the new party, the AICCCR dissolved itself. The declaration of its birth was made on 1 May 1969 in the Kolkata Maidan by Kanu Sanyal.

Mazumdar and some others were not present on that day. After that the party went underground.

The formation of a revolutionary party signalled the beginning of a new phase, most tumultuous and bloody phase in the Communist revolutionary movement in India. During that phase, the CPI(ML), led by Charu Mazumdar, withdrew from mass, legal organizations and open mass movements and concentrated on forming secret guerrilla units and adopted the policy of annihilation of class enemies in the countryside and also police personnel and others who came to the latter's defence. The aim was to destroy feudal power and establish revolutionary committees led by landless peasants as organs of people's power. This battle of annihilation of class enemies spread to Kolkata and district towns thereby initiating a battle for area domination—the capture of *paras* or localities. Various areas of the countryside in different states became storm centres of agrarian revolutionary struggles. They got a lot of popular sympathy and support.

The main centres of struggle in West Bengal were, besides parts of north Bengal, Debra-Gopiballavpur region in undivided Medinipur and large parts of district Birbhum, although 'annihilation of class enemies' took place in various other places in the state. This movement, or rather the peak period of it, was short-lived, from late 1969 to early 1971. Appeals were made time and again to the youths and students, by the leadership to go to the villages and integrate themselves with the peasantry. Charu Mazumdar gave a historic call in August 1969 to the youths and students to leave their homes and go the villages to integrate with the peasantry and become declassed. Following the call some of them left their homes and never returned.[24] This call spread far and wide and struck root. In fact, the impact on students and youths was considerable. Revolutionary minded students left their schools, colleges, and universities; went to the villages to disseminate revolutionary politics, integrate with the masses; and organize the peasantry to get rid of the 'man-eating system'.

However, this had to be a long-drawn process—leading groups going to a village, seeking to mix with the people to be one of them, gaining their trust and confidence, and then getting shelter in their homes. Once peasants are convinced about the necessity of their mission and consider it their own they join the cause and, thus, a mass base is created. The process is painful and time consuming. The middle-class urban cadre is confronted with a new reality totally different from that in which he was reared; he has to fight against great adversity and also against himself. Moreover, shelters are not readily available; these are to be created. Under such circumstances, what would the young generation cherishing a revolutionary change do? Add to this the notion of quick victory as is projected by Charu Mazumdar in such articles as 'Make the '70s the Decade of Liberation', or his statement, 'When I talk of the decade of the seventies, I cannot think beyond 1975'. It was from early 1970 that the Naxalite movement along with annihilations became an urban affair as well, aimed at the capture of areas spread over the city of Kolkata and also elsewhere. This development was peculiar to West Bengal and not to other states.

Annihilation of Class Enemies

When did the annihilation of class enemies commence? And where was it? The new phase of struggle began in November 1968 in the Srikakulam district of Andhra Pradesh and the guerrilla actions against select class enemies were backed by other actions, e.g. confiscation of property.[25]

When did the first action in West Bengal occur? *Deshabrati* published a report of the killing of an oppressive *jotedar* at the hands of the guerrillas in the Kharibari area of Naxalbari (a report originally published in a national daily).[26] That action seems to have taken place either in late December 1968 or early January 1969 and one of the first carried out by the secret guerrilla squads before the revolutionary party was born.

In West Bengal, the formation of guerrilla squads generally began in the latter part of 1969. The first instance of annihilation of oppressive feudal elements after the formation of the CPI(ML) was that of an oppressive usurer-cum-*jotedar* in village Dharampur under Gopiballavpur police station area in the then undivided Medinipur district.[27] That action took place on 2 September 1969. It is notable that unlike the previous instance where the death of a *jotedar* in Kharibari was described as *nihato* (killed), here in Gopiballavpur, the death of a moneylender-cum-*jotedar* was described as *khatam* (annihilated in Urdu). Henceforth, the word *khatam* was introduced into the Bengali vocabulary and used to describe such actions since then.

Party Organization

Besides the Central Committee, other committees were formed at state, district, area, and border levels. These committees, quite naturally, were set up in the new phase. The salient features of the earlier phase were ideological discussion and struggle, expression of new thoughts through new periodicals; in fact, the Naxalbari struggle became one of the most important topics of discussion in the *para*s, at street corner gatherings, coffee houses, and roadside tea stalls, at homes and campuses—everywhere. Besides Naxalbari, other topics included in discussions were the Cultural Revolution in China and the Vietnamese people's historic national liberation war against American aggression.

The CPI(M) as a party was breaking up; people were coming up in support of Naxalbari and armed agrarian revolution. Sections of the youth and students who did not have any previous association with politics were drawn to the new movement. So many processions took place in different localities. There were instances of intellectuals forming separate revolutionary groups, but joining the CPI(ML) after its formation. One thing is clear. In the earlier phase, there was hardly any dependence on firearms. People were everything then. Later, when the CPI(M) started using weapons such as bombs, pistols, and guns against the radicals, the revolutionaries were forced to use firearms too.

The earliest instance of physical clash between the CPI(M) cadres and the dissidents took place in Kolkata on 28 June 1967 which, according to Sumanta Banerjee, 'was to be a prelude to one of the bloodiest chapters of fratricide in the history of the Indian Communist movement'.[28] It occurred over the occupation of the office of *Desh-Hitaishi*, the CPI(M)'s Bengali weekly which, during that transitional phase, was under the control of Sushital Roy Chowdhary, who had been supporting Naxalbari through its articles. The CPI(M) cadres in large numbers attacked the dissidents and captured it because of their numerical superiority. The attack on the Naxalite sympathizers was started by those who could not combat them politically. The most common method was to enter the homes of the Naxalites, beat them, and intimidate them and their parents with disastrous consequences unless they desisted from going the Naxalbari way. Amal Bhattacharya, a schoolteacher of Hindu Vidyapeeth, Baguiati and Naxalite sympathizer, was detained in his own school for hours together by his own teacher-colleagues affiliated to the CPI(M); he was later freed by his own students.[29] The CPI(M) activists were emboldened to engage in such acts because, by then, the CPI(M) was in power in West Bengal and so the police force was under their control. On 10 April 1969, a protest procession organized by the Dum Dum Committee of the AICCCR against the murder of workers was fired upon by the CPI(M) in Belgharia. Next day, Shobhon Chakraborty, a school student, was seriously injured by CPI(M) goons. Such attacks followed at regular intervals.[30] In the Dum Dum area, Kanak Adhikari, a Naxalite sympathizer and teacher of Kamala Girls' High School in Dum Dum, was killed by the CPI(M) and in retaliation, Ananta Dutta, a local CPI(M) leader, was killed by the Naxalites. This was how clashes began in Dum Dum. At a time when Naxalite youths were being butchered by the police and paramilitary forces in Kolkata and districts, Promod Dasgupta, a top CPI(M) leader instigated the police by saying, 'Why are the Naxalites not being shot? Are contraceptives affixed to police bullets?'

That was the period when homemade guns known as pipe-guns were improvised and frequently used in clashes by all parties, the Naxalites, CPI(M), Congress hooligans, and various lumpen elements hired by ruling parties to get rid of the Naxalites. Printed posters that decorate the walls of the streets of Kolkata today were yet to make their appearance. Generally, however, street walls were then decorated with artistically written slogans with black tar—known as street-wallings. Along with that, one could witness stencil pictures of Mao's bust with his message, 'Political power grows out of the barrel of a gun' written in loud letters on the top. The creator of Mao-stencil was Debabrata Mukhopadhyay, an artist by profession. Stencils were reproduced in large numbers and all the towns and cities were thus decorated with Mao's bust pictures.

Ever since the India-China War of 1962, there had been a spate of anti-China films being screened in the cinema halls in India. It seems that the object of the Indian ruling classes was to rouse a feeling of hostility towards Socialist China and poison the relations between the people of the two countries. In mid-1969, at least three such films were shown in the halls of Kolkata and district towns. These were *Prem Poojari*, *Satranj*, and *Ashim Darshan*. Of these, *Prem Poojari* was a rabid anti-China film meant to denigrate Mao and Socialist China. The radicals in large numbers countered it by attacking the cinema halls, burning down the screens and forcing the authorities to stop the screening of those films.[31] In the case of *Prem Poojari*, thousands of revolutionary youths and students displayed their revolutionary spirit in the city of Kolkata, a 'nightmare of the ruling classes'. In a brief well-organized guerrilla action, they simultaneously stormed thirteen cinema halls in Kolkata and the suburban areas where this film was being played, explained to the audience their object, stopped the screening; and made bonfires of the reels, furniture, and screens.[32]

Gradually, open activities became difficult. Street-wallings could not be done in broad daylight. So they were done at night. One or two persons wrote the slogans, while others kept vigil so that their comrades could be alerted if police vans appeared.

Workers in the Revolutionary Movement

The working class tried to wage militant struggles throughout 1967. However, the revisionist leadership exercised considerable influence on the organized workers. With the propagation of the politics of Naxalbari, many workers started coming out of the revisionist fold and the formation of revolutionary workers' unions commenced. Though in minority, they could put up a stiff political fight against the revisionist trade union leaders. With the advance of the armed agrarian revolution in the countryside, a new phase started. A number of workers responded to the call of revolutionary party, left their jobs, and went to the rural areas to take part directly in the agrarian revolution. Another advanced section led by the party organized political demonstrations or industrial strikes in Kolkata and industrial suburbs to express their solidarity with the revolutionary movement.

Militant workers led by the local units of the CPI(ML) hoisted red flags atop factories and offices. In fact, the red flag fluttered over the mills, factories, and offices in the entire port area, the Taratala-Hyde Road area, Behala-Barisha-Thakurpukur area in south Kolkata, etc. Flags were raised also over the head office and tram depots of the Calcutta Tramways Company, the Garden Reach Works which was a defence production factory of the central government and the Cossipore Gun and Shell Factory, another central government factory. Mahaprasad Bhattacharya, a worker of Angel India in the Taratala area and leading activist of the CPI(ML) of south Kolkata told me that the workers in those days innovated a new method of struggle, 'Tool-down Strike'.[33] The factory manager and other officials of the factory are entering the factory amidst sound of machines; suddenly, the whole unit is switched off and everything comes to a standstill. This tool-down strike is very effective as it punches a powerful blow directly at the management. The workers of Behala-Taratala area published the magazine *Bhit* (Foundation) which disseminated revolutionary message that was popular among the workers.[34]

Guerrilla squads of the workers were formed. In fact, workers and petty bourgeois youth formed such squads in different areas. A few big businessmen/mill-owners hated for their crimes against their own workers or people were also annihilated. Among their other targets were police officers and men, spies roaming about in disguise, Central Reserve Police Force (CRPF) and Border Security Force (BSF) troops that were deployed in Kolkata and districts in large numbers; and officers and men of the army who displayed their strength by moving in convoys. Many revolutionary workers sacrificed their lives in the process. One such worker was Anil Chakrabarty, popularly known as Neel (a worker of Behala), who was arrested by the police, brutally tortured, sent to Presidency Jail, put up in solitary confinement and then taken out at midnight and shot dead.[35]

Deshabrati, Sasanka and Liberation

The weekly, *Deshabrati*, the Bengali organ of the West Bengal State Committee of the CPI(ML) was one of the popular magazines of the time and had a print run of 40,000. It covered news of struggles, theoretical articles, the writings of Charu Mazumdar, Mao Tse-tung, news about other lands, field investigation reports, etc. But the most popular of all was the column called 'Patrikar Duniyay' (In the World of the Newspapers) written by Saroj Dutta, one of the leading Left intellectuals of the communist cultural movement of the 1940s and the editor of *Swadhinata*, the Bengali party organ of the undivided CPI during the 1950s, under the pen name of 'Sasanka'. In his inimitable style, he assailed the bourgeois press, exposed the reactionary and dubious role of eminent personalities and defended the book burning, the desecration of Gandhi's statues, and other iconoclastic activities of the radical youth and also agrarian revolutionary movement by making a reinterpretation of our past. I would refer to only one instance among many. A report came out in some national dailies citing a statement made by the Home Minister of Andhra Pradesh that the struggle in Srikakulam had come to an end. However, barely one or two days had gone by, when the report of the annihilation of a hated class enemy came from the same place where Subbarao Panigrahi and Nirmala Krishnamurthy were killed earlier by the police. Saroj Dutta's editorial bore the heading, 'What appeared to them to be a Full Stop has now proved to be actually a Comma.'[36] I distinctly remember how that editorial became a source of much amusement to us.

The central organ of the CPI(ML) was *Liberation*, edited by Suniti Kumar Ghosh and published from the same press in Kolkata, until both the offices were raided and seized by the police on 27 April 1970. Its last legal issue had a circulation of 4,000 copies.[37] After that, both *Deshabrati* and *Liberation* went underground. Since then, the publication of *Deshabrati* was decentralized, with Niranjan Bose coordinating the task as before. The publication of *Liberation* remained centralized, although it became irregular owing to difficulties of its underground existence.

Urban Youth and Students in the Revolutionary Movement

At a meeting with revolutionary youths and students, Charu Mazumdar said that the existing education system of our country teaches the students how to not get integrated with the masses, but how to get isolated from them. So he called upon them to plunge into 'the revolutionary struggle here and now instead of wasting your energy in passing examinations'.[38] The existing situation of overall economic crisis with virtually no scope for employment brought the situation to a breaking point and the whole education, attending classes, and sitting for examinations appeared to be a futile exercise. When there was no future for the youth, Mazumdar showed the path of revolution as the way to a bright future for the people—a future that would ensure total development of masses following the path charted by Mao. That path of revolution would not be a path of roses, but one that would require immense suffering and sacrifice. It was in this way that the 'man-eating system' would be uprooted and a new, socialist society would be born. To the youths and students, this call was something new; no one else had given such a call before. They responded positively. One after another left their schools and colleges and went to villages to integrate themselves with the peasants. Others directed their attacks against educational institutions, government property, hoisted red flags atop educational institutions, government offices, etc., burnt down books written by national leaders like Gandhi, and took part in iconoclasm.

'The world is yours as well as ours, but in the last analysis, it is yours. You young people, full of vigour and vitality, are in the bloom of life, like the sun at eight or nine in the morning. . . . Our future depends on you.' This quotation from Mao Tse-tung adorned the walls of Kolkata and district towns. The early days of the decade of the 1970s were truly the days of the revolutionary youth. At the annual convocation at Jadavpur University held on 2 January 1970, two graduate students, Dilip Chakraborti of Applied Physics and Santanu Goswami of Civil Engineering departments went up to the podium and refused to take the degrees raising slogans, 'We do not want degrees, we want jobs'.[39]

Gradually, new targets of attack came up. An important feature relating to education in West Bengal was the disruption of examinations by a section of examinees on the plea of stiff questions. The CPI(ML) leadership tried to give that spontaneous tirade against educational institutions a bigger meaning. It began from early 1970 and very quickly gained momentum. These institutions were described as 'semi-colonial' in nature and hence deserving destruction. Thus, from one educational institution after another, one government office after another, documents, files, question papers, and answer scripts went up in flames and red flags were hoisted atop buildings. This was a widespread feature in West Bengal, in Kolkata and district towns.

There also took place desecration of statues and portraits of Gandhi and other political and social leaders such as Vidyasagar, Rammohan, Subhas Chandra Bose, etc. There were also book burning and other defiant activities. Urban actions started from March 1970. To start with, these were spontaneous actions in solidarity with the battle of annihilation of class enemies going on in the countryside. On 2 March, students of Presidency College ransacked the room of the principal and decorated the wall with slogans and stencilled portraits of Mao Tse-tung. They demonstrated against the bureaucratic system of education in the nearby Calcutta University campus on the same day.[40] The second United Front government of West Bengal ended on 16 March 1970 and on 24 March, the offices of the vice chancellors of both Jadavpur and Calcutta universities were ransacked and slogans such as 'All reactionaries are paper-tigers'; 'Under this educational system, the more you read, the more foolish you become'; 'Down with the rotten Yankee culture'; etc., were written on the walls. Mao's stencilled pictures were also painted as usual.[41] On 10 April, students invaded Gandhi Bhawan, an auditorium in Jadavpur University, pulled down and destroyed a life-size oil portrait of Gandhi and also made a bonfire of a large number of books written by Gandhi as also books on Gandhi.[42] Very quickly such actions spread to other institutions in Kolkata and district towns. Slogans that decorated the walls were 'Burn down the ideology of Gandhi in the red flame of Chairman's Thoughts'; 'China's Chairman is our Chairman, China's Path is our Path'.

My Days at Presidency College

I joined the Presidency College as a History student in 1970. The college was located in central Kolkata, which incidentally was one of the hubs of revolutionary activism of the new generation. Located on College Street, it had Hare School next to it and the main campus of the Calcutta University close by on the same side of the road. On the opposite side of the college there stood the Hindu School and behind it was the Sanskrit College, which was converted into an army barrack during the Revolt of 1857, when Ishwar Chandra Vidyasagar was its principal. On the other side of the street there stood the Coffee House, one of the centres of heated exchanges over current issues, also of numerous scuffles and battles between the radical students and those affiliated to the CPI(M) and police actions. The College Street area was the scene of many a battle. Tram cars and buses plying along the street were set on fire at regular intervals.

When one entered the main building of Presidency College, one was greeted with such slogans as 'Naxalbari Lal Selam' (Red Salute to Naxalbari). Once you go upstairs from the first floor to the second you are greeted with that ever memorable slogan that was a part of Charu Mazumdar's letter written to a comrade, 'It is no time for repentance; it is time to flare up like fire'. In respectful memory of Panchadi Krishnamurthy of Srikakulam, students wrote in black tar on the wall leading to the Teachers' room, 'Comrade Krishnamurthy's blood beckons for more blood'. 'Make the Seventies the Decade of Liberation' was the title of an essay written by Mazumdar that became a slogan—a rallying cry during those tumultuous days. On one part of the wall on the second floor was written that oft-quoted statement of Mao, 'A revolution is not a dinner party, or writing an essay, or painting a picture, or doing embroidery; it cannot be so refined, so leisurely and gentle. . . . A revolution is an act of insurrection, an act of violence by which one class overthrows another.' The relationship between the students and the principal was far from cordial during those days and Presidency College went without any Principal for quite some time. Students pasted an advertisement on the upper wall of the portico in the main building, which was quite amusing: 'Post lying vacant—College Principal. Qualification: Body skin should be as hard as that of a rhino'. Slogans on the walls were written skillfully only at select places, and always had an artistic touch. They were devoid of spelling mistakes and the handwriting was good.

By then, we had started getting copies of *Deshabrati*. It was available also in the students' common room. New copies were kept secretly on the table. *Frontier,* a radical weekly edited by Samar Sen, was also available. The rear portion of the library and the students' canteen were where we had our *adda,* and there was also the Ghosh

Cabin where we went to have *kachuri* during breaks. Parimal Ghosh, Kushal Gupta, Amit Banerjee, and myself used to talk after class hours about the reality around us. Copies of *Deshabrati* were also pasted on the walls at street corners. However, it was a bit risky to read it in an open space.

I can distinctly remember the day I was entering the college through the main gate. On the gate was pasted a notification. It bore the picture of a bespectacled frail man. A price of Rs.10,000 was declared on his head, dead or alive, by the government. He was a person with very bright piercing eyes, the creator of Naxalbari, the leader of the Indian revolution. By then, Charu Mazumdar had become a legend.

Iconoclastic Activities

Closely following on the heels of book burning there came the smashing of statues of national leaders such as Gandhi and Nehru and also social reformers associated with the 'Bengal Renaissance' who were held responsible for the future plight of the Indian people. The youths and students drew inspiration from the revolutionary peasant struggle of the past and judged those 'eminent' personalities by just one yardstick: Were they on the side of the people or on the side of the people's enemies? In fact, under the impact of revolutionary struggles of the peasants, not only politics, but history and culture too were subjected to re-evaluation from the standpoint of revolutionary democracy. These iconoclastic activities of the youths and students were carried out spontaneously without being directed by the party, but in keeping with the central political line and the mood of the people. But once these started, the party leadership defended and provided theoretical justification of these actions.

The first article in defence of image-breaking entitled 'On Gandhi' came from Saroj Dutta and was originally published in *Deshabrati*.[43] In August 1970, Charu Mazumdar wrote an article defending such actions and calling upon the youth not to confine themselves to such activities, but to join the armed peasant struggles in the villages. Mazumdar argued that the youth movement was neither isolated nor complete in itself:

It is the call of this agrarian revolution which has made the students and youths restive and they are directing their attacks against the images of those persons who have ever tried to put down the flames of armed revolution of the peasant masses by preaching the message of peace and reform. That is why this struggle of the students and youths is part of the armed peasant struggle.[44]

Saroj Dutta in his essay 'In Support of Image-Breaking', justified such actions also from historical perspective by saying, 'This is not a negative action. They are destroying statues to build new statues . . .; they are destroying Gandhighat to build Mangalghat (after Mangal Pande, the rebel sepoy and hero of the 1857 uprising).' He added:

One might ask, are the youth doing all these fully aware of their political implications? The revolutionary people do not enact revolutionary actions, conscious all the time of all the implications. Have they analysed the records of the work of those, whose statues they are destroying? No. . . . But still, they are doing the right things. . . . They are not burdened with any revisionist past as is the case with their elders.

He then, like Charu Mazumdar, reminded his readers that the roots of urban actions lay in the raging storm in the countryside. 'A storm is raging over the cities; its epicentre is in the sea of the peasant masses of the villages. The storm has arisen from the depression caused there by the peasants' guerrilla struggles under the leadership of the CPI(ML).'[45]

It is pertinent to point out that the revolutionary youth and students sought to resolve a number of ideological and cultural issues in a hurry, rather than through debates and patient ideological work. However, it can be argued in their defence that those stormy days hardly permitted any patient work. There were also people both inside and outside the party who had reservations about the manner in which the revolt took place as also the individual killing. Sushital Roy Chowdhary came out with a document in which he held that some sort of distinction should be made between Gandhi and the Congress leaders on the one hand and social reformers and writers like Rammohan, Vidyasagar, and Tagore, on the other hand. While he supported the attack on the former, he felt that the latter were intellectuals of a bourgeois democratic revolution and so should not be made targets of attack.

Despite reservations and criticisms coming from several quarters, this iconoclastic offensive, without doubt, shook the roots of the pro-establishment culture and gave a powerful blow to the establishment historians. This shock therapy achieved a permanent gain in the realm of history and culture, and except for the diehard historians of the establishment, serious scholars revised their past evaluations of the 'Bengal Renaissance' and of national leaders like Gandhi in the days to come.

Sometime from late 1970, the state forces started making inroads into Naxalite ranks. Anti-social lumpen elements were planted by the police amidst the Naxalites; they acted as police informers and were instrumental in the arrests and killing of Naxalite youths. Besides these, police informers masquerading as beggars were placed in key spots, e.g. gates of cooperative houses, to keep an eye on the activists and pass on information to the police about their movements. Some such beggars were also killed by the Naxalites.

Fake Encounter Killings by State Forces and the Cossipore-Baranagar Bloodbath

In those times, Kolkata looked like a war base with policemen and troops spread over the city and police and army trucks and cars equipped with wireless sets, constantly patrolling the streets. One day, while I was travelling in a tram from Shyambazar 5-point crossing to College Street, I noticed the whole area on the left from Fariapukur to the lane near Mitra cinema hall encircled by army men and search operations being conducted by the police from one house to another for apprehending Naxalites. Such things became almost daily features in Kolkata. All young boys in their teens and twenties were rounded up by the police, some released and some taken to the police stations where they were tortured and some were killed either in the lock-up itself or at night on the street. Kolkata was then under Congress rule led by the chief minister, Siddhartha Shankar Ray, who initiated a policy of cold-blooded murders of Naxalites—later known as 'fake encounter killings'.

The first cold-blooded murder in Kolkata was that of Kajal Banerjee, a young revolutionary of Taltala in central Kolkata, on 11 August 1970. When Kajal's father went to Lal Bazar to bring back his son's body, neither the body nor his wrist watch was handed over to him. A large number of people went to the burning ghat to pay their last respects to the departed soul and wrote in charcoal black 'Comrade Kajal Lal Selam' (Red Salute to Comrade Kajal) on the wall. Many people in the locality went without meals on that day. People literally wept for him. Transport came to a standstill. Cinema halls were closed. Many other areas of Kolkata came to a halt on that day.[46]

That was followed by the brutal torture and murder of Samir Bhattacharyya, another young revolutionary, inside Shyampukur police station in north Kolkata in August 1970. Amal Bose, then a professor of Political Science, Maulana Azad College and my father's colleague in the same college, who stayed very near the Shyampukur police station, told me much later that every night they heard screams of young men from the police station because of police torture. It is significant that the people refused to cooperate with the police and provide information to them about the revolutionaries. In various areas, the people joined in indignant protest when the armed forces of the state murdered CPI(ML) cadres and sympathizers. After the murder of Samir, the whole of Kolkata observed *hartal* (total shutdown) for one day and life in north Kolkata remained paralysed for three days.[47]

The police officials made it a pastime to shoot and kill young men in the streets and elsewhere. They would sometimes make a show of releasing them, ask them to leave and then shoot them from behind. An article published in a Kolkata daily stated: 'Sources say a private screening of a Hollywood crime thriller was held for a secret audience of police officers. The film featured a sequence in which prisoners were set free and then shot from behind. Sources say this strategy was carried out in devastating detail right in Calcutta (as well as elsewhere in West Bengal).'[48]

In a statement, MP Jyotirmoy Basu, said that he as well as three other MPs from West Bengal 'received letters at Delhi from a *sanyasi*, who sits in one of the burning ghats in Calcutta. He mentioned in his letter that every day and night he was watching the policemen coming between midnight and early morning and burning bodies of young people, aged between 14 and 30'.[49]

The police indulged in orgies of murder from time to time. On 19 November 1970, they arrested eleven young men from central Kolkata, took them to Barasat in north 24-Parganas and killed them. The dead bodies lay scattered on the streets. On 19/20 November, about 1,500 policemen in 44 vans under the charge of Debi Roy, DC, Detective Department raided the Beliaghata Housing Complex and searched 556 flats, captured four youths, including Ashok Bose, an Electrical Engineering student of Jadavpur University and shot them dead. A party of MPs, after investigation, dismissed the police claim of a bomb fight as a cock and bull story.[50]

However, the carnage that took place in Cossipore-Baranagar during 12–14 August 1971 was something totally new in its methods and also surpassed all others in its magnitude. It beggars description. *Frontier* reported thus:

Murder of sorts is a familiar thing nowadays. But Baranagar-Cossipore carnage was neither familiar nor secret. It had broken new ground and set a new pattern with the most ominous sign of the shape of things to come. . . . More than 150 boys were butchered within two days . . . others who were not young had also to die... The boys were murdered because they were nonconformists and Naxalites. Not all of them were activists. . . . The police were officially withdrawn and given the strictest instruction not to interfere. . . . Practitioners in murder and mayhem were brought in. . . . It started in broad daylight. . . . Who were the killers? They were euphemistically called 'resistance groups'. . . . They get protection money from the business houses; they extort money from the people on the plea of defending the locality; they are on the payroll of the police for supplying intelligence about the Naxalites. But actually who are they? They are gangsters and murderers. . . . It was a bloody sadistic settling of accounts. Dead bodies were everywhere—bodies with heads cut off, limbs lost, eyes gouged out, entrails ripped open. . . .[51]

What was the role of the CPI(M)? 'The Baranagar people know that the CPM cadres who had in the past made a strategic retreat from the area of operation due to the Congress threat, were allowed to come back and they helped the Congress (R) [later Congress (I)] killers flush out the extremists.'[52] In fact, the leadership instructed their cadres to identify the houses of the Naxalite sympathizers which they did by pasting black tar on their house-walls.[53] What was the official reaction of the ruling Congress party? S.S. Ray, the chief minster visited Baranagar and 'was conducted to the place of incidents by the killers themselves. . . . The ominous sign is the exhibition of total hypocrisy on the part of the political leaders. . . . Fascism is not a figure of speech, it is a grim reality.'[54]

Revolts in Prison and Prison Breaks

The youths and students converted prisons into centres of revolt. Physically battered while in police custody, they could nevertheless, carry into prison the spirit of rebellion which had inspired them outside. They faced prison walls and overcrowded wards, solitary confinement, *dandaberi* (iron-rods tied up to the legs) and other forms of torture perpetrated by the jail authorities. As noted earlier, the CPI(ML) line was that of rejection of legal forms of struggle in a revolutionary situation. In keeping with that spirit, it was the party's instruction that the imprisoned cadres should not seek release on bail nor should the middle-class prisoners ask for classification as political prisoners, which would entitle them, because of their social status, to facilities denied to cadres of worker and peasant origin. To get release from prison they should break the prison. That was the central policy of the CPI(ML).

The appalling conditions in jails, the savage persecutions and insults made clashes with the prison staff inevitable. Thousands of Naxalites were behind bars in various jails of West Bengal, not to speak of others in other states. Thousands were held under MISA and many more thousands as under-trials, each on several charges, mostly fictitious. Life in prisons was one of constant struggle and some of them couldn't bear it.

There was only one way of escape from prison: jail breaking. Jail breaks and jail revolts constituted another feature of the early '70s involving considerable bloodshed and sacrifices. In all the four prisons in the city of Kolkata—Dum Dum, Presidency, Alipur Central, and Alipur Special—there were revolts, jail breaks and attempts at jail-breaks, and the killing of Naxalite prisoners in large numbers. This has been revealed in quite a few prison memoirs.[55]

Role of Women in the Naxalite Movement

From processions and meetings in the earliest phase to the prison the visibility of women activists was definitely less than that of men. The guerrilla squads both in the urban and rural areas were formed almost totally by men, the notable exception being Andhra Pradesh where many women became activists and died fighting even in the early days. However, among the eleven souls who fell to police bullets on 25 May 1967 in Naxalbari, eight were women. In the Naxalbari area, there were some women who led from the front in the countryside. In the city of Kolkata, there were some known activists who were imprisoned such as Malaya Ghosh, Seuli Guha, Meenakshi Sen, Rajasree Dasgupta, Barnali Bhattacharya, Krishna Bandyopadhyay, Kalpana, Khuku, Rita, and others.

The role of women in the first phase in Kolkata was more pronounced than in other areas. They took charge of arranging shelters for fugitive comrades, treating the sick, acting as couriers, etc. A mother prevented a male activist's arrest by making him sleep on the same bed with her own married daughter.[56] Such actions taken by mothers and daughters reveal the extent to which the ideology and the sacrificial spirit of the Naxalite activists could make people consider them as their own and thus enable them to overcome social inhibitions.

According to some people, anti-social activities had come to a stop due to Naxalite activism. It was easy for people to sleep without even locking the doors. Crimes such as theft, robbery, eve-teasing or molestation of women seldom took place during this period, at least in the city of Kolkata. A number of lumpen elements were influenced by radical politics; they joined the movement and died fighting.

Conflicts over the Tactical Line within the CPI(ML), State Offensive, Arrest and Death of Charu Mazumdar in Lal Bazar Police Lock-up

From late-1970, the situation in Kolkata and elsewhere changed to the advantage of the Indian State. The West Bengal government under S.S. Ray regime and Indira Gandhi as Prime Minister pursued a ruthless policy to get rid of the Naxalites. Thousands of activists and leaders were either wiped out in cold blood or sent to prison. Many became homeless and were forced to take shelter elsewhere. *Paras* previously under Naxalite control were taken over by the ruling Congress party hoodlums. The CPI(M) cadres, who had been the former allies of the Congress in their joint mission to wipe out their common enemies, the Naxalites, were themselves made new targets of attack. Hundreds were killed by the Congress goons.

Contradictions cropped up within the CPI(ML) over such aspects of party line as annihilation of class enemies and rejection of mass organizations, mass struggles as well as all other legal forms of struggle. It was accentuated by the 'Suggestions' ('Eleven Points') from the Communist Party of China (CPC) that Charu Mazumdar received from Souren Bose after the latter's return from China in early 1971. There were eleven issues over which the CPC voiced its disagreement. There were some leading activists who held that those who did not accept the revolutionary authority of Charu Mazumdar were to be treated as class enemies. Two members of the South Calcutta Committee, Agni Roy and Kamal Sanyal, were murdered allegedly by this group, which was also opposed to the demands raised for discussion over the CPC's 'Suggestions'. In early July 1972, Mazumdar met Abdul Rauff and K.G. Satyamurthy from Andhra Pradesh in Kolkata and accepted most of the 'Suggestions' from the CPC and started to change his line. However, his arrest on 16 July from Middle Road and death in Lal Bazar lock-up put an end, for the time being, to the process.

Charu Mazumdar's death marked the end of a tumultuous phase in the history of the Communist revolutionary movement in India. His failing health could not withstand the mental and physical torture in the forms of uninterrupted interrogation, denial of essential medicines, and sleepless nights. His adversaries assured themselves, after they put his body on the funeral pyre that the spectre of revolution that had been haunting them had at last been laid to rest.

For me, as also for many others, there was, for many days total darkness all around. However, the death of the legend did not mark the end of the movement, but the beginning of a new phase. This new phase was also attended initially by splits, introspection, and attempts at reorganization and mergers. On my part, I could not continue my studies anymore. I left home to take part in a struggle that I considered worth fighting for.

Epilogue

Samar Sen, an intellectual of repute and editor of *Frontier*, wrote:

> . . . Naxalbari exploded many a myth. The upheaval was such that nothing remained the same after Naxalbari. People had to readjust their position vis-à-vis every aspect of the system: political, administrative, military, cultural. . . . Admittedly, the Naxalites raised more problems than they solved. But the very problems they raised and tried to solve in a hurry had never been raised with such force of sincerity before or after Telangana. This is their achievement.[57]

The Naxalbari and the Maoist revolutionary communist movement that followed after the setback of 1972 was a real turning point in the history of modern India. This movement boldly addressed certain crucial questions that had plagued the Indian communist movement for a long time. The questions raised by it are as follows: What is the character of the Indian state—an independent bourgeois state or a semi-feudal, colonial state? Was the Independence of India real or sham? Was the Indian National Congress truly 'Indian' and truly 'National'? What is the character of the Indian bourgeoisie: comprador or national? Why have the Indian ruling classes adopted a development policy of abject dependence on imperialist capital, and not one of self-reliance? Why should there be an imperialist stranglehold on politics, economy, society, and culture in a country which claims to be independent?

Politically, it upheld and re-established, in the Indian soil, the Marxist theory that 'force is the midwife of the old society pregnant with a new one' and rejected the parliamentary path of transition to socialism. This rejection was an important turning point in the politics of the country. Second, following the path as charted by Mao Tse-tung, Charu Mazumdar emphasized that the Indian revolution—an agrarian anti-feudal and anti-imperialist revolution led by the working class—would be a protracted one leading to the creation of liberated base areas in the countryside, their expansion, and the ultimate seizure of political power throughout the country. Third, Mazumdar also stressed the importance of the role of the peasantry and held that bourgeois intelligentsia could play a role by integrating themselves with the peasants and workers. His call to the youth and students to go to the village to integrate themselves with the peasantry had never been given before by anybody in our country. In the next phases of the Maoist movement this policy was carried forward by the new leadership. All these became an integral part of revolutionary Communism in India and there could be no turning back. On the other side, the Indian Prime Minster declared in 2004 that the Maoist movement was the 'greatest single threat to the security of the country' thereby acknowledging the gravity of the situation from the point of view of the Indian State.

Socially, the movement in its first phase, that is the phase portrayed in this essay, influenced mainly the petty bourgeois youth, students, and intellectuals, as also sections of the peasantry and the working class in West Bengal and other states. Later, vast areas of central and eastern India, particularly the mineral-rich Adivasi areas became the 'heartland of rebellion'. In the first phase, middle-class people of Kolkata were deeply touched by the self-sacrifice of the youths and students, although many among them were neither in agreement with their method of struggle nor with some of their slogans.

Intellectually, the movement affected human ideas in different ways. One of course was the reassessment of our past history in the wake of the iconoclastic activities of the youths and students. Besides new assessments about the limitations of the Gandhian national movement, the revisionist role of the CPI and the CPI(M), the comprador nature of the Indian big bourgeoisie, the myth of Indian Independence and many other issues, the movement signalled the beginning of the study of 'history from below' in our country. Major roles were played here by those who were engaged in this battle in the realm of superstructure.

The movement made people feel that our country actually was not an independent country; rather it was being controlled by imperialist powers in a new and big way. It also taught people about the uselessness of the parliament—a pigsty—a place where whoever goes becomes a villain. 'Je jay Lankay sei hoy Raavan' (Literally, 'Whoever goes to Lanka, becomes a Ravana'; an allusion to the mythological Demon King Ravana who was the ruler of Lanka and eventually killed by the god Rama), is a popular oft-quoted statement that perfectly fits in the context. That decade also made many people believe that unless some basic changes were brought about, unless we stood on our own feet and cast off all dependence on foreign capital and technology and took the destiny of our country in our own hands, we were totally doomed.

The next phase (1972–7) of the movement was characterized by splits of the CPI(ML) into groups, re-assessment of past struggles, and also mergers. It also witnessed the emergence of the civil rights movement in West Bengal (Association for the Protection of Democratic Rights, 1972 and the Andhra Pradesh Civil Liberties Committee, 1973). In the face of the countrywide Emergency (1975–7), creation of a fascist Raj throughout the country, brutal suppression of democratic voices, and incarceration of thousands of political dissenters, struggles continued and so did attempts at unity and mergers. Many of those who were released from prison after the general elections of 1977 and the formation of a new ministry, became politically inactive, some returned to their studies, some got associated with the civil rights movement demanding unconditional release of political prisoners, while others got involved in the task of reorganizing the revolutionary forces anew on a new basis. Urban guerrilla actions in Kolkata and elsewhere became things of the past and people's movements were confined mainly to open processions, street corner meetings, and conventions.

Notes

1. See Suniti Kumar Ghosh, 'Report on Struggles in the Wake of Naxalbari: A Supplement', in *The Historic Turning-Point: A Liberation Anthology*, vol. II, Kolkata: S.K. Ghosh, February 1993, pp. 341–58.

2. Abhijit Das, *Footprints of the Foot Soldiers Experiences and Recollections of the Naxalite Movement in Eastern India 1960's and 70's*, Kolkata, Delhi: Setu Prakashani, January 2015, pp. 34–5.

3. Interview with Siddhartha (Ajit) Saha, a student activist of those days, dated 30 April 2016.

4. Suniti Kumar Ghosh, *Naxalbari Before and After Reminiscences and Appraisal*, Kolkata: New Age, 2009, p. 139.

5. *Deshabrati* (In the service of the country), year 1, no. 2, 13 July 1967.

6. Ibid.

7. See 'Naxalbari Krishak Sangamer Samarthane Janasabha', *Deshabrati*, year 1, no. 4, 17 July 1967.

8. *Deshabrati*, year 1, no. 4, 27 July 1967.

9. See Das, *Footprints of the Foot Soldiers*, p. 5. The song, written originally in

Bengali by Dilip Bagchi, was rendered into English by Abhijit Das, who was known by his pen name, Jayanta Joardar. Jangal Santhal was one of the leading Adivasi figures of the movement.

10. Amit Bhattacharyya, *Storming the Gates of Heaven: The Maoist Movement in India, A Critical Study, 1972–2014*, Kolkata: Setu Prakashani, 2016, p. 52. On 25 May 1967, a large number of people—mostly women—gathered under a banyan tree by the side of a road leading to Kharibari. The police opened fired on the crowd as a result of which eleven persons including eight women, two six-month-old babies, and a boy died. It is notable that contrary to the figure (seven) mentioned in the song, the number of women who fell to police bullets was eight. The names of all of them are inscribed on a memorial column erected in Naxalbari.

11. Amit Bhattacharyya, *Karasmriti Sattarer Mashaal* (Prison Days Blazing Memories of the Seventies), Kolkata: Setu Prakashani, January 2014, p. 13. Kangsha, an oppressive ruler was killed by Krishna, a mythological hero born in prison. The full name of Kanu Sanyal was Krishna Kumar Sanyal. In this song, Krishna is Kanu Sanyal and Kangsha represents the repressive State. That explains the significance of the song. Kanu Sanyal was another leading figure of the movement coming after Charu Mazumdar in importance.

12. *Deshabrati*, 11 January 1968.

13. Bhattacharyya, *Karasmriti*, p. 15.

14. Interview with Siddhartha Saha.

15. *Kalpurush*, year 1, no. 5, August 1967.

16. *Aneek*, year 9, nos. 11 & 12, May–June 1973.

17. *Deshabrati*, 22 August 1968.

18. *Jugantar*, 19 November 1967.

19. *The Statesman*, 6 October 1967.

20. Sumanta Banerjee, *In the Wake of Naxalbari: A History of the Naxalite Movement in India*, Calcutta: Subarnarekha, 1980, p. 121.

21. Nguyen Van Trois, a Vietnamese patriot, was arrested by the police of the US puppet government of South Vietnam headed by Ngo Din Diem on the charge of making an assassination attempt on the life of Robert McNamara in Vietnam. He was killed by a firing squad. Just before his death, he told the press that he wanted to make Vietnam free and shouted at the top of his voice, 'Long Live Vietnam'.

22. *Deshabrati*, 28 November 1968.

23. *Deshabrati*, 17 April 1969.

24. *Liberation*, vol. II, no. 11, September 1969. Translated from the Bengali as published in *Deshabrati*, 21 August 1969.

25. See the Srikakulam District Committee's report in *Liberation*, vol. II, no. 7, May 1969, pp. 68–9.

26. 'Naxalbarite guerrilla-der haate Jotedar nihato' (Jotedar killed in the hands of the guerrillas in Naxalbari), *Deshabrati*, 16 January 1969.

27. 'Medinipurer Krishak Guerrilla-der haate Jotedar Khatam' (Jotedar annihilated in the hands of Peasant Guerrillas in Medinipur), *Deshabrati*, 5 September 1969.
28. Banerjee, *In the Wake of Naxalbari*, p. 121.
29. Interview with Siddhartha Saha, dated 16 August 2014.
30. *Deshabrati*, 24 April 1968.
31. *Deshabrati*, 29 May 1969; See also, *Deshabrati*, 12 March 1970 and 9 April 1970.
32. See Ghosh, 'Report on the Struggles in the Wake of Naxalbari', p. 355.
33. Mahaprasad Bhattacharya was a leading member of the South Calcutta Committee of the CPI(ML). He was arrested and incarcerated in Presidency Jail, Kolkata during 1972–7. The present writer could have long interactions with him while in prison during 1974–7. See, Bhattacharyya, *Karasmriti*, pp. 18–19.
34. Ibid.
35. Conversation with Mahaprasad Bhattacharya sometime during 1974–7.
36. See Saroj Dutta [Editorial], 'Ora jake Danri bhebechhilo, ekhon dekhchhe ta Comma' (What appeared to them as a Full Stop has now proved to be actually a Comma), *Deshabrati*, 19 February 1970.
37. Suniti Kumar Ghosh et al., *The Historic Turning-Point: A Liberation Anthology*, vol. I, Calcutta: S.K. Ghosh, 1992, pp. 20–1.
38. See Charu Mazumdar, 'A Few Words to the Revolutionary Students and Youths', *Liberation*, March 1970.
39. See Shipra Roy, 'Chhatra Andolan: Jadavpur Viswavidyalaya (1956–2005)', unpublished Ph.D. dissertation, Jadavpur University, Kolkata, 2015, p. 73.
40. Debashis Bhattacharya, *Sattorer Dinguli* (Days of the Seventies), *Protham Parba* (Part 1), Kolkata: Ekhon Bisombad, January 2000, pp. 21–4.
41. Ibid.
42. Ibid.
43. Sasanka, 'Gandhi Prosonge' (On Gandhi), *Deshabrati*, 6 June 1970.
44. Charu Mazumdar, 'Forge Closer Unity with Peasants' Armed Struggle', *Liberation*, vol. III, no. 3, August 1970.
45. Sasanka,'Murti-bhangar Samarthan-e' (In Support of Image-breaking), *Deshabrati*, 20 August 1970.
46. Piyasha Bhattacharya Dasgupta, 'Aaguner Parashmoni', *Ebong Jalark Charu Mazumdar*, no. 12, year 18, nos. 1–2, April–September 2015, pp. 277–8.
47. *Deshabrati*, 5 September 1970; See also, Ghosh, 'Report on Struggles in the Wake of Naxalbari', p. 353.
48. *The Statesman Miscellany*, 21 June 1992.
49. For this and other reports, see, Samar Sen et al., eds., *Naxalbari and After: A Frontier Anthology*, 2 vols., Calcutta: Kathashilpa, June 1978.
50. For the report of the investigation team, see *Frontier*, 12 December 1970.

51. *Frontier*, 18 September 1971.
52. Ibid.
53. See Bhattacharyya, *Karasmriti*, p. 20. It is reported that some lower-ranking CPI(M) cadres passed on the information of the approaching operation to some of the Naxalite activists.
54. *Frontier*, 18 September 1971.
55. See Azizul Haque, *Karagare Athharo Bachhar*, Kolkata: Dey's Publishing, vol. 1, 1990; vol. 2, 1991; Malaya Ghosh, *Lalbazar-e Choushotti din*, Kolkata: Setu Prakashani, 2013; Bhattacharyya, *Karasmriti*.
56. *Rakte Lekha Itihas Cossipore-Baranagar-er Ganahatyar Tadanta Report*, Kolkata, 1994.
57. See Samar Sen et al., eds., 'Foreword', in *Naxalbari and After: A Frontier Anthology*, vol. 1, Calcutta: Kathashilpa, June 1978.

11

AN EPILOGUE TO NAXALBARI

Calcutta, 1970s–2000s

Parimal Ghosh

The Maoist upsurge in West Bengal towards the end of the 1960s was perhaps the single most important political movement independent India has ever seen. Commonly referred to as the Naxalbari movement, it posed a challenge to the Indian State, its institutions and its laws, and indeed, the basic premises on which it had, and still continues to, rest its claim to legitimacy. This is something that no other political opposition has ever done, or ever thought of doing. Our entire thinking of our modern past was put under severe scrutiny and found to be wanting by partisan ideologues. This in turn led to a re-examining of many of our dearly cherished fables about our past and rethinking of our modernity by the academia, thereby fundamentally changing our understanding of ourselves.

No movement worth its name is really an episode, an event in time. Movements are processes that necessarily have a long pre-history. Naxalbari's roots can perhaps be traced as far back as when independent India was born. The Partition of the country and the resultant displacement of millions triggered the collapse of a certain lifestyle, and its associated worldview. There was terrible bitterness among Bengalis, a sense of betrayal, which was strengthened by a perceptible loss of power on the all-India stage. A sense of victimhood seemed to overtake them, from which I suppose, they/ we have not yet recovered. I would like to believe that all these went into the process which led to the spirit of Naxalbari, apart from, and perhaps more than the ideological tussle that had broken out within the Communist movement in India, in the wake of the Sino-Indian War in 1962 and the Sino-Soviet split.

Naxalbari was thus the apogee in a long build-up, almost a cathartic release for the Bengali society as a whole. At the same time, as it often happens, it also delivered a lesson to the Bengalis— as to what a revolution would be really like. A crucial element in the build-up to it had been the germination of a Left-liberal outlook, taking off from the post-Rabindranath Tagore reaction to lyrical romanticism and broad humanism of the master. After Naxalbari's decisive defeat by the mid-70s, this Left-liberal outlook came to be tempered by a large dosage of pragmatism. Indeed, what is generally not recognized is that the defeat had been brought about not merely by brutal police repression but by this retreat of the *bhadralok* literati, the cultural elite, who since the Second World War and the famine of 1943, had come to be integrally connected with the political Left. The Left Front government that came to power in West Bengal in 1977, and hung on till its comprehensive defeat in 2011, very openly put any hope of a revolution on the back-burner, and except for some fringe Maoist groups, nobody noticed. Bengal politics today is marked by this pragmatism, and too often, of late, by shallow populism, catering to the existential needs of the underclasses. Romantic dreams of a total transformation of the society are gone forever.

This essay shall examine the story of Calcutta, and with that, inevitably, to an extent that of West Bengal too, in the context of this retreat. This will not be a connected, all-round narrative account of the decades that followed Naxalbari, not certainly up to the present times. In order to capture the essence of what we have called the retreat, the strategy shall be to provide an overview of some of the climactic points of the process—political, economic, social, and cultural.

The Prelude

Calcutta, it might be remembered, had been the capital of British India till 1911, and almost till the 1930s the commercial and industrial hub of the country. Bengal was blessed with coal and iron, besides having a well-functioning port on the river Hooghly. In the mid-1850s a degree of industrialization had begun centring round Calcutta and factories started to appear, up and down on both banks of the river. Jute spinning and weaving became a major industry as it was the time when gunny sacks had become the principal packing material. Jute had been a traditional crop of Bengal and the poor were known to use jute cloth for winter wear. Dundee in Scotland had by then become the world capital of jute industry, but by mid-nineteenth century it made good sense to set up the industry in Bengal where raw jute was easily available, especially from eastern Bengal. Over time paper, glass, and engineering factories were also set up around Calcutta. Besides, tea plantations in north Bengal and coal mines in the Asansol-Dhanbad belt came to have their head offices located in Calcutta. The city thus became the preferred home base for a thriving business community, mostly Anglo-Scottish, but which from the 1930s also began to include Indian businessmen—in the main Marwaris. In keeping with this, the city came to develop infrastructure catering to the requirements of the corporate world. Till the late 50s or early 60s, Calcutta's hotels were reckoned to be the best in India—for a long time the Great Eastern was described as the finest to the east of Suez, its theatre halls, and restaurants, and bars with their live cabaret shows, enjoying a reputation all over the subcontinent.

The point to note, of course, is the general absence of the Bengali elite in this circle. Since the beginning of the nineteenth century, wealthy Bengalis had preferred to invest in land, i.e. in zamindari estates which ensured a comparatively guaranteed, large income, while the rank and file middle class had taken to English education, leading to employment in government or mercantile offices, and also to the professions. Over the decades the Bengalis, thus, came to be known as good professionals, lawyers, and doctors, as a nation of clerks, people who were cultured and into social reform and political idealism. These were the *bhadralok*, a category unique to the Bengalis, initially dominated by the upper castes, but then gradually turning into an open category for others with education and a certain avowed allegiance to *bhadra* values. The word *bhadra* literally means polite, and by early twentieth century had come to indicate those who accepted, at least notionally, the broad agenda of reformism, emanating from a belief in the Bengal

Renaissance of the nineteenth century. Whether the arrival of a succession of outstanding individuals, starting from Rammohun Roy, through Bankimchandra Chattopadhyay, Ishwar Chandra Vidyasagar, Rabindranath Tagore et al., with their respective vision of reform, social, political, and literary, qualified to be called a renaissance, has been debated for long by scholars—in as much as this reformism had remained largely confined to the English educated. The point though, would still stick that for the *bhadralok* this was vital to their identity formation. And one common element that can be easily recognized in this was, excepting for a miniscule minority of them, the *bhadralok* was neither a businessman nor an industrialist.

By the mid-thirties, thus, Calcutta was a city in Bengal, in which the overall political and administrative control was in the hands of the British, so was the economy, but in this sphere the Marwaris were poised to make important inroads. Bengalis constituted the political opposition, and the city's cultural life was also totally dominated by them. It is possible that this systemic alienation from the political and economic decision-making processes gradually turned the Bengali *bhadralok* into a dissenting voice at a pan-Indian level in the subsequent decades. Indeed, till the very end, Gandhi, with his creed of non-violence, never really could establish a hold on the Bengali psyche, and Bengal has always had a long tradition of violent/terrorist/revolutionary politics, much closer to the heart of her native people. That is where perhaps, the seeds of the subsequent Bengali fascination with left politics, germinated.

Independence and After

West Bengal was in turmoil from almost immediately after Independence and the consequent Partition in August 1947. If the massive inflow of refugees from East Pakistan, i.e. erstwhile eastern Bengal, and poor efforts at their rehabilitation by the Central government, especially when compared with what happened on the western frontier, constituted one standing grievance, then the other was the so-called 'freight equalization policy' of the central government, in effect since 1952, which so heavily discriminated against the mineral-rich states of eastern India, including West

Bengal. Briefly, the policy had aimed at encouraging balanced industrialization by promising equal tariff through central subsidy for transportation of essential commodities, such as iron and coal, throughout India, denying thereby the benefits that ought to have naturally accrued to the mineral-rich states. On top of this was the industrial stagnation that began to bite from around the mid-60s and affected West Bengal generally more than the rest of the country, in as much as this was then a more industrialized state. The upshot was a chronic unemployment crisis which fuelled discontent among the middle and the lower classes. These combined with an acute and continuing food shortage to render the state almost ungovernable for the incumbent government under the Congress party. Further, the situation seemed to lend a certain credibility to the growing leftist cultural hegemony among the *bhadralok*, which indeed had become evident since the 1930s. The outcome was that in 1967 for the first time a non-Congress government came to be installed—in the main a coalition of Communist Party of India (Marxist) or CPI(M) and Bangla Congress, a break-away faction of the Congress party.

By the benefit of hindsight one can perhaps claim that spring was in the air then. It seemed that all that had been promised in the writings of the litterateurs who arrived in the wake of Tagore—for that matter in his later writings too—in the productions of Group Theatre, i.e. the theatre movement that had evolved in Calcutta inspired by the ideals of the Indian People's Theatre Association (IPTA) founded in 1943, the music that flowed from the same source, the new aesthetics of cinema—all seemed to have reached a glorious fruition. This was not the revolution that everybody seemed to be dreaming of, but surely many came to view it as a definitive step towards it.

But then started what I would prefer to describe as a process of brutal realization as to what even a tentative step towards a purported revolution could mean in real life. The left parties, immediately upon coming to power, decided to fulfil what had been its basic political agenda for long, i.e. to seize and distribute excess and illegal landholdings under *jotedars*—the big, settled farmers who held virtually zamindar-like power in the countryside. There was strong protest from the Bangla Congress, whose representative in the coalition cabinet Ajoy Mukherjee, was also the Chief Minister, and from the opposition Congress party. What was more, the Left parties soon became involved in inter-party struggles among themselves in their attempt to expand their respective party's spheres of influence through rival land grabbing expeditions.[1] The turmoil thus begun reached a critical state when the peasant rebellion in Naxalbari exploded in May 1967. This was led and organized by the more radical section within the CPI(M), who had firmly come to believe, not without good reasons one might say, that now that the CPI(M) had become involved in government formation and therefore in formal administration, the task of actually leading a revolution, and therefore of overthrowing the state, would be postponed indefinitely.

The uprising in north Bengal was followed by the formation of a new Party, Communist Party of India (Marxist-Leninist) or CPI(ML) in 1969, with a call for launching an immediate revolution and eschewing of all electoral, even democratic practices. Charu Mazumdar, the party chief, proclaimed what came to be known as his annihilation line. Seizure of excess and illegal holdings of land and their distribution among the landless and poor peasantry, it was said, were not enough; class enemies had to be physically eliminated by guerrilla squads. Thus, it was believed, class enemies shall flee from their areas, liberated zones would appear, and at some point in the future as the number of such zones multiplied, the big cities shall be surrounded and captured. This was sincerely believed to be an application of Mao's tactic for conducting a revolution as expounded by his the then trusted Lieutenant Lin Biao, in which the leading role was to be played by the peasantry. How far this was a true reflection of Mao's thinking, or how far were the conditions in China in the 1920s and 30s comparable to the conditions in West Bengal/India of the late 1960s and early 70s, were questions occasionally raised by comrades, but somehow these did not properly register. In the meantime, young men and women, mostly students, truly idealists, who had become utterly disillusioned by the prevailing political system in the country, took up arms and waded into the revolution. First, the countryside and later the cities, especially Calcutta, became the site of vicious guerrilla strikes, and ruthless police and military action.

No doubt, there were large segments of the middle class, as much as of the poor, who were truly inspired by the self-sacrifice and heroism of the guerrillas against impossible odds. The CPI(ML) leadership paid the ultimate price—most of them either died in police custody or were shot in staged encounters, and through their deaths proved that while they might have been mistaken in their political thinking, they were not false to their beliefs. But the unpalatable fact would still remain that, for perhaps the larger society, the subsequent restoration of *status quo ante* came as a much sought after relief. To my mind, now was revealed the shallowness of the political rhetoric that Bengalis/Calcuttans had been listening to since the 40s and 50s. Now began the process of retreat.

A Rethinking of Strategy

The defeat of the Naxalbari movement, in a manner of speaking, represented the defeat of a classical Leftist way of thinking about transforming India, violent and revolutionary, which would once and for all liquidate the semi-feudal conditions in which majority of India's villages still survived, and there would begin a glorious journey from subjecthood to free citizenship for the country's teeming millions. Now that the body fabric of India had proved to be too strong and resilient, a strategy had to be devised of learning to live with it.

By 1977 when the Left Front came to be reinstated, the decay of Calcutta had become palpable. It had become clear by then that from the mid-60s onwards, Calcutta and West Bengal had been caught in a downward spiral. West Bengal's share in India's industrial output had declined by half—from about 20 per cent to around 10 per cent. The only aspect of the city that appeared to flourish was trade and commerce, largely concentrated in the Burrabazar area, and the only economic activity that caught any visitor's eye was the ubiquitous presence of the city's hawkers, 'sprawling over the city's footpaths, roads, buses and trains'.[2]

Upon coming to power, one of the first things the Left Front openly acknowledged was that under the given system their powers were limited, and the most they could hope to achieve was to provide relief to the toiling masses. There was now clearly no question of changing the system, and the only option open was to tinker with it and try to make it more livable. The two early measures that the Left Front is most remembered for were the so-called Operation Barga and the introduction of the three-tier panchayat system. Strictly speaking, these measures pertained to the conditions in the interior villages, but I refer to them here because nothing better illustrated the spirit of the changing times. Operation Barga aimed at official registration of the sharecroppers, i.e. the *bargadars*, in land records, so as to make it difficult for the landholding classes to dislodge them. By no means was this an implementation of the cherished ideal of investing the landless peasantry with the right of ownership of the land they tilled, but this was no doubt more than what the rest of India could think of. Registered sharecroppers were thus virtually turned into permanent fixtures, but without the formal right of ownership. This in turn, though, had two consequences that had not been anticipated before. First, given the high density of population in the state, 615 as against the all-India figure of 216,[3] and therefore the inevitable fragmentation of holdings, it would become increasingly difficult for the beneficiaries to hold on to their land in the later years. This was all the more because of the changing nature of agriculture requiring progressively higher investment in chemical fertilizers and high yielding variety of seeds. Till the end the Left Front was unable to move towards co-operativization or consolidation of holdings, and without such a vision for the future, Operation Barga was not likely to benefit the peasants in the long run.[4] Second, very soon the Leftist party managers realized that registration of sharecroppers antagonized rural landholding classes, who still controlled electoral behaviour of the people. One way out, and indeed that soon became the principal tactic, was to provide space for elements from these classes within the party machinery, but of course that only meant the tinkering with the system soon became the stuff of another fantasy. Indeed, the backing of the rural middle classes remained crucial for the Left Front throughout their tenure in establishing and then maintaining its control over the Panchayati structure, the three-tier system of local government, and through that over the Bengal villages.[5]

As for the city of Calcutta, once the revolutionary option was ruled out, Left Front had to fall back on what had been the policy of the previous Congress governments, to try and improve the civic amenities of the city—installing proper sewerage in the city's slums, providing for potable water supply, prevention of waterlogging during the monsoon months, and to try and ease the anarchic traffic conditions in the city—briefly, to make Calcutta more livable.

Way back in 1961, the West Bengal state government had established the Calcutta Metropolitan Planning Organization to prepare a comprehensive plan for Calcutta Metropolitan District (CMD). About five years later the Basic Development Plan (BDP) for the CMD, 1966–86, appeared, which was a master plan for water supply, sewerage and drainage, and traffic and transportation in the context of Calcutta as the metropolis in eastern India. This, however, came at a time of economic stagnation, industrial unrest, political instability, deteriorating law and order, declining investment and so little happened till the mid-1970s, when the Calcutta Metropolitan Development Authority (CMDA) was set up.[6]

It should be noted that this was the first time that an exercise of this scale was being attempted in India. In 1955 the Delhi Development Authority (DDA) had been set up, and the first master plan for Delhi drawn up in 1962, but that plan had focused on land use in Delhi and regulations thereof. The BDP for Calcutta, on the other hand, aimed at estimating within the given timeframe the likely demands on the city's civic services, in the context of Calcutta's pre-eminent position in eastern India. The exercise had become imperative given the terrible living conditions of the city's poor. Following the cholera epidemic of 1958, Dr B.C. Roy, perhaps the most pragmatic chief minister West Bengal has ever had, invited the World Health Organization (WHO) to examine the insanitary conditions of Calcutta, and to suggest measures towards improvement. Teams from World Bank and Ford Foundation followed, and the BDP was based on their reports.[7]

But what was the result of all this? No doubt there were some developments in several vital aspects in the lives of the city's poor. Cholera almost seized to occur through improvement in environmental sanitation. Of some 2.6 million slum dwellers, 1.7 million were benefited by such changes as paved alleyways, electric connection, supply of potable water, and introduction of sanitary latrines. Yet what remained undone was also of stupendous dimension. As one keen observer noted:

> . . . If one were to visit Calcutta in 1986 after a gap of twenty years, one would scarcely believe that any one ever cared for the city or its environ, much less that there was a plan for its development. Poverty and decay writ large everywhere, almost all major streets overflowing with hawkers and their stalls or wares, some like the ancient Bowbazar completely choked with garbage, endless traffic snarls, arterial roads dug up but never restored, the dilapidated, unkempt look of structures lining the famous thoroughfares like Dharamtalla, College Street, Baghbazar and Ashutosh Mukherjee Road, the sprawling slums showing no signs of shrinking, busy city centres like the Dalhousie square turned into a vast eating place, even the once resplendent Esplanade and the surrounding maidan reduced to a slum, the frequent plunge of vast areas into total darkness, the agony of the rainy season, an hour's rain being sufficient to submerge most parts of the city, the deadly pollution of air and water, the never failing outbreak of gastro-enteritis in summer, squalor engulfing almost the entire city—the contrast with what Calcutta was even in 1966 is too stark to be missed or dismissed as the product of 'casual empiricism' or statistically insignificant impressions. . . . The state of municipalities adjoining Calcutta is scarcely better. One has only to take a round of Howrah maidan to know what squalor can mean.[8]

The real problem lay in the finances. The BDP had anticipated and indeed relied for its success on massive investment by the central and the state governments, but these were at best intermittent and meagre. International aid from the World Bank or the IDA did not come as additional resources, and too often were channelized as central assistance or grants.

Learning to live with the system was also evident in other aspects of the Left Front's governance, though sometimes it took a little time to become visible. An example of this would be its industrial policy, and the associated attitude towards industrialists in generally, which in turn, was related to its overall approach towards the question of Kolkata.

Thus, in 1977, while the Left Front was aware that the olden days of militant posturing towards industrial corporations were perhaps gone forever, it needed time to acknowledge it upfront. Hence, the industrial policy that it adopted at the beginning contained several elements which harked back to an earlier age of Marxist purity. For instance, it was said that the government would aim among other things, at 'lessening the stranglehold of the monopoly houses and multinational firms on the economy of the State', 'encouragement of indigenous technology and industrial self-reliance', 'the gradual expansion of the public sector', and 'increasing the control of the actual producers, that is, the workers, over the industrial sector'.[9] It was quite strident in declaring: 'In the years since Independence, the multinational companies and big houses have utilized the profits realized from West Bengal's industries either for supporting the lavish style of living of the owners and top executives or for setting up industries elsewhere, or for remitting funds abroad.[10] Only a part was utilized to set up new units (the stimulus for which too was often provided by public sector investment).' The multi-national companies should be made to toe the line of the state government and re-invest in the state, 'along lines previously agreed to and vetted by the Industrial Advisory Council'. 'There can be no question of allowing new multinational units to come in.'[11]

These were, indeed, very brave words, given the actual state of affairs. There was no escaping the fact that things at the time were 'most disappointing'. Accumulated losses of public undertakings stood close to Rs.150 crore. There were more than forty public undertakings in the state, and several of them existed only in name. They had generally failed to function as independent business propositions: 'Even a cursory examination reveals that these undertakings are mostly Government departments, masquerading as companies and corporations.' 'In most instances their overheads are disproportionate to their contribution to output and employment generation.'[12]

As a way out the policy proposed that labour-intensive handloom and powerloom projects should be encouraged. It was observed that products like footwear, or crude engineering items, made by small units were often bought over by big companies or multinational companies who then sold them under their brand name. With support and technological guidance these small producers could generate output and employment. Further, producers' cooperatives should be encouraged with financial subsidy.[13]

In order to implement such a policy, it was finally declared that there should be 'a major modification in the allocation of powers between the Centre and the States in such matters as industrial licensing, the regulation of industries and arrangements concerning institutional finance. The Industrial Development and Regulation Act must be suitably amended so as to enable the State Governments (to) assume powers to investigate into the affairs of individual industrial units.'[14] Further, that:

The public financial institutions should also review their conventional policies about guarantees and collaterals. This is particularly important in the context of the need to provide adequate credit to small artisans and unemployed young persons. The State Government may indicate to the institutions, including the banks, certain targets for fulfillment in the matter of credit allotment to different economic groups. Continuous appraisals should take place to ensure that the targets are fully reached.[15]

It should be clear from even a cursory reading, that much of this policy rested on a large dosage of pious hope. India was, after all, a federal state, and banks and financial institutions functioned under central laws. Led by the then redoubtable finance minister Ashok Mitra, campaigning for restructuring the Centre-state relations would remain a major plank in Left Front politics through the 80s, but at the end of the day, the dream of bringing about any fundamental change in the power equation was perhaps a non-starter. Similar was the hope that the financial institutions should relax their policies about guarantees and collaterals so far as unemployed young persons were concerned. The Left just refused to recognize that all these were desperate attempts to ride two horses pulling at different directions, one towards a fundamental restructuring of the society, and the other running within the overall rhythm of India's political system.

Without a clear and practical policy direction the situation continued to worsen. For quite sometime this would not matter in as much as the Left Front continued to win elections, largely because of its success on the rural front. Land reform and installation of Panchayati Raj continued to pay rich dividend, besides in agricultural productivity, thanks to introduction of high yielding variety of seeds and shallow tube wells for round the year irrigation, the state made noticeable progress. Rate of decline of poverty was also one of the fastest in the country. In the industrial sector though, the downhill slide continued. West Bengal's share in India's industrial output declined from 9.80 per cent in 1980–1 to 4.70 per cent in

1995–6, and in keeping with it, during 1980–97 organized private sector employments went down from 10.8 lakh to 7.99 lakh.[16] There were other tell-tale signs which confirmed the same account. Thus, whereas in 1985–6, 10 per cent of India's import and export passed through Calcutta airport and its port: by 1998–9 the figure stood at about 4 per cent. In the mid-60s, West Bengal was second from top among the larger states in terms of industrialization, but by 1995–6 it was way down at the bottom, just ahead of Uttar Pradesh. In terms of infrastructure, again, West Bengal had been fourth in 1971–2, and stood at fourteenth in 1997–8.[17]

It is possible to argue that the Left Front through the 1980s were focused on the rural, agrarian front, and hence the decline of the industrial sector occurred. The fact, though, would still remain that for still sometime to come the Left did not master the language necessary to open any meaningful dialogue with either the central government or the captains of industries.[18]

While the dismal urban situation had been generating its own pressure, the first break came with the opening up of the Indian economy. In 1991, faced with a balance of payment crisis India pledged 20 tons of gold to Union Bank of Switzerland and another 47 tons to Bank of England. Pressured by the International Monetary Fund (IMF), Government of India had to undertake structural reforms in international trade and investment, including deregulation of investment procedure, privatization, reforms in tax regime, and measures for controlling inflation. This was followed in 1993 by the dismantling of the freight equalization policy.[19]

To start with the Left Front was suspicious of the new stance of the central government, and believed that it signified its capitulation before international big capital. Gradually, however, it came round to a new understanding, that it could be seen as an opening which could be used to West Bengal's advantage. On 23 September 1994, it came out with its new industrial policy, jettisoning much of what had held so dear since the late 1970s. The most important feature of the new policy was that now for the first time Left Front declared that it was welcoming 'foreign technology and investment as may be appropriate, or mutually advantageous'. Further, that it 'recognizes the importance and key role of the Private Sector in providing accelerated growth'. It specially welcomed private sector investment in power generation and in improvement of roadways and communication, in development of Growth Centres.[20]

The Left Front, thus, after much heart burning and dilly-dallying, arrived at a position which it had sought to avoid for so long. The first signs of a changing mentality was seen in a sector about which the Left had been traditionally a little uneasy. Almost since the very beginning leftist trade unions had resisted computerization of public services, especially in the banking sector, on the ground that it would lead to job loss. Yet in the post-liberalization years it was in the sphere of Information Technology (IT) that some success was achieved. In 1992–3, IT industry in West Bengal began with six units registering themselves with the Software Technology Park, Calcutta. The industry took off from 1999 to 2000 when 138 firms made an entry and export figures began to climb. In 1998–9 export stood at $40 million, and at $1,790 million in 1999–2000. It was believed that by 1910 the state would be one of the top 3 states in India in IT, and would contribute 15–20 per cent of the country's total IT revenue.[21]

In keeping with the same spirit, in the post-liberalization period, the Left also sought to relieve the overcrowding in Calcutta by trying to build a new township further to the east of Salt Lake— the Rajarhat-New Town complex. In 1998 West Bengal Housing Infrastructure Development Corporation acquired some 3,070 ha. of arable land, affecting the lives and livelihoods of around 1,31,000 inhabitants.[22] According to the master plan the township was to be laid out in four sections with a central business district. The principal allocation was to be for residential use, and for the rest the intended beneficiary was to be firms devoted to IT. Among present occupants there are several IT companies, both regional and multinational, institutions devoted to higher education, a major private hospital, hotels, and several malls. The point to be noted is that the principal part of the housing is in the way of high-rise complexes, thereby indicating the future character of the township.[23]

As a recent commentator has reminded us, 'Rajarhat used to be a fertile agricultural area dotted with villages with long histories of settlements, ponds, orchards, flower nurseries and substantial waterbodies.' Two-thirds of the people were Muslims or Dalits, and most were fishermen or farmers. Landholdings were small, and people survived through 'trade and transport of fresh produce and fish' to Calcutta.[24] It was assumed that they would now be absorbed as 'servants, housekeepers, drivers, cleaners, cooks, etc.' Some indeed were. There were others who used their compensation money to build added space to their homes and rent it out to migrants from elsewhere who came to work in the informal sector.[25] But there were many more perhaps, mostly young men, who inevitably got sucked into semi-criminal activities through the so-called 'syndicates'. These were cooperatives of building material suppliers, constituted by the unemployed youth of the surrounding areas, and operating with impunity by virtue of political patronage. There is plenty of anecdotal evidence in the press which suggests that today it is impossible to start any construction project in the New Town area without contracting with one of the many 'syndicates', and the building material that one is forced to accept is invariably overpriced and is of questionable quality. Because of political protection the police, so the stories go, typically do not act even on receiving complaints. The syndicates started more or less at the same time as when the land was acquired, i.e. when the Left Front was in power, but since 2011 under the new regime, things are widely believed to have gone out of hand.

It is obvious we can make sense of the Rajarhat New Town phenomenon only in the context of the post-liberalization shift in Left Front politics and also in our—the citizens'—mentality. Calcutta now became the site for major urban transformations, and the objective became to build a millennial city. The political project nicely dovetailed with the growing demand from those who could afford it—'a world-class township that would be integrated into the circuits of global capital and yet would bypass the poverty and squalor in the existing core city'.[26] It almost seems that the Left Front was in a hurry, driven to prove that though freshly converted, it had quickly mastered the logic of continuing primitive capitalist accumulation. It, however, stumbled in its next venture.

In 2001, Buddhadev Bhattacharjee became the Chief Minister of Bengal, replacing the old patriarch Jyoti Basu who had been at the helm since 1977. The much younger man, Bhattacharjee appeared to many as representing the new white hope, and indeed, was able to inject a new energy in the drive for industrialization. Bhattacharjee led business delegations to Thailand and to Italy. A new belief began to sprout that given its geographical location in eastern India, West Bengal could become India's gateway to South-East Asia, and thereby become a vital component of the central government's 'Look East' policy.[27] But then came the farcical denouement of Nandigram and Singur. In 2005, an MoU was signed with Indonesia's biggest conglomerate, the Salim Group, involving an investment of Rs.50,000 crore in West Bengal to set up a Special Economic Zone (SEZ) in East Medinipur. And in 2006, in the aftermath of state general elections in which the Left Front scored a resounding victory, Bhattacharjee announced that the TATA group had agreed to build two factories, one for what was called the world's cheapest car, to be priced at Rs.1,00,000, and another for pay-loaders at Singur, in Hooghly district. Unlike in IT, though, setting up a SEZ or building motor car factories involved acquisition of land. The two projects, Salim's and TATA's, required acquiring 38,650 acres and 1,000 acres, respectively, of farmland and triggered a virtual peasant rebellion at both locations. To suppress it the police, and CPI(M)'s musclemen resorted to brutal aggression. The principal opposition party, Trinamool Congress (TMC), a break-away faction of the old Congress party, organized a blockade at Singur, besides being involved in the large-scale resistance in Nandigram. The civil society in Kolkata, shocked and angered by the scale of the state-sponsored violence and the obvious callous indifference of the Left Front government, lent a powerful voice to the opposition. And the inevitable result of all these was the total rout of the Left Front in the next general elections of 1911.[28]

The new dispensation under TMC led by the mercurial Mamata Banerjee has declared time and again that while it was committed to the cause of industrialization, it was not interested in forcibly acquiring land for the benefit of private capitalists. This has created an impasse in today's context in which different state governments are engaged in a cut-throat competition to attract investors to their respective backyards with large concessions. Further, the growth rate of agricultural productivity in West Bengal has been slowing down for sometime now, and it is obvious that for hundreds of thousands of young people who enter the labour market every year, agriculture will never be the panacea. Small-scale industries do offer some hope, but these can really function as adjunct to larger units as suppliers and sub-contractors. In the absence of larger units, these are not likely to deliver. On the other hand large-scale industries are bound to be capital-intensive, which again would absorb only those who would have the necessary skill. Whither West Bengal, then?

Let us look at some broad data available in the daily press. *The Economic Times* reported in November 1915 that according to central government figures GDP growth rate of West Bengal, at 7.15 per cent, was actually better than figures posted by Maharashtra (5.66 per cent), Karnataka (7.05 per cent), and Punjab (5.32 per cent).[29] Further, in terms of industrial growth too West Bengal had performed creditably. Where Karnataka had registered 4.36 per cent, Maharashtra 4.01 per cent, Tamil Nadu 3.64 per cent, West Bengal had recorded a growth rate of 5.05 per cent.

A more analytical picture is available from *The Telegraph*'s report of 16 October 2015. Dipankar Dasgupta, a former Professor of Indian Statistical Institute, Calcutta, on the basis of Reserve Bank of India data source and publications of the Ministry of Commerce and Industry, Government of India, demonstrated that West Bengal in the post Nandigram-Singur era had not done too badly, according to growth rate of per capita net State Domestic Product (SDP) figures. In 2008–9 it had fallen to 3.05 per cent, but this was in keeping with the all-India figures, and could well have been due to an overall crisis arising from the sub-prime debacle in the US. In the last year of Left Front rule it actually recovered well to 5.08 per cent, falling again to 2.71 per cent in the first year of the new regime under TMC, but registering 6.26 per cent in 2012, a little above 6 per cent in the year after and 6.42 per cent in 2014–15.

Sector-wise analysis reveals a more complicated picture. Neither agriculture nor industry, it seems were real contributors to the rising per capita figures. The real 'saviour', according to Dasgupta, was the service sector. The segment comprising real estate, ownership of dwellings, and business services registered a growth rate of 9.66 per cent in 2013–14, and of 10.60 per cent in 2014–15, while banking and insurance hovered around 13.46 per cent. The state also did well in tackling its debt liabilities, and by the budget estimates of 2015, these stood at 35 per cent of gross SDP, compared to 41.9 in 2011.

All in all, West Bengal appears to have weathered the embarrassment of Nandigram-Singur well, and gradually settled down into a low-level service sector based equilibrium.

The question though, would still haunt us, as to what went wrong with the Left Front. The tectonic shifts in the Indian economic and social spheres following liberalization knocked it out would be the simple answer, and to a large extent it could be the right answer. The succeeding government under TMC, by refusing to acquire land for industrialization, and by offering to take care of the immediate existential needs of the poor and the needy, appears to promise protection from the shocks of these shifts. This has evidently served it well, and it has won the just concluded elections to the state assembly very handsomely indeed. The CPI(M) led Left Front, on the other hand, was bent on sailing with the new wind, still thinking in terms of a transformative project of changing the world, albeit a change of a very different character from what it used to think of four decades earlier. There was necessarily a price to pay, a price which we at that point of time, and still today are unwilling to pay. It could be because conditions were not propitious, the demographic pressure was far too much, the idea of democracy was too deep-rooted, and large scale displacement of people necessarily had political consequences. Was it then only the miscalculations in Nandigram-Singur that brought about the downfall? Thirty years of virtually unchallenged rule, I am leaving out the last term because by then its ouster had become a foregone conclusion, had left the CPI(M) supremely complacent, guaranteed power had encouraged corruption and nepotism at every level of the administration. Or perhaps it was the other way round, in order to ensure that power should remain secure the party had infiltrated its elements everywhere, thereby encouraging long-term incompetence. For placement anywhere in the official establishment allegiance to the party had become the only criterion. The party had also become unsure of its social base. If in the late 60s it generally was the underclasses—the peasantry and the workers, the refugees, the underpaid office workers and teachers—then from the late 70s it became occupied with the land question. Later it dithered between propitiating the upwardly mobile middle classes and the wealthy, and offering protection to those who fell victim to liberalization.

This brings us to the question of ourselves, how we the people of West Bengal, were moulded and transformed, by this long epilogue to Naxalbari.

The Changing Profile of the Citizen and the City

Apart from its effect on the destiny of the Left, and the politics of West Bengal, Naxalbari rebellion also left its impression on the society and culture of Calcutta. We have already suggested that part of the reason behind Naxalbari's defeat lay in the retreat of the Bengali *bhadralok*, almost recoiling from the spectre of revolution that emanated from the guerrilla strikes, and counter-strikes from the police and the paramilitary in and around the city. It was this mentality of the retreat that appears to have left an indelible mark on the Bengali psyche.

One way to understand it would be to see how the Bengali *bhadralok* today consider their habitat.

Traditionally the residential areas of the city are known as *paras*, and it is likely that the notion of the *para* is a leftover from a rural past. There was a time when Bengal villages were divided into different *paras*, or sectors, in which dwelled people of the same ritual strata, *bamunpara* for the brahmins, *kayetpara* for the kayasths, *jelepara* for the fishermen, *kumorpara* for the potters, and so on. As the city of Calcutta developed under British tutelage the native part of the city also came to be recognized in terms of different *paras*, but with one significant difference. In urban conditions, locational segregation in keeping with ritual hierarchy was difficult to maintain, and *paras* gradually turned into neighbourhoods where people of the same social strata lived. It was not as if there were no economic or social differences among a *para*'s residents, but a *para*, nonetheless evoked a spirit of a homogenous identity. It signified to the residents a sanctified arena of almost a network of putative familial relationships, in which an unwritten, but universally recognized, code of conduct operated based on mutual trust, deference and allegiance to the *para*.

A fundamental aspect of *para* life was that the residents depended on each other for their social existence. Hence, a necessary pre-condition of a functioning *para* was that neighbours should stand by each other when they were needed. As the old city expanded, first southward in the 1930s, and, later eastward, in the 50s and 60s, the old *para* spirit gradually began to dissipate. The social bonding that had developed across generations in the older parts of the city in the north, i.e. where native Bengalis had traditionally lived, understandably could not be immediately recreated in the newer areas. Yet, the habit of bonding was not totally forgotten either. This was particularly so in the so-called *jabardakhal colonies* or squatters enclaves built by refugees from East Pakistan on vacant land owned either by the government or by some absentee or careless landlord, because there residents still needed mutual aid and cooperation to tide over the difficult times. Even in more settled areas, the *para* spirit used to be evident in religious gatherings, as during Durga Puja, or on social occasions as in a wedding.

And then the political turbulence of the late 60s and early 70s, climaxing in the Naxalbari movement, dealt a mortal blow to the idea of the *para*. Calcutta's *paras* became exclusive 'liberated zones' for different political parties, and little tolerance was shown to any dissident voice. The Naxalite rebels, and the political formations which opposed them, the CPI(M), the Indian National Congress under the leadership of Indira Gandhi, the continuous inter-party fights, along with short-term opportunistic alliances between formations to face up to a stronger opponent in the area—all combined to destroy perhaps for all time to come the ethos of the *para*. Where the old *para* was home territory, providing assurance and lending an identity, and where for that reason, the residents felt free as long as one observed the universal code of conduct based on trust and deference, in the new circumstances one had to be on one's guard and be aware as to which group was in charge. After 1977, i.e. when CPI(M) came to be reinstated, and remained in power for the next 34 years, *paras* became the base from which the party grew upwards and outward. The ubiquitous local committees became the overarching authority, which came to control virtually every aspect of the *para* life, starting from the annual Durga Puja celebrations, the local library, down to who should occupy which corner of the pavement for setting up a kiosk at what rate of contribution to the local party office. In the olden days senior residents of the *para* commanded at least a show of deference from those who were younger, and there were certain professions, that of the medical practitioner, the lawyer or a senior teacher or professor, which naturally commanded respect, and they were the people who upheld the sanctity of the *para*, they were the moral guardians so to say. With the emergence of the local committees, this moral order of the *para* disappeared for all time to come.

If the middle class thus turned inward, unable to face up to the local committees' growing clout, then the social space vacated was quickly occupied by the growing presence of a new category of people. Two processes worked in tandem to produce the difference. First, the industrial decline led to a large-scale shift from manufacturing and service to trading and transport, over a long period from the 50s onwards.[30] And second, the relative prosperity of the agricultural sector through the 70s and 80s implied that a new rural middle class was emerging. The two together brought about a significant change in the profile of the Bengali society. The CPI(M) had already established its hegemony over the countryside through its land reform and installation of the panchayat system. Now it began to accommodate the up and coming rural middle class. A key figure in this was the village schoolmaster.[31] In an important step the Left Front had very early assumed the responsibility of paying the salaries of school and college teachers, the consequence of which was that in the villages, teachers in government aided schools suddenly came to attain a degree of financial respectability, and a new social status. Their educational qualification almost invariably indicated some degree of economic strength of their families, and therefore also a measure of control over land. Taken together, the schoolteachers of Bengal villages rapidly turned into local level party managers, and through them increasingly the rural middle class found a niche for itself in the party hierarchy.

As the industrial working class declined, and the *bhadralok* went into retreat, the CPI(M) gradually shifted its attention to these increasingly visible elements in the society. By no means were/are they a homogenous class-like category. If at one end of the spectrum we have the rural middle class, who at one end combined a degree of financial ease with the backing of a powerful party machinery, the lower grade government employees whose salaries had become a little more respectable over the years, or the innumerable small business people and pavement stallholders, then at the other end there were/are the autorickshaw drivers, the hawkers, tens of thousands of daily commuters to the city who provide all kinds of vital services to the residents, ranging from domestic work to maintenance and auto repair. There is one common element though, which binds them together, and that is their anxiety to be recognized as legitimate social beings. They are not desperately poor as the landless peasant, nor do they live the hand-to-mouth existence of the slum dwellers of yesteryears. It is not improbable to find colour TV sets in their homes, or college going students. They have access to media information, invariably possess cellphones, are knowledgeable about soccer and cricket world cups, and additionally are aware of their importance to every political formation that wishes to contest elections. They do not dream of earth-shaking transformative projects like the left-liberal *bhadralok* of the past used to do. They are hard-nosed, street-smart, and therefore have little illusion about ideology of any kind. From the late 80s onwards they had constituted the rank and file of the CPI(M), but had no compunction about shifting their allegiance to TMC in 2011, as the CPI(M) went into decline after the debacle at Nandigram and Singur. Their only consideration appears to be which political party would provide them with that extra leeway which makes their lives a little easier in the city.

Perhaps this is the biggest impact that Naxalbari had left for the posterior, the death of romance in the political imagination of the city. Introduction of Operation Barga and the installation of the panchayat system were the last gesture of that political romance, involving the twin goals of bringing land to the tiller, and the administration closer to the people. As we saw, neither of these two moves bore fruit, and the inherited power structure of the society could not really be dismantled. The rather reckless drive for industrialization after the elections of 2006, as if emulating the spirit of the triumphant bourgeoisie of a bygone age, was exactly that—it was late by at least a hundred years. Given the democratic set up, which the Left indeed had nurtured so well for so long,

acquisition of land at such a large scale was a sure recipe for a
political disaster. A hundred years ago the displaced people would
have been absorbed in the new factories. That was not going to
happen in the present state of technology.

Post-Left Front, the present dispensation under TMC does not
speak of any transformative project. Its own shibboleth is *unnayan*,
or development, meaning thereby governmental projects of various
kinds, which provide for the existential needs of the people,
ranging from offering rice at Rs.2 a kg., to free gift of a bicycle for
a school-going girl child. To be fair, there is plenty of anecdotal
evidence which suggests that *unnayan* has reached interior villages
too, with paved roads and electric lines, and it is possible, that this
approach would serve the party well in future. Also, it must be kept
in mind that given the conditions of West Bengal, it is doubtful if
any project based on a grand vision would at all be possible in the
near future.

Yet, Kolkata[32] the city, has been changing all through. Since 1984
we have had a metro service, and today the average office-time
commuter cannot imagine life without it. The first shopping mall
came up in the mid-1990s, but the mall culture really took off after
the liberalization of the economy, in the years after 2000. Today
the city and its surrounding areas has more than twenty, and it
seems there shall be more in the future. The city also has several
new flyovers, the first in the post-liberalization period being the
Gariahat flyover inaugurated in 2002. In the years that followed
three more appeared, considerably easing traffic congestion in the
city. The second Hooghly Bridge has been in operation since 1994,
and that again has helped in easing congestion in the north and
central part of the city by drawing to the south a large segment of
the incoming vehicular traffic from across the river.

Another extremely significant change in the post-liberalization
years was in the world of Indian television. Where in 1991
Indian viewers had access to only two channels, both controlled
and owned by the Indian government, by 1996 they could view
more than fifty, mostly owned by private players. The first private
operator was STAR (Satellite Television for the Asian Region) of
Hong Kong, but alongside there came to be any number of Indian
operators offering entertainment and news programmes in almost

all regional languages.[33] Today, the world has indeed come on view in Indian homes in a manner that was unthinkable in the 1990s. This in turn has had effect on our lifestyle, in our preference for consumer goods, the way we dress, and even in the manner in which we interact with our fellow citizens. Even up to the mid-1990s, almost the only car that was seen on Calcuttan and Indian roads, was the Hindustan Motors' Ambassador. In continuous production with minor improvements from 1958 to 2014, it was a derivative of a British car, the Morris Oxford III model which had had a run from 1956 to 1959. Most of us were not aware how ancient the Ambassador really was, nor did we care very much. In many ways it was quite the great leveller, it was owned as much by the super-rich and the powerful as by the upwardly mobile middle class. Today the entire range of cars to be had anywhere in the world are available in India, and it is possible to identify more or less precisely the financial standing of a person by the make of the car they drive.

Kolkata today, thus, is a very different place from the Calcutta of the late 60s and early 70s. If there is anything left, then it is the memory, a nostalgia for a lost moral order. The manner in which the city responded to the villagers' resistance at Nandigram and Singur against the Left Front's forcible acquisition of land for industrialization, the depth of passion that was displayed in the almost continuous street demonstrations, was evocative of that nostalgia, indicating a refusal to accept repression beyond a point. The same passion is also in evident in the campuses of our universities, in the student movements that flare up from time to time against perceived acts of injustice on the part of the present government. Political romance, suggestive of an imagined grand narrative, is dead. Its moral foundation still survives.

Notes

1. This was a period of acute political instability arising from dissension among the partners of the United Front. There were no less than four ministries and three phases of President's Rule between 1967 and 1972.
2. Amaresh Bagchi, 'Planning for Metropolitan Development: Calcutta's Basic Development Plan, 1966-86: A Post-Mortem', *Economic & Political Weekly*, vol. 22, no. 14, 4 April 1987, pp. 600–1.

3. See, http://rcwb.in/rcwb/wp-content/uploads/2012/07/4.-Density-of-Population-India-and-West-Bengal-2011.pdf, accessed 17 May 2016.

4. By 2001, West Bengal emerged as the most densely populated state in India, with per sq. km. density standing at 904 as against the all-India figure of 324. See, Planning Commission, Government of India, 'Introduction; Table 3', *West Bengal Development Report 2010*, New Delhi: Academic Foundation, 2010, p. 25. By 2002–3, in West Bengal almost 89 per cent of the land was under marginal farmers, i.e. those whose holdings ranged from 0.2 to 0.4 ha. Ibid., p. 50.

5. See Dipankar Bhattacharya, 'New Challenges for Bengal Left: Panchayat Poll Pointers', *Economic & Political Weekly*, vol. 28, nos. 29 and 30, 17–24 July 1993, pp. 1491–4.

6. This is a collection of six separate tracts. K.C. Sivaramakrishnan, 'Calcutta 2001: Triumph of Survival', in *Calcutta 1974*, Calcutta Metropolitan Development Authority, n.d., p. 5.

7. Bagchi, 'Planning for Metropolitan Development', p. 597.

8. Ibid., p. 598.

9. *A Review of Industrial Growth in West Bengal*, Commerce and Industries Department, Government of West Bengal, March 1978, para 1.

10. Ibid., para 2.

11. Ibid., para 8.

12. Ibid., para 10.

13. Ibid., paras 5–6.

14. Ibid., para 11.

15. Ibid., para 20.

16. Abhijit Banerjee et al., 'Strategy for Economic Reform in West Bengal', *Economic & Political Weekly*, vol. 37, no. 41, 12 October 2002, p. 4203.

17. Ibid., pp. 4204–5.

18. On this see, Deepita Chakravarty and Indranil Bose, 'Industrializing West Bengal?: The Case of Institutional Stickiness', Working Paper No. 83, February 2010, Centre for Economic and Social Studies, Hyderabad.

19. Mukesh Kumar, 'Impact of Economic Reforms on India', *International Journal of Informative and Futuristic Research*, vol. 1, no. 7, March 2014, see, http://www.ijifr.com/searchjournal.aspx, accessed 16 March 2016.

20. *West Bengal Industrial Policy*, see, dcmsme.gov.in/policies/state/westbengal/ipwb.htm, accessed 23 March 2016. Also see, Chakravarty and Bose, 'Industrializing West Bengal?'.

21. *West Bengal Development Report 2010*, pp. 77–8.

22. Ishita Dey et al., eds., *Beyond Kolkata: Rajarhat and the Dystopia of Urban Imagination*, New Delhi: Routledge, 2013, p. 3.

23. Ratoola Kundu, 'Making Sense of Place in Rajarhat New Town: The Village in the Urban and the Urban in the Village', *Review of Urban Studies, Economic & Political Weekly*, vol. 51, no. 17, 23 April 2016, p. 95.

24. Ibid.

25. Ibid., pp. 96–7.

26. Ibid., p. 98.

27. Chakravarty and Bose, 'Industrializing West Bengal?', p. 11.

28. On this see, Dwaipayan Bhattacharyya, *Government as Practice: Democratic Left in a Transforming India*, Delhi: Cambridge University Press, 2016, pp. 155–9. A crucial difference between the acquisition in Rajarhat in the late 90s, that the Left Front could get away with, and that proposed in Nandigram and Singur in 2006 when it could not, was of course that on the earlier occasion the Trinamool Congress was still not born.

29. 'Bengal's GDP Growth surpasses UP, Maharashtra', *The Economic Times*, 27 November 2015.

30. On this see, Pabitra Giri, 'An Analysis of the Growth of Small and Medium Towns in West Bengal, 1951–1981', in *Urbanization, Migration and Rural Change: A Study of West Bengal*, ed. Biplab Dasgupta, Calcutta: A. Mukherjee & Co. Pvt. Ltd., January 1988.

31. See, Dwaipayan Bhattacharyya, 'Agency: School Teachers', in *Government as Practice: Democratic Left in a Transforming India*, Delhi: Cambridge University Press, 2016.

32. Calcutta was always called Kolkata in Bengali; it became its formal name from 2001.

33. *India Netzone*, 'History of Indian Television', see, www.indianetzone. com/42/history_indian_television.htm, accessed 1 May 2016.

EDITORS AND CONTRIBUTORS

ANURADHA ROY is Professor, Department of History, Jadavpur University. Her research is focused on intellectual and cultural history, with special reference to the life of the Bengali *bhadralok* and *bhadramahila* (men and women of the educated upper and middle classes). She has authored/edited a dozen books in Bengali and English, most of which are related to the nationalist and communist culture in Bengal. Among the books authored by her are *Nationalism as Poetic Discourse in Nineteenth Century Bengal* (2003), *Bengal Marxism: Early Discourses and Debates* (2014) and *Cultural Communism in Bengal, 1936–1952* (2014), a monograph on the women Novelists of ninteenth-century Bengal and a collection of essays titled *Itihaser Hark Gero* (Different Knots of History, 2019).

MELITTA WALIGORA is Assistant Professor at the Department of Asian and African Studies, South Asia Studies Seminar, Humboldt University of Berlin. She teaches topics related to South Asia, focused mainly on Bengal: intellectual and cultural history, social structures, gender relations and urban history. She has published many articles (in German and English) in different journals and contributed to edited volumes. She has edited a book about gender relations: *Draupadi und Kriemhild: Frauen, Ehre und Macht im Nibelungenlied und Mahabharata*, Heidelberg 2008. Among her recent publications are a book about the city of Kolkata: Kalkutta. Moderne Stadt am Ganges, Berlin 2015, and a collection of portraits of women living in Kolkata, based on interviews with them: *Ich wollte nie so leben wie meine Mutter*, Heidelberg 2017.

AMIT BHATTACHARYYA is a former Professor of History of Jadavpur University. His main areas of interest are economic history of modern India, Maoist movement in India, civil rights movement, environmental history, ancient and modern China, banned literature and prison memoirs. Author of a number of books, he has such books to his credit as *Swadeshi Enterprise in Bengal 1880–1920*, *Swadeshi Enterprise in Bengal 1921–47*, *The*

Chinese Civilization 2207 BC–206 BC, Transformation of Modern China 1840–1969, Storming the Gates of Heaven The Maoist Movement in India A Critical Study 1972–2014, Human Rights in India Historical Perspective and Challenges Ahead (ed.), *Karasmriti Shottorer Mashaal* (Prison Blazing Memories of the Seventies) and *Spring Thunder and Kolkata: An Epic Story of Courage and Sacrifice 1965–72.*

RITWIKA BISWAS is Associate Professor of History at University of Calcutta. She has authored a monograph *Radical Face of Democratic Liberalism: A Study of Communist Politics in West Bengal 1947–77* (2011) and has also contributed significantly to journals and books.

SRILATA CHATTERJEE was Professor of History at University of Calcutta at the time of her untimely death in 2017. She had authored two monographs: *Congress Politics in Bengal 1919–39* (2003) and *Western Medicine and Colonial Society: Hospitals of Calcutta c.1757–1860* (2017). She also had a number of articles and book chapters to her credit, and had worked on a Documentation Project on the Calcutta Medical College.

SUCHETANA CHATTOPADHYAY is Associate Professor of History at Jadavpur University, Kolkata. She studied at Jadavpur University and the School of Oriental and African Studies, University of London and has been a visiting scholar at Maison des Sciences de l'homme, Paris. She has contributed to various anthologies and journals, including *South Asia Research* and *History Workshop Journal*. She is the author of *An Early Communist: Muzaffar Ahmad in Calcutta 1913–29* (2011). *Voices of Komagata Maru: Imperial Surveillance and Workers from Punjab in Bengal* (2018) is her recent monograph.

SWATI CHATTOPADHYAY is Professor of History of Art and Architecture at the University of California, Santa Barbara. She is interested in the ties between colonialism and modernism, and in the spatial aspects of race, gender, and ethnicity in modern cities that are capable of enriching postcolonial and critical theory. Winner of a number of awards, she is the author of *Representing Calcutta: Modernity, Nationalism and the Colonial Uncanny* (2005) and *Unlearning the City: Infrastructure in a New Optical Field* (2012).

PARIMAL GHOSH is former Professor of History at Department of South & Southeast Asian Studies, University of Calcutta. Some of his important publications are *Colonialism, Class and a History of the Calcutta Jute Mill Hands* (2000) and *Brave Men of the Hills: Anti-British Resistance and Rebellion in Burma, 1825–1932* (2000). His most recent book is *What happened to the Bhadralok?* (2016).

MICHAEL MANN is Professor of Modern History and Culture of South Asia at Humboldt University. Prior to that, he was a research fellow of the German Research Foundation (Deutsche Forschungsgemeinschaft) and Gerda Henkel Stiftung. His most recent publications include *South Asia's Modern History: Thematic Perspectives* (2015) and *Wiring the Nation: Telecommunication, Newspaper-Reportage and Nation-Building in the Age of Globalisation, c.1850–1930* (2017).

SUKANYA MITRA is Assistant Professor of History at Loreto College. She has presented papers in conferences and workshops at various places including Yale University (2015), Hong Kong University (2014) and University of Goettingen (2010). One of her major publications is the essay 'Visually Imagining the City: Urban Planning in 1950s Calcutta and Surjyatoran' in *Calcutta: the Stormy Decades* edited by Tanika Sarkar and Sekhar Bandyopadhyay (2015). She is currently working on a paper titled 'From New Town to Smart City: Vision, Conflicts and the Politics of Development in Rajarhat', presented at an international seminar at the Centre for Studies in Social Sciences, Kolkata.

ALKA SARAOGI is a noted novelist and short story writer in Hindi, based in Kolkata. She has a number of published works, and is a recipient of the 2001 Sahitya Akademi Award for her first novel *Kalikatha: Via Bypass* (1998). She has published six novels and is widely translated into major European languages.

TANIKA SARKAR is former Professor at the Centre for Historical Studies at Jawaharlal Nehru University. Among her well-known monographs are *Bengal 1928–34: The Politics of Protest* (1987), *Words to Win: A Modern Autobiography* (1999), *Hindu Wife, Hindu Nation: Community, Religion, Cultural Nationalism* (2001), *Rebels, Wives, Saints: Designing Selves and Nations in Colonial Times* (2009). She has to her credit a number of edited books too, which include *Calcutta: The Stormy Decades* (2015, co-edited with Sekhar Bandyopadhyay).

KAUSTUBH MANI SENGUPTA is Assistant Professor of History at Bankura University, India. Previously, he was a post-doctoral fellow at the Transnational Research Group on 'Poverty and Education in India' funded by Max Weber Stiftung, Germany. He has published essays in journals like The Indian Economic and Social History Review, Studies in

History, Economic and Political Weekly, South Asia Research and Anustup (Bengali). Currently, he is working on his monograph, tentatively titled *Carving Calcutta: Space, Economy, and Law in Eighteenth-century Bengal.*

AVIRUP SINHA is Assistant Professor of History at Deshapran Mahavidyalaya. He has been awarded MPhil for his research on 'Urban Development, Public Health, Sanitation and the Refugee Question: A Case Study of Calcutta and Its Neighbourhood 1939–1966'.

INDEX

www.ingramcontent.com/pod-product-compliance
Lightning Source LLC
Chambersburg PA
CBHW031301310326
41914CB00116B/1774/J